S0-CFT-527

THE STUDY OF

FOREIGN LANGUAGES

THE STUDY OF

FOREIGN LANGUAGES

edited by
JOSEPH S. ROUCEK
Queensborough Community College
of the City University of New York,
Bayside, N.Y.

PHILOSOPHICAL LIBRARY
NEW YORK

97590

407
R854

Copyright, 1968, by Philosophical Library Inc.
15 East 40 Street, New York, N. Y. 10016
Library of Congress Catalog Card No. 68-13396
All rights reserved
Printed in the United States of America

TABLE OF CONTENTS

Related Problems

PREFACE

America's history is largely the result of vast folk migrations. Our society was created by the intermingling of migrants speaking all kinds of languages and dialects. The problem is, obviously, still with us, since, in spite of new information and new theories uncovered by diligent research workers in the various branches of linguistic science, the teaching of the English language, as well as the foreign languages, has been under a constant barrage of criticism.

Inseparable from the typical American problem of how to successfully teach good English is the problem facing the teachers of foreign languages in the United States. Both World Wars demonstrated how deficient the Americans are in "getting along" when sent abroad, even after many years of special training in a foreign language in the American educational institutions. It is still more difficult for the diplomatic, commercial, and "intelligence" instructions of the United States to secure well-trained Americans able to communicate reasonably well with foreigners abroad, or on their visits here!

To too many American teachers, language is nothing more than one of the means of communication. But under the impact of cultural anthropology, sociology and psychology, we know today that every language is not limited to isolated spoken or written words; it can be understood only within the total cultural framework, since it is related to a common background of beliefs, interests, and sentiments—the total background of each language's culture complex.

Thus foreign language teaching in the United States is today in a transitory stage. All the evidence shows that public high schools have not kept pace with the revolution in language instruction; in fact, less than forty percent of all public high school students were studying a foreign language in 1966—a striking contrast to the nearly eighty percent who were taking a second language in private schools.

The changing nature of our comprehension of teaching foreign languages, the new methods used, and experimented with, are a phenomenon which needs constant synthesis and reinterpretation. This is the aim of this volume, which has been prepared by specialists deeply interested in facing this problem from overall, as well as particular, viewpoints.

The editor must gratefully acknowledge the help and criticism of Dr. Dagobert D. Runes, President of the Philosophical Library, who initiated the project. Also, our thanks to Dr. Rudolf Sturm of Skidmore College, who has helped with the integration of the chapters devoted to the teaching of the leading non-English languages.

Joseph S. Roucek

THE FRAMEWORK

The Anthropological View of Language and Culture

VICTOR SOLOMON

University of Bridgeport

THE WISEST of men observed long ago that "Death and life are in the power of the tongue".[1] This ancient dictum may explain the riddle of the catastrophe at Hiroshima. There is a lingering suspicion that the nuclear carnage which ended World War II was the result of a slip of the tongue! When the Allies at Potsdam issued the famous surrender ultimatum, the polite reply of the Japanese Emperor contained the word *Mokusatsu*. The Domei news agency, so the story goes, made the fatal mistake of translating the ambiguous word into English as "ignore," which invited the atomic bomb. What a difference the more acceptable rendering of *Mokusatsu* ("reserving an answer until a decision is reached") could have made! Death and life are indeed in the power of the tongue! This was demonstrated again, though less spectacularly, in the linguistic differences involving French and Flemish which toppled the Belgian regime and led to the resignation of King Leopold in 1950.

Anthropologists agree that the passing of a primordial, inarticulate beast and the genesis of a new wonderful creature are intimately connected with that magnificent organ which has the power of life and death. "For speaking with the tongue is one of the properties of a human being", states Maimonides, "and a benefit that is granted to him and by which he is distinguished".[2] The versatile Hebrew twelfth century philosopher-physician cites biblical texts: "Who hath made man's mouth?"[3] and "The L—rd G—d hath given me a tongue of them that are

1

taught",[4] to emphasize the Judaic concept that speech is a most precious divine gift which is exclusively human.

In fact, man is distinguished from the beast primarily in his ability to use symbols as a means of communication. Speech is the most obvious and universal system of symbols. This system of symbols we call language has been the most valuable tool ever invented by or given to man. It is the basic tool which he uses not only for communication horizontally (with other men) but also vertically (with generations gone and others still to come). How fascinating a mystery speech is that it enables man to pick up thoughts of others and experience them in a meaningful way. It is also his indispensable means of "communicating with himself"—we call this process "thinking." It is his outlet for expressing feelings and emotions, (a matter of tremendous concern to students of psychology). With it he reaches out to control the environment, express his will, practice magic or religion, pass on his ideas to contemporaries and create a "tradition" for those who will follow. He can shoot words instead of arrows and bullets to describe his hate and frustration and he can use them to communicate friendship and love. Words also serve as toys for grownups, who "play" with speech.

Words have the power to convey moods as well as to create them. One theory which might interest votaries of the tonsorial arts, and should certainly delight men of meager mane, ascribes our loss of body hair to the power of words. "Verbal grooming", it is suggested, made the delousing (social) activities of the primates obsolete! The social millennium may put the barbers out of business altogether!

Speech, A Unique Attribute of Man

Charlton Laird is very emphatic about the primacy of language in the existential condition of man: "Without language, no humanity".[5] True, animals are capable of some measure of communication. However, it is limited to signals of warning, expressions of fright, and noises which reflect instinctual needs. Only man is capable of conveying *abstract information*. "If language", states Laird, "is intimately related to being human, then when we study language we are, to a remarkable degree, studying human nature. Similarly we may expect language to be what it is because human beings are what they are".[6] Irving

J. Lee agrees. "Without language", he writes, "life suddenly takes on a humanless garb." He hastens to add that "language is the unique ingredient in man, for where it does not exist, there abides little that is human."[7]

Anthropology has discovered more eloquence and valuable data regarding the origins and development of peoples in muted tongues than from standard physiological criteria, including shapes of skulls and other sources of evidence enshrined in human remains. We know more about the mysterious beginnings of the Basques and the Hindus from the scientific study of their languages than from other ostensibly "exact" scientific disciplines.

"Man is the weakest reed in the universe—but he is a thinking reed", observed Blaise Pascal. "And he is a sounding reed as well," added Michael Girdansky, multidiscipline student of linguistics and the natural sciences.[8] With this "sounding reed," man is capable of producing the most powerful force on earth: language. Subatomic physics has exposed the basic substance of matter as energy or even vibration. Mass is an illusion. The intangible stuff which comes out of that "reed" then, is identical with the ultimate building blocks of the material universe. Words can certainly move mountains . . . and they frequently do!

Origins of Speech: An Exercise in Guesswork

How did this whole language business begin? Laird suggests that men have a "native genius for language".[9] In his view, the development of language was a ubiquitous universal development and not an isolated incident. The rest is shrouded in mystery and confusion. This is not intended as a complaint about a lack of theories. On the contrary, there is no dearth of theories. But the only definite ideas concerning the origins of language are a miasma of uncertainty and guesswork. "In short, we know nothing about how language started and we have not even the materials from which we might hope to find out."[10] Strange that this "greatest invention of all time"[11] from which man derives his definition as "a languagized mammal"[12] should continue to baffle scholars in this scientifically sophisticated age of nuclear physics and space exploration.

In the sphere of linguistics, distinguished scholars resort to the fanciful prattle of babies in an attempt to describe their theories. The fanciful "terminology" reveals an abundance of

3

imagination and a minimum of accuracy. The plethora of theories and the innumerable compounds to which they contribute include three popular hypotheses[13] which deserve to be mentioned. These are (seriously) the celebrated "Ding-Dong," "Poo-Poo," and "Bow-Wow" theories. Briefly, the "Ding-Dong" theory sees a logical and necessary relationship between the sound of a word and the thing to which it refers. In other words, Alley Oop called an axe, "axe" because it looked like it should be called an "axe"!

The "Poo-Poo" theory suggests that primitive language resulted from natural exclamations triggered by emotional experiences such as fear, surprise, etc.

The "Bow-Wow" theory intimates that our primeval ancestors were attentive listeners to nature's sounds, and when they succeeded in imitating them, language was born. The technical term for this theory is "onomatopoeia". This theory represents the transition from the biological to the anthropological categories.

The biological hypothesis does not concern us here. This is so because in the absence of a universally acceptable definition of "man" we must be reconciled to the *anthropological* view that "man without language was, by definition, not yet man". Thus, the anthropological hypothesis is on alien territory when it seeks to discover "origins" of language in terms of "forms of communication". Actually, the anthropological hypothesis should confine itself to recorded linguistic material and extant languages of primitive peoples. We are compelled to acknowledge our limitations, and confine our area of research to a relatively small time-span and a circumscribed lode of currently available evidence. Speculation beyond these boundaries, as Revesz warns, is a usurpation of prerogatives which belong to other disciplines.[14] In fact, Revesz views all the traditional theories, the anthropological hypothesis included, with a jaundiced eye.

Anthropology, Language and Culture: Definitions

"Anthropology" and "language" have been mentioned time and again in this chapter and soon "culture" will join our active vocabulary. It might prove profitable to establish working definitions of these terms in true Socratic tradition, to ensure clarity and precision in this discussion.

4

"Anthropology" comes from the Greek *anthropos,* meaning "man", and *logos,* which may be rendered "theory". Thus, anthropology is that branch of science which studies the human species. The ancient Greeks anticipated the development of our Western scientific outlook; anthropology is no exception. Anaximander provided intimations of the modern theory of evolution which anthropologists consider basic to their discipline. Evolution, in its broadest sense, deals with the question of survival. Anthropology focuses on human survival with special attention to adaptation to "conditions of life". Generally, three factors are involved: environment, race and culture. Corresponding to these divisions, anthropology flows into three branches which are invariably known as anthro-geography, physical anthropology and cultural anthropology. (A fourth division called "ethnology" attempts to synthesize and correlate the three branches.)

Cultural anthropology, which is our present concern, is generally conceived as tripartite in composition: language, material culture (e.g., arts and crafts), and moral culture (understood in terms of social institutions).

What emerges from this schematization is a three-part telescope beginning with "anthropology", out of which comes "culture", which in turn produces "language". As our study continues we shall discover that this relationship involving anthropology, culture and language is an oversimplification and that the bonds are more than structural. It will become abundantly evident that the three are intimately related and *interdependent.* Thus anthropology is meaningless unless it includes culture, and culture is inconceivable without language. That anthropology is predicated on the existence of language is already a *sine qua non.*

To continue with our definitions. What is "culture"? There are almost as many definitions as there are anthropologists. One popular statement defines "culture" as: "All those historically created designs for living, explicit and implicit, rational, irrational and nonrational, which exist at any given time as potential guides for the behavior of man".[15] A more comprehensive definition declares that "Culture is the way of living which any society develops to meet its fundamental needs for survival, perpetuation of the species, and the ordering of social experience. It is the accumulation of material objects, patterns of social organization, learned modes of behavior, knowledge, beliefs, and all other

5

activities which are developed in human association. Culture, then, is man's contribution to his environment."[16] In other words, everything in man's environment which is "man made" (and we do mean *everything* from art and literature to dams and skyscrapers) is included in "culture".

Where does language fit into the picture? No people known to anthropologists has ever been without a language. Few will dispute the claim that "pre-linguistic" is coextensive with "pre-cultural"—and it might as well be added "pre-human"! Where a human being is raised in total isolation from society and denied the experience of cultural transmission from other human beings he does not use language. (Such pitiful creatures are called "feral men"). Language requires groups or social organizations for fulfillment. Language as a "thinking" tool follows speech employed by man in his role, as Aristotle put it, of a social animal.

"Language is fundamental to the learning of culture", declares a college handbook in sociology. "If culture is a river, then language is the bed in which the river flows".[17] By now it is patently clear that language and culture are in a symbiotic embrace. Both culture and language are universal. Both are subject to the paradoxical dynamics of continual change in which flux and stability coexist. (Change does not disturb what Diamond calls "communal organicity"— one of the instruments "by which a whole community is organized and works, and it is also the expression of that working organization".)[18]

Language is the "vehicle of culture," the means through which men communicate to produce culture, and by means of which culture is preserved (in oral traditions or written documents). It has also been observed that women play the major role in the transmission of both language and culture. These treasures of mankind represent the cumulative results of a working partnership between language and culture extending back to the beginnings of man. The question as to which of the two is the "senior partner" privileged to make all the decisions will be considered when we cross the Rubicon of linguistics.

Returning to definitions, language is best described as a means of communication between human beings, consisting of a conscious effort on the part of one person to come in mental contact with another person or persons. It has already been

6

pointed out that language serves other highly utilitarian purposes: as an outlet for human emotions and as a form of "play". The great social anthropologist Bronislaw Malinowsky emphasized the social role played by language, the importance of a "good morning" greeting as a generator of good will. In this respect it is a powerful social force welding together individuals and groups. Speech, according to Malinowsky, is used primarily to fulfill a "social function". The transmission of information is of secondary importance. S. I. Hayakawa, the well-known pioneer in general semantics, agrees that speech as a vehicle for communicating information is secondary. The primary function of speech is to give expression to our "internal condition" as part of an activity of "noise for noise sake" intended to establish communion between people. The most vital element in speech, says Hayakawa, is pre-symbolic language which expresses feeling and not the intellectualized symbolic language which we usually identify with "language" in conventional definitions. Thus a person who does not "understand" the sacred language used in religious ritual can still be inspired by the worship service because of the content of pre-symbolic language.[19]

The more traditional definitions of language were restated in this post-semantic and meta-linguistic decade by Girdansky: "Language is a set of *arbitrary symbols* (words) which are placed in *orderly relationship* with one another according to conventions accepted by the speakers, for the transmission of messages".[20]

The many roles of language include international relations, national rivalries, and politics. It serves as a powerful instrument in the nurture and social development of children. Through it they develop a sense of self and broaden their interaction with others. It also helps them to internalize the attitudes and behavior of fellow human beings. As Henry James observed, speech, the medium of communication, is the question to which all of life must return.

The Indo-European "Cousin's Club"

Scholars speculate that most languages originated in one universal parent language. The vast family of languages spoken by half the population of the world is descended from "Indo-European". The origins of this tongue are shrouded in the mists of time. In all probability the facts were consigned to oblivion before the invention of writing. This may be the reason for the absence of documentary evidence dating back to the time when Indo-European was a living language. At best the historical lexicography of this mysterious tongue can help us deduce the "most probable forms" of basic roots. In the end we must concede that all is hypothetical.

The Indo-European ancestor of the vast complex of modern languages underwent a binary fission resulting in Eastern (Satem) and Western (Centum) divisions. The former, in turn broke into Indo-Iranian (Aryan), (which developed into Indic, Sanskrit and Pali, Prakrit, and the modern Indian dialects); and Baltic-Slavic (giving rise, via Baltic, to Lithuanian and the neighboring tongues, and through Slavonic to Czech, Polish, and the various Russian dialects). The Western (Centum) branch had more progeny. To this group belongs Modern Greek and its Classical and Hellenic forebears; Celtic and its colorful offspring; as well as the Romance languages which hark back to Latin and Italic. Finally, this group embraces the Germanic (Teutonic) subdivisions of East (Gothic); North (Scandinavian) and West-High (Modern German). Our own English language comes to us from West Germanic Low by way of Anglo-Saxon and Middle English; Plattdeutsch, Dutch, and Flemish are also part of this happy family of active tongues.

English . . . and It Grew . . . and Grew . . . and Grew . . .

The evolution of the English language involved a host of intricate factors. Demands of society stimulated the growth of a complex language with millions of words from the matrix of the limited Indo-European vocabulary. Other remarkable changes occurred. The inflected ("welded") Latin and Anglo-Saxon emerged after a complicated metamorphosis in an uninflected English. In this respect English is more akin to Chinese. A lingering suspicion, however, persists that the streets of ancient Rome echoed to a distributive, or uninflected, "spoken" Latin. Actually, English itself underwent a departure from the inflectional system between Beowulf and Chaucer when it settled down to a distributive grammar.[21]

Other factors contributed to the growth of the English language. Vocabulary increased through "specialization" (i.e.,

8

an associational relationship between a general word and a particular object), and "generalization" (i.e., when a specialized word assumes a general character in the process of application). Dynamics of word formation operated on many levels. "Differentiation" gave words greater precision, and "compounding" created a variety of new word constructions by means of the appending of prefixes and suffixes. "Amelioration" made some humble words respectable, while "pejoration" had the reverse effect on less fortunate ones. Taboos, moral preferences, aesthetic sensitivities, and religious considerations also played important roles in the development of the language. "Powder room" took over where "toilette" once reigned, only to beat a hasty exit when "bathroom" arrogantly stepped in. Today newer words are knocking at the door. Clever substitutes and circumlocutions were invented to describe bodily functions and sacred words. This is how "gosh" began its career under the sponsorship of Charles Dickens. Conversely, erstwhile less than respectable and outright vulgar words became acceptable. "Jazz," originally a Negro-Creole colloquial term for sexual intercourse, became a legitimized name for the great musical phenomenon of American culture.

And the English language continued to grow. All speech is a human activity, and every aspect of language is directly determined by human nature. It is natural for human beings to borrow, so language (and culture in general) did its share of borrowing. The alternative would be to stagnate and become sterile. Commerce is one of the most important factors in the growth of English. Invasions and religious changes made modest contributions, but trade did much more for the development of English. Every shipment of continental goods brought bags of linguistic stowaways. In addition, the general northward movement of culture from the Mediterranean basin helped enrich the language.

Words are very important, but so is the formula by which they are joined into phrases and sentences. What arranges them in patterns that make sense and communicate meaning is known by that terrifying word "grammar." If, those poor old souls, my well-intentioned but overzealous spinster teachers, could only read what I am doing to their sacred grammar right now, they would turn over in their proverbial graves to the delight of every

9

modern linguist! First, we ought to inquire: "What is English grammar anyway?" The reply is a babel of speculations, opinions, and fanciful ideas. But no one really *knows* the answer. Modern grammarians agree that English grammar has its roots in Anglo-Saxon, both oral and written, with the oral playing the dominant role. Paralleling what has been observed in regard to vocabulary, grammar is as fickle as a college queen on campus. What is acceptable form today may be obsolete tomorrow, and what is wrong now may be stylish later. Even scholars in the field find it taxing to keep up with the subtleties of changes in grammar. Complexity compounded by havoc accompanies expressions which assume a meaning not conveyed by the parts of which they are composed. An example of "rules" of grammar resistant to rhyme and reason is the "wandering" preposition which has become the scandal of English grammar. Verbs have become vague; one may "catch" a train, a cold, or a ball!

English grammar simply refuses to be identified in "neat" definitions. "Grammar," says Laird, "is not a set of rules," but an integral part of language and inherent in language. It is "whatever the users of a language do with the symbols of meaning (i.e., words) . . . in order to express extensive and complicated meanings."[22]

Modern grammarians reject the Grammar School attempt to identify grammar with "Latin" grammar. Even a conservative New England lexicographer like Noah Webster understood that English grammar should be pursued to its Anglo-Saxon origins and not shoehorned into Latin "rules" which have pinched the sensitive toes of many a chagrined Huckleberry Finn. An awareness of this point is especially important in view of the generally accepted principle (already alluded to above) that language exerts its greatest influence through speech, not the written word. Illiteracy, until recently, attended to that. The invention of writing and the printing press are factors worthy of consideration, but they have still not replaced the spoken word as the foundation of language. A professor of linguistics (unless he is a bachelor) will "tell-his-wife-off" with a greater volume of vocabulary than he could ever put into his printed books (and with a more lively and entertaining choice of words). Noteworthy is the fact that the bulk of spoken English is Anglo-Saxon while the dictionary remains a repository of Latin terms.

Endless Change

Heraclitus, the pre-Socratic philosopher, observed that "no man steps into the same river twice". In the light of modern scientific insights one may safely add that the stepper-into-the-water is also not even the *same man!* Change is the fundamental principle in language past, present, and future. For one thing, speech is one of the most democratic of human institutions. Language is created not by scholars in ivory towers or book-worms in libraries, but by all classes of people, in the market place, the street, and the home. The purely subjective will of the users of a language will determine in the long run what is "right" and what is "wrong"—and they reserve the prerogative to change their minds without notice. Thus any search for universal "laws" or "rules" of language is futile. All that can be found even by the most assiduous student of speech are universal principles—general statements.

Change in language occurs also as a result of the "playful-ness" of people as mentioned earlier. Slang occasionally becomes a respectable Cinderella; but then it is no longer slang, at least until the inexorable rule of Heraclitus intervenes. And it steps in primarily when culture and society, the matrix of language, change and in turn demand change. Even as this is being written the English language is growing fast, very fast, hardly able to keep up with itself!

"Tell me son" runs a paraphrase of a jaded ethnic pun, "is change good or bad for the English?" Linguists concede that we must learn to live *with* it because like the weather, there is nothing that can be done *about* it. The basic goal in language should not be "perfection" but "appropriateness." Our complex society has become a global community in dire need of a system of communication sufficiently flexible to meet the ever-changing needs of a world-in-flux which can destroy itself with a single misunderstanding.

Although language change is obviously necessary and even desirable, it requires the midwives of Care and Standardization. A certain measure of ambivalence is healthy in this area. Standards should be "restrictive," not "coercive." Such restrictive agencies of standardization do exist in the form of schools, homes,

11

publishing houses, broadcasting companies, and dictionaries. However, what gives life to language is "currency" and acceptable meaning through usage; and the final arbiters are the people who use it. Yet it is important to maintain a reasonable balance between man's need to express himself freely and the discipline of social convention. Even in primitive societies, it has been observed, educational, kinship, economic, and other social agencies maintain a stabilizing influence on language.

Writing, Spelling and Punctuation

Speech has been given all the bouquets till now. It is about time that at least a few petals be tossed in the direction of "writing". Laird who was quoted earlier extolling the importance of language saw fit to conclude: "without written language, no civilization".[23] Writing is the faithful preserver of ideas and discoveries. Each generation reads the written records of earlier ages and leaves its own deposit in the vast treasury of culture preserved in the written word. Deprived of the subtleties of expression and gesture, which are a natural concomitant of speech, written language was compelled to substitute *style*, in itself a cultural contribution.

Writing is thousands of years old. When man was able to record his thoughts in symbolic marks, he took one of the biggest leaps in "recorded" history. That was the moment when history began! Egyptian hieroglyphics mainly provided symbols for words or syllables, not individual sounds as do our letters of the alphabet. Our alphabet, like so much of the furniture in the language household, has an obscure origin. We do know, however, that it is of Semitic ancestry, borrowed by the Greeks from the mercantile Phoenicians, who found the little signs a practical asset in their commercial activities. The Greeks thus obtained a valuable cultural tool and a sophisticated notion of communication which represented the culmination of a long process of development.

Spelling (orthography) was far from uniform until the Renaissance when the invention of printing revolutionized many things, spelling included. George Bernard Shaw has voiced the impatience of many contemporary linguists who bemoan the inadequacy of our alphabet. Why is "rite" wrong if it means "correct" in the context of a given passage? The advent of printing also helped standardize punctuation, a relatively late invention.

Linguistics: A Scientific Approach to Language

Linguistics, placed appropriately in the Dewey decimal classification between sociology and the natural sciences, is probably the most exact of the social sciences. Names associated with the development of linguistics include De Saussure, Bloomfield, Sapir, Jespersen, and others. It begins by analyzing the simplest sound or expression unit, the *phoneme* which is analogous to an element in chemistry and is hard to define except "as a minimum feature of the expression system of a spoken language by which one thing which may be said is distinguished from any other thing that might have been said".[24] It goes on to the meaningful combination of phonemes called *morphemes*. Phonemes have no meaning in themselves; they are part of the "expression structure" of a language. Morphemes do have meaning; they are part of the "content structure" of speech. The branch of grammar concerned with meaningful arrangement of linguistic forms (e.g., prefix, suffix, etc.) is called *morphology*. *Syntax* is the branch of grammar devoted to the proper arrangement of words to form phrases and sentences. The approach of linguistics is predicated on the hypothesis that people talked long before they wrote, and that the origins of language are to be found in the *spoken* word. Language patterns emerge from this study. One example of a linguistic pattern which yielded to this method of research is the hopeless "ng" that never opened an English word; and linguists assure us that it never will! The Eskimos, however, have no compunction about using it as a prefix. Which only proves that one man's poison is another man's blubber! An Eskimo can, if he wishes, speak a perfect "nglish."

Linguistics, then, is an attempt to understand language not by means of extrinsic "rules," or concepts provided by other disciplines, but from the point of view of its internal structure. Frans Boas, the giant of anthropology, taught that cultural anthropology must appreciate language differences on the basis of "arbitrary selection"—i.e., each culture selects from the vast universe of possibilities its own model of reality—and the language with which to describe it. Why? or how? No one knows.

13

Linguistics does not hesitate to borrow insights from other disciplines such as anthropology, psychology, acoustics, and physiology. On the other hand, it reciprocates with contributions of its own to these generous sources of human knowledge.

The complex structure of language is reduced by some linguists to two dynamically interacting parts: expression (sound) and content (ideas, thoughts, etc.). Others prefer to think of language in terms of three basic structural parts: content (the most stable), expression (which is more amenable to change), and vocabulary (which is the least stable).

Differences in the phonemic systems of various languages are what make some foreign languages "sound like Chinese" to us. In fact, the phonemic system of Chinese differs radically from the Indo-European patterns to which our ears are accustomed. Chinese consists mostly of morphemes. English contains a mixture. The discovery of the phoneme revolutionized linguistics and helped make it one of the most precise of the social sciences. It eliminated much of the vagueness associated with the study of language. Linguistics, moreover, enjoys a position of special favor in the social science family because of the wealth of structural material at its disposal. In spite of the notorious imponderables connected with language, linguistics has succeeded in eliminating a considerable amount of the chaos endemic to language study, so that it is even possible for linguists to forecast developmental patterns and, as has been noted, insist that no English word will *ever* begin with "ng".

Scholars were in for a big surprise when they tried to find the "original" language in the primitive society of our time. They were amazed to learn that the language of our contemporary primitives is adequate for their particular way of life, and in some instances, extremely rich in precision, nuance and complexity. The Australian aborigine, for example, possesses a list of kinship titles more impressive than ours. In fact, sociologists have observed that the entire kinship system of these "primitives" is more highly developed than our own. The same is true of Polynesian, which has a wealth of sailing terms; and Eskimo, which offers a wide variety of terms for every nuance in quality of snow. Aztec, on the other hand, is deficient in vocabulary for snow, ice, cold, and related frigid items. It is evident that language reflects the experience of people. However, we

14

shall soon find in the Whorfian hypothesis a radical reinterpretation of the relationship between language and culture.

In turning the corner to this fresh orientation in linguistics, it should be emphasized that linguists generally agree that the terms "correct" and "incorrect" cannot be applied to any form of expression. The most that may be said critically about anything in language is "acceptable" or "unacceptable". All the new insights notwithstanding, they admit that language is arbitrary, irrational, and capricious.

Metalinguistics and a Revolutionary View of Language and Culture

The conventional view of language as a mere reflection of human conditions and a product of culture and society was challenged by Benjamin Lee Whorf, a brilliant young engineer at M.I.T. Strange that the most fascinating modern notions concerning language dynamics should come from an amateur linguist who never even wrote a book! Whorf was a bold pioneer with the courage to probe the outer space of linguistics. During a tragically brief life he accomplished for linguistics what Einstein had done for physics. In his system of metalinguistics, most of which was unpublished at the time of his death, Whorf argues that language is more than a system of sounds. Language, he said, contains a "hidden metaphysics." Building on notions already anticipated by Sapir, he demonstrated that language is a unique *view of the world*—and of culture. More, it is a general frame of reference with the power to mold the thought and behavior patterns of its habitual users. Language has three functions in the catechism of the metalinguist: To communicate with fellow-humans, to communicate with oneself (i.e., to think), and to fashion one's outlook on life.

The quintessence of Whorf's metalinguistics is an introduction to "a new principle of relativity, which holds that all observers are not led by the same physical evidence to the same picture of the universe, unless their linguistic backgrounds are similar, or can be calibrated".[25] Whorf begins with the problem: "What is the relativity between the mechanism of language, such as vocabulary, inflection and sentence formation on the one hand and either perception and organization of experience on the broad patterns of behavior on the other?"[26]

15

Metalinguistics suggests that the picture of the universe shifts from language to language. Translation cannot solve the *real* problem of communication. Some language systems are simply not equipped with the requisite linguistic conceptualization machinery to convey basic messages. In his study of the Hopi language he discovered not merely a different collection of words or grammatical rules. What he discovered was a distinct and unique philosophy of life that could only be made intelligible through the Hopi language to one who understands the Hopi language on its own terms. To illustrate, the Western mind, conditioned by centuries of Indo-European preoccupation with materialistic notions, perceives time as a *thing*. Therefore, in our society, "one day plus four days equals five days" makes sense. A day which is merely a time segment is conceived as a distinct *object*, like an apple. Who can quarrel with the correctness of "one apple and four apples equals five apples"? To the Hopi, time is a *process*, not a *thing*. Therefore it cannot be itemized as "one day" or "one hour." It is more like a snowball which grows bigger as it rolls down a hill. The Hopi fails to see "spaces" between time segments like the spaces which make five apples five distinct entities.

Linguistically, the Western mind lives in a "split-level" world of things (nouns) and actions (verbs). Time itself is frequently qualified by materialistic terms like "gone by," "killed," "taken," etc. The hapless Hopi listens and shrugs his ancient shoulders.

Notions of time, relationship, and plurality are handled differently by different linguistic families. Culture cannot remain unaffected by linguistic influences. This is of paramount importance to statesmen whose "understanding" of how others think may determine the future of the human race. What does "democracy" mean to nations who subscribe to other language systems for conceptualization? Shades of *mokusatsu!* What does the future hold for communism in China in view of the (to us) peculiar multivalued nature of the Chinese language which tolerates countless nuances of value between "good" and "bad," "right" and "wrong"? Dialectical confrontations and collisions thrive on the moral polarizations peculiar to our Indo-European heritage. Communism was brought to China by zealots who learned their dialectical materialism in Russian, which is an

16

Indo-European language. Can the Chinese language convey the "either-or" ultimatum of Karl Marx to the Chinese speaking (and thinking) masses? Unfortunately, we must wait for the answer to this existential question. In the meantime we can hope that metalinguistics is correct in the belief that language not only expresses thought but shapes it—and that culture is linguistically determined through the "linguistic system" built into the human mind.

Whorf expressed the hope that a correct "understanding of language" will usher in a "great phase of human brotherhood." He believed that a "scientific understanding of diverse languages . . . is a lesson in brotherhood in the universal human principle. . . . It causes us to transcend the boundaries of local cultures, nationalities . . . to discover in the mystique of relative linguistics the secret reality that 'all men are equal'."[27] Whorf was not without his critics. Feuer and Lennenberg disagreed with him on many points.[28]

Anthropology Speaks to Language and Culture

Anthropologists have not ceased to offer new insights to students of culture and language. Anthropology reveals that cultural evolution does not necessarily proceed from the simple to the complex. A poignant example may be found in a comparison of primitive and civilized kinship systems. The family in our sophisticated Western society is much weaker than its equivalent among the Australian aborigines. Concomitantly, the Australian "bushman" has a richer vocabulary to apply to his kinsmen than does his American cousin. Emile Durkheim and Bronislaw Malinowsky insist that the family is the basic unit in society upon which society depends for stability. Language is learned in the context of the family and is transmitted through it. The sociological implications are terrifying in view of the precarious condition of the American family. Even metalinguists should be alarmed! Consider the Chinese character for "good" or "happy": it is a combination of logograms expressing "wife" and "child." Happiness and family to the Chinese are coextensive linguistically and culturally.

Anthropology also tells us that culture is diffused from society to society in a continual process. And culture goes with language either as passenger or as the "vehicle of culture".

Another vital contribution of anthropology in this area has been the demolition of ethnocentricity. The "better-than-thou" attitude, anthropology teaches, can only isolate people and stunt culture. The same applies to language. The ancient Greeks and Romans were notoriously ethnocentric. Every non-Greek was despised as a "Barbarian." Of pertinent interest to us is the linguistic implication of the term: *barbaroi* means "stutterers"! The cultural and linguistic snobbishness of the Greek was inherited by his Western successors. The Slavic-speaking peoples referred to Germans with the equivalent of "dumb-mutes," "unable to speak." (Hence the Russian *nem'ets,* Polish *n'miec* and Hungarian *nemeth.*) Anthropology-become-preacher declares that all cultures and languages should be approached objectively. In the interest of science they must be studied from the standpoint of their intrinsic values.

The study of other languages is practical for many reasons. It can serve as a potent antidote to ethnocentrism. At the same time it provides a basis for comparison to appreciate our own language better. "What do they know of English who only English know."[29]

Finally, anthropology has discovered that human behavior is influenced by culture in various ways. Each society, in keeping with its particular value system, transmits patterns of behavior and conduct to the individuals who belong to it. Thus language, acknowledged as the "vehicle of culture," or at least as one of its most important parts, emerges once again as a shaper of human behavior, and through the human personality, of society itself.

The Challenge of Language to Modern Society

"When I use a word," Humpty Dumpty said in a rather scornful tone, "it means just what I choose it to mean—neither more nor less". "The question is," said Alice, "whether you *can* make words mean so many different things." "The question is," said Humpty Dumpty, "which is to be master—that's all." Little did egotistical (and probably ethnocentric) Mr. Dumpty realize that the Chinese do not even have a word for "word"!

Nonetheless, Lewis Carroll has touched questions that concern serious students of language and culture. What is the power of language? How much control do we have over speech? How much influence does it exercise over us? To what extent can we determine the function and development of language?

The answers to these questions do not come so easily to us as they did to the glib hero in Alice's fairytale. Many disciplines are developing an increasing interest in this subject and they may help us find the answers. Anthropology has been the keenest patron of language and culture. Recently, sociologists and social psychologists have been stirred by the vast possibilities inherent in this study. Now even philosophy sees in language one of the few fundamental sets of forms.

In spite of all this ferment, Western thought and technology have outstripped the traditional language equipment which remains an unprecise system based on archaic sources and is resistant to reform. We are simply running out of words needed to describe all the new things and concepts which have come into being since Beowulf, Chaucer, and Michener. More, our "global community" must acquire means of communication, universally intelligible, with which to "talk things over." Some think that English meets all the requirements of an international language. Others deride this claim as an example of ethnocentrism and cultural imperialism. *Life* magazine recently editorialized on a statement by William Benton, American ambassador to UNESCO and former senator from Connecticut, in which he suggested "that the U.S. should team up with Britain in a drive to confirm English as the world's international tongue." He suggested that our country ought to make the teaching of English (as Benton put it) "a major goal in the conduct of its foreign policy."[30]

Serious scholars agree with Benton but from more altruistic motives. They are the ones who believe that English is the most suitable tool for the job: it has the widest geographical distribution, is spoken by a vast numerical segment of the world's population, and has the qualities needed for a medium of human heritage. It is fair to caution the idealists of monistic inclination who look to an international language as a panacea for world problems not to get their hopes up too high. Too many wars have been fought by men who cursed each other in the same language on both side of the line.

Perhaps Einstein had the answer when he called for a "science language" as an international tongue.[31] But, so the story goes, only twelve men understood Einstein when he was at his best!

Of more vital concern is the frightening reality of widespread illiteracy involving half of the world's population. Simeon Potter urges us to ". . . create and secure for present-day society a 'climate of literacy' in which alone national democracy is able to function and world government can be achieved."[32] As mankind strives through enlightened governments and international agencies toward the realization of this ideal, responsible people everywhere must guard against the abuse of language by those who would harness this "vehicle of culture" to the four horses of the linguistic apocalypse: propaganda, politics, vulgarity, and selfishness. The potentialities for good and evil are magnified by the power of the "newer languages"—the vociferous public media of radio, television, photography, etc., which can distort and focus the contents of communication as never before.

Conclusion

This study ends as it began, with a recognition of, and respect for, the awesome power of the tongue. Without language there could be no communication, history, education, culture, thinking—no society! Essentially, the anthropological view of language and culture finds its most meaningful expression in the realization that man is man precisely because he possesses the uniquely human phenomena of speech and culture. It takes note of the ostensibly divisive factors inherent in a complicated and multiculture world inhabited by "the sons of Shem, after their families, after their tongues, in their lands, after their nations."[33] However, anthropology in uncovering clues to a universal antediluvian language and by revealing principles common to all language systems has confirmed the ancient report that "the whole earth was one language and of one speech"[34]—and that there is more hope for a mankind divided against itself than a casual observer of current events might be willing to concede.

VICTOR SOLOMON, born in New York City, received his B.A. at Yeshiva University from which he was graduated with honors in 1951. He was granted an M.A. in Education at Hunter College in 1953. In 1955, Yeshiva University's Theological Seminary conferred upon him the traditional Ordination. He continued his graduate studies at Temple University, where he earned a Doctorate in Religion and Philosophy in 1960. In 1967, he completed an intensive training program at the Postgraduate Center For Mental Health in New York, and was awarded an S.T.M. in pastoral counseling by the New York Theological Seminary. He is on the faculty of the University of Bridgeport where he once taught in the Foreign Languages Department, and now teaches sociology and philosophy. He serves in the active pulpit of the distinguished Congregation Ahavath Achim in Fairfield, Connecticut, and devotes much time to counseling. His appointment to the faculty of the Jesuit Fairfield University in 1965 was an historic event for that institution. Dr. Solomon is author of the unique *A Handbook on Conversions to the Religions of the World* (1965), and a frequent contributor to a wide variety of learned journals reflecting the broad sweep of his erudition. He is a consulting editor of the *Indian Sociological Bulletin* and a member of Delta Tau Kappa, International Social Science Honor Society.

FOOTNOTES

1. Proverbs, XVIII
2. Moses Maimonides, GUIDE FOR THE PERPLEXED. Translated by Shlomo Pines, Chicago: University of Chicago Press, 1963, III, 8, 435.
3. Exodus, IV, 11.
4. Isaiah, L, 4.
5. Charlton Laird, THE MIRACLE OF LANGUAGE. New York: Premier, 1965, 224.
6. *Ibid.* 17.
7. Irving J. Lee, LANGUAGE HABITS IN HUMAN AFFAIRS. New York: Harper, 1941, 3.
8. Michael Girdansky, THE ADVENTURE OF LANGUAGE. Englewood Cliffs, N. J.: Prentice-Hall, 1963, xiii.
9. Charlton Laird, *op. cit.*, 1.
10. *Ibid.*, 24.
11. *Ibid.*, 23.
12. *Ibid.*, 16.
13. Speculation concocted "Child Speech" theory. Theories of the priority of song, psychological predisposition, priority of gesture, language and theories based on ethnology and the pathology of speech.
14. Geza Revesz, THE ORIGINS AND PREHISTORY OF LANGUAGE. New York: Philosophical Library, 1956, 20.
15. Clyde Kluckholn, and William H. Kelly, "The Concept of Culture" in THE SCIENCE OF MAN IN THE WORLD CRISES. Edited by Ralph Linton, New York: Columbia University Press, 1945, 97.
16. Joseph S. Roucek, and Richard L. Warren, SOCIOLOGY, AN INTRODUCTION. Totowa, N. J.: Littlefield Adams, 1966, 8.
17. Leo Charles Daley, COLLEGE LEVEL SOCIOLOGY. New York: Monarch, 1963, 14.
18. Arthur S. Diamond, THE HISTORY AND ORIGIN OF LANGUAGE. New York: Philosophical Library, 1959, 14.
19. S.I. Hayakawa, "The Language of Social Cohesion" in LANGUAGE

AND LITERACY TODAY, by Patrick D. and Mary E. Hazard, Chicago: Science Research Associates, 1965, 60-8.
20. Michael Girdansky, *Op. Cit.*, 3.
21. "Distributive" refers to the use of words rather than changes in form. E.g., "The hat of the man" instead of "The man's hat."
22. Charlton Laird, *Op. Cit.*, 130.
23. Charlton Laird, *Op. Cit.*, 224.
24. Hazard and Hazard, *Op. Cit.*, 56.
25. Benjamin Lee Whorf, "Science and Linguistics," in John B. Carroll, (editor), LANGUAGE, THOUGHT AND REALITY, Cambridge: M.I.T. Press, 1964, 214.
26. Paul Henle, LANGUAGE, THOUGHT AND CULTURE. Ann Arbor: University of Michigan Press, 1958, 4.
27. Benjamin L. Whorf, *Op. Cit.*, "LANGUAGE MIND, AND REALITY", 263.
28. See Bibliography.
29. Simeon Potter, LANGUAGE IN THE MODERN WORLD, Baltimore: Penguin Books, 1964, 131.
30. LIFE, September 9, 1966, Editorial Page.
31. Albert Einstein, "The Common Language of Science" in Donald E. Hayden and Paul Alworth, (editors), CLASSICS IN SEMANTICS. New York: Philosophical Library, 1965, 324-5.
32. Hazard and Hazard, *Op. Cit.*, 13.
33. Genesis X, 31.
34. *Ibid.*, XI, 1.

Selected Bibliography

BOOKS

Diamond, Arthur S., THE HISTORY AND ORIGIN OF LANGUAGE. New York: Philosophical Library, 1959. Traces the development of language from the prattle of primitive men requesting action, to a sophisticated modern examination of the physiology of speech. Suggests that divergent theories about the origins of language contain elements of truth.

Girdansky, Michael, THE ADVENTURE OF LANGUAGE. Englewood Cliffs, N.J.: Prentice-Hall, 1963. Peppery description of language in terms of linguistics, anthropology, culture and perpetual change.

Hayakawa, S. I., LANGUAGE IN THOUGHT AND ACTION. New York: Harcourt, Brace and World, 1964. A distinguished general semanticist reveals the subtle unarticulated language of genuine communication used in conversation.

Hazard, Patrick D. and Mary E., eds., LANGUAGE AND LITERACY TODAY. Chicago: Science Research Associates, 1965. A symposium in which noted authorities attempt to redefine literacy in the idiom of the contemporary situation. They deal with spoken, written, and printed language in general and English in particular, as well as the "other languages" of the mass media.

22

Henle, Paul, ed., LANGUAGE, THOUGHT AND CULTURE. Ann Arbor: University of Michigan Press, 1958. An integrated study of language involving the disciplines of anthropology, philosophy, psychology, sociology, linguistics, and literary criticism, based on academic symposia.

Hertzler, Joyce O., A SOCIOLOGY OF LANGUAGE. New York: Random House, 1965. A sociological approach to language, with special emphasis on international, interpersonal and intercultural characteristics and uses of language. Related social problems and social advantages are analyzed.

Hoijer, Harry, LANGUAGE IN CULTURE. Chicago: University of Chicago Press, 1954. A multidisciplinary study of language and culture, with scholars in anthropology, philosophy, linguistics, psychology, history, etc., participating. Special attention is given the Whorfian hypothesis which attempts to interrelate language and other aspects of culture.

Laird, Charlton, THE MIRACLE OF LANGUAGE. Greenwich, Conn.: Premier, 1965. (Also New York: Fawcett, 1953.) A popular and witty exploration of language in the context of history and civilization.

Lee, Irving J., LANGUAGE HABITS IN HUMAN AFFAIRS. New York: Harper, 1941. Language, its uses, abuses, and misuses are analyzed from the standpoint of general semantics. Speech can be the balm of the humanitarian and the weapon of the demagogue.

Pei, Mario, THE STORY OF LANGUAGE. Philadelphia: J. B. Lippincott, 1949. A panoramic view of language which surveys its structure, development, social function, manifestation in a variety of spoken tongues, problems in acquiring fluency, and the question of an international language. Combines scholarship with literary style in an introduction to language and culture.

Potter, Simeon, LANGUAGE IN THE MODERN WORLD. Baltimore: Penguin Books, 1964. An excellent introduction to modern linguistics by one of the acknowledged authorities in the field.

Revesz, Geza, THE ORIGINS AND PREHISTORY OF LANGUAGE. New York: Philosophical Library, 1956. An analysis of the prehistory of language and the methodological approaches to its study. The significance of language is considered in the context of general human development, and is explored intensively only up to the beginnings of the current language systems.

Sapir, Edward, LANGUAGE: AN INTRODUCTION TO THE STUDY OF SPEECH. New York: Harcourt and Brace, 1949. A profound study in linguistics by an original scholar who has had a lasting influence in the field.

Saussure, Ferdinand de, COURSE IN GENERAL LINGUISTICS,

translated by Wade Baskin. New York: Philosophical Library, 1959. The cornerstone of modern linguistic theory. Marks the beginning of structural linguistics.

Watmough, Joshua, LANGUAGE: A MODERN SYNTHESIS. New York: New American Library of World Literature, 1956. A synthesis of language theories current in diverse disciplines. The author's Theory of Selective Variation is developed in this volume.

Whorf, Benjamin Lee, LANGUAGE, THOUGHT AND REALITY (selected writings, edited by John B. Carroll). Cambridge: The M.I.T. Press, 1964. Selected writings of the father of "metalinguistics" in which he creates a "metaphysics of language", demonstrating that an intimate relationship binds human thinking to human language and that thought and culture are shaped by language.

ARTICLES

Black, Max, "Linguistic Relativity: The Views of Benjamin Lee Whorf." PHILOSOPHICAL REVIEW, LXVIII, 1959, 228-38. A philosophical critique of Whorf's metalinguistics which relates language, culture and mental process. (On the appearance of LANGUAGE, THOUGHT AND REALITY, listed in the Bibliography of Books.)

Bock, Philip K., "Social Structure and Language Structure." SOUTHWESTERN JOURNAL OF ANTHROPOLOGY, XX, 4, Winter 1964, 393-403. An anthropologically oriented search for analogies between language structure and the structure of other aspects of culture.

Feuer, Lewis S., "Sociological Aspects of the Relation Between Language and Philosophy." PHILOSOPHY OF SCIENCE, XX, 2, April 1953, 85-100. Challenges the doctrine of linguistic primacy in the development of philosophy and finds the concept of linguistic relativity inadequate.

Haas, Mary R., "The Linguist As A Teacher of Languages." LANGUAGE, XIX, 1943, 203-8. Best results in learning foreign language are obtained through imitation of a native speaker under the guidance of a trained linguist.

Hall, Edward T., and Whyte, William F., "Intercultural Communication: A Guide To Men of Action." HUMAN ORGANIZATION, XIX, 1, Spring 1960, 5-12. Demonstrates practical value of anthropological knowledge as an essential aid in dealing with people of other cultures.

Hertzler, Joyce O., "Toward A Sociology Of Language." SOCIAL FORCES, XXXII, 2 December 1953, 109-19. Demonstrates the need for a sociology of language among the special disciplines in the family of "sociologies."

Hoijer, Harry, "Linguistic and Cultural Change." LANGUAGE, XXIV, 1948, 335-345. A study of the interaction of language and culture in the context of discernible patterns of flux affecting both.

Kluckhohn, Clyde, "Notes on Some Anthropological Aspects of Communication," (with reply by A. L. Kroeber), AMERICAN ANTHROPOLOGIST, LXIII, 5, part 1, October 1961, 895-912. The manner of, and extent to which, language-culture as the matrix of experience inevitably influences communication.

Labov, William, "Phonological Correlates of Social Stratification." AMERICAN ANTHROPOLOGIST, LXVI, 6 part 2, December 1964, 164-75. Demonstrates through an empirical study a relationship between linguistic change and sociological phenomena.

Lennenberg, Eric H., "Cognition in Ethnolinguistics." LANGUAGE, XXIX, 1953, 463-471. One of Whorf's chief critics disagrees with some of the implications in the Whorfian hypothesis.

Maclay, Howard, "'An Experimental Study of Language and Nonlinguistic Behavior." SOUTHWESTERN JOURNAL OF ANTHROPOLOGY, XIV, 2 Summer 1958, 220-9. An experiment designed to test the validity of the metalinguistic hypothesis.

Orr, William F., and Cappannari, Stephen C., "The Emergence of Language." AMERICAN ANTHROPOLOGIST, LXVI, 2, April 1964, 318-24. A novel interpretation of the evolution of speech and language in neuro-anthropological terms.

Osgood, Charles E., "Semantic Differential Technique in the Comparative Study of Cultures." AMERICAN ANTHROPOLOGIST, LXVI, 3, part 2, June 1964, 171-200. A scholarly effort to circumvent "language barriers" to objective understanding of cultures, through the identification of a universal framework underlying affective and connotive aspects of language.

Schrader, George A., "Existence, Truth and Subjectivity," (in a symposium on Existentialist Thought), THE JOURNAL OF PHILOSOPHY, LIII, 23, November 8, 1956, 759-71. The value of linguistic analysis in current philosophical disputations.

Sommerfelt, Alf, "The Common Bases of Human Language." INTERNATIONAL SOCIAL SCIENCE JOURNAL, XVII, 1965, 145-6. Brief testimony to the fundamental unity of human language.

Modern Languages and Modern Living

FRANCESCO CORDASCO AND LOUIS ROEDERER

Montclair State College, Montclair, New Jersey

WITHIN A DECADE, supersonic transport plus the mammoth plane capable of carrying more than five hundred passengers (which is already a reality in the Soviet Union) will make world-wide air travel almost as easy as a bus ride downtown. By 1970, COMSAT satellites will also make it possible for a single TV broadcast to blanket the globe.

As a matter of simple fact, we are entering, or have already entered, the age of quasi-instant communication. However, as is often the case in human affairs, once more technological progress is centuries ahead of man's preparedness to deal with progress itself and with his fellow man. This, however, is not the result of a complete lack of foresight and endeavor.

World Language

As far back as the seventeenth century, Descartes was considering the feasibility of a single language to facilitate communications between savants of the day; but he had more specifically in mind a sort of algebraic language to condense scientific information.[1] Moreover, Latin was still widely used among the scholars of the time, which took the urgency out of Descartes' idea.

In fact, it was not until the middle of the 19th century, with the gradual disuse of Latin as a scientific or philosophical tool (plus the decline of French at the very moment when several new languages were coming to the fore on the international scene) that the need of a universal medium of communication became a necessity. Answering this need, some individuals created "constructed" languages from the end of the 19th century and on. Among those which elicited the greatest inter-

26

est were: Volapuk, Esperanto, Ido, Latino sine flexione, Inter-lingua and Novial.[2]

For all these efforts, the world-wide use of a single language failed to materialize. By the most optimistic estimates, the number of adherents for each of these languages (those capable of reading and writing them) never went much beyond two hundred. In many cases, the figure remained much lower.

The lack of response to the efforts of the few merely reflects, on the universal scale, an attitude which is rather prevalent amidst Anglo-Americans: the "let them learn our language" attitude.

Language Study Abroad

The movement in favor of learning English as a second tongue, already in evidence before World War II, has been accelerated since then by the ever-increasing number of Americans overseas, by the constant need of American products, American technology and capital, and by the attraction of the American way of life—even in Communist countries. No doubt, the learning process is facilitated by the existence of a "basic English" language composed of about a thousand words which can be mastered in less than six months by an average person or by a child.

Will this "basic English" solve the problem? Will Japanese audiences be able to understand TV programs directly relayed from the U.S. without dubbing, in the same manner as a Japanese airline pilot understands the control tower when he brings his plane in for a landing at San Francisco's airport?

Human Values of Languages

Even if this optimistic picture ever became true, at the very best only half of the problem would have been solved. The other part of the problem is our side of the picture, as long as the other fellow can understand us and we cannot understand him.

However, we must be careful if we want to avoid wrong ideas. The mere knowledge of a language cannot in itself enable us to truly comprehend the way of life, or the thinking, of a foreigner. For that matter, such a comprehension is impossible in an absolute sense even when two persons speak the same language and live in the same environment. The contemporary

27

American scene, for one, gives enough evidence of this fact of life.

Yet, it should be emphasized that knowing the language and civilization of a country would make it possible to achieve a high level of communication, of "understanding" between people of different nationalities. This is so nearly a truism that it would not need a demonstration or arguments.

Of course, except for the establishment of a single world language, the curse of Babel will never be entirely lifted from our shoulders, even if one learns as many as six or ten languages. On the other hand, even the knowledge of only one foreign language and civilization will help us come out of our self-imposed isolation. And this is no mere luxury today. It is already a necessity and will be still more so tomorrow in a world where people will spill over national boundaries, and where languages and cultures will be jumbled together at the touch of a TV dial.

With each passing day, science fiction is becoming less and less fiction. Technology has already entered a new millennium whereas, linguistically, it could be argued whether or not we are as well off as those who lived two thousand years ago when Greek and Latin were the Lingua Franca of the Mediterranean World.

English as a World Language

A majority of the people in every continent of the world learns English as a second language. As a result of such combined numerical and geographical spread, English has become the most widely used vehicle of communication in the modern world. It is ahead of Chinese, which is localized in concentrated areas of the Asiatic continent and a few pockets like Formosa and Indonesia. English also ranks ahead of Russian in numerical and geographical spread even though the teaching of Russian as a second language outside the Iron Curtain has taken a sharp rise since Sputnik.

French, Spanish, and German had been overtaken by English as a second language at least as far back as World War I, and the gap has steadily increased since World War II despite the continued use of French by former colonial territories of the French Union. In fact, on the home grounds of these languages (as well as in the rest of Europe, including the Soviet Union) English is often taught from a minimum of three years in the secondary school to as many as nine years beginning in the elementary schools.[3] Needless to add, culture is taught at the same time and students (except for those living behind the Iron Curtain) have ample opportunities, through summer exchange programs, to get a firsthand acquaintance with the people whose culture and language they are studying. This is done in England in most cases. The study of "American" as opposed to "English" is limited even though interest in things American is keen. A dent, albeit a relatively small one, has been made in the above pattern, thanks to the presence abroad of teachers of American literature and language on Fulbright scholarships.

Languages in the United States

Generally, the average American school still has a long way to go to catch up with the levels attained in most European schools where students reach near fluency in English besides learning another foreign language or two.

Quite naturally, a primary concern of American schools has been to teach English to the immigrant who had little or no knowledge of the language. Unfortunately, for reasons which are not altogether clear, this education was accompanied by gradual disuse of the "old country language." From the second generation on, knowledge of the language and civilization of the country of origin had practically disappeared in most instances.[4] Ethnic links are often maintained only for a generation or two through membership in a church, a club, and still more rarely, a school where the "mother tongue" is used.[5] The "melting pot," the absorption of foreign elements, remains the goal of the American system of education, and quite understandably so. No serious attempt is made to preserve cultural heritages and, again, it is only fair to repeat that the schools cannot be all things to all their pupils at once. Where the preservation of the mother tongue is concerned, the burden is actually on the family and the individual concerned. Thus, it is all the more striking to notice that for years second generation immigrants had generally shunned, rather than sought, the study of their language where such study was possible in the school.

Furthermore, there has been no general protest by parents either when their progeny neglected such opportunities or when language courses were altogether cancelled by the schools for "lack of sufficient enrollment or interest." As Marjorie C. Johnston, Director of the Instructional Resources Branch, United States Office of Education, rightly observed: "The educational system has the dual role of shaping and being shaped by the society it serves."[6]

Thus, it must be a double reflection of the changing climate regarding foreign languages that following a prolonged slump between World War I and World War II, the study of languages is not only encouraged by federal and state authorities at present but that such study is no longer considered as a stigma of "foreignness" by the students themselves. Yet, for all federal and local incentives, Marjorie C. Johnston notes: "Foreign languages study is not yet considered by the public, or even by some language teachers, to be an integral part of general education. Foreign language is the only academic area of the curriculum to which children are not introduced as a matter of course before grade seven."[7]

According to figures mentioned in the same source, the national average of children studying languages in elementary schools (the most appropriate time to begin such study) is about 3 per cent; at the secondary level, almost 40 per cent of schools have no offerings in modern foreign language, and a two-year program (which is inadequate) is still the standard in most school systems. No wonder one hears, again and again, the usual complaint about the two years of language taken in school as being without lasting benefit.

The picture is somewhat brighter in colleges and universities. About 32 per cent of accredited institutions have a foreign language entrance requirement; about 86 per cent have a foreign language requirement for the B.A., although few professional schools have such requirements.

Need for Foreign Languages

In general, European schools manage to prepare a number of students sufficiently skilled in languages to satisfy the needs of governments, of business, and of the teaching profession (although the demand for skilled teachers often outstrips the supply in Europe as in the United States).

The situation is different in the United States. For instance, the Armed Forces have found it necessary to set up their own language program. The U.S. State Department has an in-service language instruction program. Industry and business, more often than not, have recourse to cram courses purporting to give the executives headed for a foreign assignment the rudiments of the language which they will be using. Many corporations with extensive overseas corporations send their executives to specialized institutes, or they may even create their own schools. All of which goes to show the frustration of the military, the government, and business in their search for personnel trained in language on and above professional skills.

The number of governmental positions overseas gives an interesting indication of such needs:[8]

Department	Overseas
Dept. of Army (civilians employed)	25,000
Dept. of Navy (civilians employed)	20,000
Dept. of Air Force (civilians employed)	15,000
Dept. of Agriculture	1,000
Dept. of Interior	3,000
Dept. of Commerce	3,000
Dept. of State	6,000
U.S. Information Agency	1,000
Agency for International Development	4,000
Peace Corps	10,000

Regarding the need for language skills in the United States, we quote from the same source:

. . . Within the United States, however, there are many economic opportunities for persons with language skills. A survey of the want ads in six successive Sunday editions of the NEW YORK TIMES showed nearly 1,000 requests for persons with a knowledge of one or more foreign languages. The jobs were for 382 men and 605 women, and required a good working knowledge of Spanish, French, German, Italian or a combination of any of them in that order. The greatest demand was for secretaries, followed by secretary-stenographers, accountants, teachers, typists, translators, bookkeepers, salesmen, hotel workers, and teletype operators . . .[9]

These figures speak for themselves. Furthermore, the demand for language skills can only increase in the following fields: transportation, travel, hotel, banking, advertising, journalism, publishing, translating, import-export, mining, engineering, and other foreign business operations.[10] The United Nations and various international organizations, such as the Pan American Union, are another source of constant demand for language-trained specialists. And finally, the teaching profession, both in the United States and abroad, makes the greatest demand of all on the reservoir of linguists.

In most situations (all other things being equal) there is an increasing tendency in present recruitment policies to give preference to the multilingual candidates over the monolingual—which makes sense in a shrinking world where the knowledge of a foreign language and civilization will at least give useful insight in more than one situation, not to mention the cases where such knowledge will be indispensable.[11] However, this practical aspect of the importance of modern languages is not the utmost consideration one should bear in mind when facing the problem of communication on a world-wide basis. William Parker has, perhaps, best expressed the critical need:

The person who has never comprehended, spoken, read, or written a language other than his mother tongue has little or no perspective on his own language, particularly its unique structure, and, more important, he has never penetrated the rich areas of learning and experience lying beyond monolingual communication. His linguistic horizon is fixed. Though he may have acquired insights into other cultures through music or art, though he may even have travelled widely in other lands, he has never experienced directly a different culture in terms of the spoken and written symbols with which it uniquely reveals itself. Born a citizen of a multilingual world, he is, among the educated of that world, conspicuous in his limitations. If he does travel, he cannot help advertising his single-culture orientations. His interests may be wide, his international outlook generous, but abroad he must either hope to meet with people better educated than himself or else communicate lamely through interpreters; and at home, if he wishes to learn about other cultures, he must depend always upon translations (when they exist) or knowledge at second hand.[12]

FRANCESCO CORDASCO, a sociologist, is Professor of Education at Montclair (New Jersey) State college, and Educational Consultant to the Migration Division of the Commonwealth of Puerto Rico. He has taught at New York University, City College of the City University of New York, and Long Island University. His books include *Research and Report Writing; A Brief History of Education; Shaping of American Graduate Education; Educational Sociology: A Subject Index of Doctoral Dissertations. . . .* He has also written articles on the minority child; ethnicity and the schools; curriculum; and related problems.

LOUIS ROEDERER is Associate Professor of French at Montclair State College, and former chairman of the Modern Language Department at Montclair State College. He served as legal advisor to the United Nations Relief and Works Agency (UNRWA) during World War II, and has taught at the International College of the American University of Beirut. He is a graduate of the University of Lyon, and former chairman of the Foreign Language Department of the Stony Brook School in New York.

FOOTNOTES

1. "Constructed Languages." MODERN LANGUAGE ASSOCIATION, FL Bulletin #52 (1956-57).
2. *Ibid.* For further details on these languages see Mario Pei, ONE LANGUAGE FOR THE WORLD. New York: Devin-Adair, 1958.
3. Eric Kadler and Bernard Flam, "Some Notes on Foreign Language Teaching in Other Countries." MODERN LANGUAGE JOURNAL, XLVIII, November 1964.
4. See in this connection, F. Cordasco, ed., Leonard Covello, THE SOCIAL BACKGROUND OF THE ITALO-AMERICAN CHILD. A Study of the Southern Italian Mores and Their Effect on the School Situation in Italy and America. Leiden [Netherlands]: E. J. Brill, 1967.
5. "Bilingualism and the Bilingual Child: A Symposium." MODERN LANGUAGE JOURNAL, XLIV, March and April, 1965.
6. Marjorie C. Johnston, "Designing Foreign Language Education for World Understanding—A Shared Responsibility." MODERN LAN-

GUAGE ASSOCIATION, FL Bulletin #52 (1956-57), 33.
7. *Ibid.*
8. Richard T. Hardesty, "Translating Foreign Languages Into Careers." INDIANA LANGUAGE PROGRAM, Bloomington: Indiana University, 1964, 10.
9. *Ibid.*, 25.
10. "The Role of Foreign Languages in International Business and Industry." MODERN LANGUAGE ASSOCIATION, FL Bulletin #54, June, 1957 (reissued 1965).
11. William R. Parker, "Why a Foreign Language Requirement?" COLLEGE AND UNIVERSITY, Vol. XXXI, Winter 1957.
12. *Ibid.*, 27.

Selected Bibliography

BOOKS

Covello, Leonard, THE SOCIAL BACKGROUND OF THE ITALO-AMERICAN CHILD: A STUDY OF THE SOUTHERN ITALIAN MORES AND THEIR EFFECT ON THE SCHOOL SITUATION IN ITALY AND AMERICA, edited and with an introduction by F. Cordasco, Leiden [Netherlands]: E.J. Brill, 1967. A detailed study of the "assimilation" of the minority child by the American school.

Ferrero, Guglielmo, THE UNITY OF THE WORLD. New York: Albert and Charles Boni, 1930. General review of political and linguistic problems in the light of world unity aspirations; Americanization of the world.

Hymes, Dell, LANGUAGE IN CULTURE AND SOCIETY. New York: Harper & Row, 1964. Several studies by world-known linguists.

Jespersen, Otto, LANGUAGE, ITS NATURE, DEVELOPMENT AND ORIGINS. London: George Allen and Unwin Ltd., 1954. Concise history of the science of linguistics and of the development of language from its origin; a basic introduction.

Lee, Irving, LANGUAGE HABITS IN HUMAN AFFAIRS. New York: Harper, 1941. Practice and application of language; a clear and brief introduction to the subject.

Parker, William R., THE NATIONAL INTEREST AND FOREIGN LANGUAGES: DISCUSSION, GUIDE, AND WORK PAPER. Washington, D.C.: U.S. Government Printing Office, 1957. An excellent position paper with elaborate data on foreign languages and the national interest.

Pei, Mario A., ONE LANGUAGE FOR THE WORLD. New York: Devin-Adair, 1958. Succinct presentation of the need for, and uses of, a universal language; various solutions proposed; bibliography needed.

Potter, Simeon, LANGUAGE IN THE MODERN WORLD. Baltimore: Penguin, 1965. An excellent non-technical discussion of language needs.

34

UNESCO. THE TEACHING OF MODERN LANGUAGES. Paris: UNESCO, 1953. An invaluable assessment of the postwar methodologies.

ARTICLES AND PAMPHLETS

Hardesty, Richard T., "Translating Foreign Language Into Careers," INDIANA LANGUAGE PROGRAM. Bloomington: Indiana University, 1964.

Johnston, Marjorie C., "Designing Foreign Language Education for World Understanding—A Shared Responsibility." MODERN LANGUAGE ASSOCIATION, FL *Bulletin* #52 (1956-57).

Kader, Eric and Bernard Flam, "Some Notes On Foreign Language Teaching in Other Countries." THE MODERN LANGUAGE JOURNAL, XLVIII, No. 7, November 1964.

Modern Language Association of America, "Bilingualism and the Bilingual Child: A Symposium." MODERN LANGUAGE JOURNAL, XLIX, March and April 1965.

——, "Constructed Languages." MODERN LANGUAGE ASSOCIATION OF AMERICA, FL Bulletin #52. [C. 1956-1957].

——, "The Role of Foreign Language in International Business and Industry." MODERN LANGUAGE ASSOCIATION OF AMERICA, FL Bulletin #54, June 1957 (reissued 1965).

Parker, William, "Why a Foreign Language Requirement?" COLLEGE AND UNIVERSITY, Winter 1957.

VALUES AND PROBLEMS
IN FOREIGN LANGUAGE LEARNING

The Value of Second Language Learning

L. CLARK KEATING
University of Kentucky

THE REASONS that have been given for the study of a second language are as varied as the place, time, and circumstances that have produced them. Ever since men have had the experience of meeting, trading and fighting with other nations, or marrying their daughters, the value of learning a second tongue has been obvious. In the United States the early settlers and pioneers found extremely useful the occasional Indian who learned English or the rare individual among their own number who learned an Indian language. Such interpreters made dealing with the Indians, in peace or in war, an easier matter. The exchange of ideas, goods, and services among the several communities of European settlers was also rendered easier by the presence of the translator-interpreter. In those early days, however, little thought seems to have been given to any systematic teaching of a second language. A possible exception was the theology curriculum, which included Latin, Greek, and Hebrew because these languages were regarded as indispensable for the reading of the sacred texts in the original languages. No similar urgency seems to have been felt about teaching the modern languages, and when students with secular intentions began to enter the schools, they usually accepted the curriculum as they found it and absorbed Latin and sometimes Greek along with future clergymen, since the concept of a specialized education for the various walks of life had not yet been born.

Early History of Language Study in the United States

In the eighteenth and nineteenth centuries the concept of providing those who could afford it with a literary and cultural orientation began to find favor along the Eastern Seaboard, and gradually the curriculum of British universities began to be imitated on this side of the Atlantic. Foreign languages were among the subjects brought into the curriculum at this time. French was introduced at Harvard in 1735, and at the College of William and Mary in 1779.[1] The history of the nineteenth century thereafter reveals a gradual introduction of language instruction in the programs of higher education until the eve of the First World War when nearly every college in the United States taught one or more foreign languages, though their study was but infrequently compulsory. If one asks why language study suddenly assumed enough importance to find a place in the curriculum, a few explanations suggest themselves. Ticknor, Longfellow, and Lowell, and men like them went to Europe as part of the "grand tour" that was coming into vogue as a kind of finishing school for college graduates of means and refinement. On their return the use to which these travelers put their language was by and large the study of foreign literature in the original, with little hint of mere vocational use. The second language, or even the third one, when acquired, was seen as a pleasant adjunct to an upper-class education, and its presence (if justified by theory, which it seldom was) found an adequate basis in purely aesthetic and intellectual considerations. The high schools of the country meanwhile, unlike the Eastern preparatory schools which imitated the colleges in this as in most other things, took to languages slowly and without much doctrinal justification for their inclusion in the curriculum. At the same time the normal schools, agricultural and mechanical colleges, as well as the engineering schools, tended to affirm then, as they do now, that there were few reasons for offering their students an opportunity to study foreign languages. It was assumed by the leaders in technical education, and their assumption was seldom challenged, that persons engaged in teaching, farming or engineering could carry on their trade or profession without the knowledge of a second language. This was about where matters stood at the outset of the First World War. Then by a kind of perversely nationalistic reasoning diffi-

37

cult to understand today, attitudes toward language learning in the United States changed drastically.

The First World War

The study of French was given an unprecedented impetus by our involvement with France as an ally in the First World War. In the schools enrollment in French soared. Among the general public, classes for adults were organized and taught by self-styled specialists. YMCA's and church groups sponsored the study of French from Maine to California, and America was treated to the spectacle of previously isolationist adults striving mightily and with patriotic zeal to master a foreign language.[2] Viewed in retrospect, most of these programs seem to have been ill-conceived, ill-taught, and all but useless, at least from a purely linguistic point of view. Few persons in the volunteer classes actually achieved any proficiency in French. Furthermore, it is difficult even now to see just what these enthusiastic would-be French speakers expected to accomplish. Apparently second language learning was felt in some obscure way to be connected with the war effort, and may be compared (I trust not too unkindly) to the cheering which youthful zealots believe to be an actual help to an embattled football team. Perhaps the best thing that can be said of this linguistic fiasco is that it did no harm. If Americans did not learn to speak fluent French in their night classes, at least their instruction taught them a few things about France, and their attitude toward second-language learning, if affected at all, was turned in the direction of giving them some sympathy for the trials of their children who were attempting the same task with rather more success in high school.

At the same time a disastrous linguistic event occurred— the abandonment of German. By a logic even stranger than that which motivated the study of French, it was assumed that to study German, which came to be called the language of the enemy, was to impede the war effort, to display sympathy for our adversaries, and to waste time that could be better employed. The result was a drop in German enrollment at all levels, sometimes to the vanishing point, all in the name of patriotism. Naturally a few sensible persons in public life, and a few educators, pointed out the folly of this proceeding. If anything, the crisis required more German speakers rather than less. They were needed in many fields for the conduct of the war, to help in reading and interpreting German scientific publications, and to prepare for a postwar world in which problems concerning Germany, whether she was victorious or defeated, might be expected to loom large on the international horizon. Nothing could stem the tide, however, of an irrational anti-Germanism which went so far as to demand the elimination from the English language of the German names of well-established culinary specialties, such as sauerkraut, which became "liberty cabbage".

The Postwar Period

During the period between wars language study in America deteriorated in quantity and quality. Many of the educationists of the day started to attack it as an unjustifiable preemption of school time, urging its total elimination or, where this was impossible, its reduction to a mere two-year program.[3] Latin fought back, suicidally as it finally appeared, by insisting on the transfer value of the "discipline" involved in learning Latin grammar, and when this argument proved hollow, the Latinists finally adduced, when it was almost too late, many good solid arguments for studying the ancient languages, namely, their linguistic relation to English, their usefulness to the student of science, law, and medicine, and the cultural values to be obtained, under proper instruction, from the study of peoples whose civilization had contributed so much to the Western European culture upon which our own is built.

The modern languages were also in a precarious state. It took a generation to undo the damage done to German under the mistaken banner of patriotism. Spanish began to demand "equal time" with French, its claims spearheaded by persons in parts of the country that felt more ties with Spanish than with French because of the presence of Spanish-speaking people in the local community. Italian also began to make a bid for inclusion in the curriculum, but this move was, or appeared to be, mainly motivated by a desire on the part of Italo-Americans to foster in their descendants an interest in the homeland of their ancestors. Be that as it may, Italian studies, although they got off to a good start, have never assumed a commanding position in the race for second-language supremacy. Meanwhile the advocates of the study of Spanish as a second language began to exploit what they regarded as an impregnable argument, connected as it was with monetary considerations. The value of Spanish, it was said, was bound up with the bright future of our commercial dealings with Latin America.[4] A growing commerce obviously would require a knowledge of Spanish. Latin America was already our best customer, and her importance as a commercial center and outlet for American goods was said to be barely in its beginning phase. French, meanwhile, carrying on after the impetus of her wartime popularity, gained first place after Latin as the second language in our schools.[5] Meanwhile, also, many of the schools of education discouraged or tried to discourage all study of languages as a colossal failure in the public school. The opponents of foreign language study frequently advanced the not untenable argument that languages in the United States were being taught badly wherever they were taught. Language teachers, so the argument ran, were badly prepared, which meant that very few of them were equipped to impart a passable accent in the foreign language to their students. It was also urged that few American students would discover any value in the languages they were being forced to study, and that of all those who were exposed to foreign language, only a handful would ever acquire enough competence in any one of the four areas, that is, speaking, understanding, reading, and writing, to justify the use of a large block of time. After all, the curriculum was already hard pressed to provide even minimum instruction in the important fields of science and social science, let alone in literature or the humanities.

Language teachers reacted by trying to maintain the *status quo*. They spent little time in pointing out values of second-language learning, which seemed to them self-evident. Whatever arguments or reasons that might have been alleged as to the value of second language study—whether justifying its place in the curriculum as a basic skill, or as valid part of a general education—were all but lost for a time in a discussion of aims, methods, and an assumed right to a place in the class schedule.[6] In the long run, these discussions were probably of more value for the profession of language teaching than as a rebuttal of the educationists' position. For a mere rethinking of the purposes and values of language study might have turned up many ingenious arguments in its favor only to have the battle lost in the classroom where languages were so badly taught that no rational goal could be attained. As it happened, the discussion of methods then engaged in proclaimed that the chief value of second language study lay largely in having students achieve a reading knowledge. Since hindsight is better than foresight it can now be seen that this reading aim, which was expected to replace the fourfold goals of speaking, understanding, reading, and writing, was as ill-chosen as the methods that were supposed to impart it were ill-conceived. But through their deliberations concerning principles and practices the teachers came at last to the realization that methodology was not irrelevant to teaching, and that if they wished their subject to have its place in the curriculum, they had better teach it well.

To critics the language teachers gave assurance that with the new reading goals better performance would be forthcoming from both teacher and student. Exceptionally and occasionally, a few language teachers made a pronouncement in behalf of the virtues of language learning *per se* or persuaded a good-natured businessman or a professional educator to do the same. When they did so, the arguments used were relatively few in number, and from time to time they even included a plea on behalf of language study for its disciplinary value, but such outbursts were quickly silenced by vigilant colleagues. Most modern language teachers had noted, and with reason, that the discipline argument had backfired when used by the teachers of the classics. They were, therefore, abnormally sensitive on the subject and wished to let the argument of disciplinary value of language study alone. More popular and more cogent were the assertions that language study would make the reading of foreign materials possible, thereby opening vistas of cultural appreciation. This argument was mainly advanced in favor of French, though it is difficult to see why it should be any less important to understand the Germanic or the Hispanic culture. Spanish clung by and large to its commercial argument, bolstered constantly by chamber of commerce pronunciamentos to the effect that a vast program of Latin-American commercial development was just about to get under way. German made a fair comeback, for Germany had made a rapid recovery from the war, and her scientific

41

and literary achievements were such as to entitle her to a place in our studies. The popularity of the language was also abetted, beyond a doubt, by the inevitable reaction against France when it became apparent that her postwar governments were not always conducting their affairs along the lines that Americans expected or desired. Still French held its own and even increased its lead not only numerically but proportionally.

The Second World War

The Second World War was to effect a drastic change in many American attitudes, and not least in the attitude toward language study. Apparently sufficient ridicule had been heaped upon the "liberty cabbage" kind of thinking to prevent a repetition of such nonsense, and so immediately after the disaster at Pearl Harbor, the Armed Forces began to tackle the problem of teaching Japanese to selected groups of men of the Armed Forces. The methods were modern, motivation was high, and the results achieved were notable. German was also intensively studied as was Italian, the other language of the Axis Powers. For the first time intelligence officers were trained in Japanese and German in such a way that they could actually function with native fluency in the language. French took its usual upward turn and Spanish did likewise. Then since the Soviet government was our ally, as was China, we turned for the first time to the study of Russian and Chinese, long neglected by our schools and colleges. Special classes in foreign languages were established under government auspices, with adequate financial backing, respectable standards of instruction, and a determination to do the job which had been all but totally lacking in the well-meant but sporadic efforts of American adult language students during the First World War. Businessmen were dispatched to Latin America who actually spoke Spanish and Portuguese. And if more skills were needed, courses in both languages were made available. In fact, the interest in Portuguese was a wartime phenomenon, for though a few colleges had long since promoted Portuguese studies in a desultory way, the total result from the national point of view had been all but nil. Russian specialists knowing how to speak Russian were sent to Russia or to the front. This was the linguistic miracle of the war years: the decision to train Americans in strategic positions in foreign languages and the carrying out of that decision by effective instructional implementation of the goals set up.

The lesson was not lost on the American people. They saw that languages could be taught effectively, and that if we put our mind to it, we as a people are capable of learning and using a second language. For the first time in our history our collective consciousness also caught the message that we cannot and dare not rely solely on foreign interpreters and translators when national security is at stake. With the realization of these facts went a frequently expressed impatience with the results heretofore achieved by conventional methods. Unfair comparisons were made between the teaching done in the public schools and that done in the Armed Forces. It was unnoticed that the Army and Navy had two to four students in a class in comparison with the thirty-five or forty students in classes in the schools; that they hired the best teachers and paid them well, that they chose their students on the basis of aptitude tests, relieved them of all other duties, plied them with expensive gadgetry, and, to crown it all, frequently commissioned enlisted men who achieved success in the language program. All this should have been noticed if any fair comparisons were to be made. Unfortunately, the public was not alone in missing the point. Many language teachers failed to draw the conclusion that favorable conditions would mean better results in schools and colleges also. There were even some teachers who had themselves achieved phenomenal results under the optimum conditions supplied by the Armed Forces who were content to go back to their large classes, their dull methods of instruction and the limited goals of little reading and less comprehension. Thus the lessons learned about language teaching in the Armed Forces were all but lost.[7]

The Foreign Language Program and FLES

Actually it took two outsiders to stir up the language profession generally to a realization of its true potential. William Riley Parker, executive secretary of the Modern Language Association, was the first of these. He belonged to the profession of English teaching, a field with which modern foreign language teachers make little common cause despite their membership in a common association. Dr. Parker was appointed to a UNESCO

43

commission to study the problems of foreign language teaching in the United States. The commission was appalled at what it learned, namely, that the United States was behind every other civilized nation in the length of time given to language study and in the results achieved. The report of the commission, chaired by Dr. Parker, was entitled *The National Interest and Modern Foreign Languages,*[8] and this document did far more than describe the *status quo.* In its pages, Dr. Parker undertook to state the case for languages in the modern world. The report sees value in language study for all, and not content with merely proclaiming this faith, Dr. Parker undertook to do something about it. He created within the Modern Language Association a Foreign Language, or FL, Program. Beginning in a small way, the association soon assembled a core of experts dedicated to the value of language study for the citizen and determined to effect a revolution in the way languages are taught. The story of that successful struggle, which produced among other things the summer training of language teachers under NDEA institutes, themselves an outgrowth of Parker's action on the national scene, is not germane here, but important is the fact that the new program, unlike the study of the nineteen twenties, was not content merely to discuss the improvement of language instruction. It sought also to examine its whys and wherefores, to establish an ideological basis for its existence, and, in a word, to establish a basis for believing in the value of language study. In monthly chats with the membership, in a column entitled *Strictly Personal,* printed in the front pages of the association's previously stuffy and scholarly journal,[9] the secretary strove to state the case for languages, to prod the conservative in method, and to preach the gospel of more and better language teaching in America.

The second outsider to abet the revolution in America's language consciousness was Dr. Harold MacGrath, a professor of education who had become United States Commissioner of Education. Confessing that, like many of his colleagues, he had once questioned the value of language teaching in the public schools, he went on to say in a famous speech in May 1952[10] that in the world of today America must prepare to take a place of leadership, and that leadership could hardly be exercised intelligently by a monolingual nation. Further, taking a lesson from Montaigne, Commissioner MacGrath stated his conviction that the best time to teach a foreign language to an individual is before he reaches the age of twelve. He proposed therefore a massive program of foreign language instruction in the elementary schools, to be continued all the way through high school, and to be abetted by college training for all individuals who went that far in their education. The result of this speech was an astounding display of public enthusiasm and a burgeoning of language programs in elementary schools. This FLES (Foreign Language in Elementary Schools) program was a kind of hit-or-miss affair whose results were excellent in one place and poor in others. But this does not concern us here. What is of importance for this chapter is the fact that the effective response of the American people proved beyond the shadow of a doubt that they accepted Dr. Parker's basic premise without cavil, that is, that a nation in a position of world leadership cannot afford to be monolingual, and this conviction has been a powerful stimulus to language study in high school and college as well as on the elementary level.

Foreign Language in the Graduate Schools

Still another area of education that has always interested itself in foreign languages is the graduate school. Ever since the famous Flexner report, entitled *Universities: American, English, German*,[11] and even before, American graduate schools have insisted that all candidates for the Ph.D. degree should have a reading knowledge of two foreign languages. With but slight variation, or the occasional substitution of Russian, Spanish, or some other language directly connected with the candidate's field of research, French and German have been required. But complete agreement on this point has never been reached, and although of all people the graduate faculties of our universities might be expected to be unanimous on the value of language, either as a research tool or as a prerequisite to graduate education, such is not the case. Members of the faculty of nearly every graduate school in America will recall wryly, no matter which side of the debate they have been on, the endless discussions between the proponents of language and the revisionists. The latter want either to do away with language requirements altogether, claiming, incredible as it may seem, that nothing of value is produced in their field, except in English, or they wish to substitute some other subject for language skill. In answer to such revisionists, and hoping to end the argument at least for a time, the American Association of Graduate Schools issued this statement in October 1951:

> Nor is it desirable in a period when different countries are coming more and more into contact with each other to allow the future leaders of thought to isolate themselves behind the barrier of their own language . . . The whole case against languages is based upon a concept of graduate work as technical training rather than as training in scholarship. In fields where technical training rather than scholarly training is desirable, some other degree than the Doctor of Philosophy should be conferred . . . and the Ph.D. should be retained for scholars.[12]

Summary

In summary, we find ourselves currently in the position of having a great many more arguments in favor of second language learning and more arguments both strong and weak for their value to the people of a modern nation than we have ever had before. And, as this chapter has endeavored to demonstrate, all reasons for studying a language, all estimates of its value to the individual and to the nation, have to be considered in the light of the circumstances that rule our times. Surveying, then, the currently accepted values of language study, it would appear that they may be divided into approximately four categories, all of which have to do with communication in one way or another.

The first may be called vocational. The trader who goes to another country to sell goods or to purchase them undoubtedly sees linguistic skills as an indispensable adjunct to the job. Without language he cannot explain to the American Indians, Hottentots, or neighboring Mexicans what it is that he has to sell or what its uses and virtues are. Similar also is the missionary, who from time immemorial has been the world's most prolific user of foreign language skills. The Wycliffe Bible translators today are working with more than five hundred tongues in an effort to put Christianity within the reach of savage tribes by means of the printed word. Significantly, neither the missionary nor the salesman needs propaganda to convince him of the value of knowing a foreign language. But there are other trades and professions that have come slowly and reluctantly to the realization that knowledge of a foreign language is well-nigh indispensable. Among these is diplomacy. Not until recently did official diplomacy take language skills seriously. It was President Truman who declared during his presidency that he expected to demand language competence as a criterion for appointment to the diplomatic service, but it was not until the Administration of John F. Kennedy that a massive attempt was made to make such a policy work by appointing to top diplomatic posts persons with the requisite linguistic skills. Now under a monolingual President, Lyndon Johnson, the application of the policy is spotty. Many American ambassadors speak the language of the country to which they are accredited, many do not. Meanwhile, equally effective language skills would appear to be needed for all the staff members of a modern complex embassy. Unfortunately, linguistic skill, while preferred for overseas service is not actually required, though the State Department at least makes an effort, with varying success, at on-the-job language training throughout the world.[13]

Second in importance as an unarguable value of language learning is its usefulness as a key to important foreign material published in the foreign language and unavailable in English. Indeed, the variety of persons to whom comprehension of some species of foreign material is sometimes necessary would run the whole gamut of human endeavor. The college researcher or scientist comes readily to mind, but the dairyman, the lawyer, the physician, the government clerk, the teacher, and the preacher may all find themselves, at one time or another, in a position to need foreign language skills in some degree. Of course, in our increasingly complex world useful material may turn up in Swahili or Hindi as well as in French or German, but most sensible persons believe that this is a poor excuse for not knowing one or more of the tongues that most frequently bear upon the problems that we are likely to encounter. A secondary but increasingly frequent need to comprehend foreign material is demonstrated at international conferences where Americans

47

sometimes discover to their chagrin that they are the only ones present who cannot understand speeches given in one or more of the major world languages other than English. Thus whether in oral or written form, we find ourselves, far more than our grandfathers, almost constantly in need of foreign language skills.

Closely related to the value of language for comprehension is the by no means less important though far more subtle value of such skills for their psychological effect in international affairs. The American alluded to above who knows no foreign language irritates those who speak more than one language by his provincialism. He is certainly less likely to understand the point of view of his foreign interlocutor since he has not had the cultural orientation that frequently accompanies language study. And it is this cultural orientation that is our third major value connected with the acquisition of a second language. The world has shrunk, so the saying goes, and anyone who has ordered something from Paris and has received it in a couple of days can feel as well as know that this is so. Since nations cannot live any longer all to themselves, isolated by their mountains or oceans, it behooves us to understand each other a little better. Whether we like it or not the world's peoples are on the move. Asians, Africans, and Europeans occupy chairs in our universities.[14] Students from those continents come to live in our homes, their businessmen visit our factories and our Rotary luncheons. Simple common sense requires us to have a modicum of appreciation and understanding for the way other people live. Tourism, business, education, politics, and, unfortunately, war bring the peoples of the earth into each other's backyards. Language is no guarantee of universal peace or understanding as witness the Israelites' destruction of those who could not pronounce "shibboleth" acceptably, but in our world the chances for understanding are statistically increased with a modicum of linguistic knowledge.

Last but not least, it has come to be recognized that language learning is somewhat different from any other subject in the curriculum, whether in elementary school or university, and that languages, even when halfway decently taught, give the student an insight into the processes of human thought that is not possible from the study of the mother tongue.[15] The latter is learned so early in life that the process is not remembered at all. We think in our native speech without being able to observe ourselves thinking. Not so a foreign language. It requires of us a dedication that is unique. It uses new muscles, and new synapses. It gives new concepts and new insights regarding man's processes of thought. It makes a strange world less strange. It is another dimension of life.

L. CLARK KEATING, born on August 20, 1907 in Philadelphia, received his B.A. degree from Colgate University (1928), M.A. (1931) and Ph.D. (1934) from Harvard. He also studied during the summers at Middlebury College (1928, 1929), Heidelberg (1931) and Madrid (1933). He taught at Colgate University (1928-1929), Macalester College (1934-1936), Monticello College (1936-1937), University of Illinois (1937-1939), George Washington University (1939-1957), where he was appointed chairman of the Romance Languages Department (1946-1957). In 1957 he became chairman of the Romance Language Department at the University of Cincinnati, and from 1963-1966 was chairman of Modern Foreign Languages at the University of Kentucky where he is Professor of French. Among his publications are: *Studies on the Literary Salon in France, 1550-1615, Teaching a Modern Language* (with C.C. Gullette and C.P. Viens); *Critic of Civilization: The Writings of Georges Duhamel;* in addition he has authored ten textbooks, and has published articles in *MLJ, FR, Hispania, School and Society, Symposium, Romanic Review,* etc.

FOOTNOTES

1. R. D. Cole and James B. Tharp, MODERN FOREIGN LANGUAGES AND THEIR TEACHING. New York: Appleton-Century, 1937, 1-2.
2. While still a small boy the present writer remembers being taken to some of these sessions.
3. C. C. Gullette, L. Clark Keating, and Claude P. Viens, TEACHING A MODERN LANGUAGE. New York: Appleton-Century-Crofts, 1942, 3.
4. Chauncey D. Snow, MODERN FOREIGN LANGUAGES AND INTERNATIONAL BUSINESS RELATIONS. Washington, D. C., 1940, 2.
5. Cole-Tharp, *Op. Cit.,* 11.
6. *Ibid.,* Ch. IV.
7. A SURVEY OF LANGUAGE CLASSES IN THE ARMY SPECIALIZED TRAINING PROGRAM, prepared for the Committee on Trends in Education of the Modern Language Association of America, 1944, *passim.*
8. Washington, D. C.: Government Printing Office, 1957.
9. Publications of the MODERN LANGUAGE ASSOCIATION.
10. Conference on Foreign Language in the Schools, Saint Louis, Missouri, May 1952.

11. Abraham Flexner, UNIVERSITIES, AMERICAN, ENGLISH, GER-MAN. New York: Oxford University Press, 1930.
12. Meeting of the Association of American Graduate Schools. October 1951.
13. Released time is allowed embassy personnel overseas in order to study the language of the country.
14. The University of Kentucky, for example, has foreign members on its teaching staff.
15. For a discussion of the new thinking about the nature of language, see John B. Carroll, "The Contributions of Psychological Theory and Education Research to the Teaching of Foreign Languages," TRENDS IN LANGUAGE TEACHING, edited by Albert Valdman, New York: McGraw-Hill, 1966, Ch. VI.

Selected Bibliography

BOOKS

Brooks, Nelson, LANGUAGE AND LANGUAGE LEARNING, THEORY AND PRACTICE. New York: Harcourt-Brace, 1960. One of the best expositions of the new theory of language teaching. Since it was written it has been outpointed in various technical aspects, but it is still a good general statement of what language learning is all about.

Childers, James Wesley, FOREIGN LANGUAGE TEACHING. New York: Center for Applied Research, 1964. A workmanlike account of language teaching today including a certain amount of historical background.

Cole, Robert D., MODERN FOREIGN LANGUAGES AND THEIR TEACHING, revised and enlarged by James Tharp, New York: Appleton Century, 1937. An old and completely outdated work, but it is indispensable for a look at the evolution of language study in America, especially in the third and fourth decades.

Finocchiaro, Mary. TEACHING CHILDREN FOREIGN LANGUAGES. New York: McGraw-Hill, 1964. One of the most recent and best books on the subject.

Gullette, C. C., Keating, L. Clark, and Viens, Claude P., TEACHING A MODERN LANGUAGE. New York: Appleton-Century-Crofts, 1942. Outdated but useful for some of the bibliographies and historical material.

Lado, Robert, LANGUAGE TEACHING, A SCIENTIFIC APPROACH. New York: McGraw-Hill, 1964. An excellent statement of the use and value of structural linguistics in the teaching of language.

Parker, William Riley, THE NATIONAL INTEREST AND FOREIGN LANGUAGES, prepared for UNESCO. Washington, D.C.: Government Printing Office. An historical and telling propaganda document that states the case for language study in America.

Politzer, Robert L., FOREIGN LANGUAGE LEARNING, A LIN-
GUISTIC INTRODUCTION. Englewood, N.J.: Prentice-Hall,
1965. A cogent account of the problems encountered in teaching language with linguistic principles.
Valdman, Albert and Others, TRENDS IN LANGUAGE TEACH-
ING. New York: McGraw-Hill, 1966. A well-edited series of
technical papers on various aspects of language learning. Each
writer is an expert in his field.

PAMPHLETS

Doyle, Henry Grattan, A SURVEY OF LANGUAGE CLASSES IN
THE ARMY SPECIALIZED TRAINING PROGRAM, prepared
for the Committee on Trends in Education, Modern Language
Association of America, New York: 1944. As the title implies
this short report sums up the findings of the ASTP as observed
by a committee.
Huebener, Theodore, "Vocational Opportunities for Foreign Lan-
guage Students." MODERN LANGUAGE JOURNAL, National
Federation of Modern Language Teachers' Association, St.
Louis, 1949. An answer to those who can think of few reasons
for studying a foreign language.
Peyre, Henri, THE NEED FOR LANGUAGE STUDY IN AMER-
ICA TODAY. New York: French Cultural Services in the United
States, 1956. A clear and cogent statement regarding the need
to overcome America's monolingualism.
Snow, Chauncey D., MODERN FOREIGN LANGUAGES AND IN-
TERNATIONAL BUSINESS RELATIONS. Washington, D.C.,
1940. A useful statement from the business point of view. Mr.
Snow thinks language is as good as money for a businessman.

The Development of Skills, Attitudes and Sensibilities

P. JOHN GEORGEOFF

Purdue University

HISTORICALLY, teachers of foreign languages in the United States have employed methods derived from the humanistic tradition in education.[1] This tradition applied Latin grammar methods to the study of foreign languages and was essentially deductive and analytical in nature. Primary emphasis was placed upon mastery of grammatical rules and through them, the acquisition of reading ability in the language. Proficiency in the language was generally tested by requiring the students to translate from the language into English, and the reverse. Although the development of skills of an oral-auditory type—the ability to speak the language and to understand it when spoken at a normal rate of speed—was not altogether ignored, it was usually relegated to a secondary role. Possibly, for students of a nation relatively isolated from the rest of the world, reading and writing ability was rightly the most important objective in the study of a foreign language; since few of them spent more than two or three years in such study, and fewer still ever had the opportunity to use it orally.

From time to time, various methodological changes were proposed in foreign language teaching during the first decades of the twentieth century. In 1902, Wilhelm Viëtor developed a direct or oral method of teaching languages at the University of Marburg, Germany.[2] This system was introduced in the United States as early as 1911. Although the technique was tried in a number of institutions, generally in modified form, it made little headway. Indeed, in 1929, in a report sponsored by the Carnegie Foundation titled, *The Teaching of Modern Foreign Languages in the United States*, Algeron Coleman continued to stress reading ability.[3] This remained the emphasis during the thirties and the early forties.

With the entry of the United States into the Second World War, it soon became apparent that the global nature of the conflict demanded large numbers of persons possessing a command of languages which hitherto had received little or no attention in American institutions—languages such as Japanese, Malay, and Melanesian Pidgin. Methods had to be developed which produce a good working knowledge of the language in as short a time as possible, with the ability to communicate effectively being the prime requisite. The method developed by the Army Specialized Training Program, the most important of the various programs set up to provide military personnel with training in foreign languages, involved two specialists:

¶ 1. A native speaker with a cultured command of the language; and

¶ 2. A linguistic specialist to analyze phonemically the structure and phonetic patterns of the language.[4]

This method soon was to have a tremendous impact on the teaching of foreign languages in American schools. The emergence of the United States as a first-rank world power following the war, with global responsibilities and commitments, brought into continued focus the importance of large numbers of its citizens' having a working knowledge of at least one foreign language. Increased international trade, the expansion of air travel, continuing requirements of the military, the development of foreign assistance programs, such as the Marshall Plan, the Agency for International Development, and more recently, the Peace Corps, all have served to emphasize the need for both language specialists and for persons who, though trained in other professional areas, possess a knowledge of foreign languages.[5]

This need has brought about a reappraisal of the instructional methods used in foreign language teaching, with the result that much experimentation is taking place, resulting in new techniques and approaches.

Methods

Most of the newer techniques are considerably refined and based upon the Army methods developed during the Second World War, improved as a result of experimentation and teacher experience. A veritable revolution in the teaching of foreign languages has thus taken place in the United States. The New Approach, as it is frequently called, takes a number of forms, but regardless of the particular methodology it may use, usually has an audio-lingual emphasis—especially in the beginning. Reading, writing, and grammar are introduced at a later stage, for students of secondary or collegiate level. In some "systems," reading and later writing are taught even in the elementary grades after the children have become acquainted with the language through audio-lingual techniques; in any event, the work is carefully graded by increasing level of difficulty, with specific attention being given to sentence structure. Although vocabulary development is viewed as important, it is considered a natural development as the various sentence structures of the language are mastered, and not as an isolated end in itself, as was often the case formerly.[6]

The theory forming the basis of the audio-lingual approach maintains that foreign languages can best be learned in the same way in which the individual learns his native tongue.[7] The infant hears his parents and others speaking all around him even before his eyes can focus upon objects. As he becomes older he begins to isolate and repeat the various sounds that he has heard about him. Soon he begins to utter meaningful words and phrases, although still in rudimentary and poorly constructed structural form. By the age of five or six, however, his growth in speaking ability has reached a well-developed stage, with only a few elements still needing to be perfected. His school years are spent primarily in learning to read and write his mother tongue. Thus, with respect to language development, "ontogeny recapitulates phylogeny"—each individual in his development follows the general course through which the entire race has passed before him.

In the audio-lingual approach, the foreign language is taught in a manner duplicating the stages through which the student has passed in learning his mother tongue.[8] The new language is first presented as a system of sounds to which the student listens as they are presented in meaningful phrases at a spoken rate normal for the particular language. The material selected is short and simple in its construction and carefully graded as to difficulty, but nevertheless it *is* authentic: it is spoken naturally as the natives of the country would speak it, and it concerns meaningful topics. By the process of listening, repetition, imitation, and memorization, he learns or "internalizes" these phrases. Soon he can understand conversations relating to everyday situations, stories about his peers in foreign lands, biographical descriptions of important historical figures, accounts of significant events in the past, and selections from newspapers, books, and magazines. In learning a foreign language, the student must thus first learn how to listen.

Subsequently, his ability to speak the language develops from listening to it spoken, the two skills being closely related to each other. The student hears the sound patterns (phrases) that are spoken and attempts to imitate them. In the process, the teacher assumes three roles: he serves as a model which the students imitate; as a judge evaluating the accuracy with which the students imitate the intonational patterns; and as a director who provides practice in coordinating ears, tongue, and facial expressions and gestures.

It is obvious, therefore, that repetition or drill is an important means by which students develop the ability to speak another language, but such reinforcement is most effective when it is meaningful to the learners.[9] Consequently, the phrases and simple sentences which are selected for practice should be appropriate to the interest and the level of the students; the words and phrases should be related to the daily life of the foreign country where the language is spoken; and the content should be presented in a systematic, sequential manner, each new skill being built upon those which the students have already developed.

Several classroom procedures can be used to provide the students with meaningful practice in the foreign language:[10]

"Canned" Dialogue. This technique utilizes a situation from daily life as the basis for the dialogue. Such themes as these are quite common: "A Day in School," "My Family," "At the Restaurant," and "On the Train." The dialogue is memorized by the students and then re-enacted in class. Although the newer textual materials that are now available include dialogues of this type, it may sometimes be necessary or advisable for the teacher to

develop his own, with or without the participation of the class in the project.

Some suggestions for the development of dialogues therefore follow: (1) The dialogue should be short, not more than seven or eight lines; (2) The number of roles required should be kept at a minimum; (3) The material should provide a means to review previously learned material and an opportunity to master new material.

Any number of procedures can be used in working with the "canned" dialogue in class, depending upon the abilities of the students, their maturation level, and similar factors. One possible approach is given below:

1. Before introducing the dialogue, the teacher should review the difficult expressions or idioms so that all students understand the content thoroughly.
2. The teacher then reads the material several times to the class at a normal rate of speed.
3. The class repeats the material in unison.
4. Various members of the class are then called upon to read individually the roles in the dialogue.
5. Finally, some of the students are asked to re-enact the dialogue from memory in front of the class.

The "canned" dialogue permits students to learn phrases and sentences which would be most useful to them in a foreign country. It also helps them to gain confidence in speaking the language by repeating the dialogue before the class, with the addition of suitable gestures and expressions. The device is also appropriate for a small group activity in which several students rotate their roles. One of its disadvantages, however, is that much of the material learned is appropriate for only one specific situation and is not useful in a wider range of circumstances. Moreover, the repetition of memorized content in this manner can produce boredom and disinterest after a while.

Dramatization is an extension of the "canned" dialogue approach, for it is a series of situational dialogues forming one coherent, sequential whole. The preparation of dramas is especially effective with elementary school students and with extracurricular foreign language clubs at the secondary and college level. It is advisable that the skit or play be a fairly short one

56

and that it serve as a genuine learning experience. Moreover, understanding should be stressed; otherwise, students may learn to say their parts fluently without comprehending the meaning and without clearly understanding the plot.

"Free response" or impromptu dialogue. This approach utilizes a particular theme or topic, but permits the students to respond as they wish within the broad, general framework which it presents. It has as an object the utilization of language patterns which the students already possess and the reconstruction and application of these to other situations. In this manner, students will gradually develop the ability to think in the foreign language. Because of the minimal ability of beginning students to use the language, a considerable amount of English must at times be interjected during the course of the dialogue, thus limiting the effectiveness of this method.

Discussion. Pictures in the form of photographs, travel posters, cartoons, or paintings may provide topics for discussion. Especially effective are those having situational themes that are in keeping with the students' age, interests, and language competency.

Likewise, realia can be utilized for discussion purposes, such as a doll dressed in a native costume of the country whose language is being studied or a model of a "typical" room in a home of the particular foreign country. Even simple classroom items can serve this function.[11]

From a psychological point of view, the use of pictures and objects for discussion has the advantage of associating abstract words and expressions with the concrete objects themselves, or at least with their pictorial representations. Of course, not all situations can be readily portrayed, and there are many concepts, such as loyalty, love, obedience, and duty, which can be conveyed in graphic form only with great difficulty—if at all. Moreover, pictures and objects can sometimes lead to misunderstandings. An eraser has color, shape, specific function (is it an ink or a pencil eraser?), and chemical composition. What exactly is being portrayed may not be clear.

Lastly, stories and expository articles can also serve as a source for discussion material. The reading by the teacher of such works provides students with opportunities to hear long passages that are integrated around a central theme, on the basis of which a series of questions and answers can be formed having a variety of sentence patterns. Difficulties arise, however, if the materials read contain words with which students are unfamiliar, if the structure of the sentences is complex for the ability level of the students, if unusual idioms are included, or even if cognates and combinations of known words are used.

Folklore. The use of folklore from the country or countries whose language is being studied can also serve as a means to facilitate learning.[12] Such lore includes proverbs, songs, customs, dances, and folk-games, a study of which can be combined with drill sessions on new expressions and grammatical structures that have been introduced.

By this means, not only are language-study objectives being realized, but the students are also being exposed to authentic elements of the foreign culture in a manner designed to motivate interest. Care should be taken, however, that the words and idiomatic expressions are those in contemporary and national usage, rather than those which may be archaic or dialectical. Otherwise, considerable time can be spent on the study of material which has little utilitarian value and which cannot meet the objective of elementary communication in the language.

Reading

Within the last few years, the audio-lingual approach to the teaching of modern languages has been increasingly subject to criticism.[13] The critics maintain, for the most part, that too much emphasis has been placed upon developing the student's skills in listening and speaking and that not enough consideration has been given to what they consider to be the equally important areas of reading and writing. They further contend that the results for the audio-lingual method have not been as spectacular as some of its proponents have claimed and that experimental data substantiating these claims has been lacking. These criticisms have produced a trend in language teaching toward a more eclectic approach, with both the audio-lingual techniques, as well as those of reading and writing, being given commensurable attention.

Reading done in the study of foreign languages has several purposes.[14] Students may read intensively to obtain information, to develop their vocabulary or knowledge of idioms and dialecticisms and to perfect some skill or skills such as reading for speed or comprehension. Intensive reading, which may be silent or oral, is usually closely controlled by the teacher with the objectives being clearly stated to the students; these may be such things as reading to answer specific questions, to discover how the new words are used, or to locate particular idiomatic expressions. On the other hand, in *extensive reading*, which most frequently is carried on silently, the students read a mass of material for the purpose of general comprehension, rather than for specifics with respect to structure or information. Extensive reading is also guided by the teacher, especially in the early stages of language study. Material that is read extensively usually is assigned during the lesson period and then is read by the students as part of their out-of-class assignment. Most teachers follow up this work by an oral or written evaluation. Extensive reading which is less rigidly controlled by the teacher can be termed *supplementary reading* and takes place after the students have developed some facility with the language.

The intensive reading lesson needs, of course, a greater degree of planning on the part of the teacher if it is to be successful. The suggestions given below are primarily for this type of lesson, but some of the ideas are also applicable to the extensive form:

1. The reading matter should be introduced so that the interest of the students is aroused.
2. Care should be taken to anticipate difficulties in vocabulary, idiomatic expressions, and grammatical structure so that these can be discussed when the material is presented to the students.
3. A variety of approaches should be employed to make the material meaningful: resource persons, realia, audiovisual materials, newspapers and periodicals, discussion and lecture.
4. The form of class reading should be varied: oral reading of the selection by the teacher or pupils, choral reading, silent reading, and the reading of dialogues.
5. A number of drill patterns should be used to reinforce the new material. Part of these may be assigned as out-of-class activities.

6. Some technique should be employed each time to summarize the lesson. Such a technique can involve the rereading of the material, a re-statement of the new concept for a review of the new words and terms.
7. Provisions should be made for frequent evaluations.

Writing

The ability to write a foreign language stems from the ability to speak and read it. The point at which students should begin to write the language they are studying is also at present in dispute, with partisans of the audio-lingual approach contending that writing skills should be introduced after some facility in listening, speaking, and reading has been reached.[15] The pendulum seems to be swinging the other way, however, with writing skills being developed simultaneously with the others. Although research implications are not clear, the approach seems to be a sound one—at least for older students in secondary schools and colleges—for all these language skills are interrelated and interdependent upon each other.[16]

Writing a language can proceed at several levels.[17] The simplest is writing by *imitation*: copying the material from a text or reader. At a somewhat more complex level is writing from *dictation*, since this demands several additional skills. Although the nature of the language ultimately determines what skills need to be developed before students can learn to write it, in most cases they will need to develop the ability to listen (in order to differentiate between sounds and their relationship to the orthography of the language), they will need to know the grammatical structure, and they will have to master the mechanics of punctuation.[18]

Any material which the students have studied is suitable for dictation, usually a short paragraph at first, with the material read gradually being lengthened to include two or more paragraphs. Later, unfamiliar material may be selected for dictation, provided care is taken to use only selections which are on the ability level of the students. The following procedure for giving dictation is suggested:
1. The teacher reads the material at a normal reading rate, with the students listening, no attempt being made to write it.

2. The teacher then re-reads the material slowly a phrase at a time.
3. The teacher re-reads the material again at a normal rate of speed, but pausing after each sentence in order to give the students time to make any corrections which they deem necessary.

Requests by the students for further re-reading of the material should be discouraged, since two of the skills which they need to develop through dictation are the ability to listen in the foreign language and the ability to retain passages which they have heard.

After the dictation has been completed, some means should be used to evaluate the work of the students.[19] The teacher may collect, grade, and return the papers at the next class session; she may have one student write on the blackboard where his work can be corrected to serve as a key by which the rest of the class can check their work; or she may utilize an opaque or overhead projector in which a correct copy of the dictation has been inserted.

Drill patterns may form another level of writing in a foreign language.[20] Depending upon the particular drill pattern selected, students can on occasion be given considerable freedom in their range of responses. They are thus being prepared to make the transition to writing compositions in the foreign language.

This transition is also facilitated through the re-writing of material in the foreign language. Students can be given practice in changing indirect speech to the parts of a play in dialogue form, or in re-writing in letter form an incident from a passage in a book.

The most complex type of writing ordinarily found in foreign language teaching is the *composition*, a form which permits students considerable independence in sentence structure and vocabulary, if not in subject matter.[21] In the beginning, the teacher probably should prescribe the theme of the composition so that the vocabulary and sentence structure will be familiar to the students. At this stage the teacher may even provide an outline for the students to follow. When the students have gained sufficient experience and have developed a larger vocabulary, they can be assigned themes on topics of their own choosing.

The writing of compositions is one of the most effective

means in learning a language, for it provides the students with opportunities to review, to reinforce their knowledge structures, to learn new words and expressions, and to repeat those that they already know.

Vocabulary Development. One of the most important elements in the study of a foreign language is the acquisition of a vocabulary extensive enough to meet the learner's needs.[22]

As with the development of other skills in learning a foreign language, the acquisition of a vocabulary takes place at the understanding, speaking, reading, and writing levels. Of course, the depth of meaning attached to a particular word varies significantly among students, even though all of them may be able to use it at each of the levels. Much is contingent upon two interrelated factors:

1. *Scope of Understanding.* Are they able to define the word? How many of its several meanings do they know?
2. *Scope of Utilization.* Do the students actually use the word to communicate in the language? Can they use it when needed in terms of all its possible shades of meaning?

Students learn new words of new meanings for partly familiar words in at least three ways:

1. Through visual clues including
   a. Picture aids
   b. Sight words
   c. The configuration of pattern of the word
   d. Unusual features which the word may possess
2. Through an emphasis on meaning
   a. Context
   b. Compounds of words already known
3. Through analytical methods
   a. Phonetic analysis
   b. Structural analysis
   c. Dictionary study

The exact extent to which the above methods are employed depends upon the study habits and skills of the learners as well as on the nature of the language. Not all of these methods, therefore, are applicable in every situation.

Students learn a large number of the new words incidentally, in the course of their study of the language; direct teaching for vocabulary development is nevertheless quite essential.[23]

Teachers can help students to build their vocabularies in several ways:

1. Time should be allotted in class in which new words are introduced.
2. Questions can be phrased so as to require students to use the new words when replying.
3. The new words should be used as much as possible when a lesson is summarized on the chalkboard.
4. Audio-visual aids should be selected which will clarify and enrich the meanings of the new terms.
5. Class activities should be planned which will require the frequent use of the new words, such as in dialogues, written assignments, quizzes, tests, and discussions.

Grammar. With the introduction of the audio-lingual approach to the teaching of foreign languages, less emphasis has been placed upon formal grammar.[24] The emphasis now is upon "structural patterns" of the spoken language. Grammatical concepts are presented as "keys," "rules-of-thumb," or in "notes." Grammar is learned as similarities and differences in the sounds, inflections, and structures. Only a minimum of formal principles are introduced—those absolutely essential for an understanding of the logical coherence of the language. Later, when the students have gained some competence in the language, more extensive consideration of grammar is undertaken. Grammatical understanding develops through use of the language and does not precede its use. It follows from a study of the language, rather than serving as a pre-requisite for its study.

Thus the current consensus seems to be that grammatical understanding is essential in the study and mastery of a foreign language. The difference between the "old" and the "new" methods therefore is not *whether* students need to know the grammar of the language they are learning. Rather, these questions are raised: *When* should students be introduced to grammar? *How* should it be presented? And *how much* of it do they need to know in order to communicate effectively in the language of their choice?

Drill. Suggested below are several drill patterns that can be used to reinforce the study of a foreign language.[25] These patterns can be used both in beginning stages and later, when some

63

proficiency in the language has been developed; they can be employed both with audio-lingual approaches and with those emphasizing reading and writing. The patterns which are described use English for illustrative purposes, but may be used in teaching various languages.

1. *Repetition.* This is the basic form of drill. The students simply repeat the statement which they have heard.

2. *Substitution.* One word (or more) is replaced in the sentence, such as a definite article for a demonstrative adjective or a noun for a pronoun:

> The girl is intelligent.
> That girl is intelligent.
> (or)
> The boy will go.
> He will go.

3. *Transformation.* One word (or more) is changed to another form or forms, such as a plural to the singular, an interrogative to a declarative, and a positive form to its negative.

> The boys are here.
> The boy is here.
> (or)
> Will he go?
> He will go?
> (or)
> He is a senior.
> He is not a senior.

4. *Integration.* Two independent statements are combined to form one sentence:

> The boys are happy.
> (and)
> They are going on a picnic.
> The boys are happy because they are going on a picnic.

5. *Expansion.* A sentence is lengthened by the inclusion of one or more additional words or phrases.

> The coffee is hot.
> The freshly-brewed coffee is steaming hot.

6. *Contraction.* The sentence is shortened by using one word in lieu of a clause or phrase.

The man who was an electronic specialist repaired the circuit.

The electronic specialist repaired the circuit.

7. *Completions.* The student inserts a word or phrase in the blank space to complete the sentence.

I like to eat ————.

I like to eat apples.

8. *Translations.* English sentences are translated into the foreign language, and sentences from that language are translated into English. The basic structure of the sentence is retained when the translation is made; for instance, declarative sentences remain declarative, and the same word order is followed insofar as possible.

Translating as an element in language study is being questioned, however.[26] Many authorities feel that such exercises are helpful only at an advanced stage of language work, when translating can help the student perceive the relationship of two languages in which he is already competent. Translating thus can help students understand the similarities and differences in structure, vocabulary, and power of expression of the respective languages.

P. JOHN GEORGEOFF, Associate Professor of Education at Purdue University, Lafayette, Indiana, holds a B.A. from Harris Teachers College, an M.A. from Washington University, and a Ph.D. from George Peabody College. Dr. Georgeoff has taught modern languages to elementary school classes, and methods courses at the university level. In addition, he has traveled widely in Europe and has lived in several other countries for extended periods. During 1960 he was a Ford Fellow studying abroad, and in 1964-65 he became the recipient of a grant from the Inter-University Committee on Travel Grants to do research in Bulgaria.

FOOTNOTES

1. Adolphe E. Meyer, AN EDUCATIONAL HISTORY OF THE WESTERN WORLD. New York: McGraw-Hill Book Company, 1965, 156-157; and J. Wesley Childers, FOREIGN LANGUAGE TEACHING, New York: The Center for Applied Research in Education, 1964, 1-28.
2. E. D. Wooley, "Five Decades of German Instruction in America." MONATSHEFTE FÜR DEUTSCHEN UNTERRICHT, XXXVI, November 1944, No. 7, 359-370; Otto Jespersen, HOW TO TEACH A

FOREIGN LANGUAGE. London: George Allen and Unwin, 1947, 1-10; and Childers, *Op. Cit.*, 32.

3. Algeron Coleman, THE TEACHING OF MODERN FOREIGN LANGUAGES IN THE UNITED STATES. New York: Macmillan. (Publication of American and Canadian committees on foreign languages, Vol. XII). See also the complete report: American and Canadian Committees on Modern Languages Publications. Vols. I-XVII plus A SUMMARY OF REPORTS ON THE MODERN FOREIGN LANGUAGES. New York: Macmillan; and Toronto: University of Toronto Press, 1927-1931.

4. A complete description and analysis of the methods employed in the military language training programs during World War II appears in the following book: Paul F. Angiolillo, ARMED FORCES' FOREIGN LANGUAGE TEACHING. New York: S. F. Vanni, 1947.

5. See: Theodore Huebener, WHY JOHNNY SHOULD LEARN FOREIGN LANGUAGES. Philadelphia: Chilton Books, 1961, 1 ff.; and William Riley Parker, THE NATIONAL INTEREST AND FOREIGN LANGUAGES, Washington, D.C.: U. S. Department of State, U. S. National Commission for UNESCO, 1949, 1 ff.

6. For brief histories of language teaching see: Simon Belesco, ed., MANUAL AND ANTHOLOGY OF APPLIED LINGUISTICS, Boston: D. C. Heath, 1961; Nelson Brooks, LANGUAGE AND LANGUAGE LEARNING: THEORY AND PRACTICE, New York: Harcourt, Brace, and World, 1964; and Robert Lado, LANGUAGE TEACHING: A SCIENTIFIC APPROACH. New York: McGraw-Hill, 1964.

7. Robert A. Hall, Jr., NEW WAYS TO LEARN A FOREIGN LANGUAGE. New York: Bantam Books, 1966, 27-28.

8. *Ibid.*, 17-40.

9. John M. Stephens, THE PSYCHOLOGY OF CLASSROOM LEARNING. New York: Holt, Rinehart and Winston, 1966, 108-118.

10. See also Hall, *Op. Cit.*, 49-83; and Theodore Huebener, HOW TO TEACH FOREIGN LANGUAGES EFECTIVELY, rev. ed. New York: New York University Press, 1965, 13-47.

11. Hall, *Op. Cit.*, pp. 118-124.

12. Robert A. Hall, Jr., INTRODUCTORY LINGUISTICS. Philadelphia: Chilton Books, 1964, Chapter LXIX; and Charles F. Hockett, A COURSE IN MODERN LINGUISTICS. New York: Macmillan, 1958, Chapter LXIII.

13. John B. Carroll, "Wanted: A Research Basis for Educational Policy on Foreign Language Teaching." HARVARD EDUCATIONAL REVIEW, XXX, Spring 1960, No. 2, 128-140.

14. Nelson Brooks, LANGUAGE AND LANGUAGE LEARNING (2nd edition), New York: Harcourt, Brace, and World, 1964, 164-173.

15. *Ibid.*, 165-166.

16. *Ibid.*

17. *Ibid.*, 173-179.

18. Childers, *Op. Cit.*, 49-50.

19. Robert Lado, LANGUAGE TEACHING: A SCIENTIFIC APPROACH. New York: McGraw-Hill, 1964, 145-146.

20. Childers, *Op. Cit.*, 53.

21. Edward M. Stack, THE LANGUAGE LABORATORY AND MODERN LANGUAGE TEACHING (rev. edition). New York: Oxford Uni-

versity Press, 1966, 178-183.
22. Lado, *Op. Cit.*, 114-130.
23. *Ibid.*, 120-129.
24. Childers, *Op. Cit.*, 30-32; 56-57.
25. See also: Lado, *Op. Cit.*, 90-113.
26. See: Childers, *Op. Cit.*, 57; Lado, *Op. Cit.*, 53-54; and Stack, *Op. Cit.*, 137-138.

Selected Bibliography

BOOKS

American and Canadian Committees on Modern Languages, Publications. Vols. I-XVII plus A SUMMARY OF REPORTS ON THE MODERN FOREIGN LANGUAGES. New York: Macmillan; and Toronto: University of Toronto Press, 1927-1931. This historic series of volumes surveys the teaching of modern languages in the United States and Canada and reports the results of one of the most extensive studies of its type ever conducted. The recommendations emphasize methods that facilitate mastery of reading and writing skills in foreign language study. Still important today as one of the best statements supporting the traditional approach to the teaching of modern languages.

Angiolillo, Paul F., ARMED FORCES' FOREIGN LANGUAGE TEACHING. New York: S. F. Vanni, 1947. A comprehensive, thorough analysis of the audio-lingual techniques used by the military in teaching modern languages during World War II.

Bahlsen, Leopold, THE TEACHING OF MODERN LANGUAGES, translated from German by M. Blakemore Evans. Boston: Ginn, 1903-1905. This book is one of the first in English describing the methods developed by Wilhelm Viëtor and others in Germany for the direct or oral teaching of modern languages. It is important today primarily for its historical significance.

Belasco, Simon, ed., MANUAL AND ANTHOLOGY OF APPLIED LINGUISTICS. Boston: D. C. Heath, 1961. Discusses the place of linguistics in the teaching of modern languages. Also contains selected readings on the subject.

Brooks, Nelson, LANGUAGE AND LANGUAGE LEARNING, 2nd edition. New York: Harcourt, Brace, and World, 1964. Considers the function of language in society and the process by which language skills are acquired. Expresses the current thought in the field.

Carroll, John B., THE STUDY OF LANGUAGE. Cambridge, Mass.: Harvard University Press, 1953. Describes various methods used in the study of foreign languages, including those utilized by the armed forces during World War II. A plea is made to view language as culture, especially in light of the increasing association of the world's peoples with each other.

Childers, J. Wesley, FOREIGN LANGUAGE TEACHING. New

York: The Center for Applied Research in Education, Inc., 1964. The purpose of this volume is threefold: (1) to give a brief history of the changing status of foreign language teaching in the schools and colleges of the United States; (2) to highlight the principal methods of teaching foreign language today; (3) to review research which has been done in the foreign language field and to show how this research has influenced the teaching of languages (1900-1963 time span).

Council for Cultural Cooperation of the Council of Europe, RESEARCH AND TECHNIQUES FOR THE BENEFIT OF MODERN LANGUAGE TEACHING. Strasbourg: Council of Europe, 1964. Techniques are discussed for making the introduction to languages both easier and quicker, even for the least gifted. They are not designed for the training of teachers (although the latter may find them useful), but to serve non-language specialists who in the modern age have increasing need of one or more languages for contacts with other countries in connection with their work.

Fotitch, Tatiana, ed., TEACHING FOREIGN LANGUAGES IN THE MODERN WORLD. Washington: Catholic University of America Press, 1961. Contains the proceedings of a workshop conducted by the Catholic University of America during June 1960.

Hall, Robert A., Jr., NEW WAYS TO LEARN A FOREIGN LANGUAGE. New York: Grosset & Dunlap, Inc., 1966. This paperback book attempts to present in semipopular form the techniques of language-learning, with special emphasis being given to modern linguistic analysis.

Holton, James S. and others, SOUND LANGUAGE TEACHING: THE STATE OF THE ART TODAY. New York: University Publishers, 1961. Provides specific helps to foreign language teachers, administrators, and board-of-education officials for answering the many questions that are being asked by the public today regarding language laboratories and sound language teaching.

Huebener, Theodore, HOW TO TEACH FOREIGN LANGUAGES EFFECTIVELY. rev. edition. New York: New York University Press, 1965. The purpose of this book is to suggest practical instructional procedures to teachers of modern foreign languages. Various methods of instruction are presented and a generous collection of illustrations, examples, model lessons, games, and devices are included. Over forty complete lesson plans for the teaching of French, German, Italian, and Spanish have been included to illustrate different aspects of language instruction.

Jespersen, Otto, HOW TO TEACH A FOREIGN LANGUAGE. London: Allen and Unwin, 1956. A general methods book on the teaching of modern foreign languages. Although written some time ago, it is still methodologically sound.

Lado, Robert, LANGUAGE TEACHING: A SCIENTIFIC AP-
PROACH. New York: McGraw-Hill, 1964. Presents some of
the major areas the language teacher should be familiar with
to follow a scientific approach to the teaching of foreign language. Some of the areas presented are linguistics, techniques
of testing and teaching, human learning, the languages laboratory, reading, writing, teaching machines, programmed learning,
cultural content and literature, and the target and source
languages.
Meras, Edmond A., A LANGUAGE TEACHER'S GUIDE, 2nd edition. New York: Harper and Brothers, 1962. A methods book
for teachers and prospective teachers of modern languages. An
excellent discussion is included reviewing the advances made
during the last half century in the methodology of foreign
language teaching.

ARTICLES

Green, John A., "On Improvement in Teaching the Oral Skills."
THE FRENCH REVIEW, XXXIX, April 1966, 748-757. Discusses techniques to improve the audio-lingual approach in the
teaching of modern languages. Presents some excellent suggestions to make the language laboratory period more interesting.
Guerra, Emilio, "The Teaching of Modern Foreign Languages."
HIGH POINTS, LVI, October 1964, 6-13. Surveys the modern
techniques employed in teaching foreign languages in secondary
schools. Although no new findings are presented, current procedures and trends are summarized very well.
Hayes, Alfred S., "New Direction in Foreign Language Teaching."
MODERN LANGUAGE JOURNAL, XLIX, May 1965, 281-293.
Proposes a series of new directions for the teaching of modern
languages. It contains excellent ideas for relating psycholinguistics to existing methods of programmed instruction. The
author also suggests "a great intensification of listening practice,
a heavy underscoring of the audio in the audio-lingual-visual."
Kelly, Leo L., "Dialogue Versus Structural Approach." FRENCH
REVIEW, XXXVII, February 1964, 432-439. Contrasts the dialogue versus the structural approach in the study of a modern
language. He concludes that the two methods need not be in
opposition to each other, but rather that they can complement
each other. Dialogues can provide practice in the use of each
new element as it is introduced and serve as means to integrate
these new structures with those previously learned.
Lambert, Wallace and Henri, C. Barek, "Conditioning of Complex
Verbal Sequences." CANADIAN JOURNAL OF PSYCHOL-
OGY, XIV, June 1960, 87-95. Describes an attempt to condition
a complex verbal response by means of selective reinforcement.
The subjects used in the experiment were college students.

Lambert, Wallace, *et al.*, "Development Aspects of Second Language Acquisition." JOURNAL OF SOCIAL PSYCHOLOGY, XLIII, February 1956. Reports the results of a study investigating the problem of linguistic enculturation. The findings indicate that vocabulary development proceeds rapidly; but that culturally related aspects, as evidenced in word order, stereotyped response, associational form and content, and pronunciation, are persistent.

Leutenegger, Ralph R., *et al.*, "Auditory Factors in Foreign Language Acquisition." MODERN LANGUAGE JOURNAL, IL, January 1965, 22-31. Reports the results of a study which attempted to develop techniques to predict potential abilities of students for language acquisition.

O'Connor, Patricia and W. F. Twaddell, "Intensive Training for an Oral Approach in Language Teaching." MODERN LANGUAGE JOURNAL, XLIV, Part 2, February 1960, 1-42. Six months of full-time work were spent on the task of converting a body of experimental language-teaching material into the basis for a teacher-training seminar. This publication describes and discusses the seminar material which was thus developed.

Oinas, Felix J., ed. "Language Teaching Today." INTERNATIONAL JOURNAL OF AMERICAN LINGUISTICS, XXVI, Part 2, October 1960. Report of the Language Laboratory Conference held at Indiana University, 1960, 1-204. A report of the Language Laboratory Conference held at Indiana University, January 22-23, 1960. This volume contains the papers presented at the conference. The general theme was the use of language laboratories and programmed learning in the teaching of foreign languages in the high schools and colleges.

Popper, Evelyn, "More Time with the Audio-Lingual Approach." HIGH POINTS, XLVII, February 1965, 55-57. Suggests that more time is needed in using the audio-lingual approach at the junior high school level. Proposes that its introductory use be spread out over a two-year period through an enriched program of activities and materials.

Smith, Henry Lee, Jr., "Descriptive Linguistics and the Future of Modern Language Teaching." INTERNATIONAL JOURNAL OF AMERICAN LINGUISTICS, XXVIII, No. 1, Part II, January 1962, 40-51. A paper given at the Second Language Laboratory Conference held at Purdue University, March 23-25, 1961. The author discusses the role of descriptive linguistics in the improvement of language teaching.

Starr, Wilmarth H., "Proficiency Tests in Modern Foreign Languages." *PMLA*, LXXVI, May 1961, 7-11. An address given at the General Meeting on the Foreign Language Program in Philadelphia, December 29, 1960.

Insights into the Nature of Meaning and the Symbolizing Function of the Human Mind

HENRY WINTHROP

University of South Florida

THE IMPORTANCE of language teaching is deeply related to the whole province of verbal meaning and to the processes by which the human mind conveys such meaning through a variety of symbolizing functions. For this reason we shall review some of the fundamental phenomena in the realm of meaning, since all refinements and extensions of language and all translations from one language or code into another language or code are cogently related to the problem of faithfully rendering the *intentions* underlying symbol-making and symbol-using activities. Even where the work of symbolization is *nonverbal* in nature, as in dreams, art, and ritual, the discussion of the purposes in human life served by such nonverbal activities, must be undertaken obviously by means of language. In this sense language is the most basic and widest vehicle for conveying meaning and understanding of the functions of symbolization. For all these reasons this chapter will therefore be devoted to a review of *some* of the central work which has been done in exploring the nature of meaning and the symbolizing functions of the human mind. A staggering volume of work has been done in both these connections, and the present chapter can only make a modest attempt to *select* some of the more significant and interesting contributions which have been made along both these lines. Limitations of space will therefore make it necessary to exclude much of significance and value. What has been chosen for treatment here, in the estimation of this writer, has a direct bearing on the problems associated with the teaching and the translation of foreign languages, and it is this educational objective which will

71

be the explicit criterion that shall govern the choice of topics which follow.

The Functions of Discourse

Charles Morris[1] has devoted himself to the task of analyzing and classifying the content of human language in terms of the vast variety of purposes to which human discourse ministers. Language which fulfills special functions can be classified into what Morris calls *types of discourse.* In order to arrive at what he regards as the most useful taxonomy for the classification of language into the special functions it serves, Morris makes use of two different criteria. The first criterion makes use of a classification of language by the type of meaning its *signs* are intended to convey. In the present context, of course, these signs are *words.* The second criterion classifies the sign complexes (e.g., words, phrases, and idioms) of language by the *use* or *function* to which they are put.

The first of Morris' two criteria is referred to as the *mode* of *signifying* of signs. In Morris' work there are four modes of signifying: *designative, appraisive, prescriptive,* and *formative* modes. A *designative* sign or word is one which signifies the characteristics or stimulus-properties of stimulus-objects. An *appraisive* sign is one that signifies something as having a preferential status for behavior. A *prescriptive* sign signifies that certain types of related responses in behavior or, if you prefer, a certain pattern of behavior, is called for. For purposes of this discussion, in which we are forced to avoid unnecessary, qualifying, technical detail, we can regard a *formative* sign as a symbol or word which has strictly "logical" or "formal" functions.

The second criterion for the classification of signs used by Morris is, as I have already mentioned, to stress their *use* or *function* rather than their mode of signifying. There are four such uses: the *informative, valuative, incitive,* and *systemic* uses. The *informative* use of signs occurs when they are produced to cause someone to act as if something had, has, or will have certain characteristics. The *valuative* use of signs occurs when they are produced in order to cause preferential behavior towards something. Signs are *incitive* when they are intended to bring out more or less specific ways of responding to something. Signs are *systemic* when they are used to organize behavior that other signs—verbal or nonverbal—tend to provoke. When signs are used *adequately* they are said to be convincing if they are informative, *effective* if they are valuative, *persuasive* if they are incitive and *correct* if they are systemic.

Classifying the words (signs) of language by both *mode of signifying* and by *use* or *function,* yields a four-by-four schema, exhibiting the sixteen major types of discourse found in Western languages. Thus, to take only four examples, *scientific discourse* is designative-informative; *poetic discourse* is appraisive-valuative; *religious discourse* is prescriptive-incitive; and *metaphysical discourse* is formative-systemic.

The value of Morris' schema for teachers of languages and literature lies in the fact that it illuminates the different types of meaning-function which written or spoken discourse may have. It recognizes that complex human behavior needs all these types of discourse and that communication is poorly served if we imagine that any one of these types can do service for all the others. There are students and teachers—usually trained in science or technical philosophy — who uncritically assume that the *structured* language of science, on the one hand, or that of mathematics and logic, on the other, are the only models for all *linguistic* communication. This is not so. The former types of discourse require chiefly designative-informative signs; the latter two, formative-informative signs. If, however, we are trying to convey the power of great literature, if we are trying to sensitize individuals to religious insight, or if we are trying to make subjects aware of the moral issues of a complex situation, then the appropriate types of discourse are *designative-valuative, prescriptive-incitive* and *appraisive-incitive.* Each type of discourse is geared to dealing with its own special meaning-functions.

There is a special value for teachers of foreign languages, in looking at their problems in terms of Morris' schema. The value is that the schema provides a cautionary measure in effecting translations. To take one type of discourse as an example, if one has to translate religious discourse from language A into language B, the *sign complexes* (words, phrases or clauses) should be functionally equivalent in the two languages. For any given type of discourse, it should be possible to standardize by conventional agreement the *sign complex equivalencies* of the two languages for the given type of discourse. Such standardization (which will obviously always fall far short of perfection) can heighten the effectiveness of translation and minimize the incidence of *linguistic distortion in translation.*

The degree of *distortion in translation* is in principle measurable, and I have tried to indicate elsewhere[2] some of the methodological techniques which may perhaps prove useful in effecting such measurement. In the present connection, however, I should like to suggest that an interesting consideration which might be explored experimentally is the hypothesis that the maximum degree of distortion in translation occurs when one type of discourse in one language undergoes translation into *another* type of discourse in a second language, in linguistic situations in which the sign complex equivalencies have been improperly established or not established at all.

Structured Meaning in Human Communication

With the progress of science and of well-shored-up human knowledge, the need has become ever greater for the use of communication in what has come to be called the highly rigorous *language of structure.* The language of structure, so central to the development of scientific theory, has been richly dealt with by Nagel.[3] *Structured* language, which is the type of language we employ to achieve painstaking rigor in the communication of ideas and intellectually complex concepts, is the language *par excellence* of the sciences, of logic and mathematics, of technology, and of all those areas of human inquiry in which complex *ideational* meaning is to be clearly conveyed and made *public* or *intersubjective.* In terms of Morris' schema, the language of structure would involve *predominantly* designative-informative, prescriptive-informative, and formative-informative types of discourse. To a lesser extent, structured communication may also be found in other types of discourse, such as designative-incitive (legal) and designative-systemic (cosmological).

Because the attributes of the language of structure are very potent in effective communication, because structured communication is beginning to be increasingly needed and used by modern man, and because it is perhaps the one type of discourse which has been undergoing the most rapid development, the understanding of *structured meaning* and the properties of structured language are matters of the greatest importance to language teachers. An understanding of the properties of structured language becomes a major responsibility of the foreign language teacher for several reasons. Increasingly in the modern university, students who specialize in one of the sciences or mathematics are finding it necessary to take a course or two in scientific readings in French or German and occasionally in another foreign language. Some of the students who are specializing in science or mathematics seriously expect to be busy reading periodicals in foreign languages. In connection with their chosen professional fields, many expect to be busy doing a great deal of translation from foreign languages into English, or the reverse. A good many of our students wish to prepare more effectively for their doctoral language examinations, which are taken most seriously at some institutions of higher learning.

Apart from all these practical considerations, however, some familiarity with the properties and limitations of structured language as a vehicle for communication is indispensable in a general sense for the foreign language teacher. To one who intends to make language teaching his or her profession and who recognizes that man manipulates his world, pushes out the frontiers of human knowledge and dispels confusion regarding some of our most important issues by clarifying them through language, some knowledge of the most general properties of structured language is clearly vital.

It is being increasingly recognized in many quarters that the most important scientific breakthrough of the twentieth century thus far has been computer technology, because of its anticipated social effects. Since the heart of the modern computer is its programming and since computer programming depends upon the *highly structured properties* of logical and mathematical languages, it behooves all those who deal with language to become familiar with structured language as a major vehicle for applied scientific and technical progress. The language of structure has not only helped to deepen and advance man's knowledge and shed a flood of light on traditional puzzles and problems about which man has speculated throughout history, but at the same time the language of structure has now been exploited in such a way as to help to fulfill a whole range of man's practical needs. These needs are met by computer services in industry, in scientific research involving what is called *simulation theory,* and even in the first faint beginnings of artistic production as in some of the current experiments on computer music.

For all the preceding reasons and many more which cannot be expanded upon because of space limitations, those concerned with the teaching of languages should become acquainted with some of the most general findings to date which have been achieved in research on the language of structure. The reader can of course deepen his knowledge of the nature of meaning by a serious reading program in the literature which is devoted to research on the language of structure. A good beginning can, I think, be made through the work of such men as Vaihinger,[4] Pap,[5] and Walker[6]. With increasing background in this area the reader can make it his business to read some of the journals devoted to advancing the *philosophy of science,* a field which, among other things, is extensively devoted to research and new ideas concerning the language of structure. In the material which follows I propose to highlight a few major considerations on the problem of meaning concerning the language of structure, which have achieved a somewhat general consensus to date.

The Meaning Functions of Language

Language can be regarded as falling into three categories, insofar as attention is focused on its *meaning-function.* These three categories which reveal the major uses of language are *syntactics, semantics* and *pragmatics,* a classification which we also owe to Charles Morris.[7]

Syntactics is interested in the relations among terms of discourse, such as the relation of words to one another or of symbols to one another within a discipline such as mathematics. An example of a syntactic sentence would be one in which the concept of a *triangle* was defined as a plane, three-sided figure.

Semantic statements are assertions which deal with things, events, processes, situations, and relationships given by nature and *discovered* by man rather than *invented* by man. In short, semantic statements deal with "states of the external world" rather than any psychological states of man himself. Those things in the external world to which attention is paid through a semantic assertion, are called "referents." A semantic statement is one which tells us something about such referents. Thus "Water is a wetting, compressible medium" is a semantic statement which, however, is still sufficiently vague as to require further refinement for greater precision. On the other hand, the statement, "A molecule of water consists of two atoms of the element hydrogen, combined with one atom of the element oxygen," is a semantic statement of far greater precision. Even here, however, further precision can be achieved if we can clarify what is meant by "element."

Pragmatic statements tend to reveal the relationship of words, phrases, and ideas to their users. Thus, although the average, linguistically unsophisticated person may believe he is making *a statement about something in the world* when he stands before a canvas and says "This painting is beautiful," he is mistaken. He is really making an elliptical statement about one of his own, internal psychological states, that is, he is furnishing us with information about one viewer's reactions to a painting. Statements of this type have been spoken of as being in the "quasi-material mode of discourse."

The value of the preceding tripartite classification of the meaning-functions of language for language teachers lies in the fact that much confusion, both in language description and language translation, may derive from mistaking language intended to express one of these functions for language intended to express another. Thus a sliding scale of meaning may result from mistaking the pragmatic functions of language for its semantic functions. Suppose a passage in language, A, which clearly tries to describe the pragmatic and *evaluating* reactions of a character to something in his milieu, is translated by a *philosophically naïve* translator into a passage in language, B. If this translation is executed in such a way that the translated passage appears to be saying something about an object, situation, or event in the character's milieu rather than about the character himself, then accuracy has been sacrificed and intent has been lost. Clearly, sophistication about language functions should so govern the process of translation as to constrain the translator to choose *only those words of the language into which the passage is being translated*, which will express the same *mode* (syntactic, semantic or pragmatic) as that of the original language in which the passage appeared. An awareness of these meaning-functions of language will constrain a translator or a teacher of foreign languages to think in terms of the *modal equivalences* of the original and translated passage and therefore, derivatively, of the vocabulary of the translating language which will most suitably establish such a modal equivalence.

The Propositional Function

One of the more important gains which has been made historically in our understanding of the language of structure is a more precise knowledge of the nature of that basic unit of all discourse, the proposition. In particular, our knowledge has been enhanced with respect to the valid functions of the proposition and its limitations in discourse. Almost every reader is familiar with the structure of a proposition from an undergraduate course in logic or linguistics or perhaps from some other field. Here we need only to remind him that the most general features of a proposition are that it contains a subject and a predicate and some asserted relationship between the two. Thus, "Academics are unworldly," "John is the father of Mary" or "The lieutenant originated the plan of attack" are all examples of propositions. Fewer readers, perhaps, are familiar with what is called "the propositional function," a linguistic and logical device which has received major consideration in the work of Bertrand Russell.[8] A propositional function, unlike a proposition, is an assertion which has the *structure* and *grammatical form* of a proposition, but is without content. When we say that a propositional function is an assertion which is without content, we mean that a *predicate* is asserted about a subject term which is *variable*. Thus the assertion "X is a dog" is a propositional function. We cannot tell whether a propositional function is true unless we substitute a given value for the variable involved. If X is Lassie, the function becomes a proposition which is true. If X is Man O' War, a champion race-track horse some decades ago, we get a proposition which is false.

The importance of the propositional function for language teachers and for those who are concerned with effective language translation is that research has revealed that *nearly all human judgments* are made in terms of propositional functions. As a result many of the subject terms of our assertions are *really and implicitly variables*. One result of this for language translation and even, for that matter, for communication within a single language, is that the specific value which A had in mind for the variable, X, in the propositional function which he expressed in language 1, may not be the specific value for the variable, X, which B has in mind when the variable term is translated into a propositional function expressed in language 2. Let us provide an illustration of what we mean.

Consider the assertion "A liberal is likely to try to introduce needed social change without delay." If by a "liberal" you mean the type of politician or statesman to whom the public generally attaches this label, in democratic countries like the United States and England, the statement will be true. If, however, by a "liberal" you mean the type of politician or statesman in certain Latin-American countries which are dominated by the military, you have an entirely different situation. The type of politician or statesman in some Latin-American countries who is frequently referred to there as a "liberal" by those who hold to a traditional outlook and who wish to preserve the status quo, would be regarded as quite conservative or even at times reactionary in the Anglo-Saxon democracies. Thus the assertion which we have placed in quotes at the beginning of this paragraph would be true on the whole when read in English in the United States or the United Kingdom, and false when read in Spanish in certain Latin-American countries.

Thus, in the teaching of foreign languages, it is important to recognize that statements in the form of propositional functions are likely to appear ridiculous or incredible in translation if one merely translates the variable term into its *lexicographic* equivalent in another language. Judgment will appear to have gone awry. The proper way to prevent this in translation is to find or coin a word or phrase which gives us the true meaning-equivalent of the *variable* term in the *language of translation*. Since the reader (and often the hearer too) may replace the lexicographically translated variable by a constant which is different from that intended by the original writer or speaker, misunderstanding is likely to increase. It is therefore best, when making a translation, to ask oneself just *what is intended* by the terminology of the assertion when couched in the original language, rather than to seek to find the most precise, lexicographic equivalent of that terminology in the language into which it is to be translated. Words and phrases, which are often really cryptic variable terms, may reflect neither a specific idea nor a specific judgment, as they are used in propositional functions. A cryptic variable makes for open ambiguity unless caution is exercised. The dictionary may therefore often prove to be a poor crutch for the task of translation and the achievement of fairly accurate communication.

Conclusion

In the author's opinion a considerable increase in power and efficiency can be derived when the teacher of foreign languages is conscious of the meaning-intentions of language and the symbol-functions of language. The teacher of foreign languages is already adept at dealing with the *expressive* functions of language, via literature and the humanities. The *ratiocinative* functions, however, that is, those concerned with the refinements of rigor for purposes of communication, offer ground for considerable improvement in the activity of teaching mastery of a foreign language and achieving accuracy in the task of translation. Although some familiarity with the material discussed in the present chapter can help the teacher of foreign languages considerably in perfecting his command of, and discrimination between, the two functions of language just mentioned, it is the ratiocinative function which can be more richly mastered through a knowledge of the considerations touched upon in this chapter. It is the author's conviction that material of this type should become a permanent part of the educational equipment of the foreign language teacher.

HENRY WINTHROP, professor and chairman, Department of Interdisciplinary Social Sciences, University Of South Florida, has pursued graduate studies in both the natural and social sciences. He received his Ph.D. (1953) from the New School for Social Research, his M.A. from George Washington University (1940) and his B.S. from the College of the City of New York (1935). He has taught the social sciences and philosophy. Dr. Winthrop now serves as an editor on fourteen professional journals, among which are the *Journal of Human Relations, Journal of Humanistic Psychology* and *Journal of Existentialism.* He is the author of close to four hundred professional publications which have appeared in well-known professional journals. Dr. Winthrop is listed biographically in *American Men of Science, Who's Who in the Southeast* and *Who's Who in American Education.*

FOOTNOTES

1. Charles W. Morris, SIGNS, LANGUAGE AND BEHAVIOR. New York: George Braziller, 1955. See Chapter 5 "Types Of Discourse," 123-86 and the *Glossary* to this volume, 345-56.
2. Henry Winthrop, "A Proposed Model and Procedure for Studying Message Distortion in Translation." LINGUISTICS. No. 22, June 1966, 98-112.
3. Ernest Nagel, THE STRUCTURE OF SCIENCE. PROBLEMS IN THE LOGIC OF SCIENTIFIC EXPLANATION. New York: Harcourt, Brace & World, 1961.
4. Hans Vaihinger, THE PHILOSOPHY OF 'AS IF'. A SYSTEM OF THE THEORETICAL, PRACTICAL AND RELIGIOUS FICTIONS OF MANKIND. London: Routledge & Kegan Paul Ltd., 1952.
5. Arthur Pap, ELEMENTS OF ANALYTIC PHILOSOPHY. New York: Macmillan, 1949.
6. Marshall Walker, THE NATURE OF SCIENTIFIC THOUGHT. Englewood Cliffs, N.J.: Prentice-Hall, 1963.
7. Charles W. Morris, FOUNDATIONS OF THE THEORY OF SIGNS, Volume 1, Number 2 of the International Encyclopedia of Unified Science. Chicago: The University of Chicago Press, 1938.
8. Bertrand Russell, INTRODUCTION TO MATHEMATICAL PHILOSOPHY. London: George Allen & Unwin, 1948. See Chapter 15 "Propositional Functions," 155-66.

Selected Bibliography

Morris, Charles W., SIGNS, LANGUAGE AND BEHAVIOR. New York: George Braziller, 1955. See Chapter 5 "Types Of Discourse," 123-86 and the *Glossary* to this volume, 345-56. This volume aims to lay the foundation for a comprehensive and fruitful science of signs.

——, FOUNDATIONS OF THE THEORY OF SIGNS, Volume 1, Number 2 of the International Encyclopedia of Unified Science, Chicago: The University of Chicago Press, 1938. This is a classic monograph executed by Morris three decades ago. It was one of the earliest contributions to the systematic study of *semiosis*, defined as the process in which something functions as a sign.

Nagel, Ernest, THE STRUCTURE OF SCIENCE. PROBLEMS IN THE LOGIC OF SCIENTIFIC EXPLANATION. New York: Harcourt, Brace & World, 1961. This is a recent and somewhat advanced textbook devoted to scientific method or to what, in the terminology of section 2, is called the language of structure. It is one of the more distinguished of the recent textbooks which have appeared in this field.

Russell, Bertrand, INTRODUCTION TO MATHEMATICAL PHILOSOPHY. London: George Allen & Unwin, 1948. See Chapter 15 "Propositional Functions," 155-66. This volume was intended by its author to be an introduction to the subject matter of mathematical philosophy.

Vaihinger, Hans, THE PHILOSOPHY OF 'AS IF.' A SYSTEM OF THE THEORETICAL, PRACTICAL AND RELIGIOUS FICTIONS OF MANKIND. London: Routledge & Kegan Paul Ltd., 1952. This book is a classic in its field. Essentially it is concerned with the nature and function of "fictions." A fiction, broadly speaking, is a linguistic device which aids us in advancing knowledge but need not be true in any objective or scientific sense.

Walker, Marshall, THE NATURE OF SCIENTIFIC THOUGHT. Englewood Cliffs, N.J.: Prentice-Hall, 1963. This is one of the most interesting volumes on the language of structure available to the general reader. It deals with the relationship of science and philosophy, models in mathematics, models in the natural and social sciences, and the relationship of science to ethics.

Winthrop, Henry, "A Proposed Model and Procedure for Studying Message Distortion in Translation." LINGUISTICS, No. 22, June 1966, 98-112. This paper is concerned with a description of novel types of experiments which can be conducted in order to measure the characteristic degree of linguistic distortion which occurs for a translation between any two languages. Statistical procedures are described for defining and measuring *operationally* what is meant by *degree of linguistic distortion in translation.*

Language, Ethnocentrism, and Culture Conflicts

PANOS D. BARDIS

University of Toledo

> *And did not Spinoza think in Judeo-Portu-
> guese, obstructed by and contending with
> Dutch?*

MIGUEL DE UNAMUNO

> *The Yugoslavs understand Russian and the
> Russians understand Yugoslav, but neither
> understands the other.*

DAGOBERT RUNES

FROM THE biblical account of Babel, the polyglot and cosmo-
politan city in the Plain of Shinar with its magnificent seven-
story *ziggurat,* to the most modern linguistic study, man has in-
defatigably investigated every aspect of one of his truly spectacular achievements: language.

Before analyzing the findings of these investigations which
deal with ethnocentrism and culture conflicts, it seems necessary
to define some of the most important terms employed in the
present essay, namely, language, culture, nation, nationalism,
ethnos, and ethnocentrism.

1. *Language,* from the Latin *lingua,* "tongue," may be defined as a "system of communication by sound, that is, through
the organs of speech and hearing, among human beings of a
certain group or community, using vocal symbols possessing
arbitrary conventional meanings."[1] It may also be asserted that
"language, as it is usually understood, is a system of sounds, or
rather of the habits of producing them by the speaking organs,
for the purpose of communicating with other persons, that is,
of influencing their actions, decisions, thoughts, etc."[2] One of
the most famous definitions of language is that by Edward Sapir,

83

an anthropologist — anthropology has investigated linguistic phenomena more than any other social science has — who stated in 1921 that language is "a purely human and non-instinctive method of communicating ideas, emotions, and desires by means of a system of voluntarily produced symbols." Language, then, is almost completely social, since we acquire it through contacts with other human beings, but also an individual phenomenon, as it exists as a constellation of habits in each person, on whose experiences it is based, never being identical to that of any other individual. In other words, language consists of *phonemes* recurring in certain patterns. Phonemes are minimal groups of typical acoustic elements, which we usually express by means of phonetic alphabets — English is composed of forty-five phonemes. The recurrent patterns, on the other hand, may be *morphemes,* the smallest meaningful units of linguistic form (such as *town* and *s* in *towns*) or *tagmemes,* the basic meaningful units of grammatical form.

Language must be distinguished from the concepts of *standard language* and *dialect.* The former is a subtype of a "language which has gained literary and cultural supremacy over the other dialects and is accepted by the speakers of the other dialects as the most proper form of that language."[3] A dialect, however, is a "specific form of a given language, spoken in a certain locality or geographic area, showing sufficient differences from the standard or literary form of that language, as to pronunciation, grammatical construction and idiomatic usage of words, to be considered a distinct entity, yet not sufficiently distinct from other dialects of the language to be regarded as a different language."[4]

A further distinction, according to F. de Saussure's famous terminology, must be made between *la langue* ("tongue," but "language-system" is a more accurate term) and *la parole* ("speech"). A *tongue* is a code, potential, social, fixed, slow-moving, and psychological, whereas *speech* is the encoding of a message, actualized, individual, free, ephemeral, and psychophysical.[5]

2. *Culture,* from the Latin *colere* (to care for), includes material and nonmaterial inventions and discoveries of an artistic, economic, ideological, linguistic, philosophical, political, religious, and social nature, which are socially transmitted, and which are aimed at the control of man's environment. In 1850, Gustav

Klemm (1802-1867), a German scholar who anticipated Darwin's theory of evolution, emphasized the transmission aspect of culture from generation to generation. Similarly, in 1871, Edward Burnett Tylor (1832-1917), the noted English anthropologist and author of *Primitive Culture,* observed that the acquisition of cultural habits presupposes social life. These and myriad additional definitions of culture, according to Alfred Kroeber and Clyde Kluckhohn, are of five types, namely, descriptive, genetic, historical, normative, and psychological. The science investigating purely cultural phenomena is known as *Kulturologie,* a term introduced by Wilhelm Ostwald (1853-1932), a German chemist and philosopher who wrote *Naturphilosophie.* Leslie A. White has suggested *culturology* as the English equivalent to *Kulturologie.* The primary vehicle employed in transmitting the aforementioned components of culture is language, which also constitutes an exceedingly important cultural element.

3. A *nation,* from the Latin *nasci* (to be born), since the French Revolution of 1789, has been defined as the people of a politically independent state who possess the sense that they constitute a unique political group because of their common cultural or racial background.

4. *Nationalism,* an ideology aimed at the establishment of an autonomous state, began as an intellectual movement in the eighteenth century which was gradually transformed into the conscious political force of the French Revolution. Although this force was conceived as the prelude to cosmopolitanism, by 1900 it had degenerated into a conservative, parochial, chauvinistic ideology. It thus led to the fragmentation of empires and constant catastrophic conflict. Today nationalism is flourishing among both leftists and rightists, while in Africa and Asia what is becoming dominant seems to be a composite of democratic and nationalistic ideas.

5. An *ethnos,* or *ethnic group,* is a group of people united by cultural or racial bonds which its members adopt rather unconsciously. In the original Greek, *ethnos* had many meanings, including the following: a nationality, as "the Median nation" (Herodotus, *Histories,* I, 101); a number of tribes living together, as those of the Lycians (Homer, *Iliad,* XII, 330); a social class, as "the class of serfs" (Plato, *Laws,* 776d); and sex, as "the female sex" (Xenophon, *Oeconomicus,* VII, 26).

6. *Ethnocentrism* refers to the tendency to evaluate outsiders in terms of the social norms of one's own group, or, as William Graham Sumner (1840-1910) said, the conviction that "one's own group is the center of everything." This implies that, unlike *cultural relativism* and *xenocentrism*, ethnocentrism includes a generalized intolerance of the behavior patterns of outsiders.

Animal Culture and Language

In *The Descent of Man*, Charles Darwin avers that the "habitual use of articulate language is, however, peculiar to man. . . . That which distinguishes man from the lower animals is not the understanding of articulate sounds, for, as every one knows, dogs understand many words and sentences . . . . It is not the mere articulation which is our distinguishing character, for parrots and other birds possess this power. Nor is it the mere capacity of connecting definite sounds with definite ideas; for it is certain that some parrots . . . connect unerringly words with things, and persons with events. The lower animals differ from man solely in his almost infinitely larger power of associating together the most diversified sounds and ideas" (Chapter 3). Darwin also states that among birds "the members of the same species utter the same instinctive cries expressive of their emotions" (*ibid.*). These and later scientific observations regarding culture and language among animals may be summarized as follows:

1. Ants, bees, and other animals do have some form of social organization, as well as a rudimentary language.

2. Animal cries are characterized by extreme simplicity.

3. Such cries present a high degree of uniformity for each individual and species.

4. There is no conclusive evidence that animals are capable of accurate imitation of sounds.

5. They do, however, possess and express elementary emotions.

6. Their simple experiences seem to be transmitted genetically and not, as in the case of humans, socially.

7. Also unlike humans, animals are almost completely integrated into their social roles.

8. Animal societies lack religion and codes of ethics.

9. Therefore, true cultures and genuine languages among animals are nonexistent.

Origin and Number of Languages

One may assert, then, that, in view of the numerous functions of language, especially that of social communication, *Homo loquens* (speaker) is superior to *Homo fabricans* (tool-maker). This was realized even in ancient times. In Greece, for instance, innumerable treatises on rhetoric were published quite early. Euripides (484-407 B.C.), the celebrated Attic tragedian and painter, frequently confessed that his philosophy and style were influenced by rhetoric. The Sophists, Greece's professors of rhetoric and the art of litigation, considered language more than important. In fact, Aristophanes (445-380 B.C.), the Athenian giant of the Old Comedy who wrote a play about the Sophists' pedagogical philosophy, presented Socrates as their leader who apotheosized *glossa,* or language: "there are three gods, chaos and clouds and language" (*Clouds,* 424).

This valuable cultural invention appeared so long ago that its true origin is lost in the misty beginnings of man's prehistory. Some scholars, therefore, believe that it is impossible to know the origin of language, while others are convinced that language and society were born at the same time. Other authors aver that this invention took place in China, Egypt, and Mesopotamia in early Pleistocene times. It seems at least certain, however, that articulation of a spontaneous nature, and not conscious imitation, generated human speech. It appears equally certain that man's first words represented concrete objects rather than abstract meanings. Perhaps it is significant that the Latin *anima* (soul), is associated with the Sanscrit *aniti* (breath), a more concrete phenomenon. On the basis of recent research, one may further conclude that the theory of monogenesis, advanced by Italy's Alfredo Trombetti, is incorrect, since man's innumerable languages do not actually derive from a common ancestor.

The most important theories dealing with the origin of language may be summarized as follows:

1. *Bow-wow* or *onomatopoeia*: according to Johann Gottfried Herder (1744-1803), the German father of a modern religious humanism, language began with man's imitation of animal sounds: "bleat," "cuckoo," and the like. In *The Descent of Man,*

Darwin states that, under the influence of Hensleigh Wedgwood, F. Farrar, and Max Müller, he was convinced "that language owes its origin to the imitation and modification of various natural sounds, the voices of other animals, and man's own instinctive cries, aided by signs and gestures" (Chapter 3).

2. *Ding-dong*: Max Müller (1823-1900), the great Anglo-German philologist, saw the origin of language in the association between sound and sense.

3. *Family-tree, pedigree,* or *tree-stem* theory: an original language family gave birth to new tongues which later advanced independently.

4. *Gestural* theory: Piaget's belief was that primitive man made hand, body, and foot movements which were accompanied by simple cries. These cries were gradually standardized and finally became words representing the corresponding actions.

5. *Interjectional* or *pooh-pooh* theory: man's first words derived from interjections which constituted reactions to various emotions.

6. *Nativistic* theory: also by Müller, this theory emphasizes an inherent tendency in early man to translate external impressions into vocal sounds.

7. *Sing-song*: Otto Jespersen (1860-1943), the Danish grammarian and philologist, asserted that language had its origin in primitive man's chanting and courting cries.

8. *Yo-de-ho*: Noire saw an association between man's first words and the vocal sounds that accompanied his strenuous physical activities.

Whatever the origin of human speech was, man's languages are virtually innumerable. Meillet and Cohen's *Les Langues du Monde,* for instance, describes 10,000 languages and dialects.[6] The Indians of North and South America alone developed about 2,000 tongues. In the Soviet Union the number of languages is at least 120, not including the numerous additional dialects. Some of these, like Byelorussian, the tongue of the White Russians, are spoken by millions of natives. Ukrainian, from the Russian *u kraya,* at the border, is represented by 35,000,000. Ginukh, Karagassian, and Vodian have less than 1,000 speakers each. Armenian and Georgian are two of mankind's oldest tongues. The official and most advanced Soviet language, with an alphabet of thirty-three letters, is Russian, spoken by 115,000,000 native Russians. Some of the tongues in the rest of the world, together with the number of people speaking them (in millions), are as follows:

Arabic	80	Italian	55
Bengali	75	Japanese	95
Bulgarian	7	Korean	33
Catalan	5	Norwegian	4
Czech	10	Polish	33
Danish	5	Portuguese	75
English	250	Spanish	140
French	65	Tibetan	6
German	100	Vietnamese	24
Greek	10	Yiddish	5

Language and Culture

Homo neanderthalensis, who lived 100,000 to 50,000 years ago, must have had some form of language, since his brain size was about 1,400 cubic centimeters, and since his knowledge of tools and burial customs required a vehicle of cultural transmission. Besides, it is now definitely established that culture and language are more than closely related. Indeed, it is legitimate to speak of the linguistic and nonlinguistic components of culture, which means that culture and language appeared at about the same time.

One of the most interesting indications of this association between, for example, morphemes and culture is the fact that the Arabs have created at least a thousand words for "camel." It is also true that culture areas and language families tend to coincide. Among American Indians, for instance, despite exceptional cases such as the Arawakan and Chibchan languages, this coincidence has been quite common. Here are a few examples: the Californian culture area and the Californian Penutian languages; the Mayan tongues and the Meso-American culture; the Arctic culture areas and the Eskimo-Aleut language family. This last association, of course, may be explained in terms of geographical homogeneity, relative isolation, and west-east migration in a short period of time.

The culture-language relationship, however, does not include identical rates of change. In some instances, as among the

89

Athapaskans of California and, especially, the Uto-Aztecans, culture may change faster. In other cases, as among the Penutians of California, it is language that undergoes a more rapid change. But ordinarily culture presents a lower degree of stability than language.

A further difference between cultural and linguistic phenomena is that the former tend to be more conscious. Nevertheless, in both instances, form is imparted less readily than content and is identified only when culture and language are quite advanced.

Still, it must be stated most emphatically that culture and language are linked together so strongly that knowledge of the latter is inadequate without some acquaintance with the former. This partly explains why translation is usually difficult and occasionally impossible. According to a French translator, "*Les traductions sont comme les femmes. Quand elles sont belles, elles ne sont pas fidèles; et quand elles sont fidèles, elles ne sont pas belles.*" An analogous problem is found in *Variety Magazine's* celebrated headline, "Stix Nix Hix Pix." Few people outside the entertainment world will understand that this means that movies about rural life do not sell well among rural residents.

One of the most famous theories about language and culture is the Sapir-Whorf hypothesis. The main points of this hypothesis are the following:

1. Language is a guide to social reality.

2. To a great extent, the real world is unconsciously built up on linguistic habits.

3. Language conditions all our thinking about social problems and processes.

4. No two languages are sufficiently similar to represent the same social reality.

5. Different societies live in distinct worlds, but the same world is never represented by different labels.

This distinction between grammatical and semantic phenomena, however, is overemphasized here. As Driver and Murdock have indicated, for instance, social structure and semantic categories in kinship terminology are not highly associated. In general, the correlation between culture and semantic phenomena appears to be greater than that between culture and various grammatical and phonological patterns.

Linguistic Change

The absurdity of ethnocentrism becomes more evident when we examine linguistic diffusion, change, and the like. Here only a few aspects of the fluidity of language will be considered.

The first known work on the origin and subsequent instability of human tongues is Plato's *Cratylus,* a witty, humorous, and technically perfect dialogue. Dealing with the speculative theories of that time, the work introduces two of Plato's teachers, Cratylus and Hermogenes. The latter was a follower of the philosopher Parmenides and an advocate of linguistic conventionalism. Attacking this theory, Socrates says to Hermogenes: "By adding and subtracting letters, people change the meanings of names completely . . . our beautiful modern language has altered 'obligation' and 'hurtful' in such a way that each now means the opposite of what it meant in ancient times" (418a-b).[7]

More conventionally, St. Jerome (342-420 A.D.) wrote to the Spanish Pope Damasus I (305-384 A.D.) that he disapproved of the doctrine "one *usia,* three *hypostaseis,*" since in ancient Greek these words were synonymous, meaning "substance" (*Epistulae,* XV, 3-4). Apparently, the great Ciceronian scholar was blissfully unaware of the fact that, like every other language, Greek was constantly changing, and that most theologians were then employing the new form of Greek.

Modern authors have also investigated various aspects of language change. Three of the ways in which such change occurs are *generalization, specialization,* and *metaphorical extension.* In the first, the "same symbol may come to denote a *more extended class* of objects, so that it no longer denotes with accuracy the more specific things it may once have symbolized. Thus 'paper' once denoted papyrus . . . today it symbolizes not only the product of rags, but also the product of chemically treated wood pulp."[8] In specialization, the "same symbol may become restricted in its application to a smaller range of objects . . . . Thus the word 'surgeon' once meant anyone who worked with his hands; today it is restricted to those with special medical training."[9] The third "source of change in the meaning of words arises when their application is broadened . . . . Thus 'governor' originally meant a steersman on a boat."[10]

Empirical evidence regarding the formation of new words

91

in historical times indicates that these usually derive from other known words. Some of the techniques employed in such derivation are as follows:

1. *Affixture*: attachment of prefixes (kind, unkind) and suffixes (kind, kindness).

2. *Association*: use of names of persons (Swedish botanist Anders Dahl, dahlia) and places (Geneva, gin).

3. *Backformation*: derivation by analogy and mistaking another word (sculptor, to sculpt, like actor, to act).

4. *Blending*: combination of elements of distinct words that usually have similar meaning (breakfast, lunch, brunch; chuckle, snort, chortle; these are called *portmanteau* or *telescope* words).

5. *Composition* or *compounding*: combining existing words (*components*) to form new words (*compounds*) that often mean something different from what the parts denote (day's eye, daisy). This is typical of German and Greek.

6. *Conversion* or *functional shift*: employing an existing word as a new part of speech (boat, to boat).

7. *Derivation*: borrowing a word from a foreign language and changing or retaining its meaning (Greek *angelus*—messenger; Latin *angelus*—angel).

8. *Echoism* or *onomatopoeia*: imitation of natural sounds (crack, splash, whirr).

9. *Folk etymology, popular etymology,* or *misunderstanding*: popular modification of strange words resulting in familiar-sounding ones (Middle English agnail, hangnail; sparrow grass, asparagus).

10. *Gradation* or *vowel gradation*: changing internal vowels in a consonantal structure to produce distinctions in meaning (ride, road, raid).

11. *Shortening*: omission of a word element (periwig, wig).

12. *Suggestion*: creating a new word through suggestion by another, as by a pun (two-door automobile, Tudor), acoustic proximity (Greek chaos, Van Helmont's gas), word segments (NAtional soZIalist, Nazi), and the like.

Language and Nationalism

Two New Testament verses speak of language as a criterion distinguishing a nation: "Thou wast slain, and hast redeemed us to God by thy blood out of every kindred, and tongue, and people, and nation" (Revelation 5:9); and "A great multitude, which no man could number, of all nations, and kindreds, and people, and tongues, stood before the throne" (7:9). Many centuries later, on September 18, 1773, Dr. Samuel Johnson remarked, "I am always sorry when any language is lost, because languages are the pedigree of nations." Johann von Herder further asserted that a national language is the guardian of the nation and its civilization. Similarly, according to a Czech proverb, "As long as the language lives, the nation is not dead." The Welsh also sing, "If the enemy has ravished the Land of Wales,/ The Language of Wales is living as ever." A modern author has added the following: "Nationalities are usually linguistic groups . . . a common language has been, in the great majority of instances . . . a symbol and agency of unity,"[11] as well as "probably the strongest single reenforcing factor in nationality."[12] It is no wonder, then, that the adjective of a nationality ordinarily represents its language (French, Greek, Polish, Spanish, and so forth), while the slogan "One country, one people, one language" is fairly universal.

Evidence of such association between language and nationalism is abundant. In the United States of America, for example, Noah Webster, who published *Webster's Blue-Backed Speller* in 1783, stressed linguistic homogeneity as a means to national unity. "A national language," he observed, "is a bond of national union." Indeed, his dictionary and, particularly, his speller were so successful in this respect that Jefferson Davis wrote: "Above all other people we are one, and above all books which have united us in the bond of common language, I place the good old Spelling-Book of Noah Webster." Perhaps it is significant that Josef Dobrovsky (1753-1829), the Catholic priest who became the father of comparative Slavic philology, was also an ardent Czech nationalist. Then, numerous nationalistic movements have sought success by reviving the folk languages of their respective lands: Brittany, Denmark, Ireland, Israel (Hebrew), Norway, Poland, Scotland, Wales, and others. It is interesting to add that immigrants are frequently the first to organize a linguistic-nationalistic movement, as did the Irish of Boston, who in 1873 founded the Phil-Celtic Society for the promotion of Gaelic—in Ireland itself, a similar movement appeared only in 1876. Some governments have even attempted to facilitate unity by legally imposing a common language on their people: India (Hindi), Pakistan (Bengali and Urdu), Philippines (Tagalog), and so forth.

Nevertheless, political and linguistic boundaries, as among the Crow and Shawnee Indians of North America, do not always coincide. This was especially true of earlier civilizations, in which language was seldom employed as a means of political suppression. In fact, the Greeks and Romans displayed little interest in imposing their tongues on other peoples.

More specifically, since language is not the only unifying force, the same political unit may include more than one tongue. Here are a few examples: Austro-Hungarian Empire (Czech, German, Italian, Polish, Romanian, Serbian, and others); Belgian Congo (about two hundred languages and dialects); Ghana (four primary languages and numerous dialects); Nigeria (five major languages and many dialects); Philippines (seven chief languages and innumerable minor ones); South Africa (Afrikaans and English); and Switzerland (French, German, Italian, and Raeto-Romanic).

Conversely, one and the same language may encompass more than one nationality, since nationality is mainly subjective, whereas culture and language are primarily objective. The following are examples of this phenomenon: Arabic (many nations in the Middle East); English (Australia, Britain, Canada, Ireland, New Zealand, United States of America, and others); German (Austria, East Germany, Luxemburg, part of Switzerland, West Germany); Portuguese (Brazil, Portugal); and Spanish (Argentina, Bolivia, Chile, Colombia, Costa Rica, Cuba, Dominican Republic, Ecuador, Guatemala, Honduras, Mexico, Nicaragua, Panama, Paraguay, Peru, Puerto Rico, San Salvador, Spain, Uruguay, Venezuela).

In the same way, although national and state boundaries may coincide, a basically homogeneous nationality may consist of more than one state (for instance, Australia, Britain, Canada). Some states, however, may comprise more than one nationality (Belgium: Flemings, Walloons). This is particularly true of large states, such as the Holy Roman Empire (Czechs, Dutch, French, Germans, Italians, Slovenes), Rome, and the Soviet Union (78 percent Great, Ukrainian, and White Russians, plus 22 percent almost fifty other nationalities, including Armenians,

Georgians, Kazaks, Lithuanians, Moldavians, and Uzbeks). Unfortunately, as the present analysis partly indicates, there is some confusion among scholars regarding the terms "nationality" (people?) and "nation" (state?). Perhaps "nationality," for ethnicity, and "government" or "political nation," for state, would be more satisfactory. At any rate, as a modern sociologist has observed, "In Europe the nationalities existed as nations-in-their-own-minds before their states were created. In Africa the states were created before most of the nationalities came into being. In Europe languages became the symbols of suppressed peoples who longed to have cultural autonomy if not national sovereignty. In Africa languages rarely become symbolic of the quest for nationhood because, from the very first, nationhood implied a supratribal entity, whereas languages remained entirely tribal and therefore prenational or nonnational or even antinational."[13]

Language and Ethnocentrism

It has been asserted that ethnocentrism, which may easily lead to conflict, has "probably been based on the linguistic as much as on any other cultural factor."[14] Languages, of course, do differ from one another. Such variation manifests itself in two basic ways: "different phonetic or ideographic elements are employed in them; and different groups of ideas are expressed by fixed phonetic and graphic elements. But the experiences which a language intends to express and communicate vary in an unlimited manner, while the language employs only a finite number of fundamental linguistic elements."[15] Nevertheless, the belief in linguistic superiority is usually unjustified. From the literary point of view, for example, a common conviction is that the simplicity of morphological structure which characterizes modern languages renders them inferior to Greek and Latin; that, unlike Italian and Spanish, English and German are not musical; and that English, thanks to its rich vocabulary, is a much better language. Practically and esthetically speaking, however, all major tongues present both advantages and disadvantages. Even the notion concerning the "limited" vocabularies of "primitive" peoples is unduly ethnocentric; for whenever a new word is needed, these peoples ordinarily function like the Greeks by creating new terms from those already in existence, or like the Romans by borrowing from other languages. Besides, the composition of a literary masterpiece depends not on the morphology, phonetic nature, and vocabulary of a given tongue, but on a high level of culture and the presence of a Dante who is able and willing to employ the vernacular.

Still, language is an indisputable index of social status even within one and the same society. In the United States of America, a minority tongue is frequently accompanied by two types of social distance, horizontal, such as voluntary or involuntary residential segregation, and vertical, namely, a lower social position.[16] It has also been estimated that the vocabulary of the lower social classes comprises about 2,000 words—although this difference seems exaggerated, a definite difference does exist. It is further significant that, in that famous hymn to physical love, D. H. Lawrence's *Lady Chatterley's Lover* (1928), the invalid husband symbolizes, among other things, class consciousness, and the gamekeeper Mellors speaks in his dialect only when he is the lady's lover. When, however, she playfully responds in the same idiom, the ex-officer becomes absolutely furious.

At the international level, ethnocentrism and language have been associated with each other ever since history began. The Slavs, for instance, long ago referred to the Germans as *niemci*, or mutes, and to themselves as "intelligible." In Old Testament times, Jephthah, one of Israel's greatest judges, employed a language test—*shibboleth*, or stream in flood—to distinguish between his own Gileadites and the Ephraimites, who could not pronounce the sound *sh* (even today this Hebrew word is often used to symbolize a group's linguistic characteristics): "Then said they unto him, Say now Shibboleth: and he said Sibboleth: for he could not frame to pronounce it right. Then they took him, and slew him at the passages of Jordan: and there fell at that time of the Ephraimites forty and two thousand" (Judges 12:6). Perhaps better known is the case of the ancient Greek word *barbarus*, or barbarian, an ironic imitation of the non-Greeks' "stammering" *bar-bar* (similar to *Hottentot* and *Tartar*). Indeed, the most frequent criticism against the aliens who became Athenian citizens was that their Attic was inadequate. In *The Birds*, Aristophanes writes, "For they were barbarians before I taught them language" (199-200). In *The Thesmophoriazusae*, he adds that a Scythian is ludicrous because his Greek is poor (1001-1006), while in *The Frogs* he includes these biting verses: "More

96

proud than Cleophon, on whose bilingual lips a Thracian swallow is shrieking dissonantly, sitting on a barbarous perch" (678-682)—Cleophon's mother was of Thracian descent, and the Greeks did not consider the swallow's song melodious. In the same play, we find that class ethnocentrism was also prevalent, as the urban resident, whose speech had been cultivated by the Sophists, often lampooned and ridiculed the peasant's idiom. Euripides himself, whose mother Cleito used to sell herbs, is ironically described as the "child of the peasant goddess" (*The Frogs*, 840). Equally sarcastic is the reference to his "sweet little phrases" (Aristophanes, *The Acharnians*, 444). Similarly, in *The Ecclesiazusae* of the same comedian, a woman, who typically expects the Greek peasant's speech to be barbarous, says: "Very well, sweetest Praxagora, and correctly. Where, miserable one, did you learn these things so well?" (241-242). In another comedy, Aristophanes satirizes even the Ionian dialect: "if, in the assembly, someone says that it is necessary to declare war, all those present, overcome by fright, will say Bah! in Ionian" (*The Peace*, 931-933). Finally, Solon, the great legislator and one of the Seven Sages, often lamented that the Athenians who migrated to other lands no longer spoke the Attic dialect.

Language and Conflict

A student of the sociological aspects of human speech has averred that language is the chief "means of establishing rapport between members of a group, and the main instrument for maintaining that cohesiveness and solidarity of groups, upon which their durability and the free and effective cooperation of their members depends."[17] In addition, language is a "binding, integrative and solidarity-producing factor within and between groups."[18] Of course, just as a shared tongue ordinarily "makes for mutual comprehension and unity, so difference of language can lead to lack of understanding, misunderstanding and disunity."[19] Some of the myriads of the empirical data pertaining to this issue may be summarized as follows:

1. Language manifests a remarkable tendency to persist. The ancient Egyptians continued to speak their tongue, despite the Hyksos, Assyrian, Persian, Greek, and Roman conquests. Breton or Armorican is still spoken in the French region of Brittany, notwithstanding two thousand years of contact with Latin, Saxon,

Frankish, German, and French. The Greeks retained their language, in spite of the Turkish occupation of 1453-1821. The tongue of the majority in a given locality is particularly capable of surviving. In Europe, this is true of Albanian, Basque, Caucasian, and Celtic; in India, of Dravidian and Kolarian; in Bolivia, of Aymara; in Brazil, of Tupi; in Mexico, of Maya and Nahuatl; and in Peru, of Quechua. Cases such as the adoption of Latin in Gaul after Julius Caesar's military triumphs are exceptional.

2. The Greek amphictyonies, antiquity's "United Nations," were not quite successful in their pursuit of peace, although the linguistic bonds that united the member states were very strong.

3. The Romans, whose linguistic success in Gaul was not repeated in Britain, made Latin their empire's national and official language. In the East, however, as St. Augustine (354-430 A.D.) informs us, they never really attempted to outlaw the tongue of the Greeks (*De Civitate Dei*, XIX, 7). In fact, the Eastern provinces were granted two distinct correspondence departments, one under the procurator *ab epistulis Latinis* and the other under the procurator *ab epistulis Graecis*. And, although the magistrates of the East employed Latin officially (Lydus, *De Magistratibus*, III, 68), most trials were carried on in Greek (Valerius Maximus, *Factorum ac Dictorum Memorabilium*, VIII, 7). Emperor Caracalla himself, on May 27, 216 A.D., conducted a trial in the city of Antioch primarily in Greek. It was Emperor Diocletian (284-305) who tried to unify the entire Roman Empire linguistically (Libanius, *Speeches*, I, 34), and, according to the *Saturnalia* of Macrobius, had some success in this respect. But, under Arcadius (395-408), judges were directed to pronounce sentences in Greek, and, as we can see in Justinian's *Novellae Constitutiones* (VII, 1), this language soon prevailed almost completely. It is no wonder, then, that few Greeks bothered to study Latin—for instance, Herod Atticus, the celebrated rhetorician of the second century A.D. and teacher of Emperor Marcus Aurelius (Fronto, *Epistulae ad M. Aurelium*, III, 2). Of course, as we are told by St. John Chrysostom (347-407 A.D.), the great church father of Antioch, the Greeks who wished to study Roman law had to learn Latin (*Against the Detractors of the Monastic Life*, III, 5). This is also indicated by Libanius, the rather ethnocentric orator and St. John's teacher, who was critical of those who pursued Latin studies (*Speeches*, I, 214). Most

educated Romans, however, spoke both Latin and Greek, since the latter was considered the tongue of intellectual giants (Cicero, *De Oratore*, II, 2). Cicero (106-43 B.C.) further informs us that some of his countrymen even disdained the study of their own "primitive" language (*Brutus*, 247). In addition, Polybius (204-122 B.C.), one of the greatest historians of antiquity, mentions that numerous authors, particularly those who dealt with historical subjects, wrote in Greek. One of them was the senator Aulus Postumius, whom Marcus Porcius Cato satirized for his attempt to write a serious history in Greek, in whose preface its author apologized for his linguistic barbarisms (Polybius, *Histories*, XXXIX, 1). Cicero himself, who studied in Athens and Rhodes, mastered Greek perfectly, as many of his writings reveal. At the same time, like Vergil, Rome's brilliant orator, philosopher, and statesman proved that great works could actually be written in Latin. Accordingly, the prestige of Greek began to decline—the days were over when Quintus Ennius (239-170 B.C.), the father of Latin poetry, had to compete with the author of the *Iliad* and *Odyssey*.

4. Most great religions have attempted to organize and unify vast geographical areas by means of a "universal" language. The Roman Catholic Church, for example, employed Latin, but, since a common tongue is not sufficient for international unity, the Reformation replaced this ancient language with the various vernaculars of northwestern Europe.

5. In England, after the Norman conquest of 1066, "the members of the new ruling class were sufficiently predominant to continue to use their own language . . . . For two hundred years . . . French remained the language of . . . the upper classes in England. At first those who spoke French were those of Norman origin, but soon through intermarriage and association with the ruling class numerous people of English extraction must have found it to their advantage to learn the new language . . . . The language of the masses remained English."[20]

6. In North America, as far as we know, the Cree, Montagnais, and Naskapi were never at war with those who shared the same language with each of these groups. But conflict between tribes that differed linguistically was common—for instance, Xaihais versus Bella Bella or Tsimshian; and Tlingit versus Eskimo or Haida. The hostility between the Nootka and those

who spoke their tongue was rather exceptional. In general, peace prevailed among North America's linguistically homogeneous groups.

Language differences, then, are ideologized and nationalized before they become sources of conflict. But even in such cases strife is not inevitable, since other factors may generate peace or war. In fact, unity and disunity themselves often become ideologies that may diminish or reinforce linguistic and other differences. Therefore, "a linguistically more united world need not be a more peaceful world any more than a world less concerned with religion and religious differences, or with folkways and ethnic differences, has become less dangerously bellicose. The array of human differences that may become ideologized is endless."[21]

Before closing this section, it seems necessary to include brief accounts of a few modern cases of language conflict which illustrate some of the preceding points.

1. *Belgium.* The present linguistic crisis in Belgium goes back to the revolution of 1830 when this country was formed as a combination of Flanders (Dutch) and Wallonia (French). "For more than a century, the prosperous Walloons dominated things from their industrial southern strongholds; the northern Flemings were the poor relations. After World War II the balance shifted. The population advantage moved to the Flemings —5,250,000 to 4,000,000—and industry flocked to the cheap labor supply of Flanders. Flemish nationalism flourished, and Flemings bitterly protested that, although Dutch and French had official parity, French was still the language for Flemings who wanted to rise to the top. Few Walloons, they complained, bothered to learn Dutch."[22] In 1962, the Flemings legislated a line across Belgium running south of Brussels—which is officially bilingual[23] —and north of Liège. The plan made French (actually, a French dialect called Wallonian) official in the south, and Flemish (a West Germanic variant of Dutch) in the north.

One of the resulting problems was that the Walloon minority has been legally forced to send its children to Flemish schools. It was for this reason that in 1965 a group of 324 Wallonian-speaking Belgians protested to the European Court of Human Rights, in Strasbourg, France.

The line has also placed the great University of Louvain,

where Erasmus studied between 1517 and 1521, inside the Dutch-speaking section. The school itself, which never offered Flemish courses until 1932, is now the scene of linguistic warfare between its Dutch and French halves. Needless to add, very few of the two thousand non-Belgian students (total enrollment: 20,000) speak Flemish.

2. *Canada*. France controlled Canada between 1534 and 1763. In 1867, the British North America Act united New Brunswick, Nova Scotia, Ontario (Upper Canada), and Quebec (Lower Canada), thus creating the Canadian federation. Later additions—Alberta, British Columbia, Manitoba, Newfoundland, and so forth—resulted in the modern nation comprising ten provinces and two territories.

About 20 percent of the Canadian population regard French as their native language. Indeed, the French Canadians have preserved their culture and tongue so zealously that the country's official languages are French as well as English. Most of the French-speaking Canadians are found in Quebec, where two distinct educational programs have been developed, one Catholic and French-oriented, and one Protestant and English-oriented—the second is also the only pedagogical system in the remaining nine provinces.

Such bilingualism has recently generated numerous problems, which a Canadian Royal Commission in 1963 described as the "greatest crisis" in Canada's history. Although this diagnosis is somewhat hyperbolic, these problems are definitely serious. Unfortunately, French Canadian nationalism has often been viewed as a purely linguistic phenomenon, as if the economic, political, social, and other forces which are in operation were nonexistent. In a brilliant study of the subject, a Canadian scholar has wisely emphasized the following thesis:

> *"les notions de groupe ethnique et de relation ethnique sont très peu utiles pour expliquer les relations du Québec avec le reste du Canada et le monde international. Ces concepts . . . mettent trop l'accent sur l'aspect linguistique et culturel et négligent les autres niveaux de la réalité sociale et économique. Sous le couvert de la langue, c'est un système de valeurs, une forme d'organisation sociale, des techniques même, que l'on veut promouvoir ou sauvegarder . . . sous la lutte ethnique se*

101

*révèle une définition de la societé globale idéale; défini-
tion qu'une élite en possession du pouvoir ou à la recherche du pouvoir veut rendre collective.*"[24] The same
author has explained, "*Le nationalisme canadien-français s'est toujours présenté comme l'affirmation de la
langue française au Canada et plus généralement en
Amérique du Nord . . . . Mais au-delà de cette attention
particulière portée à la langue, ce que les nationalistes
ont voulu affirmer, c'est une nation, un type de société,
sinon de civilisation. Plus qu'un effort pour conserver
une langue, le nationalisme canadien-français a été et
continue à être une représentation collective de ce que
devra être le Canada français.*"[25]

3. *India.* This vast republic became autonomous by the
terms of the India Independence Act of 1947, and adopted a
modern constitution on January 26, 1950. With a heterogeneous
population of 480,000,000 (1966 estimate), the country has been
facing myriad problems, one of which is that of language. According to two Banaras Hindu University scholars, the "language
problem of India has become Problem Number One after Independence. But it is an exaggeration to say that this problem
brought India and its unity to a verge of collapse."[26] Nevertheless, the problem is difficult to solve, since the country's sixteen
states and six territories, resulting from the 1956 States Reorgani-
zation Act and legislation passed in 1960, are, to a certain extent,
distinct linguistic entities.

The gravity of this situation becomes obvious when we consider the vast variety of languages spoken in India. Indeed, isolation is common and communication difficult, as, according to
the census of 1951, there are 845 tongues and dialects in the
country, 63 of which are not even Indian. Some of these languages, together with the number of people (in millions) speaking each of them, are as follows:[27]

Assamese	7	Marathi	33
Bengali	34	Oriya	16
Gujrati	20	Punjabi	11
Hindi	133	Tamil	31
Kannada	17	Telugu	38
Kashmiri	2	Urdu	23
Malayalam	17		

The choice of a national language has been particularly problematic. Regarding English, which "unified all the people in the country for the first time, both culturally and administratively";[28] which, under Britain, was taught primarily to those planning to function as administrators and civil servants; and which is still the common means of communication in higher education and other pan-Indian activities, Lord Reading said that in India's legislatures, the "debates take place in English, rarely is a speech made in another tongue, especially in the Central Legislature, where otherwise a member from Madras could not understand a member from the Punjab, a member from Bengal could not understand a member from Burma. It is the lingua franca." Even before 1947, however, leaders such as Mahatma Gandhi advocated the adoption of Hindi as a national language—actually, Gandhi supported Hindustani, the tongue of the masses, and not Hindi, which prevails among the elite.[29] Similarly, Pandit Nehru advised: "We must have an all-India language. This cannot be English or any other foreign language although I believe that English, both because of its world position and the present wide-spread knowledge of it in India, is bound to play an important part in our future activities. The only all-India language that is possible is Hindi or Hindustani or whatever it is called."[30] But the adoption of Hindi as an official language has been followed by violent riots, for instance, in southern India, where the Tamil-speaking mobs of Madras protested: "WE ARE INDIANS. WE ARE NOT HINDIANS."

"By far the most difficult problem, which looks to the unwary as the most easy and innocuous, is the medium of instruction for higher education."[31] College textbooks in English, the language which became common after the famous Macaulay Minute of 1835, are comparatively few. Those in the local tongues are not only fewer, but also inadequate, as these idioms lack most modern scientific terms. At the lower levels, where Hindi, or some other native language, is emphasized, the transfer of pupils is exceedingly problematic. And where English is taught, instruction is so rudimentary that the student encounters formidable obstacles when he commences his college training.

It seems, then, that the issue to which the Indians devote too much energy, "namely, the official link language for India,

103

is probably beset with least difficulties. Hindi is bound to become the official language of India. It is only a question of time —and English is bound to remain as the language of the elite, scientists and technologists. It is the question regarding the other three problems that must worry us,"[32] that is, a medium of instruction, a language for competitive examinations throughout India, and a court language.[33]

4. *Switzerland*. This federal republic, with a population of 5,560,000 (1961) and one of the most democratic constitutions (1848) of all time, is composed of twenty-two cantons which enjoy a high degree of local autonomy. In nineteen of these cantons, the dominant language is German. The country, however, recognizes four official tongues, French, German, Italian, and Romansh, the corresponding population percentages being 21, 72, 6, and 1. Romansh, a Raeto-Romanic dialect spoken by most of the people in the mountain valleys of Graubunden, achieved official status in 1938, but is now gradually becoming extinct.

According to a Louvain University scholar, the unity which has prevailed in Switzerland "is undoubtedly due to the fact of diversity which extends throughout all phases and levels where the Swiss must express themselves and act in unison. The overlap of economic, political and cultural interests is so complex that the cleavages are constantly neutralized and never protrude sharply enough to endanger the internal unity. They are attenuated by other loyalties."[34] The religious equilibrium— for instance, 46 percent Catholic, 53 percent Protestant—has intensified the prevailing linguistic harmony. In addition, the low taxes, the well-organized economy, and the absence of war— the country's neutrality has never been violated since 1815— have generated a unifying prosperity.

As has been stated by a sociologist at the University of Bern, however, since the end of the Second World War, "the ethnic-cultural equilibrium has been disturbed by an unprecedented influx of immigrants which in the end aroused Swiss public opinion to manifestations of xenophobia and had a deleterious effect upon the external relations between Switzerland and Italy."[35] In this way, the percentage of Italian-speaking persons in the alien population, which was about 30 in 1941, rose to much more than 50 in 1960. The corresponding percentages in

104

the total Swiss population were 5.2 and 9.5.[36]

One of the solutions to this problem was restrictive measures that "finally succeeded in halting the influx of foreign workers and even in reversing the movement to some extent."[37] Another measure was the learning of languages, at which the Swiss have been adept, in view of their emphasis on tourism and foreign trade. Moreover, in German-speaking Zurich, although only 7 percent of its population declared Italian as their native language in 1960, "all streetcar signs and inscriptions were translated into Italian . . . . In many communities the schools are offering special language classes for Italian children and evening language courses for adults are offered not only by schools but also by many large plants which employ foreign workers."[38]

In brief, the Bern sociologist concludes that "the long-run effects of the postwar influx of foreigners will be less disturbing . . . . The current restrictions on immigration have effectively halted the inflow and there is no reason to assume that those foreigners . . . cannot be assimilated. Indeed, the wave of xenophobia has receded . . . . But the recent events in Switzerland serve to remind us that intergroup relations are always delicate . . . . It also demonstrates how close the relationship between international relations and cultural tensions remains."[39]

International Languages

In the story of Babel, the Hebrew name for Babylon, we are told that "the whole earth was of one language, and of one speech . . . . And the Lord said, Behold, the people is one, and they have all one language; and this they begin to do: and now nothing will be restrained from them, which they have imagined to do. Go to, let us go down, and there confound their language, that they may not understand one another's speech" (Genesis 11:1, 6-7). For a long time, countless scholars have tried to put an end to such confusion of tongues, and to promote international understanding and cooperation, by creating a universal language. Convinced that linguistic chaos constitutes a major source of international misunderstanding and conflict, idealists of the nineteenth and twentieth centuries have been particularly energetic in this area. Obviously, at least some of these creative minds forgot that the adoption of such a medium of communication itself presupposes international cooperativeness and un-

105

derstanding. Besides, the techniques employed thus far have been so inadequate that interlinguistics, the science of universal languages, remains practically primitive. For the sake of completeness at least, let us outline some of the results of these indefatigable efforts.

1. *Scientific languages.* Perhaps beginning with the *Polygraphia* (1518) of Johannes Trithemius, these are nonverbal symbolic systems of a somewhat mathematical nature. The Italian philosopher Giordano Bruno (1548-1600), inspired by the *Ars Generalis* of the Spanish missionary and theologian Raymond Lull (1235-1315), attempted to construct a language of this type. More impressive was the work of Gottfried Leibniz (*De Arte Combinatoria,* 1666), the German mathematician and philosopher who devoted a great deal of time to a thought-alphabet known as *alphabetum cogitationum humanarum.* Using signs for simple concepts, and combinations of such signs or distinct new symbols for complex ideas, the philosopher of monadology actually succeeded in inventing what was an encyclopedia, a grammar, and a logic. Naturally, this ideographic system was never completed, since it presupposed the completion of all knowledge. An analogous effort is found in *An Essay Towards a Real Character and Philosophical Language* (1668), by John Wilkins.

2. *Pasigraphic languages.* From the work of A. Müller (1681) to that of F. Gilbert (Tokyo, 1941), these plans have employed symbols similar to Chinese ideographs, their goal being to write ideas without verbalizing them, as this may be done in any tongue.

3. *Volapük* (*vol,* world; *pük,* speech). In *Über Pasigraphie und Ideographik* (1808), F. Niethammer expressed the idea that since concepts follow speech, artificial languages are of the *a posteriori* form only if they incorporate this notion and are inspired by natural languages. More specifically, emphasis should be placed on those components of natural tongues which are international. A satisfactory universal language, therefore, as Chile's Alberto Liptay stated in 1895, is discovered, not invented. Such a scheme—in reality, a systematized *lingua franca*—is Volapük, which was introduced in 1879 by Johann Martin Schleyer, a German priest, and which was based on various languages, but mainly on English. After ten years of spectacular success, Vola-

pük failed, since its autistic nature made it inadequate for international use. Esperanto and Interlingua belong to the same type of language.

4. *Esperanto* and *Ido*. Dr. L. L. Zamenhof (1859-1917), the Polish oculist who called himself Dr. Esperanto (Dr. Hopeful), created his tongue in 1887 with Neo-Latin, Slavonic, and Teutonic roots. In its vocabulary, spelling, pronunciation, grammar, and syntax, "Esperanto shows enormous simplification when compared with any national language. The *Spelling and Pronunciation* are absolutely phonetic, and there are only five vowel sounds (most national languages have twenty or more). Each letter has one sound only, and any sound is always rendered by one and the same letter."[40] Here are some Esperanto words: *arbaro,* forest; *biciklo,* bicycle; *edzino,* wife; *edzo,* husband; *homo,* man; *lerni,* to learn; *nepo,* grandson; *oficiro,* officer; *pagi,* to pay; *solvi,* to solve; *studento,* student; and *trovi,* to find.[41] Regarding the development of this system, it has been said that an "artificial language which has really been learned by adults of differing first languages can be creolized . . . . This has happened, to some extent, to Esperanto."[42] It was such artificiality that precluded natural change on the part of this tongue, as a result of which, at least fifty variants of it are now in existence. Undoubtedly, the most famous one is Ido (an Esperanto word meaning offspring), introduced by Louis de Beaufront and Couturat in 1907.

5. *Interlingua.* Giuseppe Peano, a brilliant logician and mathematician at the University of Turin, who discovered the so-called Peano area-filling curve in mathematics, in 1903 also invented *Latino sine flexione* (Latin without inflection). Modified in 1951 by the International Auxiliary Language Association, which was founded in 1924, *Latino* became a combination of modern European languages known as Interlingua.

6. *Occidental.* This artificial tongue was created by de Wahl in 1922.

7. *Basic English.* An extremely simplified type of English, this Basic (an acronym for British, American, Scientific, International, Commercial) system was originated by an educator, psychologist, and semanticist of Magdalene College, Cambridge, Professor Charles Kay Ogden (*Basic English: A General Introduction with Rules and Grammar,* 1930). Ogden's goals were three: first, to create a simple international auxiliary tongue; sec-

ond, to organize an elementary course in English for foreign students; and third, to facilitate the semantic instruction of English-speaking persons. The vocabulary, selected on the basis of utility, and not frequency, consists of 400 nouns of a general nature, 200 terms representing picturable objects, 150 adjectives, 100 so-called "operators" (particles, prepositions, verbal forms, and the like), and an additional general science list of 100 words, as well as lists for particular disciplines. Eminent men like George Bernard Shaw and Winston Churchill have supported Basic English with enthusiasm, and many works in this language have been published by the Orthological Institute.

8. *Miscellaneous languages.* New Testament Greek, Church Latin, Church Slavonic, and others may also be considered "universal" tongues. *Pidgin English,* on the other hand, is, as Bodmer and Hogben would say, a "contact vernacular," or a creolized type of English, including elements of non-English dialects, which is employed as a means of commercial communication in China, Melanesia, Northern Australia, and West Africa—the name derives from the Chinese pronunciation of "business." Finally, *Lingua Franca* (Italian for "language of the Franks") is a combination of Arabic, French, Greek, Italian, and Spanish, developed in the Mediterranean during the Crusades, and still spoken in the ports of that sea—this tongue is also called *Sabir,* from the phrase *Si ti sabir,* "if you know," in Jean-Baptiste Molière's comedy, *Le Bourgeois Gentilhomme* (1670).

Conclusion

Once Ralph Waldo Emerson remarked that "language is a city, to the building of which every human being brought a stone." Indeed, language is a city, a resplendent, magnificent city, which has been built by humans of every race, every color, and every creed. Culture itself is a radiant, scintillant galaxy of countless enchanting cities. Perhaps, then, the human race will work in harmony and peace to add more sparkling stars, more glittering, luminous jewels to this stupendous galaxy.

PANOS D. BARDIS, Professor of Sociology, University of Toledo, came to the United States on a scholarship, and received his Ph.D. in Sociology from Purdue University; he has taught at Albion College and the University of Toledo. He is the editor of *Social Science* and has 135 publications to his credit since 1955, including many poems, *Ivan and Artemis* (a novel), and *The Family in Changing Civilizations*. He has presented numerous papers at national and international conferences.

FOOTNOTES

1. Mario A. Pei and Frank Gaynor, A DICTIONARY OF LINGUISTICS. New York: Philosophical Library, 1954, 119.
2. Rudolf Carnap, INTRODUCTION TO SEMANTICS AND FORMALIZATION OF LOGIC. Cambridge, Mass.: Harvard University Press, 1961, Volume 1, 3.
3. Pei and Gaynor, *op. cit.*, 203.
4. *Ibid.*, 56.
5. Stephen Ullmann, SEMANTICS. New York: Barnes and Noble, 1962, 19-23.
6. A. Meillet and Marcel Cohen, editors, LES LANGUES DU MONDE. Paris: Centre National de la Recherche Scientifique, 1952.
7. This and other classical quotations appearing here have been translated by the present author.
8. Morris R. Cohen and Ernest Nagel, AN INTRODUCTION TO LOGIC. New York: Harcourt, Brace, and World, 1962, 119.
9. *Ibid.*
10. *Ibid.*
11. Joyce O. Hertzler, A SOCIOLOGY OF LANGUAGE. New York: Random House, 1965, 245.
12. *Ibid.*, 234.
13. Joshua A. Fishman, "Sociolinguistic Perspective on Internal Linguistic Tensions and Their Impact on External Relations." Paper presented at the World Congress of the International Sociological Association, Evian, France, September 1966, 8.
14. Hertzler, *op. cit.*, 251.
15. Cohen and Nagel, *op. cit.*, 117.
16. Hertzler, *op. cit.*, 251-252.
17. *Ibid.*, 65.
18. *Ibid.*, 226.
19. *Ibid.*, 248.
20. Albert C. Baugh, A HISTORY OF THE ENGLISH LANGUAGE. Second Edition. New York: Appleton-Century-Crofts, 1963, 135.
21. Fishman, *op. cit.*, 11-12.
22. "Belgium: The Congo of Europe." TIME, August 6, 1965, 34.
23. Jacques Brazeau, "Social Change and the Position of French and Flemish in Belgium." Paper presented at the annual conference of the American Sociological Association, Miami, Florida, August 1966.
24. Gérald Fortin, LE QUEBEC: UNE SOCIETÉ GLOBAL. Paper presented at the World Congress of the International Sociological Association, Evian, France, September 1966, 1.
25. *Ibid.*, 2.
26. S. Singh and K. V. Rao, "India's Language Problem." INTERNATIONAL REVIEW OF HISTORY AND POLITICAL SCIENCE, December 1965, 66.
27. *Ibid.*, 66-67, note 2.

28. *Ibid.*, 67.
29. *Ibid.*, note 3.
30. *Ibid.*, 67-68.
31. *Ibid.*, 72.
32. *Ibid.*, 73.
33. *Ibid.*, 71.
34. Pierre de Bie, cited in Kurt B. Mayer, "International Migration, Cultural Tensions and Foreign Relations: The Case of Switzerland." Paper presented at the World Congress of the International Sociological Association, Evian, France, September 1966, 1.
35. *Ibid.*, 2.
36. *Ibid.*, 9.
37. *Ibid.*, 7.
38. *Ibid.*, 9.
39. *Ibid.*, 14.
40. John Cresswell and John Hartley, TEACH YOURSELF ESPERANTO. London: English Universities Press, 1957, 9-10.
41. *Ibid.*, 152.
42. Charles F. Hockett, A COURSE IN MODERN LINGUISTICS. New York: Macmillan, 1958, 423.

Selected Bibliography

BOOKS

Baugh, Albert C., A HISTORY OF THE ENGLISH LANGUAGE, second edition. New York: Appleton-Century-Crofts, 1963. A detailed study of the evolution of English. Social aspects emphasized frequently.

Carnap, Rudolf, INTRODUCTION TO SEMANTICS AND FORMALIZATION OF LOGIC. Cambridge, Mass.: Harvard University Press, 1961. A two-volume work by a well-known philosopher. A systematic treatment of general semantics and a brilliant analysis of semantical research.

Cohen, Morris R., and Ernest Nagel, AN INTRODUCTION TO LOGIC. New York: Harcourt, Brace, and World, 1962. Two experts present many interesting aspects of language while dealing with the basic concepts of logic.

Cresswell, John, and John Hartley, TEACH YOURSELF ESPERANTO. London: English Universities Press, 1957. One of the best books on the history and, primarily, nature of this international language.

Hertzler, Joyce O., A SOCIOLOGY OF LANGUAGE. New York: Random House, 1965. The first comprehensive work, in English, dealing with the social aspects of language. Main emphasis is placed on the social functions of human speech.

Hockett, Charles F., A COURSE IN MODERN LINGUISTICS. New York: Macmillan, 1958. Although somewhat simplified, this long work remains an advanced analysis of every important aspect of the science of linguistics.

Meillet, A., and Marcel Cohen, editors, LES LANGUES DU MONDE. Paris: Centre National de la Recherche Scientifique, 1952. Perhaps the most important reference publication in the field of linguistics, presenting the major aspects of 10,000 tongues.

Pei, Mario A., and Frank Gaynor, A DICTIONARY OF LINGUISTICS. New York: Philosophical Library, 1954. One of the best publications presenting brief definitions of terms employed in the language sciences.

Ullmann, Stephen, SEMANTICS. New York: Barnes and Noble, 1962. A chiefly empirical survey of the new science of meaning, including numerous suggestions for further investigation.

ARTICLES

"Belgium: The Congo of Europe." TIME, LXXXVI, 6 August 6, 1965, 34. A brief account of Belgium's recent linguistic problems.

Brazeau, Jacques, "Social Change and the Position of French and Flemish in Belgium." Paper presented at the annual conference of the American Sociological Association, Miami, Florida, August 1966. A fairly comprehensive analysis of Belgium's linguistic crisis with a great deal of information on the economic, historical, legal, political, and other areas.

Fishman, Joshua A., "Sociolinguistic Perspective on Internal Linguistic Tensions and Their Impact on External Relations." Paper presented at the World Congress of the International Sociological Association, Evian, France, September 1966. An interesting and competent investigation of Karl Deutch's hypothesis that linguistic conflict would increase as the speakers of local vernaculars sought to nationalize their mother tongues.

Fortin, Gérald, LE QUEBEC: UNE SOCIETE GLOBALE. Paper presented at the World Congress of the International Sociological Association, Evian, France, September 1966. The author brilliantly concretizes the nonlinguistic forces in Canada's language crisis.

Mayer, Kurt B., "International Migration, Cultural Tensions and Foreign Relations: The Case of Switzerland." Paper presented at the World Congress of the International Sociological Association, Evian, France, September 1966. An expert and fairly long discussion of the Swiss language problem, plus several of the sociocultural forces related to it.

Singh, S., and K. V. Rao, "India's Language Problem." INTERNATIONAL REVIEW OF HISTORY AND POLITICAL SCIENCE, II, 2, December 1965, 66-73. Two able Indian scholars briefly analyze their country's language difficulties and suggest some solutions.

THE CHANGING ASPECTS OF FOREIGN LANGUAGE INSTRUCTION

High School, College, University

The Changing Aspects of Teaching German

LEO D. RUDNYTZKY
La Salle College

THE TEACHING of German in the United States is and always was very closely connected with the teaching of modern languages. Historically speaking, there are, however, three important factors which render the position of German unique: Three times during the course of the history of the United States, the teaching of German on all levels was severely impaired as a result of political considerations. These three instances, the Revolutionary War and its postwar period, the period of World War I and of World War II serve as lines of demarcation which divide the three historical chapters of German instruction in America.[1]

Historical Background

Very little is known about the teaching of German during the colonial era. There is ample evidence, however, that German thought and literature flourished in New England and that the German language was known to many American intellectuals of the time.[2] The earliest recorded instance of the actual teaching of German to groups is in the year 1702 when German was taught to immigrant children in Germantown and Philadelphia from textbooks brought over from the old country. Generally speaking,

AUTHOR'S NOTE: I regret that the more recent developments in the field, such as transformational grammar, CAI (Computer Assisted Instruction), and similar developments could not be included.

the teaching of German in the early part of the eighteenth century was fostered mainly by various religious sects—Lutherans, Dunkers, Moravians, Quakers, and others, who not only taught the language but also used it as the language of instruction in their schools.

Among leading Americans of that time, Benjamin Franklin contributed much toward the development of American education and in particular toward the popularization of German. Through his efforts the Public Academy and College was established in Philadelphia in 1749. In 1755 the Academy (the ancestor of the University of Pennsylvania) became a degree-granting institution and the first American school in which German was taught. Soon King's College (Columbia University) and William and Mary began to offer German, and other colleges and academies followed.[3]

The period of the American Revolution, however, had, as noted above, a negative effect on the teaching of German. The reason is twofold: The presence of Hessians and Hanoverian mercenaries tended to make German unpopular, and the blockades of the ports prevented the emigration process from supplying new people of the German tongue.

During the early part of the nineteenth century the interest in German was revived by Mme. de Staël's work *De l'Allemagne* (1811), by Carlyle's writings, and by the activities of men like George Ticknor, Professor of Modern Languages at Harvard. Other significant factors were the growing up of a young generation to whom the War of Independence had not been a personal experience and an influx of German-speaking immigrants.

Thus in 1816 Harvard appointed its first licensed German teacher, Meno Poehls. The University of Virginia offered German in its inaugural year, 1819. Bowdoin College began to offer German along with other modern languages in 1820, and Amherst College started German instruction in 1824. To be sure, these were humble beginnings; German was in most instances not a part of the regular inflexible curriculum, and regular professorships in German were established much later, but from here on German, along with French and Spanish, gradually gains in its struggle for respectability and soon begins to compete with the classical languages. The Master's degree in German was offered at American universities as early as the 1850's, and in 1879 Waterman T. Hewett received a doctorate in Germanics from Cornell University.[4] However, according to Zeydel, "the most important step of all was the founding of the Johns Hopkins University at Baltimore . . . Here, where German was called 'the court language of the university,' original research in Germanics found a home in the New World."[5] Thus the latter part of the nineteenth century experienced a tremendous boom in the study of German on all levels of instruction. This trend reached its zenith shortly before the eve of World War I. Indicative of this development is the establishment of the Nationaler Deutsch-Amerikanischer Lehrbund (1870), an organization of teachers of German which soon began to publish its organ the *Monatshefte*, still published today by the University of Wisconsin. Similarly significant was the founding of other professional journals such as *Modern Language Notes*, established in 1885 at Johns Hopkins University and still in existence, *Americana Germanica*, established 1897 at the University of Pennsylvania and now extinct, and *The Journal of English and Germanic Philology*, established in the same year at Indiana University and now published at the University of Illinois.

World War I, however, put a sudden end to the popularity of German. Whereas immediately prior to the war, German was the leading foreign language in American schools, in the spring of 1917, as a result of war hysteria, German was either entirely dropped or actually legislated out of existence. A few statistics as quoted by Zeydel strikingly underscore this cataclysm:

> Between 1917 and 1919 the teaching of German became practically non-existent in the public and private high schools, 315,884 (28%) of whose students had still been studying it in 1915. By 1922, four years after the end of the war, the high schools had less than 14,000 students of German, or little more than one-half of one percent of the high-school enrollment of 2,500,000. This compares with about 387,000 (15½%) in French and 250,-000 (10%) in Spanish.[6]

And also:

> In the face of a steady increase of total high-school population from 1,300,000 in 1915 to 5,400,000 in 1948, German enrollments dropped from 324,000 (24.4%) to

43,000 (0.8%). During the same period, French enrollments went from 117,000 (8.8%) to 254,000 (4.7%) while Spanish rose from 36,000 (2.7%) to 443,000 (8.2%).[7]

The recovery from the disaster of World War I began, at least on the college and university levels, in 1926 with the founding of the American Association of Teachers of German (AATG), which publishes *The German Quarterly*, performs special functions through its Service Bureau and its Placement Bureau, and furthers the study and teaching of German in general. In the same year the *Germanic Review*, a periodical devoted to research in Germanic languages and literatures, was founded at Columbia University. The period between the two World Wars was also marked by the development of various German Summer School Programs, the Junior Year in Europe Plan, and by the development of new testing procedures: prognosis tests, oral tests, and numerous standard tests, such as the then new true-and-false and multiple-choice type, were experimented with but without significant achievement.

The Renaissance of the 1950's

Whereas the popularity of German during the Second World War once again diminished, it is, nevertheless, that time which brought about a re-evaluation of the teaching methods of modern languages in general and made the American public more language-conscious. The events of the war strikingly brought out the inadequacies of language teaching in American schools[8] and gave rise to the development of the so-called "Army Method" and its emphasis on oral communication. It was not until 1952, however, that the actual revision and revitalization of modern language teaching began with the Foreign Language Program sponsored by the Modern Language Association and subsidized by the Rockefeller Foundation from 1952 to 1958. This program furthered the study of modern languages by introducing foreign language teaching in elementary schools (FLES), by helping to develop and use audio-lingual-visual aids, by constantly providing helpful information on the use of various realia and on the use of language laboratories, by encouraging the development of new methods of teaching; in short, by giving information per-

115

taining to the teaching of language on any level. Largely as a result of this program, Congress passed the National Defense Education Act (NDEA) of 1958 (Titles III, IV, and VI), the tremendous importance of which for the study and research in modern languages is now a well-known fact. Along with the other modern languages German experienced a revival. A survey conducted by C. R. Goedsche of Northwestern University presents graphic evidence of the recovery of German from 1953 to 1963:

Year	Number of Majors	Number of Graduate Students
1953	218	333
1954	277	321
1955	243	327
1956	316	341
1957	332	382
1958	437	443
1959	500	490
1960	652	588
1961	789	726
1962	928	799
1963	1,030	919

Similarly, the growth of interest in German may be seen in the increasing number of high school students participating in the nation-wide German contest sponsored under the auspices of the AATG. The first of these competitive examinations was administered to 3,316 students at some 111 test centers;[9] only three years later (1963), 6,000 students were examined in 200 test centers.[10] The number of participants is growing steadily from year to year, and now the National Association of Secondary School Principals has placed this contest on the Approved List of National Contests and Activities for 1966-67.[11]

One final statistical comparison based on figures from the United States Office of Education. In 1951-1952 United States institutions of higher learning conferred the following number of degrees in German:

Bachelor's and First Professional	Master's and Second Professional	Doctor's	Total
515	121	56	692

The breakdown for 1963-64 (excluding degrees conferred in Germanics) is as follows:

Four-Year Bachelor's	Master's	Doctor's	Total
1,591	344	75	2,010[12]

This comparison of the totals shows an astonishing increase of nearly 300 per cent. It is interesting to note that of the 2,010 total, 1,087 are women.

There is at present no state in the Union which does not offer some instruction in German, and the over-all enrollment is on the increase. Programs such as the Junior Year in Germany maintained by numerous institutions, the summer sessions for high school and college teachers sponsored by the Goethe Institut in Munich, the numerous work and study summer programs in Germany, as well as the services and programs of the National Carl Schurz Foundation help to make the study of German more attractive and more rewarding to the student.

The present situation of German in American colleges and high schools is, of course, not ideal, and there is much room for improvement. In spite of the NDEA program there is still a shortage of qualified teachers in German; the average elementary and intermediate class size is excessively large, and the time of the classes in many cases rather unfavorable;[13] the German programs abroad are often not living up to their expectation,[14] but the outlook for the future is nevertheless a bright one.

The Age of Experimentation

The present controversy in the field of modern languages between the advocates of the "New Key" and those of the more traditional approach to teaching also makes itself felt in German. On the whole, the controversy insofar as it pertains to German, seems to generate a rather constructive spirit of experimentation and of self-examination. A typical example of such type of experimentation is "The German Teaching Experiment at the University of Colorado," a program report on a two-year experiment officially entitled "Extended Classroom Experimentation with Varied Sequencing of the Four Skills in German Instruction."[15] In this experiment two groups, consisting of about 150 students each, were divided into six audio-lingual and five traditional sections and given instruction in German in the two methods. The results based on testing administered after the end of the first year indicated that:

1. The audio-lingual students were far superior in listening and speaking ability and were not significantly inferior in reading and writing ability when the two skills were measured purely. However, the traditional students were far superior in translating from English to German and the reverse.
2. There was no evidence of greater improvement in English listening comprehension in the audio-lingual than the traditional group.
3. The audio-lingual students displayed clear evidence of a more direct association between German words and their meanings.
4. The audio-lingual students exhibited a more integrative orientation toward the learning of the language, and toward the German people.

Similar experiments in the teaching of German are conducted in many institutions with variable results,[16] yet the urge for experimentation is not confined to the classroom *per se*. German on television, for example, was a very common topic in the issues of *The German Quarterly* and the *Modern Language Journal* during the last decade. For instance, Alfred R. Neumann in his article "German on Television in Houston: An Informal Report,"[17] points out that, among other things, the difference between test results on classroom work and TV work in elementary German are statistically insignificant; TV students failed and succeeded in about the same ratio as students in the university classroom.[18] Another most interesting report is Albert F. Buffington's "Teaching Beginning German by Closed-Circuit Television,"[19] the critical review of the article by Philip Rovner from the University of Maryland as well as Buffington's reply to the appraisal.[20] They provide insights into a rather complex problem of teaching German through this modern medium. Of great interest is also "German on Television at the University of Texas" by Leroy R. Shaw,[21] inasmuch as it is a report of a pioneering endeavor of a twofold use of television as a teaching medium: (1) to help meet the emergency represented by increased enrollments; and (2) to provide a kind of inservice training for the student-teacher. This report also confirms Herbert W. Reichert's claim[22] for the use of the conventional textbook in television.

The results of all these experiments of teaching German through television demonstrate the great potentiality of the new medium not only as a teaching aid but also as an important factor in furthering the interest in the subject.

Along with the experiments involving comparative studies of methods and the uses of closed and open-circuit television, there are also numerous attempts to improve the use of the language laboratory as a teaching aid[23] and to increase and facilitate the use of various technical and nontechnical devices[24] used in teaching German on all levels.

All these experiments are conducted more or less in the spirit of the "New Key," where the primacy of sound is stressed. There are, at the same time, many voices which emphasize, directly or indirectly, the importance of teaching the finer points of grammar, of stressing translation, and of introducing literature in the early stages of teaching German. For example, an attempt to approach sentence structure from a new direction with the intent of facilitating translation from German to English is made by C. V. Pollard in his work *The Key to German Translation* (1954). A very thorough, and for the teacher of German very useful, descriptive analysis of the German sentence structure is presented by Albert L. Lloyd[25] of the University of Pennsylvania; also, helpful pedagogical pointers based on parallels between English and German sentence structure are made in John T. Waterman's article "Basic Syntax for Language Learning."[26]

Experiments with introduction of lyric poetry to students of first-year College German,[27] as well as introduction and discussion of German poetry in translation[28] with students of the same level, serve to deepen the contents of basic German instruction and to add academic dignity to the subject matter.

Our survey of the present state of German instruction has up to now been confined to the teaching on college level. The age of language rebirth, nevertheless, has produced some startling changes in the teaching objectives and procedures on the high school level as well. Perhaps the most significant positive change here has been the development of the German Advanced Placement Program in secondary schools. This program originated in the educational experiment known as the *School and College*

119

Study of Admission with Advanced Standing. It was a cooperative study between twelve colleges and seventeen secondary schools, founded, as Joseph R. Reichard points out, "on the principle that gifted secondary school pupils should remain in their natural social environment until they had attained the normal age for college entrance."[29] Within the framework of this program the student of German in high school is expected to achieve by graduation the degree of competence in the language and to develop the capacity for literary interpretation normally attained in the junior year in college.[30]

Initially German played but a modest role in the Advanced Placement Program. In 1954, the first year of the experiment, there were only twenty-four German candidates for the examination.[31] Since that time both the method of the program and the testing procedures have been continuously revised and improved, the final result being a single *Advanced German Examination* first put into effect in 1964. An indication of the high caliber of the program is the *Advanced Placement German Examination of 1965* and the German section of the current *Advanced Placement Program: Course Descriptions,* reprinted in the September 1965 issue of *The German Quarterly.* According to the *Course Descriptions,* the candidate, by the time he starts the last year of German in secondary school, should be able:

1. to understand German spoken in connected discourse or in simple lectures;

2. to express everyday experiences in conversational German;

3. to read German prose and poetry of moderate difficulty;

4. to write simple German with reasonable ease and accuracy.

Beyond the acquisition of these basic skills, the advanced placement candidate should also develop a familiarity with the German language as a mode of expression distinctly different from English and a capacity for literary interpretation and critical analysis of representative German literary works. A reading list ranging from Lessing to Dürrenmatt is supplied to help achieve these aims. Thus the Advanced Placement Program in German appears to be the long missing link between secondary schools and colleges. It is quite clear that within the framework of such a program, a fuller cooperation and collaboration between high schools and colleges will be possible, the end result of which should be a more unified and more coherent educational experience of the student. The growth of the Advanced Placement Program also indicates that there is a noticeable trend toward longer language sequences on the secondary school level, which, in turn, points toward the possibility of providing the high school student, in addition to the competence in the four skills, also with a rather thorough introduction to German literature.

In all, the state of German on the high school level is, *mutatis mutandis,* that on the college level: the methods controversy rages on both levels producing, generally speaking, positive results in the re-evaluation and development of teaching techniques.

The experimentation, however, is not confined to high school and college levels. Abram Friesen of the University of North Dakota recently proposed an M.A. program in German with a new approach. Friesen urges the adoption by the American universities of a three-year M.A. program with one year of study at a German university. He proposes a fully articulated plan,[32] which, in the light of recent developments, may in the future become the German M.A. program at American universities. The student, according to Friesen's plan, would spend the first year at the American university doing regular course work in addition to taking courses specifically designed to prepare him for study at a German university. Thus prepared, the student would spend the second year at a German university of his choice. Upon his return home for the third year, he would complete his M.A. thesis and take the remaining required courses. By means of a program of this type, Friesen points out, only graduate students who are well prepared for independent study would be sent abroad. An M.A. degree within the framework of this program would provide the student with better preparation to enter the field of teaching or to continue work on the doctoral level.

The Making of a Synthesis

From the data presented in the preceding section, we are able to observe, among other things, that the experimentation in

German instruction displays two essential trends based, generally speaking, on two different principles: the primacy of sound and the primacy of meaning.

These two discernible trends as well as the recent critical reaction against the audio-lingual method[33] strikingly bring out the need for a synthesis in methodology. In regard to German, it seems that the audio-lingual pendulum is now slowly swinging from the extreme to the middle, thus creating a more meritorious approach; in short, a synthesis. The traditional method is evolving under the influence of the audio-lingual method. The audio-lingual method itself is changing under the impact of the criticism leveled against it by the traditionalists as well as by its supporters. "Though I am a thorough convert to the audio-lingual techniques, I do not hesitate to confess that I still have a sense of satisfaction when the inanities and brainlessness of the early audio-lingual stages can gradually give way to more mature considerations,"[34] writes Jack M. Stein of Harvard. The tide is definitely turning toward a more academic mode of procedure in the classroom, and the study of the German language is rapidly regaining some of the academic dignity lost during the early audio-lingual stages.

Of interest here may be a survey conducted by this author.[35] From the 226 questionnaires sent out to various instructors of German chosen at random from the AATG membership list, 108 were returned: 57 from college instructors and 51 from high school teachers. This is a gratifyingly large response, indicating a concern of a sizable number of German teachers in the United States about the present state of German instruction. The entire questionnaire cannot be reproduced here for reasons of space, yet answers given to some questions provide an interesting view of the nature of German instruction today. In one part of the questionnaire the teacher was asked to indicate what method he uses to achieve his aims in teaching elementary or inter- mediate (first or second year) German. Four possible choices were given as well as an opportunity to express one's own view. The four, in brief, were: (1) audio-lingual method, (2) direct method, (3) traditional method, and (4) combination of the above. A short definition followed each method mentioned. The result was as follows:

College
  (1) Audio-lingual method 5 (9%)
  (2) Direct method 5 (9%)
  (3) Traditional method 3 (5%)
  (4) Combination of methods 44 (77%)

High School
  (1) Audio-lingual method 3 (6%)
  (2) Direct method 3 (6%)
  (3) Traditional method 7 (14%)
  (4) Combination of methods 38 (74%)

The results here clearly indicate a tendency toward an eclectic approach to teaching both on high school and college level. Very similar results were obtained from the question regarding the aims of first- and second-year German. Both reading knowledge and the audio-lingual skills received equal emphasis by over 75 percent of the high school and college teachers polled. Rather significant may also be the question regarding introduction of literature in the first or second year of German. The difference between college and high school in this respect becomes quite apparent. Out of the 57 college instructors polled, 29 (almost 50 per cent) introduce literature in the first year of instruction; 22 (39 per cent) introduce literature in the second year; 4 (7 per cent) do not introduce literature during the first two years at all; two instructors disregarded the question. The genre of literature favored by these instructors is short story (modern), lyric poetry, and Hörspiel in that order.

In the high schools the situation is somewhat different: Only 10 teachers (about 20 per cent) indicated that they introduce literature during the first year of study; 21 (about 40 per cent) during the second year, and 20 (about 40 per cent) indicated that they do not introduce literature during these years at all. The genre favored here is fairy tale and short story.

Thus on the basis of the data presented it would seem that German is striving to regain the required equilibrium between the various facets of language learning; that the overemphasis placed on methods and mechanical devices in recent years has fortunately not been successful in completely reducing the study of the German language to a mere training process. It is hoped that the methodological synthesis which we saw in the making will place and maintain things in their proper perspective. The purpose of study of any foreign language in school or in institutions of higher education should be, and always has been, a humanistic one. Thus the formal study of the German language should have as its principal purpose the reading, comprehension, and appreciation of the literature written in that tongue.

LEO D. RUDNYTZKY received his M.A. degree in Germanics from the University of Pennsylvania in 1960. In 1960-1961 he studied Germanic and Slavic literatures at the Free University of Berlin and later transferred to Munich from which he received his doctorate in August 1965. He is currently Assistant Professor of German at La Salle College, Philadelphia, where he also serves as coordinator of the Comparative Literature Program and as a member of the Academic Senate. He is a consultant to the Catholic Renascence Society, a member of the Modern Language Association, the Shevchenko Scientific Society, the Association of American Teachers of German, and the American Association of Teachers of Slavic and East European Languages. In June 1966, he was awarded the Christian R. and Mary F. Lindback Award for Distinguished Teaching at La Salle College.

FOOTNOTES

1. Edwin H. Zeydel, "The Teaching of German in the United States from Colonial Times to the Present." THE GERMAN QUARTERLY, XXXVII, September 1964, 315-392, gives a detailed, exhaustive historical account of the subject matter.
2. Harold S. Jantz, "German Thought and Literature in New England, 1620 - 1820, A Preliminary Survey." JOURNAL OF ENGLISH AND GERMANIC PHILOLOGY, XLI, January 1942, i, 1-45.
3. Edwin H. Zeydel, *Op. Cit.*, 329.
4. Ralph P. Rosenberg, "American Doctoral Studies in Germanic Culture." YEARBOOK OF COMPARATIVE AND GENERAL LITERATURE, IV, 1955, 30-44.
5. Edwin H. Zeydel, *Op. Cit.*, 348.
6. *Ibid.*, 361-362.
7. *Ibid.*, 368.
8. Francis M. Rogers, "Languages and the War Effort." MODERN LANGUAGE JOURNAL, XXVII, May 1943, 299 ff.
9. Elizabeth E. Bohning, "The National Contest for Secondary School Students." GQ, XXXIII, November 1960, 343.
10. "Notes in Brief." GQ, XXXVI, November 1963, 495.
11. "National German Contest." GQ, September 1966, 529.
12. For dissertations in progress in German and Germanics and for doctoral degrees granted 1965-1966 see MONATSHEFTE, LVIII, Fall 1960, 256-267.

13. The information on class size and time of classes was kindly supplied by Professor John J. Mulligan of Villanova University.
14. See, for example, Diether Haenicke's article "Zum Ausländerstudium in Deutschland"; Günther Bicknese's "Akademische Programme für Undergraduates in Deutschland: Endlose Misere oder Existenzberechtigte Bildungsquelle?" and Volkmar Sander's "Study Abroad: An Alternate Solution." All in GQ, XXXVIII, November 1965.
15. See George A. C. Scherer and Michael Wertheimer, "The German Teaching Experiment at the University of Colorado." GQ, XXXV, May 1962, 298-308.
16. See William H. Clark and Margaret G. Clark, "Achievement in Elementary German Under Programmed and Conventional Instruction: A Preliminary Study." MLJ, L, February 1966, 97-100.
17. GQ, November 1956, 261-267.
18. Substantially the same results in this respect were achieved by Günther H. Gottschalk at the University of California, Santa Barbara. See "Closed-Circuit Television in Second Semester College German." MLJ, XLIX, February 1965, 86-91.
19. GQ, XXXIII, March 1960, 147-152.
20. Both in GQ, XXXIV, March, 1961, pp. 154-163 and 164-173 respectively.
21. GQ, XXIV, March 1961, 146-153.
22. "Conventional Textbooks in the Foreign-Language Telecourse," GQ, XXXII, January 1959, 34-42.
23. George A. C. Scherer, "The Use and Misuse of Language Laboratories." GQ, XXXVIII, May 1965, 335-344.
24. Eberhard Reichmann, "The Map for Pattern Practice." GQ, XXXVIII, May 1965, 345-350.
25. "On German Sentence Structure." GQ, November 1962, 511-518.
26. GQ, XXX, November 1957, 262-268.
27. Ruth J. Kichenmann, "Teaching Lyric Poetry in First Year German." GQ, XXXV, May 1962, 292-297.
28. Carl Hammer, Jr. "Poetic Translations for the German Class." GQ, XXXIII, January 1960, 14-21.
29. "The First Ten Years of German Advanced Placement: Theory and Practice." GQ, XXXVIII, September 1965, 440.
30. Ibid., 445.
31. Ibid., 441.
32. Abram Friesen, "An M.A. Program in German with a New Approach." GQ, XXXVIII, November 1965, 685-691.
33. Perhaps the most severe criticism of the audio-lingual method was triggered by Raymond F. Keating's A STUDY OF THE EFFECTIVENESS OF LANGUAGE LABORATORIES. Institute of Administrative Research, Teachers College, Columbia University, 1963, 61 pp. In the same year three interesting articles appeared in MLJ, XLVII, each criticizing the audio-lingual method from a slightly different point of view. They are: Harold B. Dunkel's "Language Teaching in an Old Key," No. 5, 203-210; Max Zeldner's "The Bewildered Modern Language Teacher," No. 6, 245-253; and Theodore Huebener's "The New Key is Now Off-Key!" No. 8, 375-377.
34. "Language Teaching and Literature." GQ, XXXVIII, September 1965, 439.

35. I wish to express my gratitude to Professor Thomas N. McCarthy, Department of Psychology, La Salle College, for his constructive comments on the questionnaire.

Selected Bibliography

BOOKS

Bagster-Collins, Elijah W., THE TEACHING OF GERMAN IN SECONDARY SCHOOLS. New York: Columbia University Press, 1915, 232 pp. An extensive treatise on various aspects and methods of German instruction prior to World War I.

Brooks, Nelson, LANGUAGE AND LANGUAGE LEARNING. Harcourt, Brace and World, New York, 1964, 300 pp. A valuable work on recent developments in language instruction with extensive bibliography (283-289) and practical suggestions regarding classroom and laboratory procedures.

Childers, Wesley J., FOREIGN LANGUAGE TEACHING. The Center for Applied Research in Education, Inc., New York, 1964, 120 pp. A comprehensive treatise on the state of foreign teaching on elementary and secondary school level with a selected bibliography (115-116).

Fotitch, Tatiana, editor, TEACHING FOREIGN LANGUAGES IN THE MODERN WORLD. Washington, D.C.: The Catholic University of America Press, 1961, 225 pp. A useful collection of essays on various facets of foreign language teaching on high school and college level.

Huebener, Theodore, AUDIO-VISUAL TECHNIQUES IN TEACHING FOREIGN LANGUAGES. New York: New York University Press, 1960, 163 pp. Practical handbook on the subject with extensive bibliography (125-160) pertaining to all areas of instruction.

Jespersen, Otto, HOW TO TEACH A FOREIGN LANGUAGE. London: George Allen & Unwin, Ltd., 1947, 194 pp.

Keating, Raymond F., A STUDY OF THE EFFECTIVENESS OF LANGUAGE LABORATORIES, A PRELIMINARY EVALUATION IN TWENTY-ONE SCHOOL SYSTEMS OF THE METROPOLITAN SCHOOL STUDY COUNCIL. Institute of Administrative Research, Teachers College. New York: Columbia University, 1963, 61 pp; bibliography (43-45).

Lado, Robert, LANGUAGE TESTING. London: Longmans, Green and Co. Ltd., 1962, 389 pp. A valuable manual on the construction and use of foreign language tests.

Moulton, William G., THE SOUNDS OF ENGLISH AND GERMAN. Chicago: The University of Chicago Press, 1963, 145 pp. A contrastive analysis of the sound systems of English and German designed to facilitate the study of German pronunciation.

Pfeffer, Alan J., GRUNDDEUTSCH. BASIC (SPOKEN) GERMAN

WORD LIST. Englewood Cliffs, N.J.: Prentice-Hall, 1964, 79 pp. An excellent word list consisting of 1,268 entries arranged alphabetically, syntactically, and in terms of frequency and origin.

Pollard, Cecil Vivian, THE KEY TO GERMAN TRANSLATION. Austin, Texas: The University Cooperative Society, 1963, 250 pp. and appendix. An original approach to the translation of German based upon the capitalized noun and eleven major rules. Appropriate reading selections from virtually all academic disciplines are included (65-250) to facilitate practical application of the rules.

Rudenberg, Werner and Pearl, Kate, 400 GERMAN IDIOMS (REDENSARTEN) AND COLLOQUIALISMS WITH THEIR ENGLISH EQUIVALENTS. London: Hirschfeld Bros., 1955, 470 pp.

Scherer, George A. O. and Wertheimer, Michael, A PSYCHOLINGUISTIC EXPERIMENT IN FOREIGN-LANGUAGE TEACHING. New York: McGraw-Hill, 1964, 256 pp. Of particular interest to the German teacher especially in regard to its description of German skill tests (108-135) and its presentation of the nationally standardized German tests (27-28, 111-112).

Stack, Edward M., THE LANGUAGE LABORATORY AND MODERN LANGUAGES TEACHING. New York: Oxford University Press, 1966, 234 pp. Authoritative report on the use of language laboratories, pattern drills, and audio-lingual exercises in general.

Thierfelder, Franz, DIE DEUTSCHE SPRACHE IM AUSLAND. Hamburg: Decker's Verlag, 1957, 2 vols. Vol. II, 358-402 give a wealth of information about the state of German instruction in the United States, inclusive historical background and recent statistical data.

Valdman, Albert, editor, TRENDS IN LANGUAGE TEACHING, New York: McGraw-Hill, 1966, 298 pp. A collection of comprehensive essays on the most recent developments in the field with references to the psychology of language learning.

ARTICLES

"The Advanced Placement German Examination of 1965." THE GERMAN QUARTERLY, XXXVIII, September 1965, 480-505.

Bicknese, Günther, "Akademische Programme für Undergraduates in Deutschland: Endlose Misere oder Existenzberechtigte Bildungsquelle?" THE GERMAN QUARTERLY, XXXVIII, November 1965, 671-684. Well-documented critical analysis of the existing undergraduate programs in Germany with constructive suggestions for improvement.

Bohning, Elizabeth E., "The National Contest for Secondary School Students." THE GERMAN QUARTERLY, XXXIII, November 1960, 343-352.

Buffington, Albert F., "A Reply to Mr. Rovner's Appraisal of Teach-

ing Beginning German by Closed-Circuit Television." THE GER-
MAN QUARTERLY, XXXIV, March 1961, 164-173.

Buffington, Albert F., "Teaching Beginning German by Closed-Circuit Television." THE GERMAN QUARTERLY, XXXIII, March
1960, 147-152.

Clark, William H. and Clark, Margaret G., "Achievement in Elemen-
tary German under Programmed and Conventional Instruction:
A Preliminary Study." MODERN LANGUAGE JOURNAL, L,
February 1966, 97-100.

Dunkel, Harold B., "Language Teaching in an Old Key." MODERN
LANGUAGE JOURNAL, May 1963, 203-210.

Friesen, Abram, "An M.A. Program in German with a New Approach." THE GERMAN QUARTERLY, XXXVIII, November
1955, 685-691.

Gottschalk, Günther H., "Closed-Circuit Television in Second Semester College German." MODERN LANGUAGE JOURNAL,
XLIX, February 1965, 86-91.

Haenicke, Diether, "Zum Ausländerstudium in Deutschland." THE
GERMAN QUARTERLY, XXXVIII, November 1965, 660-670.

Hammer, Carl, Jr., "Poetic Translations for the German Class." THE
GERMAN QUARTERLY, XXXIII, January 1960, 14-21.

Huebener, Theodore, "The New Key is Now Off-Key." MODERN
LANGUAGE JOURNAL, XLVII, December 1963, 375-377.

Jants, Harold S., "German Thought and Literature of New England,
1620-1820, A Preliminary Survey." JOURNAL OF ENGLISH
AND GERMANIC PHILOLOGY, XLI, January 1942, 1-45. An
essay with valuable historical data about the early development
of German culture in America.

Lloyd, Albert L., "On German Sentence Structure." THE GERMAN
QUARTERLY, XXXV, November 1962, 511-518.

Moeller, Jack R., "An Advanced Placement Program: Are three years
enough?" THE GERMAN QUARTERLY, XXXVIII, September
1965, 455-460.

Neumann, Alfred R., "German on Television in Houston: An Informal
Report." THE GERMAN QUARTERLY, XXIX, November 1956,
261-267.

Reichert, Herbert W., "Conventional Textbooks in the Foreign-Language Telecourse." THE GERMAN QUARTERLY, XXXII, January 1959, 34-42.

Reichard, Joseph R., "The First Ten Years of German Advanced
Placement: Theory and Practice." THE GERMAN QUARTER-
LY, XXXVIII, September 1965, 440-449.

Reichmann, Eberhard, "The Map for Pattern Practice." THE GER-
MAN QUARTERLY, XXVIII, May 1965, 345-350.

Rogers, Francis Millet, "Language and the War Effort." MODERN
LANGUAGE JOURNAL, XXVII, May 1943, 299 ff. and No. 8,
571 ff. This essay was one of the factors that brought about the

revolution in the teaching of foreign languages in the United States.

Rosenberg, Ralph P., "American Doctoral Studies in Germanic Culture." YEARBOOK OF COMPARATIVE AND GENERAL LITERATURE, IV, 1955, 30-44.

Rovner, Philip, "An Appraisal of Teaching Beginning German by Closed-Circuit Television." THE GERMAN QUARTERLY, XXXIV, March 1961, 154-163.

Ryder, Frank G., "Literature in High School—A College Point of View." THE GERMAN QUARTERLY, XXXVIII, September 1965, 469-479. A persuasive argument for the introduction of literature early in high school with helpful methodological suggestions.

Sander, Volkmar, "Study Abroad: An Alternate Solution." THE GERMAN QUARTERLY, XXXVIII, November 1965, 692-695. The presentation of a plan adopted by the New York University with the purpose of strengthening the undergraduate language program, while trying to avoid the negative aspects of the traditional Junior Year Abroad Plan.

Scherer, George A. C. and Wertheimer, Michael, "The German Teaching Experiment at the University of Colorado." THE GERMAN QUARTERLY, XXXV, May 1962, 298-308.

Scherer, George A. C., "The Use and Misuse of Language Laboratories." THE GERMAN QUARTERLY, XXXVIII, May, 335-344.

Shaw, Leroy R., "German on Television at the University of Texas." THE GERMAN QUARTERLY, XXXIV, March 1961, 146-153.

Stein, Jack M. "Language Teaching and Literature." THE GERMAN QUARTERLY, XXXVIII, September 1965, 436-439.

Waterman, John T., "Basic Syntax for Language Learning." THE GERMAN QUARTERLY, XXX, November 1957, 262-297.

Zeldner, Max, "The Bewildered Modern Language Teacher." MODERN LANGUAGE JOURNAL, XLVII, October 1963, 245-253.

Zeydel, Edwin H., "The Teaching of German in the United States from Colonial Times to the Present." THE GERMAN QUARTERLY, XXXVII, September 1964, 315-392. A detailed historical account of the subject matter with a wealth of bibliographical and statistical data.

STANDARD REFERENCE GRAMMARS
OF THE GERMAN LANGUAGE

Behagel, O., DEUTSCHE SYNTAX: EINE GESCHICHTLICHE DARSTELLUNG. Heidelberg, 1923-1932.

Curme, George O., A GRAMMAR OF THE GERMAN LANGUAGE, 2nd rev. ed., New York: Frederick Ungar Publishing Co., 1952.

Paul, Hermann, DEUTSCHE GRAMMATIK, Halle, 1916-1920.

Thomas, Calvin, A PRACTICAL GERMAN GRAMMAR, 4th ed., New York: Holt, Rinehart and Winston, 1944.

The Changing Aspects of Teaching Spanish

CALVIN A. CLAUDEL

West Virginia Wesleyan College

ANOTHER ARTICLE on Spanish teaching in the United States may seem like carrying coals to Newcastle when we consider the numerous scholarly articles already done on this subject. The best of these is no doubt the splendid work of Dr. Sturgis E. Leavitt.[1] Yet, however fine these articles may be, they are not sufficiently critical of our increasingly poor texts and methods, especially as found in the widely accepted and officially sponsored audio-lingual method, based upon pedagogical assumptions without proof. A cogent critic says, "Although this stimulus-response view of language stems from a formerly traditional view, it is a fallacious interpretation of language learning today."[2]

The study and teaching of Spanish in our country have generally been of primary importance, next to French. In 1960 Spanish showed the greatest percentage gains, from 29,767 students to 55,430, or 86.2 per cent, compared with 1959, while French was highest in actual numbers, from 55,458 to 87,543, or 57.7 per cent.[3] A recent tabulation of enrollment in the schools of New York City showed Spanish in first place with 90,000 students and French in second place with 73,000.[4]

Except for a few periods of setback, generally found in the study of all foreign languages in our country, the role of Spanish has increased phenomenally in recent years, so that next to English, it is the major tongue of the New World, extremely vital in both popular expression and literary development.

Not only the Spanish-speaking countries of Latin America but also our own United States owe a great debt to Spain for her linguistic and cultural influences, which are found in countless monuments, place names, and current words and expressions.

Our close link with Latin America also points up the importance of teaching and studying Spanish. The Monroe Doctrine stressed our close ties in international affairs. The Pan-American Union (Organization of American States) exemplifies our Good Neighbor Policy and the need for mutual protection. Close and friendly relations are more important today than ever before. Discussing our involvement in Vietnam, the extremes of a Bastista and a Castro in such countries as Cuba, a journalist recently said, "The whole continent of South America—which we ignore at our peril—is rent with the conflicting forces of reaction and revolution. Adherents of the democratic process are pitifully few and weak in almost all South American countries. The decent people have little real choice."[5] A mutual knowledge of both Spanish and English is one of the best ways of accomplishing much needed better relations.

As pointed out by Dr. Leavitt, our interest in and connection with Spanish culture and civilization preceded the American Revolution. Spain settled Mexico some one hundred years earlier than the English settled our Eastern Seaboard. A number of great American writers and statesmen were students and teachers of the Spanish language and literature. Among them were Washington Irving, James Russell Lowell, and Henry Wadsworth Longfellow, to mention only a few.

The study and teaching of Spanish were emphasized not only for literary but also for practical and commercial values in relation to trade in Latin America, for one writer refers to Spanish as "the language of literature and commerce."[6] Fine commercial courses in Spanish existed from early days in such metropolitan areas as New Orleans, which advertised itself as the Gateway to the Americas, and rightly so, since its International Trade Mart today is second to none in the world. These early practical courses were pioneering ventures in the effective teaching of the spoken language. Some of these commercial schools boasted of their language teaching. Some years ago, the president of the American Association of Teachers of French stressed their competence and good results, telling language teachers that they should try to do as well.[7]

Traditional Methods

While in some of our large metropolitan areas, which had

many Spanish-speaking persons, the teaching and learning of Spanish were accomplished most effectively through the direct use of the language, most of our instruction was by the traditional method, which consisted of readings in Spanish along with exercises to be translated from Spanish into English and from English into Spanish. Some of these early texts were fine scholarly works. This writer learned to love Spanish with one of these entitled *A Spanish Grammar for Beginners,* in which each lesson began with an apt proverb, such as the one from Cervantes, "La pluma es lengua del alma"—"The pen is the tongue of the soul."[8] Many of these traditional texts not only presented Spanish culture but also used many valid devices of teaching. Indeed some of these volumes were far better than some of our poor present-day audio-lingual texts!

Although in a large city, such as New York, Spanish might have been taught in elementary school, this language was generally begun in high school and often continued into college. In high school, elementary grammar was usually covered in a period of two years, to be followed by a review of grammar with composition, possibly accompanied by reading of a practical or cultural nature or both. "Composition" generally meant the translation of sentences from English into Spanish, illustrating textual idioms and difficulties.

Lower-level college Spanish was quite similar and varied only in increased content or rate of coverage. Elementary grammar was covered in one year, to be followed by a review grammar, accompanied by literary or practical readings dealing with the culture of Spain and Spanish America. Although numerous texts might be labelled "conversational," in reality their contents and use in class in general paid only lip-service to an oral method. While in many areas a reading knowledge of the language was the main objective, in some areas, such as New Orleans, both a conversational and a cultural ability in Spanish were required and ultimately achieved, but this high level of achievement has declined today because of regimentation into the audio-lingual method, which demonstrates "unprecedented activity—though not necessarily unprecedented success."[9]

University courses in Spanish emphasized the teaching of the language and literature in English rather than in Spanish. Such large institutions as the University of Chicago and the

University of North Carolina stressed the study of Old Spanish, dwelling in great detail on the minute study of philology. After long years of study, a person with an American doctorate in Spanish might have had many courses in Spanish literature and philology and not be able to speak the language. In fact a recent article criticizes the poor Spanish usage at present among American teachers.[10] Promotion and progress in one's profession of teaching depended and still depend largely on the number of literary and philological articles published in the various university quarterlies.

Most teachers on upper levels have in the past held themselves aloof from any discussion of or interest in methods or the teaching of lower-level courses while concerning themselves with esoteric literary questions. Some of the language quarterlies, such as *Hispanic Review*, contain only literary articles of an exclusive nature. Although some language journals, such as *Hispania* and *The Modern Language Journal*, will publish articles concerned with practical methodology and the like, most of them and their contributors concern themselves with literary criticism only. There is much need today for an all-out examination of learning, studying, and teaching practices on all levels from grade school through the university.

A major in Spanish often minored in French or vice versa. At the University of North Carolina a candidate for the doctorate was usually made to study the gamut of all the Romance languages including all the various dialects, both ancient and modern. This involved and still involves a long curriculum of courses in philology and related fields.

Less successful candidates for the doctorate might well find a position teaching both Spanish and French in some godforsaken area or perhaps teaching Spanish and coaching football. This spreading out of teaching in several fields, while the teacher may not know any one language thoroughly, has been one of the main faults of teacher and student preparation. There is a great need for teachers who are expertly trained in their specialty of Spanish. If there is not sufficient teaching for a teacher in one school, he might well share his time with another school in the community or nearby vicinity.

Many critics warn that prosperity in language teaching may indeed be short-lived unless we take careful stock, for such affluent conditions have not always existed. We have but to recall our Great Depression of 1929, around which time it was concluded that the aim of foreign language teaching was to teach only a bare reading knowledge.[11] Although some language teachers, including this writer, rejected such a defeatist trend, lean years followed, and language teachers generally apologized for their profession. Students would tell somewhat sheepishly of having had one or two years of Spanish and of not being able to utter anything in Spanish, except a couple of phrases. Consequently because of curricular changes and laxity, the classics and content subjects, such as modern languages, gradually declined in our schools, to be replaced by social studies and life adjustment courses. In our emphasis on mass education, elite subjects suffered in enrollment and prestige.

In the early 1940's, during the Second World War, language teaching in the Army Specialized Training Program (ASTP), conducted in such institutions as the University of North Carolina, where this writer was teaching at the time, pointed up the inadequacy of traditional methods. New ideas and methods were developed. The concept of area studies was created, which included not only the literature of the region but also its many political, social, and economic aspects. Native teachers were employed using the direct method. This writer used visual aids in his class with success. Foreign films were presented along with other social activities involving conversation with native speakers on the campus. Subsequent studies from this short-lived program, which was somewhat frowned upon by traditional teachers, served to focus attention on our weaknesses and to create a demand for better language teaching.

The so-called "Army Method," used in the above program, is sometimes mistakenly equated with the current audio-lingual method, which was really developed somewhat later.

An atmosphere of change became apparent. In 1953 Earle McGrath, then Commissioner of Education, stressed at St. Louis the importance of foreign languages even in elementary education and invited leaders and administrators to meet with him in Washington. The program of Foreign Languages in Elementary Schools (FLES) was launched.

As explained in this writer's chapter on "The Language Laboratory," our technological revolution considerably increased not only our media of travel but of communication, so that space and time are literally being annihilated, giving us a power somewhat comparable to that of the Seven-League Boots found in the tale of "Jack and the Beanstalk" and to that of Aladdin in the tale of "The Wonderful Lamp." Certainly space travel and television have helped to reveal most clearly the importance of speaking a foreign language. In any case the numerous electronic devices, which produced the language laboratory, helped spark a language revolution.

The launching of Sputnik by the Russians in 1957 revealed our inadequacy in both science and foreign languages. Our country then was ready for and demanded a change; consequently the National Defense Education Act (NDEA) was established, whose initial purpose and intent was to improve the quality of education in sciences and foreign languages.

Traditional language teachers, opposed to change, defaulted in their leadership, which they surrendered to other fields,[12] such as English, education, psychology, and anthropology, and to an avant-garde group of so-called structural linguists dedicated to a mechanistic method of teaching languages centered around the use of electronic devices. Under government subsidy language laboratories were set up in many schools along with summer institutes for teachers.

Alongside our traditional methods there had also existed for some years good direct methods in such institutions as Middlebury College and other private schools. At this time these better methods might have been adopted except that most language teachers were not fluent enough in the foreign languages to use such methods, which demanded a thorough speaking knowledge of the foreign tongue.

A Crash Method

Consequently, to meet mass demands, a makeshift crash method was developed and adopted, subsequently called the "New Key" and later the audio-lingual method. This latter method was contrived by the structural linguists who based their findings on Pavlovian psychology of the conditioned reflex. Language was stated to be a habit which must be taught by a "scientific" method, especially based around the mechanistic means of the language laboratory. This mechanical method along with the laboratory was presented as the logical solution for the impasse, for both teacher and student would presumably be trained by it while using it. It also served to drive out better direct methods, for the audio-lingual method became a sort of official dogma or canon of methodology.[13]

The faults do not lie in the mechanical devices of the laboratory but rather in their improper use through the procedures of the audio-lingual method. Many articles already cited elsewhere stress the weaknesses and inadequacies of this makeshift crash method. Meras' excellent article summarizes these, and he suggests our return to the good direct methods which existed in our better private schools.[14]

A recent article by Professor Hamilton contends that the audio-lingual method is a fad, although he does not offer a better alternative.[15] Professor Barrutia's reply to him begs the question. He unconvincingly answers several severe critics: A. F. Gronberg,[16] Venita Booth,[17] and Thomas R. Palfrey.[18]

Barrutia cites not only the above writers to his detriment but especially this passage from Miss Booth: "To build an entire course of study around dialogue-memorization, however, denies the student the opportunity of using the analytical skills he has learned since he began school and thereby refutes the whole purpose of public education."[19] Moreover, Barrutia displays questionable scholarship, indeed, for another point to his discredit is that the first sentence and the last two sentences of his presumed quotation from Miss Booth's article are not found in her article, certainly not in the context he presents them.[20]

Barrutia's assumption as well as that of other proponents of the audio-lingual method is that all opponents of their method are traditionalists. This writer and a number of others, such as Meras, point to a better method than both the traditional and the audio-lingual, that is, the direct audio-visual method.[21] For some years now this method has been used most successfully by the Alliance Française and its branches in the teaching of French.[22] This writer first explained these methods in an earlier article.[23]

Better Audio-Visual Method

At West Virginia Wesleyan, where the writer is chairman of the Department of Romance Languages, audio-visual methods are being used with much success in both French and Spanish on the lower levels. In French we are using the excellent texts of Gaston Mauger, *Cours de langue et de civilisation françaises.* In Spanish on the elementary level, I. A. Richards' *Spanish Through Pictures* is being used by Robert Green with good results. Also Ugarte's *Gramática española de Repaso,* a completely Spanish text, is being used on the second-year level quite successfully, along with readings in Spanish and Spanish American literature.[24] On all levels classes are being conducted in Spanish most of the time.

There is a great need in Spanish, however, for a good visual text similar to Gaston Mauger's first volume of *Cours de langue et de civilisation françaises,* somewhat modified and amplified perhaps to suit different needs.

A number of critics of the New Key have returned or have expressed a wish to return to the traditional method of teaching, or have suggested taking a middle course combining what is presumably best of the traditional and of the audio-lingual methods. The writer in one of his earlier articles pointed out how he returned to a traditional text after floundering around in a program with only a very elementary reader and no grammar at all.[25] Miss Booth tells of her fruitless efforts with the audio-lingual method and how she and her students gladly returned to traditional methods. Hamilton suggests an eclectic course between the audio-lingual and the traditional. He espouses, however, *Modern Spanish,* which is one of the most audio-lingual of texts, and thus retreats from his position of having been anti-audio-lingual and begs the question, to say the least.

As pointed out in the writer's article cited above, the student usually comes very late to the study of Spanish, often after reaching high school or even college. He has no time to waste in duplicating courses or in makeshift learning methods. Every minute counts, and he must put his time to the best and most effective use.

One of the greatest lacks in our present-day foreign language curriculum is the coordination of overlapping and repetitious courses, reflecting the over-all absence of any planned direction in both study and teaching.[26]

A contradictory situation has existed and still exists in graduate university foreign language work. While present-day requirements demand primarily of the student a writing and speaking knowledge of the language, many institutions still require the writing of long graduate research papers, including theses and dissertations in English, which often amount to academic busy-work and which require years of time and effort. At least, as some better institutions of higher learning require, such research should be in the foreign language. In any case, the average student should spend most of his time in achieving a language proficiency and over-all cultural knowledge.

As Germaine Brée aptly pointed out, we have the dual responsibility of teaching both language and literature, and this must be done by the best methods, which is not the case today, as pointed out by the above critic of our banal and "degrading" dialogue methods.[27]

In criticizing one of his student teacher's audio-lingual classes in Spanish, Dr. Meras says, "If this is typical, and I hear that it is, it would seem that the inflexibility of the total memorization system does not train students to adapt themselves even in a class with the same teacher for any variations of the fixed pattern."[28]

The above pointed criticism and the half dozen others cited cogently by Dr. Meras, not to mention the many others stressed by numerous critics from the past several years, certainly do bring into question the validity of an audio-lingual text such as *Modern Spanish,* despite its official acceptance and backing, for all the faults mentioned by these critics most aptly apply to this latter text.[29]

Immediately after the above passage, Dr. Meras tells of the far better results obtained from a direct visual approach in language teaching: "My own experience as well as that of colleagues with a Direct Method approach has shown that even before the end of the first year almost all students can follow an impromptu talk in the foreign language, especially if it is illustrated."[30]

In the key word "illustrated," Dr. Meras touches the kernel of his entire article, which is a plea for using direct audio-visual methods in foreign language teaching.

Our main problem has been and still is that of needing better-trained teachers. One article shows that the need for better-trained teachers in foreign languages is an even greater problem on college and university levels.[31]

The plethora of "guidelines" laid down in a recent official report reveals inner weaknesses of philosophy and method in language teaching throughout the United States.[32]

Our whole FLES program needs to be revitalized through the better audio-visual methods. It needs expert teachers, possibly from Spanish-speaking countries. The state of Indiana has made excellent strides in this direction in its grass-roots program.[33]

Despite poor and inadequate methods, Spanish teaching and learning in our country has always done fairly well because of our proximity to Latin America, which affords the possibility of easy contact with Spanish-speaking persons. There are numerous fine summer schools in Mexico and in other Latin countries. We need to take greater advantage of these. For some years now the cost of living in Spain has been most reasonable, and travel in Spain offers excellent opportunities for language practice and study. Such travel needs to be encouraged more and more through intensified student and faculty exchange programs.

Importance of Spanish in National Security

Our very survival may depend on the more effective spread of both English and Spanish between the Northern and Southern hemispheres. This writer was surprised to note the very poor methods of teaching English to Latin-American students in our country. Our same anti-intellectual audio-lingual methods are being used with them.

Professor Robert Mead in a recent article points out that our image in and relations with Latin America need improving, to say the least. He concludes, "Most of *Hispania's* readers are teachers of Spanish and Portuguese, and there is no need to remind them of the rewards and satisfactions which can be theirs if they will but set as their ultimate goal the improvement of international understanding in the Americas."[34] This same point was stressed by a writer some ten years ago: "We have been accustomed to consider languages as a part of liberal education. Let us learn to consider them as an imperative for international relations and national security."[35]

While visiting in Mexico recently, this writer found out

clearly why an ability to speak Spanish helps us to win friends in such countries. As a Mexican friend stated: "Do you know why we liked Mrs. Kennedy so much? Well, it was because she spoke Spanish and was so friendly!"

Every week the writer receives materials advertising various methods of teaching Spanish, usually involving quite expensive materials purchasable under NDEA subsidy through taxpayers' money, and assuring the speedy and effective teaching and learning of Spanish. While some of this material is worthy of note, most of it is not.

We have been witnessing a revolution, not only in the teaching and learning of Spanish, but also of other foreign languages. For the most part, the very same conditions and problems are prevalent in all. As in the case in all revolutions, however, there has been a growing trend toward a doctrinaire philosophy and methodology in teaching and learning foreign languages.

Time to Take Stock

Quoting the psychologist John Carroll, from his address delivered in Berlin at the International Conference on Modern Language Teaching, September 5, 1964, Dr. Meras said "There should be a rethinking of current theories of foreign language teaching to keep up with psychological theory."[36]

In this same vein another important critic said, "A clearcut viewpoint on the teaching of foreign languages has emerged and is being increasingly adopted in the schools. The time has now come for a critical appraisal of this method, in the light of the most recent conclusions on the learning process."[37]

Stressing the need for a "basic philosophy in foreign language teaching," another critic said, "I believe both native and non-native teachers should be concerned, above all, with an efficient method, suitable text materials, the development of efficient techniques, and the discussion of problems encountered in the classroom in order to avoid the deadly dull aspects of foreign language instruction of the past."[38] One might also add that if traditional instruction of the past was "deadly dull," current lock-step procedure of the anti-intellectual method exemplified in such texts as *Modern Spanish* is far worse, yet this text is endorsed by over a score of teachers and linguists. This is the paradox against which there is ever-growing criticism.

140

In summary, we have noted in the United States three methods of teaching Spanish: the traditional, the audio-lingual, and the direct audio-visual. "The third method can best be taught by one who is fluent in the language. While the poorly trained teacher may feel more at ease in the first two methods, the truly creative and well-trained teacher will feel limited and frustrated in these and much freer and at home in the latter method."[39]

CALVIN ANDRE CLAUDEL, chairman of the Romance Language Department, West Virginia Wesleyan College, Buckhannon, West Virginia, earned his B.A. and M.A. and his Phi Beta Kappa at Tulane University; and his Ph.D. in Romance Languages and Literature at the University of North Carolina. He has been a Diplômé de la Sorbonne; Chevalier dans l'ordre des Palmes Académiques; Lauréat de l'Athénée Louisianais, member of the Paul Claudel Society; Vice-President of l'Athénée Louisianais; past president, Louisiana State Poetry Society. A specialist in medieval and modern French literature, Dr. Claudel has taught at the University of North Carolina, Saint Louis University, and Beloit College. His work has appeared in *PMLA, French Review, Hispania, Kentucky Foreign Language Quarterly, New Mexico Quarterly, Georgia Review, Journal of American Folklore, Louisiana Historical Quarterly*, and others. He is listed in *Who's Who in the South and Southwest, Directory of American Scholars, Who Knows and What, Who's Who in the East*, etc.

FOOTNOTES

1. Sturgis E. Leavitt, "The Teaching of Spanish in the United States." HISPANIA, XLIV, No. 4, December 1961, 591-625.
2. Beverly Moen Bazan, "The Danger of Assumption Without Proof." THE MODERN LANGUAGE JOURNAL, XLVIII, No. 6, October 1964, 338.
3. Wesley Childers, "Foreign Language Offerings and Enrollment in Public Secondary Schools, Fall 1960." PMLA, LXXVII, No. 4, Part 2, September 1962, 30.
4. Theodore Huebener, "Fifty Years of Foreign Languages in New York City." HISPANIA, XLVII, December 1964, 784.
5. Sydney J. Harris, " 'Winning Viet Nam War' Is Meaningless Phrase." PITTSBURGH POST-GAZETTE, December 2, 1966, 10, col. 2.
6. Vicenzo Cioffari, "The Role of the Modern Foreign Languages in Our Schools." THE MODERN LANGUAGE JOURNAL, XL, No. 6, October 1956, 302.
7. Julian Harris, "Message of the President." THE FRENCH REVIEW, XXVII, No. 1, October 1953, 2.
8. M. A. De Vitis, A SPANISH GRAMMAR FOR BEGINNERS. New York: Allyn and Bacon, 1915, 1.
9. Georges J. Joyaux, "Foreign Languages and the Humanities." THE

MODERN LANGUAGE JOURNAL, XLIX, No. 2, February 1965, 102.

10. Ned Davison, "Lengua o Literatura?" HISPANIA, XLIX, No. 2, May 1966, 300-302.
11. Algernon Coleman, THE TEACHING OF MODERN FOREIGN LANGUAGES IN THE UNITED STATES. New York: Macmillan Company, 1929, 169 ff.
12. Robert F. Roeming, "Traditional!" THE MODERN LANGUAGE JOURNAL, XLVIII, No. 2, February 1964, 97.
13. Edward T. Heise, "Let's Talk Sense About Language Teaching." THE FRENCH REVIEW, XXV, No. 2, December 1961, 176-184.
14. Edmond Meras, "An Evaluation of Audiolingual Methods." BULLETIN OF THE KANSAS MODERN LANGUAGE ASSOCIATION, XL, No. 5, May 1966, 2-5.
15. T. Earle Hamilton, "The Audio-Lingual Method in the University: Fad or Panacea?" HISPANIA, XLIX, No. 3, September 1966, 434-440.
16. A. F. Gronberg, "A Teacher Looks at the Audio-Lingual Approach." BULLETIN OF THE COUNCIL FOR BASIC EDUCATION, X, No. 1, September 1965.
17. Venita Booth, "Cry Against the 'New Key'." THE TEXAS OUTLOOK, XLVIII, No. 5, 26-27.
18. Thomas R. Palfrey, "How Far Off Key Is the New Key?" TEACHING OF MODERN FOREIGN LANGUAGES IN SECONDARY SCHOOLS, Bureau of Educational Research and Services, Arizona State University, August 1965, 29-35.
19. Venita Booth, Op. Cit., 27.
20. Richard Barrutia, "Some Misconceptions About the Fundamental Skills Method." HISPANIA, XLIX, No. 3, September 1966, 443.
21. Calvin Andre Claudel, "Parroting and Progressive French Teaching." THE FRENCH REVIEW, XXXIX, No. 1, October 1965, 120-123.
22. Kenneth A. Lester, "Audio-Visual Programs in France." THE FRENCH REVIEW, XL, No. 2, November 1966, 277-283.
23. Calvin Andre Claudel, "Enseignement et repetition." L'ENSEIGNEMENT DU FRANCAIS AUX ETRANGERS, BULLETIN PEDAGOGIQUE MENSUEL, edite par l'Ecole Pratique de l'Alliance Francaise, XVII, No. 144, December 1964, 2.
24. Francisco Ugarte, GRAMÁTICA ESPAÑOLA DE REPASO. New York: The Odyssey Press, Inc., 1960.
25. Calvin Claudel, "Teaching Junior High-School Spanish." LOUISIANA SCHOOLS, XXXVII, No. 8, April 1960, 20, 35-36.
26. Ibid., p. 36.
27. Germaine Brée, "The Double Responsibility of the Foreign Language Teacher: Proficiency in the Language and Mastery of the Literature and Culture." PMLA, LXXVIII, No. 2, May 1963, 8.
28. Edmond Meras, Op. Cit., 4.
29. Dwight L. Bolinger, et. al., MODERN SPANISH, A Project of the MLA. New York: Harcourt, Brace & World, 1960.
30. Edmond Meras, Op. Cit., 4.
31. Rosalyn O'Cherony, "FLES Status and Teacher Preparation." HISPANIA, XLIX, No. 1, March 1966, 121-125.
32. F. Andre Paquette, "Guidelines for Teacher Education Programs in Modern Languages: An Exposition." THE MODERN LANGUAGE JOURNAL, L, No. 6, October 1966, 323-425.

33. George E. Smith, "An Experiment in Statewide Development: The Indiana Language Program." THE FLORIDA FL REPORTER, Spring 1966.
34. Robert G. Mead, Jr., "Literature and Politics: Our Image and Our Policy in Latin America." HISPANIA, XLIX, No. 2, May 1966, 307.
35. Vicenzo Cioffari, *Op. Cit.*, 304.
36. Edmond Meras, *Op. Cit.*, 4.
37. Wilga M. Rivers, THE PSYCHOLOGIST AND THE FOREIGN LANGUAGE TEACHER. Chicago: The University of Chicago Press, 1964, v.
38. J. Michael Moore, "Is It Time To Take Stock?" THE MODERN LANGUAGE JOURNAL, L, No. 5, May 1966, 271.
39. Calvin Andre Claudel, "Parroting and Progressive French Teaching," 122.

Selected Bibliography

BOOKS

Bolinger, Dwight L., *et al.*, MODERN SPANISH, A Project of the Modern Language Association. New York: Harcourt, Brace & World, 1960. This is a typical audio-lingual text with dialogues in translation to be memorized and with the repetitious drills. At the present time, the validity of this method is being questioned.

Coleman, Algernon, THE TEACHING OF MODERN FOREIGN LANGUAGES IN THE UNITED STATES. New York: Macmillan Co., 1929. This volume by the late Professor Coleman is the much-disputed "Coleman Report," and stresses the need for a reading knowledge only in the study of a foreign language.

De Vitis, M. A., A SPANISH GRAMMAR FOR BEGINNERS. New York: Allyn and Bacon, 1915. This is an example of an early good traditional Spanish text used in high school.

Richards, I. A., SPANISH THROUGH PICTURES, Book I. New York: Washington Square Press, Inc., (22nd printing) 1965. This is an elementary visual Spanish text, useful for a beginning course.

Rivers, Wilga M., THE PSYCHOLOGIST AND THE FOREIGN-LANGUAGE TEACHER. Chicago: The University of Chicago Press, 1964.

Ugarte, Francisco, GRAMATICA ESPANOLA DE REPASO. New York: The Odyssey Press, Inc., 1960. This is a Spanish review grammar, written in Spanish, and is useful for a class that has already had a year or so of background.

ARTICLES

Barrutia, Richard, "Some Misconceptions About the Fundamental Skills Method." HISPANIA, XLIX, No. 3, September 1966, 440-446. This article is by an apologist for the audio-lingual method who fails to prove his points and cites several opponents to his discredit.

Bazan, Beverly Moen, "The Danger of Assumption Without Proof." THE MODERN LANGUAGE JOURNAL, XLVIII, No. 6, October 1964, 338-346. This writer questions claims of mechanistic methods.

Booth, Venita, "Cry Against the 'New Key'." THE TEXAS OUTLOOK, XLVIII, No. 5, 26-27. This article is by a veteran French teacher who makes a stinging and telling criticism of the audiolingual method.

Cioffari, Vicenzo, "The Role of the Modern Foreign Languages in Our Schools." THE MODERN LANGUAGE JOURNAL, XL, No. 6, October 1956, 302-306. This article discusses the importance of foreign languages not only for literature but for international relations.

Claudel, Calvin Andre, "Parroting and Progressive French Teaching." THE FRENCH REVIEW, XXXIX, No. 1, October 1965, 120 to 123. In discussing French teaching, this article tells about the three methods of teaching a foreign language: 1) the traditional, 2) the audiolingual, and 3) the better audiovisual.

Heise, Edward T., "Let's Talk Sense About Language Teaching." THE FRENCH REVIEW, Vol. XXV, No. 2, December 1961, 176-184. This excellent article by a traditionalist warns about our increasingly doctrinaire methods in foreign language teaching.

Joyaux, Georges J., "Foreign Languages and the Humanities." THE MODERN LANGUAGE JOURNAL, XLIX, No. 2, February 1965, 102-105. This writer discusses the importance of languages in relation to the humanities.

Leavitt, Sturgis E., "The Teaching of Spanish in the United States." HISPANIA, XLIV, No. 4, December 1961, 591-625. A detailed history of the teaching of Spanish in the United States from early times to the present.

Lester, Kenneth A., "Audio-visual Programs in France." THE FRENCH REVIEW, XL, No. 2, November 1966, 277-283. This article is about the fine work of the French government in French language teaching, especially that of the Alliance Française in the direct audio-visual method.

Mead, Robert G., Jr., "Literature and Politics: Our Image and Our Policy in Latin America." HISPANIA, XLIX, No. 2, May 1966, 302-307. An excellent article tells about our image in Latin America from the past to the present in both literature and politics. It also stresses the important role of the Spanish teacher in promoting good relations.

Meras, Edmond, "An Evaluation of Audiolingual Methods." BULLETIN OF THE KANSAS MODERN LANGUAGE ASSOCIATION, XL, No. 5, May 1966, 2-5. A fine article which shows the numerous faults of the audio-lingual method suggests a shift to the direct audio-visual method, which existed in the past.

144

The Changing Aspects of Teaching French

GENEVIEVE DELATTRE

University of California, Santa Barbara

LET US IMAGINE for a moment that we are back in the years immediately preceding World War II and that we are investigating the standard procedures of teaching French in the United States. In classroom after classroom, whether in colleges or in secondary schools, we will find students engaged in various activities all of which are centered around the study of French as a written language, oddly devoid of any meaning unless it is translated into English. Its morphology is taught as essentially orthographic changes. Thus the students learn that to form the plural of nouns one adds an -*s*: *table/tables, livre/livres,* etc.; that regular adjectives form their feminine by adding an -*e* to the masculine: *joli/jolie, grand/grande, vert/verte;* that possessive adjectives of the first person singular have three forms: masculine *mon,* feminine *ma,* plural *mes.* Fill-in sentences in which an English word is provided as a cue to the French form needed are the extent of the students' required skill in manipulating French morphology. French syntax is taught through the study of intricate rules which one tries to apply by translating strange English sentences into French. Ex.: What do you think of the house the rooms of which we saw?

Learning vocabulary means identifying the written form of a word and attaching to it the lexical content of a corresponding English word. Reading and writing are the immediate goals of most French classes, but one should specify that both reading and writing are in final analysis sheer translation into or from English. We will find few attempts on the part of the teacher to go beyond this limited goal. Of course, the phonology of French must be taught, so that the students can read aloud what is printed in their textbook or what they have just written themselves. But phonology is often equated with spelling. One learns on the first day that French has six vowels: *a, e, i, o, u, y*. If the sound system of French is presented, English again is used as a point of reference: *a* as in *cat, o* as in *go, ã* as in *sank,* and no one seems too concerned about the obvious and uninhibited transfer of English speech habits to the French language. Suprasegmental features are totally ignored. Although we may find many different texts in use, by far the most popular one, and also the best for this grammar-translation-oriented teaching, is Fraser and Squair, in its various subsequent editions.[1]

I. Toward the Audio-Lingual Method

It would be unfair to imply that no classrooms could be found where French was used as an oral means of communication. Among those who had themselves a good command of spoken French, many of the Fraser and Squair era teachers heroically tried to convey their skill to their students. But their textbooks were a far more formidable obstacle to any success than the somewhat mythical lack of aptitude for foreign languages traditionally attributed to the American student. The interference of English at all levels of language learning was constantly reinforced rather than checked by the methodology used in textbooks. Teaching one to speak French was then a difficult task, while teaching one to translate French into English or vice versa was relatively easy. Syntax and morphology are certainly simpler in French than in German, for instance, and as one moves away from everyday style toward the expression of more abstract ideas, cognates become more and more frequent and thus facilitate translation into English.

The ASTP

When the sudden demands of the United States Armed Forces for language-trained personnel and their consequent organization of ASTP shook up the dormant world of foreign language teaching, French of course played a prominent part in the new program. In 1943 the publication of the Army manual for French,[2] Hall's *Spoken French,* offered a long-awaited model for materials aimed at teaching the spoken language effectively. Slowly, during the next decade, the French teaching profession began to awaken. The leadership came mostly from the universities and the colleges. In secondary schools, lack of adequately trained teachers maintained the teaching of French at a very low level of oral proficiency, and only in 1958, when the federal government finally directed its attention toward the retraining of language teachers, does one perceive any noticeable changes in teaching techniques in secondary schools.

Two Significant Experiments

Among the very early experiments undertaken by college teachers of French in an attempt to improve their teaching techniques, two appear, from a twenty-year distance, as clearly pointing the way to what has become now common procedure. In 1941, at Green Mountain Junior College in Poultney, Vermont, Frederick Eddy inaugurated what can be considered the first language laboratory by sending his students (1st, 2nd, and 3rd year) after class to a "language studio" where they could practice their listening and speaking skills as much as they needed to (a minimum of fifteen minutes a day being required for first-year students). The instructor or a qualified student assistant was present to help the students with their pronunciation or encourage them to speak. Reading material from the textbook was recorded on discs and served as models for correct pronunciation. By offering intensive individual drilling in aural comprehension and speaking, the studio allowed the instructor to devote more classroom time to reading and writing, to no detriment of the oral skills.[3]

In 1944-1945, a visitor to a University of Oklahoma's French class would have been greatly surprised. Students had no books and were learning French entirely by ear, in a systematic fashion very remote from what is known as the "direct method." The teaching material, composed by the instructor for the occasion, consisted of oral drills (not dialogues as was the case with the Army materials) based on the "echelon" technique, that is, successive transformation of sentences by substitution and/or addition.

Ex.: Avez-vous mangé?
———— les pommes?
———————— qui étaient là?
———————————— sur la table?

147

Students were introduced first to French phonology, then to French grammar, in carefully devised steps which allowed a progressive build-up of the essentials of sentence structure in French. They acquired a genuinely new set of speech habits, phonological (including those pertaining to supra-segmental features), grammatical (with minimum interference from English) and psychological (direct association between sound and meaning bypassed translation into or from English). Class time was divided between practice of new material and transfer of well-learned material into new situations to encourage students' creativity. In a small room equipped with a single phonograph, students did their daily assignments. They listened and responded to drills recorded each day by their instructor on a disc. After one semester of strictly aural-oral training, the twenty students who had volunteered for this experimental section were, in the course of the second semester, progressively led into the textbook used by the other more conservative sections of French I and finally not only caught up but surpassed the traditional group in reading and writing ability. In aural comprehension and speaking, they remained far superior and were lagging only in spelling.[4]

It was an interesting experiment, but an isolated one. The experimenter himself didn't pursue the matter much further. His department was not interested and he was engaged in other absorbing research. He never polished his material, never used it again himself, except for the initial phase of introduction to French speech habits (three weeks' work), which were later published and are still widely used throughout the country.[5] When reported in the *French Review,* however, his experiment aroused some scattered interest, and several colleagues expressed the wish to try the same teaching technique with their students. At the University of Texas, for instance, Professor Ernest Haden, using the Oklahoma material, did some further experimenting with the aural-oral method and later developed similar material for Spanish.

The Conversational Method

After 1946, we will find more and more classes where French is spoken, for the simple reason that those who are willing to teach French with more modern techniques now have a textbook available: Harris and Lévêque's *Conversational French for Beginners*.[6] The lasting success of that book, indicated by its presently undergoing a fifth revision, can best be explained by its strict adherence to the "Army method" of teaching a language through memorization of basic dialogues. Even its oblong format was directly inspired by the Army manuals. Moreover, its authors had made a real effort to reject unnecessary complexities and refinements of grammatical points in favor of the more basic aspects of the French language. Each lesson consisted of a conversation, the equivalent of which was given in English on the opposite page. Grammatical explanations were kept to a minimum, and given in separate units after students had practiced the rules through the conversations. Extensive use of directed dialogue (*Demandez à . . . Dites que . . .*) permitted active oral practice beyond the memorized conversation. In contrast to most textbooks, Harris and Lévêque, because of its simplicity, could be used by beginners either in high school or in college.

Problems Particular to the Teaching of French

In this evolution from a method of teaching oriented mainly toward grammar and translation to a method placing more and more importance on the oral mastery of the language, the teacher of French found himself faced with more serious problems than his colleagues teaching any other language. These problems refer essentially to pronunciation and arise from two important factors. First, since French and English habits of articulation and prosody are at the two opposite ends of the spectrum among world languages, very strong interferences arise. Secondly, the discrepancy in French between the spoken language and its graphic representation is such that, unless solid articulatory habits are already established, reading will lead the student to a series of false interpretations. We have all seen our students repeat model sentences perfectly one day, and the next day return to class with a disastrous pronunciation because of having substituted, while studying at home, the visual image to the aural memory. This misleading character of spelling in French applies to grammar also. The actual grammatical structure of the language is often very different from what it appears to be. Today a teacher of French faced with such problems has at his disposal infinitely more resources than his colleague of the forties or even

149

of the fifties. The implementation of the National Defense Education Act has done much to coordinate and stimulate individual efforts in all areas relevant to language teaching. I will review here only research relevant to the teaching of French, then I propose to examine the materials presently available to high school and college teachers of French and see how new data and techniques can be applied to the classroom.

II. THE CONTRIBUTION OF RESEARCH TO THE TEACHING OF FRENCH PHONETICS RESEARCH

Although research in French phonetics has a respectable history, for a long time the tools were lacking which would permit an objective and precise analysis of the articulatory and acoustical characteristics of a language and which would facilitate comparison with those of another language. These tools now exist. The spectrograph permits the acoustical analysis of speech; the speech synthesizer permits the systematic manipulation of speech components and therefore the precise study of various "accents"; the improved motion picture x-ray machine permits the filming of the vocal organs in action. It is in combining these different research techniques that Pierre Delattre undertook his comparative studies of English, French, German, and Spanish.[7] Since it is no longer impressionistic but totally objective, the comparison of French and English characteristics permits the definite establishment of the list of phonological interferences which will strongly influence American students when learning French. The importance of these interferences cannot be stressed enough. They can blur the speech of the second language phonetically and make it unintelligible, as, for instance, in the sentence *filmez la salle* heard as *fiume la sau* because of the American habit of tongue backing and retroflexing of the tip in the articulation of final or postvocalic *l*. They can also affect the speech phonemically, thus producing a different meaning than the one intended: *ce bonnet* is pronounced *ce bon nez*, because, vocalic nasality not being distinctive in English (there are no meaningful contrasts such as *mais-main* /me/mẽ/, *bas-banc* /ba/bã/), the American student tends to spread the nasality of the consonant to the preceding vowel. *C'est vu* is heard as *c'est vous*, *je veux un dollar* as *je vaux un dollar*, *ils veulent un dollar* as *ils volent un dollar* because in English lip rounding is strongly associated with tongue backing while the vowels /y/, /ø/, and /œ/ in French are at once rounded and fronted. New phonetic research instruments and the precision which they permit have thus clarified many pronunciation problems for the teacher of French. The contrast between French articulatory tenseness and American laxness can now be observed on motion pictures of comparable sentences uttered by natives of France and the U.S. (ex.: *Ces bateaux sont égaux et sont beaux* vs. *They can tow where they go for the bow*). The facial expressions (a front and profile view were filmed simultaneously) show striking muscular contraction during the articulation of the French sentence and no less striking muscular laxness for the English one.[7a] An animated cartoon, made after x-ray films, shows in slow motion the articulation of the /r/ in French, Spanish, and American-English. A minute study of hundreds of intonation patterns extracted from spontaneous utterances by French and American natives has led to a much better understanding of the structure and function of intonation in both languages, and should encourage teachers of French to pay much closer attention to intonation, both in their modeling of sentences for students' imitation and in the students' utterances.[8] This is an area of the language where fancy has reigned too long. Commercial recordings made by natives totally ignorant of the structure of their own language are mostly responsible for the erroneous intonation patterns which our students learn.

The contribution of structural linguistics to the teaching of languages, and in particular to the perfectioning of audio-lingual techniques, is a phenomenon which obviously does not concern only French. But in French more than in the other languages, the notions of phonemes, morphemes, morphophonemes, and tagmemes show how much the language in its oral reality differs from the image which traditional grammar had until now presented. If the linguists who are grappling with a structural analysis of French are still few in number, one must rejoice in the fact that the research has been done by people who are directly interested in teaching techniques and who thus have made the practical application of their work easier.

Structural Analysis

The first structural phonological study of French was made

by Georges Gougenheim back in 1935.[9] It contained a detailed study of all the phonemic oppositions which twenty-five years later would replace the pronunciation exercises of isolated sounds in French classes. In his *Système grammatical de la langue française* (1939),[10] Gougenheim analyzed the morphology of spoken French as opposed to its orthographic forms and analyzed syntax by morphemic oppositions. Robert Hall Jr.'s *Structural Sketch of French* (1948)[11] covers phonology, morphology, and syntax, and is the first attempt by an American structuralist to apply his technique of analysis to the French language. A more complete and more up-to-date structural grammar of French is currently being written by Jean Dubois, whose research promises to be very fruitful. His first volume, already published, is devoted exclusively to the structure of nouns and pronouns, and offers valuable information for the teachers interested in applied linguistics, especially those who are engaged in the preparation of instructional materials.[12] A recent article in *Le Français Moderne* by the same author,[13] on French verbs, gives a brilliant example of what new linguistic research in French morphology can produce. It is found that verbs are irregular only when traditional criteria, mostly historical or graphic, are applied. Stems rather than endings explain the structure of verbal forms, and by using criteria of basic oppositions between a few radical forms, Dubois arrives at a classification into seven conjugations, with no irregular verbs left out. The conclusion of his article opens the door to transformation grammar by hinting that further study might lead to the uncovering of one model from which all morphosyntactic variations would stem.

It was left to Albert Valdman, himself a professor of French actively engaged in linguistic research, to bring the results of structural linguistics research down from the esoteric realm of linguistic science to the level of understanding by French teachers. His original contribution has been to link theory and practice, and the guide which he prepared under the general editorship of Simon Belasco, for use in NDEA Institutes, is an excellent presentation of how structural analysis applies to the teaching of French.[14] Exercises in minimal pairs, for instance, train the students in the aural discrimination of the phonemic contrasts typical of French as opposed to English and in their accurate reproduction.

Structural analysis has also shown how liaison, a phenomenon unique to French, makes phonology, morphology and syntax closely interdependent. Pronunciation cannot be taught separately from the forms and mechanisms of grammatical structure any more than grammar can be understood outside of its oral realization. The immediately following phonemic environment (consonant, vowel or pause) and the syntactic relationship between words determine in French whether there is a liaison or not. For example, while traditional grammar classified French determiners according to their gender and number inflections as shown in their orthographic transcriptions (*il/ils, le/la/les, mon/mes*), structural analysis, by leaving morphemes in their phonemic and syntactic environment and taking into account the variations caused by liaison, arrives at the only classification true to reality. This does not necessarily multiply the number of forms, since very often an orthographic variation will have no corresponding phonemic variation (*il parle/ils parlent—/il parl/ il parl/*), or a phonemic variation will have no corresponding orthographic variation (*ils sont/ils ont—*/il sõ/il zõ/). When teaching French, then, it is evident that one must distinguish very clearly between the actual structure of the language, to be drilled orally, and its written representation, to be learned through memorization of spelling. Knowing, for instance, that the possessive pronoun of the first person has five forms and not three as stated in traditional grammars, the teacher can systematically drill his students in these five forms, first separately, then mixing them. His drills will be based on the contrasts:

/mõ/ plus masc. noun beginning with a consonant: *mon livre*

singular /ma/ plus fem. noun beginning with a consonant: *ma soeur*

/mõn/ plus masc. or fem. noun beginning with a vowel: *mon oncle; mon école*

/me/ plus masc. or fem. noun beginning with a consonant: *mes disques; mes robes.*

/mez/ plus masc. or fem. noun beginning with a vowel: *mes amis; mes oranges*

Let us give one or two more examples of the new teaching approach brought about by structural linguistics. While students

153

traditionally learned that the plural of regular nouns was formed by adding an -s, the oral realization of *l'élève/les élèves, le professeur/les professeurs, les enfants/les petits enfants* makes it clear that the plural mark in French is more often attached to the determiner than to the noun itself (here, [le] or [lez]). Likewise, when grammars prescribe the addition of an "e" to the masculine form as the mark of a feminine adjective, only the spelling is considered. Reality is much more complex, since an adjective such as "petit," for example, has four forms for the masculine singular alone: [pəti] as in *quel petit garçon!*, [pti] as in *un petit garçon*, [pətit] as in *quel petit homme* and [ptit] as in *un petit homme*, each one depending on a particular phonemic environment. The phenomenon of liaison combines here with that of the unstable *e*, another unique feature of French completely neglected by traditional teaching. Like liaison, unstable *e* affects morphology: *Jacques le prend/Je le prends*—[zakləprã/zəlprã]. Many of the problems which have always been the stumbling-block of students of French can now be clarified and solved. By establishing model structures which could then serve as a point of departure for teaching, the so-called grammatical irregularities disappear. For instance, an adjective of the type *blanc/blanche* will no longer be an exception once it is established that adjectives in French divide themselves into two structures: the type *joli/jolie*, without variations between the masculine and the feminine; and the type *vert/verte*, where the masculine equals the feminine without the final consonant. If the morphological variations due to the presence in French of an unstable phonological element (liaison and unstable *e*, called sandhi variations in linguistics) were of no interest to the teacher as long as only the written language was taught, they become very important when the teaching of oral skills becomes part of the curriculum.

In the area of syntax, linguistic research is also of interest to the teacher of French, since it permits him to better define the essential structures of French and their mechanisms (either by the notion of tagmeme or by that of transformation) and to understand the points of interference with English. If the contrastive study on the phonological level is important, as I have shown, it is much more so on the syntactical level. Only interference points need to be carefully drilled, since elsewhere the two languages function identically. It is in this perspective of contrastive structural analysis of English and French that the book by Robert Politzer, *An Introduction to Applied Linguistics: Teaching French*[15] was written, as well as the one by Valdman already mentioned. Neither of these authors attempts to be exhaustive, for their goal is, above all, of a practical nature. At present, there is no thorough contrastive structural study of English and French. But this need will soon be filled since the Center for Applied Linguistics has entrusted André Martinet with the task of doing the French volumes for their Contrastive Structure Series.

The Français Fondamental

In the domain of vocabulary study, French is ahead of the other languages, thanks to the pioneer investigation of word frequency in spoken French conducted in France by a team of researchers under the direction of Georges Gougenheim. Out of a total of 8,000 different words extracted from taped conversations, a frequency list was established. The *français fondamental,* (*1er degré*), with its 1,500 words, is the result of this objective study.[16] It is of great value to French teaching and should serve as a point of departure for all materials written for beginners.

Research on Culture

We cannot close this brief survey of recent research relevant to the teaching of French without mentioning the work now in progress by Howard Nostrand on cultural patterns. When language teaching, in the last decade, moved away from the old classical definition of culture (opposing barbarianism to civilization) to embrace that of anthropology (a way of life to be described objectively), French teachers were in an awkward position, for the language they were teaching was that of a "cultured" country par excellence, in the old sense of the word, and many of them revolted at the thought that, for instance, French eating or mating habits were to replace, in their teaching, France's contributions as a nation to the world of ideas. A more careful analysis of culture was urgently needed, and still is, in order to extract, if possible, patterns which, when put together, all contribute in the making of a particular culture as opposed to another. Then the dichotomy between trivial and refined aspects of culture will be resolved. This is what Howard Nostrand is trying to do.[17]

We have indicated here only the research which has, or can have, a direct application to the teaching of French. If one adds to it all the research dealing with language learning in general, especially that done by psychologists, it is clear that theoretically the teacher of French is better equipped today than twenty years ago.

The big question remains that of transferring the theoretical information to the classroom situation. This problem has two facets: on the one hand the diffusion of information and the training of teachers, on the other the availability of adequate instructional materials. NDEA Institutes, the MLA Foreign Language Program, professional reviews have done, and are doing, much for keeping teachers in contact with methods and new research. The availability of adequate instructional materials is crucial.

III. INSTRUCTION AT THE HIGH SCHOOL LEVEL

The pressure brought about by NDEA on secondary schools for a new orientation of their language programs made this problem most urgent at the high school level. Underneath the semblance of unity of purpose and techniques (every school now has a language laboratory, every French teacher tries, or at least knows he should try, to teach his students how to understand and speak French) still lies considerable confusion. Basic principles are not fully understood; teaching conditions (overcrowded classrooms, overloaded teachers) run contrary to the demands of audio-lingual teaching; adoption of materials is too often dictated by outside pressures (NDEA Institutes at best, publishers' representatives at worst), rather than by a wholehearted adherence on the part of the teacher to the main features of the materials chosen. Again, this is not a problem peculiar to French. Nor, I fear, are the problems attached to the development of new materials.

Requirements for Good Materials

It is not too difficult to spell out the qualifications for good materials:

1. They should be based on a scientific study of frequency of

156

words and grammatical structures in educated everyday French speech.

2. They should be well structured, so as to afford continuity of learning throughout the French curriculum with immediate and ultimate goals well defined. No abrupt change of approach or method should occur between level one and two, for instance.

3. They should present the French language in its reality, first as it functions orally (taking into consideration the phonological and grammatical traits specific to French as opposed to English), then as it appears in its graphic representation.

4. They should provide for constant integration of new and familiar material, so as to build on solid ground.

5. They should provide for both processes of language learning: imitation and creativity.

6. They should plunge the learner into the socio-cultural context of a French native of his own age. Language alone is not sufficient; modern visual aids (slides, filmstrips or films) can offer invaluable help.

So far, none of the materials presently available on the market to high school teachers will fulfill all of these six very basic requirements, for the simple reason that the passing of NDEA made their production urgent, and that publishers, rushing to the new, very competitive market, could do no better than use what individual initiative here and there had produced. Scientific construction of materials would require a pooling of experts (theorists and practitioners), which time and money factors make it very difficult to achieve.

A-LM

When NDEA Institutes required an immediate use of some model audio-lingual material, the already existing "Glastonbury material" was officially chosen, quickly polished and expanded, and it was distributed as A-LM (thus creating confusion beneficial only to the publisher between the audio-lingual method and a particular set of materials). The A-LM French series[18] is similar to the Spanish or the German one, so similar that one wonders if it actually takes into account the specific features of the French language and culture. If given the test of our six basic requirements as stated above, it will fail on No. 1 (vocabulary is chosen at random; random use of structures in the dialogues call for a

157

very high rate of waste since few of these structures can be used as basic sentences for drills); on No. 2 (level one is over-simplified, level two abruptly takes the student into a new approach of intricate basic sentences and long reading passages); on No. 5 (on level one at least, transfer of memorized material to creative expression is practically nonexistent and left to the imagination of the teacher who often neglects it); and on No. 6 (cultural content of level one is very poor and is strictly limited to language per se, cut off from its live gestural and visual environment). Its indisputable merits, and they are not negligible, lie in its skillful use of pattern drills based on structural analysis, its principle of keeping throughout level one aural comprehension and speaking ahead of reading and writing, and on its deliberate reduction, also on level one, of quantity for the benefit of quality. Because of A-LM's initially favored position as government sponsored materials, and its wide use for demonstration purposes in NDEA Institutes, we can safely attach its name to the typical high school French class of the present time.

Ecouter et Parler

Other materials are of course available. I will dismiss here the face-lifting of traditional textbooks. Adding "audio-lingual" chapters to matter already far too substantial to be digested can hardly be an improvement. The *Ecouter et Parler* series, composed by imaginative teachers with the right goal in mind but with a definite lack of technical knowledge, exclusively relies, on level one, on dialogue memorization technique (not far from Harris and Leveque's original approach).[19] Drills are only of the simple substitution type (one slot), and dialogue content is reshuffled into various new dialogues with the commendable goal of encouraging creativity. But the basic tools for language creativity are missing. If applied the test of our six requirements, the *Ecouter et Parler* materials would pass only Nos. 4 and 5. Its cultural content at level one is null. There is no articulation between the technique of level one and that of level two.

Observing an *A-LM* or *Ecouter et Parler* class, we will see students speak French, mostly repeating what they have memorized, but also, when teaching is good, responding spontaneously in French to French aural stimuli. Their pronunciation will of course largely reflect that of the teacher, even when tapes are used, but it can be very good. The most striking weakness to the outside observer will be the total absence (except for a few noble efforts on the part of the teacher to act out what he says) of situational context. Therefore, meaning remains essentially dependent on English translation (in the textbooks, dialogues are translated into English). Since most teachers nowadays avoid constant reference to English for meaning, learning French depends heavily on abstract memorization and manipulation of sound combinations too often devoid of meaning, because none of the nonlinguistic cues on which we all rely heavily in real life are present. It is as if children were learning their native tongue on the telephone.

Teaching with Films

While this problem seems to have been ignored by the official audio-lingual propagandists in the United States, it has attracted the attention of others. Films have been used for quite some time as supplementary material. They bring French culture into the classroom in a much livelier way than talks by the teacher. However, the idea of developing a curriculum entirely based on the use of films is fairly new. Many high school teachers have now adopted this technique and use the *Je parle français* films.[20] Each lesson is presented first by viewing a film and learning how to comprehend its dialogue. The situation comes alive, students can identify themselves with the people on the screen and share their daily experiences in an authentic French cultural context (filming was done on location with French native speakers, most of whom are professional actors). This is of course extremely attractive to teenagers and radically changes the classroom atmosphere. Translation is not needed because language operates in its normal live context, and what is not fully understood at first becomes clearer and clearer after repeated viewing of the film. Constant reappearance of previously learned material (each lesson has but a few new structures or words) creates a solid frame of reference for new material, providing at the same time an opportunity for overlearning. There are no drills based on a systematic manipulation of structures. Rather, drilling is done entirely by stimulus and response in context, having students react automatically but meaningfully in French to a French utterance. Memorization and imitation play an important part indeed in such a method, but more unconsciously than consciously. This is the closest approximation possible, in a classroom, of the learning conditions created by direct immersion into a native French environment. At close examination, the teaching-through-films technique, as it is applied in *Je parle français*, is closer to our ideal materials than one might think. It would rate very high on Nos. 2, 4, 5, and 6. As for No. 3 (distinction between spoken French and its graphic representation), it does not ignore it but approaches the problem in a global manner, without isolating each feature. Nothing is read or written which has not been solidly acquired orally first, and students can easily do one whole year of French without books. Writing then becomes mostly a matter of spelling, for the oral fluency in the use of structures and vocabulary remains intact when students write. They may not know the grammar abstractly, but I have never seen students make fewer mistakes in speaking or writing than those trained with *Je parle français*. Since it never uses translation to promote understanding, this method probably comes closer than any other to developing bilingualism.

The Saint-Cloud Method

Comparable to *Je parle français* in the importance given to visual aids and in the basic orientation of the course toward spontaneous response in French to certain situational cues, *Voix et Images de France* was developed by the CREDIF (Centre de Recherche et d'Etude pour la Diffusion du Français) at Saint-Cloud, France.[21] Commissioned by the Ministry of Education and assigned to a team of experts, it was constructed with great care and with no commercial profit in mind. Each lesson consists of a dialogue, recorded on tape for its presentation in class to the students, accompanied by a cleverly illustrated filmstrip, (one picture to one sentence). The students listen to the dialogue while they watch the filmstrip. The teacher intervenes only for explanation (by reference to previously learned items) of new words not made directly intelligible by the illustrations. Structural drilling takes the form of a dialogue strictly built for the learning of a few particular points of grammar. A filmstrip accompanies this dialogue also. Pronunciation is learned in context only (with another short dialogue built around phonemic contrasts). Transfer from dialogue to personal expression is done by question-answer-type exercises. As with *Je parle français*, no translation from or into English is ever necessary. Since this set of materials was developed in France for foreign students originating from many different countries, it cannot take into account interferences between French and one particular language. This is no doubt a shortcoming. Principles of structural analysis are not applied systematically either, and the absence of pattern drills is often regretted. On the other hand, its vocabulary is much more meaningful than in any of the other materials because it is that of the *Français Fondamental*. It is also based on a frequency study of structures in everyday French. The imagination used in providing visual cues to meaning is praiseworthy, and keeps the interest of the students constantly alive. The cultural content of the dialogues is quite rich, less spectacular maybe than in *Je parle français* (where one can visit all famous places in France without leaving the classroom) but more subtle because all small aspects of everyday life are presented in a referential context, authentically French. Reading and writing is not neglected, students have workbooks, but the primacy of the oral skills at the beginning is strictly observed, with a recommended pre-reading period of at least sixty contact hours.

Neither *Je parle français* nor *Voix et Images de France* is perfect, but both are the right answer to one of the very important learning problems of the audio-lingual method: if French is read before habits are well established, it engenders immediate phonological distortions. But students find it very difficult to learn entirely by ear, and visual and auditory memory can effectively reinforce each other. Books can remain closed when visual images which recreate for the learner the real context in which language communication takes place permit direct association between sound and meaning. Most French courses now use tapes in class or in the language laboratory. Films or filmstrips should be added. The classroom will come alive, memorization will concentrate on the essential, on the structure of the language, and not on the unimportant sequence of the lines of a dialogue.

IV. INSTRUCTION AT THE UNIVERSITY LEVEL

Although materials which would score perfectly on our basic six requirements cannot be found yet, there is no reason for pessimism. The new orientation of French classes in high school toward a mastery of the four skills and an understanding of French culture already has its repercussions. Freshmen entering colleges and universities are putting increasing pressure on French departments to open their classroom doors to the spoken language. For, alas, the presence of many professors of French among the leaders in the field of research and experimentation in foreign language teaching is not clearly reflected in the quality of teaching offered by college or university French departments. Free from direct outside pressures such as was exerted on high schools by the implementation of NDEA, French departments, in the organization of their lower division courses, depend entirely on the initiative of their own faculty. For various reasons often far remote from actual preference of one method or another, conservatism seems more frequent than reformism.

This slowness of university French classes to benefit from new research and techniques is clearly indicated by the slowness with which genuine audio-lingual textbooks have appeared on the market. Until very recently, French instructors who wanted to teach by the audio-lingual approach had either to write their own materials or to adapt a traditional textbook. Both enterprises require much time and expertness. Such experimental materials, often used for several years locally in mimeographed form, are now being published. The new competitive spirit of publishers in producing audio-lingual College French textbooks is the best evidence of the belated but welcome interest of French departments at large in more modern materials and techniques. If we exclude such materials as *Je parle français* or *Voix et Images de France,* which both can be used at the college level, new college textbooks are more basically similar to one another than the high school materials. They all teach phonology by phonemic contrasts (at least partially) and intensive oral practice, they all depend heavily on pattern practice stemming from a dialogue, and they all try to approach grammar structurally, by more or less skillful analysis of its mechanisms as they appear in the spoken language. Although, on the whole, they provide the French instructor with an excellent tool for teaching his students audio-lingually, some problems remain to be solved. That of time, for instance. The massiveness of most of the new textbooks (500 or 600 pages) forces the user, even if his program combines maximum classroom and laboratory practice, to an unpleasant choice between building solid linguistic foundations and finishing the book. The problem of content is also critical. Pattern practice alone does not seem a very efficient means of convincing a college student that language is culture. His motivation depends on his interest which in turn depends on his intellectual stimulation. French culture has much to offer. The author of an audio-lingual textbook is faced, then, with a serious dilemma: Should dialogues be linguistic beachheads, scientifically calculated to introduce certain phonemic or grammatical structures only, at the expense of cultural content? or should they be cultural beachheads so written as to have maximum cultural content and naturalness at the expense of linguistic rigor?

Programmed Learning

Now that French departments at universities are slowly converting to teaching French in the new key and would need a lower student-teacher ratio in order to maintain small sections, where students could have maximum oral practice, the enormous influx of students, especially in state universities, and the shortage of qualified instructors call for changes in the opposite direction. Universities are now educating the masses. Language departments caught in these contradictory trends can either convince their administrations that foreign languages deserve preferential treatment and solve the staffing problem by hiring teaching assistants or decide to change drastically the traditional teaching environment (one class to one teacher) and fully exploit the possibilities of self-instruction offered by the language laboratory. This latter solution means resorting to programmed learning and requires courage, conviction, imagination, expertness, time, and money. Programmed learning in French is still in its exploratory phase, but a few significant experiments have already been done.

F. Rand Morton, at the University of Michigan, wrote a programmed course for French similar to his pilot Spanish Course (ALLP series).[22] Starting from the principle that skills require not intelligence but automatism, Morton decided that control of expression must precede any attempt to associate it with content. Thus, *phonematization* (that is, aural discrimination and accurate echoing) is drilled first, with no association with meaning. Then, *acoustic signifiers* (phonemic changes with grammatical significance) are learned. But there again, these changes are manipulated abstractly before grammatical meaning is introduced. Lexical meaning is finally presented in the *structural patterns* phase. During the last phase, the students are to generate language by responding meaningfully to simulated conversational situations. In Morton's program, writing is not used except for phonemic transcription. The approach is rigorously audio-lingual.

Fernand Marty, at Hollins College, has experimented with a partially self-instructional program which on the contrary depends heavily on reading and writing and has none of the radical features characteristic of Morton's.[23] Between Marty's conservatism and Morton's mechanistic approach, stands Albert Valdman who may well at present offer the best model of what a French programmed course should be. His program reflects his conviction that phonology, morphology, and syntax, are not separable linguistic areas which one can learn in successive isolated phases, and that even French spelling has enough relevancy to syntax to justify its introduction as soon as the pronunciation habits are established. He has programmed his course so that the simultaneity of significance of the linguistic elements contained in an utterance be always respected.[24]

It is interesting to note that when used experimentally with University of Indiana students, Valdman's course encountered no problems seriously questioning the structure of the program, while two successive trials of Morton's ALLP French Program at the University of Akron by Theodore Mueller led to a drastic revision of the program. Not only was writing introduced early, but the total separation between expression and content in the first phases was abandoned because of the total discouragement it generated among students. Mueller's *Revised Program* seems now closer to practical applicability than Morton's original project.[25]

One needs not point out the complexity of construction of good audio-lingual programmed materials. The amateurism dominant in the writing of textbooks (including audio-lingual ones) is not permitted here. The demands of programmed courses are great: minute definition of terminal behavior (with a detailed listing of expected performances), rigorous analysis of the structure of French (and subsequent organization in minimal steps of optimum efficiency), objective testing materials. Such demands, when successfully met, should contribute greatly to the improvement of teaching materials written for a more conventional teaching environment. The pioneer research in programmed learning in French will serve the profession, independently of whether or not programmed learning becomes widely used. Such will be the case for a new research project in total self-instruction presently conducted by a team of experts (linguists, psychologists, pedagogues, electronicians) at the Center for Applied Linguistics, for the Defense Language Institute. French has the good fortune of being the pilot language chosen for that project. New mechanical devices are being developed along with the course which will permit better control when presenting the material and eliciting students' utterances. As the project develops, a careful record of procedures, trials and errors, time schedules, etc., is kept, so as to help future investigators.

Conclusion

I would not commit myself to forecasting that self-instruction will be the teaching approach for elementary French courses in the future. Current experimentation is exploring the maximum, minimum, and optimum use of self-instruction. It is not likely that high schools will ever resort to programmed learning in languages. Their road leads to an ever greater emphasis on the active use of the language, both for everyday communication and for exploration of French culture through literature and other cultural media. The presence of the teacher is needed for motivation. As for universities, both Valdman's and Mueller's experiments with large numbers of students clearly indicate that, here also, the role and presence of a teacher is indispensable if the function of the language as communication is to be preserved. Even if technical know-how developed near-perfect teaching machines, students would not learn unless they could apply what they learn to a live situation in which effective communication through language takes place on a human level.

GENEVIEVE DELATTRE (1920–   ) was born and raised in France. She received her Baccalauréat and Licence ès Lettres from the University of Grenoble. She has a M.A. degree from Mount Holyoke College and a Ph.D. in French from Columbia University. She has taught French at Mount Holyoke College, the Middlebury French Summer School, Columbia University, the University of Colorado; and is now at the University of California at Santa Barbara where she divides her time and interest between French literature and the training of teachers of French at the secondary and college level. She is the author of *Les Opinions littéraires de Balzac* and of several articles of literary criticism or methodology. She has collaborated with her husband in experiments on the audio-lingual teaching of French.

FOOTNOTES

1. W. H. Fraser and J. Squair, STANDARD FRENCH GRAMMAR. Boston: D. C. Heath and Company, 1931.
2. Francois Denoeu and Robert A. Hall, Jr., SPOKEN FRENCH, BASIC COURSE. Boston: D. C. Heath and Company, 1943.
3. See Frederick Eddy, "The Language Studio." MODERN LANGUAGE JOURNAL, XXVIII, 4, April 1944, 338-341.
4. For a detailed report on this experiment, see Pierre Delattre, "A technique of aural-oral approach." THE FRENCH REVIEW, XX, 3, and 4, January and February 1947, 238-250, 311-324.
5. Pierre Delattre, AN INTRODUCTION TO FRENCH SPEECH HABITS. New York: Holt, Rinehart and Winston, 1947.
6. Published by Holt and Company, New York, 1946.
7. See Pierre Delattre, COMPARING THE PHONETIC FEATURES OF ENGLISH, GERMAN, SPANISH AND FRENCH. Philadelphia: Chilton Books, 1965.
7a. See Pierre Delattre, "Voyelles diphtonguées et voyelles pures." THE FRENCH REVIEW, XXXVII, 1, Part 1, October 1963, 64-76.
8. See Pierre Delattre, "Les dix intonations de base du français," THE FRENCH REVIEW, XL, 1, October, 1966, 1-14.
9. ELEMENTS DE PHONOLOGIE FRANCAISE. Publications de la Faculté des Lettres de l'Université de Strasbourg, Paris: Les Belles Lettres, 1935.
10. Published by d'Artrey, Paris, 1939.
11. Published in Supplement to LANGUAGE, XXIV, 3, Suppl., July-September 1948.
12. Jean Dubois, GRAMMAIRE STRUCTURALE DU FRANCAIS. Paris: Larousse, 1964.
13. "Essai d'analyse distributionnelle du verbe." LE FRANCAIS MODERNE, XXXIV, 3, Juillet 1966, 185-209.
14. APPLIED LINGUISTICS—FRENCH, A GUIDE FOR TEACHERS, edited by S. Belasco. Boston: D. C. Heath and Company, 1961.
15. Published by Ginn and Company, Boston, 1960.
16. Centre de Recherche et d'Etude pour la Diffusion du Français (CREDIF), LE FRANCAIS FONDAMENTAL. Paris: Publication de l'Institut Pédagogique National, 1959.
17. The only published data to this date is "A la Recherche des thèmes majeurs de la Civilisation Française." BULLETIN DES PROFESSEURS DE FRANCAIS DE AATF DE WASHINGTON, May 1966.
18. Modern Language Materials Development Center, A-LM, FRENCH

(level one, level two, level three). New York: Harcourt, Brace and World, 1961-

19. Dominique G. Côté, Sylvia N. Levy, and Patricia O'Connor, LE FRANCAIS: ECOUTER ET PARLER. New York: Holt, Rinehart and Winston, 1962.
20. LaVelle Rosselot and Georges Matoré, JE PARLE FRANCAIS, A FILM-AND-TEXT COURSE IN FRENCH FOR BEGINNERS. Encyclopedia Britannica Films Inc., 1961.
21. Published in the U.S. by Chilton Company—Book Division, 1963.
22. AUDIO-LINGUAL LANGUAGE PROGRAMMING PROJECT. Unpublished report, Contract No. OE-3-14-012, U. S. Office of Education, Language Development Branch, 1964.
23. This programmed course is the first to be commercially available: ACTIVE FRENCH: FOUNDATION COURSE. Roanoke, Va.: Audio-Visual Publications, 1965.
24. For details about this experiment, see Albert Valdman, THE IMPLEMENTATION AND EVALUATION OF A MULTIPLE CREDIT SELF-INSTRUCTIONAL ELEMENTARY FRENCH COURSE. Unpublished report, Contract No. OE4-14-009 and OE5-14-002, U.S. Office of Education, 1963.
25. Theodore H. Mueller, REVISIONS OF THE ALLP FRENCH PROGRAM AND SECOND TRIAL USE AT THE UNIVERSITY OF AKRON, 1964-65. Unpublished report, Contract No. OE5-14-007, U.S. Office of Education, August 1965.

Selected Bibliography

BOOKS

Centre de Recherche et d'Etude pour la Diffusion du Français, LE FRANCAIS FONDAMENTAL. Paris: Publication de l'Institut Pédagogique National, 1959. An objective study of the 1,500 highest frequency words and the most basic grammatical structures in spoken French.

Delattre, Pierre, AN INTRODUCTION TO FRENCH SPEECH HABITS. New York: Holt, Rinehart and Winston, 1947. Three weeks of pre-reading instruction for beginners in French, with emphasis on correct phonological habits (including prosodic features).

Delattre, Pierre, COMPARING THE PHONETIC FEATURES OF ENGLISH, GERMAN, SPANISH AND FRENCH. Philadelphia: Chilton Books, 1965. Segmental and suprasegmental features of four languages are analyzed and compared by statistical and instrumental techniques.

Dubois, Jean, GRAMMAIRE STRUCTURALE DU FRANCAIS. Paris: Larousse, 1964. A rigorous structural analysis of the noun and pronoun in French. The best grammatical study thus far of this sort. Quite technical but very clear.

Gougenheim, Georges, ELEMENTS DE PHONOLOGIE FRANCAISE. Publications de la Faculté des Lettres de l'Université de Strasbourg. Paris: Les Belles Lettres, 1935. The first phonemic analysis of the French language (phonology, morphophonemics, and structure of the word). Contains in appendix a very useful chart of minimal pairs.

Morton, F. Rand, AUDIO-LINGUAL LANGUAGE PROGRAMMING PROJECT. Unpublished report, Contract No. OE-3-14-012, U.S. Office of Education, Language Development Branch, 1964. A report on the first experiment with a programmed French course at the University of Michigan.

Mueller, Theodore H., REVISIONS OF THE ALLP FRENCH PROGRAM AND SECOND TRIAL USE AT THE UNIVERSITY OF AKRON, 1964-65. Unpublished report, Contract No. OE5-14-007, U.S. Office of Education, August 1965. A report on the applicability to actual teaching of Morton's Programmed Course, and on the revisions dictated by two successive trials.

Politzer, Robert L., TEACHING FRENCH, AN INTRODUCTION TO APPLIED LINGUISTICS. Boston: Ginn and Company, 1960. The aim of this book is practical: to show how to teach French (phonology, morphology, and syntax) in its actual structural reality and by contrast with English. The part on phonology is rather weak, but the other parts are excellent and useful.

Valdman, Albert, APPLIED LINGUISTICS—FRENCH, A GUIDE FOR TEACHERS, edited by S. Belasco. Boston: D. C. Heath and Company, 1961. Contains an Introduction by Belasco on language teaching (audio-lingual method) and a detailed analysis by Valdman of French syntax, morphology, and phonology, with direct practical application to the classroom situation (drills).

Valdman, Albert, THE IMPLEMENTATION AND EVALUATION OF A MULTIPLE CREDIT SELF-INSTRUCTIONAL ELEMENTARY FRENCH COURSE. Indiana University. Unpublished report, Contract OE5-14-002, U.S. Office of Education, 1963. A report on an experiment with a programmed course in French at the University of Indiana.

Watts, George, "The Teaching of French in the United States: A History." THE FRENCH REVIEW, XXXVII, 1 (part 2), October 1963. An attempt to retrace the history of the teaching of French in the United States from the colonial days to present time. Much stronger on the past than on the present.

ARTICLES

Delattre, Pierre, "A technique of aural-oral approach." THE FRENCH REVIEW, XX, 3 and 4, January and February 1947, 238-250, 311-324. A report on a very early experiment at the University of Oklahoma on the feasibility of a pre-reading period of one semester for beginners in French.

Delattre, Pierre, "Les dix intonations de base du français." THE

168

FRENCH REVIEW, XL, E, October 1966, 1-14. A precise and practical study of French intonation.

Delattre, Pierre, "Voyelles diphtonguées et voyelles pures." THE FRENCH REVIEW, XXXVII, 1 (part 1), October 1963, 64-76. A contrastive study of English and French vowels, based on the latest laboratory experiments.

Dubois, Jean, "Essai d'analyse distributionnelle du verbe." LE FRANCAIS MODERNE, XXXIV, 3, Juillet 1966, 185-209. A very technical study of the verb morphology in French, showing how a thorough structural analysis can dispose of all the so-called exceptions in traditional grammar.

Eddy, Frederick D., "The language studio." MODERN LANGUAGE JOURNAL, XXVIII, 4, April 1944, 338-341. A report on what can be considered as the first language laboratory in the United States.

Nostrand, Howard L., "A la recherche des thèmes majeurs de la civilisation française." BULLETIN DES PROFESSEURS DE FRANCAIS DE AATF DE WASHINGTON, May 1966. The first results of many years of research on a better definition of French culture. Cultural themes are extracted from literary material and studied from a sociological point of view.

Valdman, Albert, "Not all is wrong with French spelling." THE FRENCH REVIEW, XXXVII, 2, December 1963, 213-223. An argumentation in favor of introducing French spelling as soon as pronunciation habits are well established on the basis of the close relationship between spelling and syntax.

The Changing Aspects of Teaching Russian

RUDOLF STURM

Skidmore College

In 1951 I asked a class of third-year college students in Massachusetts to define the following words: Russian, Soviet, Slav, Slavic, Slavonic, Slavish, Slovak, Slovene. One student answered that all these were immigrants from Europe, but was not sure from what country. Another thought that they all came from Russia and that the different terms are only variations for the word "Russian." A third said that Russian pertains to Russia, Soviet is another word for Communistic, and the other words are simply different names pertaining to the people of Yugoslavia. The rest of the students remained silent.[1] In 1963 I put the same question to a similar college class in New York State. This time every student knew what Russian and Soviet meant, and most knew also the meaning of the remaining words. It was a marked difference in the space of only twelve years. Is it possible that the knowledge of the Slavic world and Russia in particular made such progress within this short time? And why? A look back at the development of Russian emigration to America and at the growth of Russian studies will facilitate answering these questions.

The Russians in America

In tracing the beginnings of teaching Russian as well as other Slavic languages in the United States, we discover what has been known to sociologists all along—that especially in their early stages these studies were separated from the Russian-American population. The immigrant complex was, and still is, at work here: If you speak the language of the "old country," and as long as you speak it, you are not a full-fledged American and therefore less desirable than other Americans. Few immigrants

170

are able to afford being "less desirable," and the thought that their children would continue to remain in this underprivileged group make most of them avoid any effort at supporting the study of their native tongue or encouraging their children in this direction. You may also put it the other way and say that American colleges and universities have for several generations simply ignored the ever-increasing numbers of Russian immigrants, and with them, the Russian language and the culture of Russia in general.

The Russians reached the Pacific Ocean in their eastward push as early as the sixteenth century. A group of refugees from Novgorod went to Siberia during the reign of Ivan the Terrible, crossed the sea in about 1571, and founded a colony in Alaska. How long this colony lasted, why it came to an end, and where its inhabitants went we do not know. When the next, and more permanent, group of Russian settlers came to Alaska some two hundred years later, they found only rumors among the natives about these first settlers, and the only tangible evidence consisted of "big knives with inscriptions just like those the Russians had," that were shown them by the natives.[2]

Between 1783 and 1785 the Russian fur merchant Grigoryi I. Shelikov (spelled also Shelekhov) established a permanent colony of Russians on the island of Kodiak.[3] A little later this trading post was transferred to where present-day Sitka, Alaska, is located. To exploit these new lands, Shelikov founded the Russian-American Company which soon was given a semi-official charter and was entrusted by the Russian government with the administration of the Aleutian Islands and Alaska. In the meantime the first Russian Orthodox Church in America was built on the island of Kodiak in 1795 and the second at Sitka in 1816. Other early Russian arrivals, Alexander Baranov and Ivan Kuskov, founded a Russian trading post near San Francisco called Fort Ross.

These Russian settlements were poorly supported by the czarist government, which evidently did not foresee the tremendous potential of establishing a beachhead on U.S. territory and in Alaska. Also, any effective support from Russia was made difficult if not impossible by the promulgation of the Monroe Doctrine in 1823 and more specifically by the treaty between Russia and the United States signed in 1824. In this treaty Russia agreed to establish no settlements on the American continent or any adjacent lands south of the 54.40 parallel, on which lies the southernmost tip of Alaska. Fort Ross in California was not mentioned, but the treaty did involve its abandonment, thus putting an end to any further Russian expansion in California. Fort Ross was sold to the Americans in 1841, and the Russians withdrew to the north.[4]

The Russian-American Company remained in charge of the Alaskan possessions until 1861, when the Russian government assumed direct control. Further Russian expansion having been blocked to the east by Great Britain and to the south by the United States, the czarist government decided in 1867 to sell Alaska altogether. Within a few months after the sale there were only a dozen Russians left at Sitka, the headquarters of the Russian administration, and a score of Orthodox priests throughout Alaska attending, in a dozen churches and chapels, to the spiritual needs of the natives and a few Russian colonists. The 125 years of Russian occupation of Alaska thus came to an end. Political refugees and immigrants continued to arrive on the Pacific Coast in small numbers up to the present time, settling mostly in and around San Francisco.

Throughout the nineteenth century it seemed that the Russian government was interested more in colonizing Siberia than letting the overflow of its population emigrate to America. Only the inhabitants of the non-Russian areas of the Russian Empire and the Jews were allowed, and often even encouraged, to go to the United States. This was the time when millions of Russian citizens of Polish, Finnish, Lithuanian, and Jewish background came, mostly to the Atlantic Coast. Only trickles of ethnic Russians were among them. On the lists of American soldiers of the Revolutionary War, we find several Russian-sounding names. The first known Russian immigrant to the east of the United States was Demetrius Augustine Golitsin (or Gollitzin) who came to Maryland from Holland in 1792. In America he was ordained as a Catholic priest and then worked as a missionary in Maryland and Pennsylvania. The towns of Gallitzin in Pennsylvania and Gallitzinville in New York are named after him. Very little is known about other Russians living in the eastern part of the United States before the Civil War. Among the combatants in that war we find many in the Union Army bearing Russian names, but few in the Confederate Army.

The first Russian newspaper in America was the *Alaska Herald,* printed in Russian and English in San Francisco starting in 1868, with a subsidy from the U.S. government at the outset.[5] Since then scores of Russian periodicals, some with socialist leanings, others church-oriented, began and after a shorter or longer existence suspended publication. In 1936 six Russian dailies and ten weeklies or monthlies were published in the United States. Of these, most went out of existence or are printed in bilingual Russian-English editions. But one of the dailies, the New York City-based *Novoye Russkoye Slovo* (The New Russian Word), established in 1910, still goes on strong today.

In many instances the Russian language and customs of the "old country" were maintained by various Russian ethnic clubs and societies, from anarchist and socialist to lawyers' and physicians' associations and church-related groups. The number of these organizations, most of them short-lived, is variously estimated at from one hundred to five hundred, depending on whether you count local branches, regional groupings, etc. The largest among them, of course, is the Russian Orthodox Church, although a majority of its members do not speak Russian any more. And there are eleven towns called Moscow in the United States, from Vermont to Idaho, a dozen Petersburgs, several Volgas, Kremlins, and Ivans, all attesting to the presence and influence of Russian immigration.

According to the thirteenth census of the United States in 1910, there were 57,926 persons in the country whose mother tongue was Russian. At the same time, 1,184,382 persons listed Russia as their country of birth. (Russia, or the Russian Empire, at that time included Finland and the Baltic states of Lithuania, Latvia, and Estonia.) A similar disproportion between the number of those born in Russia, or later the U.S.S.R., and those listing Russian as their native language existed at the time of the census of 1920 and all subsequent ones. In 1920, 392,049 persons gave their mother tongue as Russian, although 1,400,489 were born in the U.S.S.R. For 1940, the figures were respectively 356,-940 and 1,040,884. For the 1960 census, the figures were 276,834 and 690,598. We can assume that many, perhaps even a majority, of the non-Russians who came to America from Russia and the U.S.S.R. spoke Russian as their second language, thus increasing considerably the number of Russian-speaking people in the United States.

Statistics from censuses prior to 1910 are nearly meaningless for the purpose of this study because the 1910 census was the first one in which an inquiry was made as to the mother tongue. The census reports state that in 1850 there were in the United States 1,414 persons who were born in Russia; in 1870, there were 4,644; in 1890, the number jumped to 182,644. But we have no way of telling how many of them were ethnic Russians and how many were Yiddish-speaking or Ukrainian-speaking immigrants from Russia.[6] Be that as it may, the fact is that there were hundreds of thousands of Russian-speaking people living in the United States since at least World War I and that they did not influence at all, for reasons indicated above, the teaching of Russian in American schools. The influence and impulse had to come from a different direction, and be of an entirely different kind, as we shall see.

The Study of Russian: A Checkered Career

The teaching of Russian, and Slavic studies in general, in the United States grew slowly and unevenly. I shall not deal here with the first attempts in colonial times and up to the end of the nineteenth century. These early attempts were dilettante in character, produced no lasting results, and being isolated instances, they created no tradition. Worth mentioning, however, are the early efforts to acquaint America with Russian culture. Significantly, they were done outside the educational system of the United States.

The first known American translator of Russian literature is William David Lewis (1792-1881), a native of Christiana, Delaware, who learned Russian while living in St. Petersburg in 1814-24. While he was still in Russia, the *National Gazette and Literary Register* in Philadelphia published his translation of a poem entitled "Stanzas," by Yurii Alexandrovich Neledinsky-Meletsky, a contemporary of Karamzin.[7] This is, as far as this writer was able to ascertain, the first Russian work printed in English translation in the United States. Later, Lewis translated some of Pushkin's poems. Another forerunner was James Gates Percival (1795-1856), poet and geologist, but his translations and linguistic studies are nearly forgotten. The work of TALVI, the

174

pseudonym of Theresa Alberta Louisa von Jacob (1797-1870) should also be noted. Born in Germany, she lived for several years in Russia before coming to America as the wife of the Reverend Edward Robinson. Her articles dealing with Russian culture and especially her book, *Historical View of the Languages and Literature of the Slavic Nations; With a Sketch of Their Popular Poetry*[8] served for many years as a source of information on Russia. By the end of the nineteenth century many of the main works of Russian literature became known of course to the American reading public. This was true particularly of the Russian novel. Principal works by Turgenev, Dostoevsky, and Tolstoy were translated, as were portions of poetry by Pushkin and Lermontov.

It was not until the very end of the nineteenth century that the first campus-based instruction in Russian language was begun in the United States.[9] The year was 1896 and the man responsible for it was the Harvard University Chief Librarian, Archibald Cary Coolidge. Leo Wiener, the first professional Slavist in America, served as instructor. In addition to Russian, Wiener offered instruction in Polish, Czech, and other Slavic languages; his many publications included an important anthology of Russian literature. One of Wiener's students, George Rapall Noyes, initiated the teaching of Russian (and Czech) at the University of California at Berkeley in 1901. Noyes also offered courses in Russian history and literature and organized public lectures on Russia and East Europe.

In spite of the low enrollment in Russian courses at Harvard and California and the lack of general interest among American educators, Russian was introduced at Yale by M. S. Madell shortly after the turn of the century, and in 1905 at the University of Chicago by Samuel Harper. At Chicago, the offering of Russian was financed by Charles R. Crane, a patron of Russian and Czech arts. Starting in 1908, C. L. Meader taught Russian at the University of Michigan. At Stanford University, Russian was introduced in 1915 by Frank Golder, who previously taught it at Harvard.

The development of Russian studies in America before World War I was a slow and unimpressive process. Russian was not recognized as a legitimate part of the curriculum, was tolerated rather than encouraged by college presidents, and enjoyed no prestige. Most of the teachers of Russian did have a touch of the pioneer spirit but lacked a sense of being a part of an elite group which of course they were not. In retrospect, George R. Noyes has described the situation in these words: "During the years before the First World War, despite the wide circulation of certain Russian authors, notably Tolstoy and Dostoyevsky, and despite a rather hazy consciousness that literature was not the only art in which Russians had won distinction, most Americans regarded Russia with condescension or even with contempt. Serious interest in Russian life and above all in the grotesque and unpronounceable Russian language, was accounted something freakish, the mark of an eccentric, almost unbalanced mind".[10]

In the period between the two World Wars, Russian studies made only a mild progress. The involvement of Russia in the First World War and the outbreak of the Bolshevik Revolution evoked much interest on the part of the American public, but the absence of normal diplomatic relations, which were not established until 1934, the meager trade, and minimal cultural exchanges between the U.S.A. and the U.S.S.R. prevented that interest from being translated into action on the campuses. Mention should be made of the introduction of Russian at Columbia University by John D. Prince, scholar and diplomat, who, together with Clarence A. Manning and Arthur P. Coleman built up a first-class Slavic Department there. On the Pacific Coast, in the meantime, Slavic studies grew especially at California, where in the late twenties and thirties three full-time instructors were teaching Russian alone. The University of Washington made Russian a part of its Department of Oriental Studies, with Ivan Spector in charge.

At the University of Texas, Russian was taught as an appendix to an extensive program in Czech, and the University of Wisconsin offered Russian as a mere complement of its numerous courses in Polish. Several smaller institutions also added Russian to their curricula, although the teaching of the language was as a rule subordinate to Russian history and social sciences. This does not mean that an integrated program of Russian studies, or area studies, as an interdepartmental discipline was taking root. That development did not materialize until after the Second World War. All told, only nineteen institutions of higher learning were offering Russian language courses in 1939.

Only three universities, Harvard, Columbia, and California, the "big three" of Slavic teaching and scholarship, were equipped to offer Ph.D. degrees in Russian.[11]

Organizational activities in the field of Russian studies in the interwar period were also of little importance. There was not a single Slavic journal published in the United States, so that American Slavists had to send their articles to the *Slavonic and East European Review* in London. A Slavic group was organized within the Modern Language Association of America in 1929; later it split into two branches, linguistic and literary, but they both led only a marginal existence. An important step was taken in 1941 with the founding of the American Association of Teachers of Slavic and East European Languages at the MLA convention in Indianapolis. Arthur P. Coleman of Columbia was elected its first president. His scholarly wife, Marion Moore Coleman, began to publish in 1942 the *AATSEEL Bulletin,* later called the *AATSEEL Journal.*

The events of World War II brought Russia to the forefront of international affairs. During the war the armed forces in this country already had such a need for Russian-speaking personnel that they organized at a number of universities intensive courses, usually nine months long, to cope with this emergency.[12] With the end of the war, the U.S. Navy and Air Force discontinued language courses, while the Army concentrated them in the Army Language School at the Presidio of Monterey, California. By then many colleges and universities had added Russian to their regular academic programs, so that in 1945 Professor Coleman found eighty-one institutions presenting instruction in Russian; in 1946 the number rose to 112, and in 1948 to 120. At that time also, Coleman estimated at 5,000 the number of Americans studying Russian in regular college courses, and about 30,000 students in private and commercial schools.

Professor Jacob Ornstein in a similar survey focused on Russian, conducted in the mid-fifties, found that in the academic year 1954-55 there were 165 collegiate institutions teaching Russian, with a grand total of some 4,000 students (a drop of 1,-000 since 1947-48). By comparison, 110,000 college students were reported as taking French that year, 95,000 Spanish, and 70,000 German. As to the methodology, about 15 per cent of the responding institutions stated that they followed a purely grammar-trans-

177

lation approach, while 80 per cent indicated that they combined the oral-aural work with the grammar-translation method.[13]

The growth of Russian in secondary schools, too, was still slow. A total of fourteen public and private high schools were reported as having taught the language at one time or another between 1945 and 1955, with nine still offering it in 1955. It was obvious that both high schools and colleges needed a much greater awareness that Russia matters to us and is more and more likely to influence the lives of the American people directly. They needed a new incentive, and above all, something that would dramatize the need.

The breakthrough came in 1957 with the first Soviet sputnik. The American parents and students alike paused to consider the undeniable success of Soviet technology. They read and thought about the lowering of American prestige in many foreign lands, which they interpreted, in some instances erroneously, as automatically resulting in a higher prestige for the Soviet Union. They realized that the Americans who speak Russian may be "the future men of destiny." Admiral Hyman G. Rickover has effectively summarized the situation when, testifying before a committee of U.S. Congress, he said: "If we are to keep our position in the world today and to influence people in international relations, we must become a multilingual people. One reason that Russia has gotten so far with other nations is that she has taken the trouble to learn to communicate with them in their native tongues."[14]

The American answer to sputnik was the National Defense Education Act (NDEA) of 1958. Sputnik touched an urgent need in the U.S.A. for more and better students of sciences and modern foreign languages or, in the words of the NDEA, "to insure trained manpower of sufficient quality and quantity to meet the national defense needs of the United States." In addition to supporting the study of sciences, NDEA, in its original version and as amended, authorized loans of up to $1,000 per year for five years to students of Russian and other needed languages. It made possible a substantial financial assistance to the states and territories for strengthening the instruction of Russian in public elementary and secondary schools. It gave money to support fellowships for future college teachers of Russian, each fellow receiving a yearly stipend from $2,000 to $2,400 for three years.

Also, it allocated funds for guidance counseling and testing and for institutes established in colleges and universities to train personnel for guidance and counseling. It authorized funds to establish language and area centers focusing on Russian and the Soviet Union (and, of course, several other areas). And the Act also authorized financial assistance for language research projects dealing with language teaching by television, audio-visual materials, and instructional films.[15]

The encouragement and direct financial support given to the study of Russian by the NDEA brought about a dramatic rise in the enrollment both on secondary school and college level. Let us recall once more the figures collected by Dr. Ornstein for 1955: 165 collegiate institutions teaching Russian to some 4,000 students. By contrast, in 1960 there were 593 institutions with some 28,000; and in 1966, 950 institutions and nearly 60,000 students. At the same time the enrollment in Russian in secondary schools also showed tremendous gains. In 1955 nine high schools taught Russian to an undetermined number of students, hardly more than 100. In 1960 there were almost 600 high schools enrolling some 9,000 students in Russian. By 1966 the number of schools rose to 2,800 and the number of Russian students to nearly 50,000. Sputnik and the NDEA brought excellent results.

Whatever other meaning these figures may have, they certainly indicate that the teaching of Russian, after an uneven and difficult development, has reached a more stable, and hopefully also a less crisis-oriented, stage. The future seems promising indeed. What we still need in the United States is a sufficient number of competent and dedicated teachers of Russian. But that is another story.

RUDOLF STURM, born in 1912, was graduated from Charles University, Prague, in his native Czechoslovakia, and later received a Ph.D. degree in Slavic languages and literature from Harvard University. He is now professor of Russian and Italian at Skidmore College, Saratoga Springs, N. Y. Before coming to Skidmore in 1958, he served on the faculties of Boston College, Yale University, Hershey Junior College where he was head of the Modern Language Department, and the City College of New York. He is the author of a number of studies and articles on Slavic subjects which appeared in the *Slavonic Encyclopedia, Harvard Slavic Studies, Books Abroad,* and other journals. His latest publication is *Czechoslovakia: A Biblio-*

graphic Guide, just released by the U.S. Government Printing Office. Professor Sturm served as secretary general of the Czechoslovak Society of Arts and Sciences in America, 1959-60 and 1962-66, and was appointed consultant to the Library of Congress, Slavic and Central European Division, 1964-65. Recently he has been named Associate Bibliographer of the Modern Language Association.

FOOTNOTES

1. In 1945 a questionnaire made up of important information about the Soviet Union was submitted to some 2,500 high school seniors throughout the United States to test their knowledge of Russian and Soviet affairs. Their answers were tabulated and analyzed by Richard W. Burkhardt in "Report On a Test of Information About the Soviet Union in American Secondary Schools," THE AMERICAN SLAVIC AND EAST EUROPEAN REVIEW, V, Pts. 14-15, November 1946, 1-28. The results revealed a distressing lack of information on Russia and the U.S.S.R.
2. For details see Theodore S. Farrelly, "A Lost Colony of Novgorod in Alaska," THE SLAVONIC AND EAST EUROPEAN REVIEW, XXII, October 1944, 33-38.
3. This and the following paragraphs dealing with early Russian immigration in America are based on several sources, among which I would like to cite Mark Efimovich Vil'chur, RUSSIANS IN THE UNITED STATES. New York: The Foreign Language Information Service, 1935; and Yaroslav J. Chyz and Joseph S. Roucek, "The Russians in the United States," THE SLAVONIC AND EAST EUROPEAN REVIEW, XVII, No. 51, April 1939, 638-658.
4. On the subject of Fort Ross consult Robert A. Thompson, THE RUSSIAN SETTLEMENT IN CALIFORNIA KNOWN AS FORT ROSS; FOUNDED 1812, ABANDONED 1841. WHY THE RUSSIANS CAME AND WHY THEY LEFT. Santa Rosa, Calif.: Sonoma Democrat Publishing Co., 1896. 34 pp.
5. Its editor, Andrew A. Honcharenko, was a Ukrainian priest who arrived in Boston in 1865, moved to San Francisco, and there founded the *Alaska Herald,* intended as a means of educating the Alaska population about the laws and customs of the United States. Honcharenko's revolutionary and radical spirit made his paper a sharp critic of the U.S. military administration in Alaska. As a result, he lost the government subsidy and the paper soon suspended publication.
6. Statistics in this and the preceding paragraph were drawn from the official reports of the U.S. Bureau of the Census covering the U.S. censuses from 1850 through 1960.
7. In the issue for January 31, 1821.
8. New York, Putnam, 1850, 412 pp. TALVI borrowed heavily from the works of the Slovak scholar Pavel Jozef Safarik.
9. Among the many sources consulted the following are of primary importance: Clarence A. Manning, A HISTORY OF SLAVIC STUDIES IN THE UNITED STATES. Marquette University Press, Milwaukee: 1957. 118 pp.; and Jacob Ornstein, SLAVIC AND EAST EUROPEAN STUDIES: THEIR DEVELOPMENT AND STATUS IN THE WEST-

ERN HEMISPHERE. U.S. Department of State, Washington, D.C.: 1957. 65 pp.

10. Noyes, "Slavic Languages at the University of California." THE SLAVONIC AND EAST EUROPEAN REVIEW, XXII, October 1944, 56.

11. Strange as it may sound, statistics on the teaching of Russian are hard to find, and are as a rule incomplete and subject to reservations. Figures used in this study are gleaned from Ornstein, *op. cit.;* Arthur P. Coleman, A REPORT ON THE STATUS OF RUSSIAN AND OTHER SLAVIC AND EAST EUROPEAN LANGUAGES IN THE EDUCATIONAL INSTITUTIONS OF THE UNITED STATES. American Association of Teachers of Slavic and East European Languages, New York, 1948. 109 pp.; and from various statistical surveys published in THE MODERN LANGUAGE JOURNAL, THE SLAVIC AND EAST EUROPEAN JOURNAL, and the AATSEEL'S NEWSLETTER throughout the years.

12. For further studies of these programs see Robert John Matthew, LANGUAGE AND AREA STUDIES IN THE ARMED SERVICES; THEIR FUTURE SIGNIFICANCE. Washington, D.C.: American Council on Education, 1947. 211 pp.

13. It is interesting to note that in a survey of methods conducted at about the same time by the MLA among teachers of all foreign languages, more than one half of the respondents reported aural-oral approach in the instruction. See PMLA, LXX, No. 4, Part 2, September 1955, 50-55.

14. Reported in THE AMERICAN WEEKLY OF WASHINGTON POST, February 28, 1960, 7.

15. The first five years of operation of the NDEA, 1959-64, are described and assessed by Donald N. Bigelow and Lyman H. Legters in NDEA LANGUAGE AND AREA CENTERS: FIRST FIVE YEARS. Washington, D.C.: U.S. Department of Health, Education, and Welfare, 1964. 131 pp. The results are highly gratifying.

Selected Bibliography

BOOKS

Coleman, Arthur P., A REPORT ON THE STATUS OF RUSSIAN AND OTHER SLAVIC AND EAST EUROPEAN LANGUAGES IN THE EDUCATIONAL INSTITUTIONS OF THE UNITED STATES. New York: American Association of Teachers of Slavic and East European Languages, 1948. 109 pp. A survey of 236 institutions, covering the teaching of language, literature, history, and area studies.

Davis, Jerome, THE RUSSIAN IMMIGRANT. New York: The Macmillan Co., 1922. 219 pp. A solid study of the subject. Features a valuable 5-page bibliography.

Horecky, Paul L., ed., BASIC RUSSIAN PUBLICATIONS; AN ANNOTATED BIBLIOGRAPHY ON RUSSIA AND THE SOVIET UNION. Chicago: University of Chicago Press, 1962. 313 pp. Includes important chapters covering language, literature, and folklore.

——, RUSSIA AND THE SOVIET UNION; A BIBLIOGRAPHIC GUIDE TO WESTERN-LANGUAGE PUBLICATIONS. Chicago: University of Chicago Press, 1965. 473 pp. A companion to the above BASIC RUSSIAN PUBLICATIONS. Emphasis on English language material. The best and most complete bibliography in the field.

James, C. V., ed., ON TEACHING RUSSIAN. New York: The Macmillan Co., 1963. 143 pp. A collection of papers on the theory and practice of teaching in England. Valuable for comparison with the situation in the U.S.A.

Magner, Thomas F., ed., THE TEACHING OF RUSSIAN: REPORTS AND PAPERS. University Park, Pa.: Pennsylvania State University, 1962. 101 pp. In fifteen papers, the writers, all specialists in the field, examine the state of teaching Russian in Pennsylvania. All levels of instruction are discussed.

Manning, Clarence A., A HISTORY OF SLAVIC STUDIES IN THE UNITED STATES. Milwaukee: Marquette University Press, 1957. 117 pp. The author is a senior Slavist, having taught at Columbia for several decades. An important contribution to the history of Russian in American colleges.

Ornstein, Jacob, SLAVIC AND EAST EUROPEAN STUDIES: THEIR DEVELOPMENT AND STATUS IN THE WESTERN HEMISPHERE. Washington, D.C.: U.S. Dept. of State, 1957. 65 pp. A very good survey, well written, reliable. Includes a 5-page bibliography.

Parry, Albert, AMERICA LEARNS RUSSIAN: A HISTORY OF THE TEACHING OF THE RUSSIAN LANGUAGE IN THE UNITED STATES. About 200 pp.; to be issued later this year. Written under the auspices of the MLA, on a contract from the U.S. Office of Education.

Spector, Sherman D., and Legters, Lyman, comps. CHECKLIST OF PAPERBOUND BOOKS ON RUSSIA AND EAST EUROPE. Albany; University of the State of New York, 1966. 81 pp. A catalog of paperbacks dealing with many fields of human endeavor, from art to literature to world affairs.

Turkevich, Ludmilla B., editor, METHODS OF TEACHING RUSSIAN. Princeton, N.J.: D. Van Nostrand Co., 1967. 216 pp. A collection of papers dealing with classroom procedures, programmed instruction, teaching by TV, touch typewriting in Russian, and several other topics. Very useful for any teacher and advanced student.

Vil'chur, Mark Efimovich, RUSSIANS IN THE UNITED STATES. New York: Foreign Language Information Service, 1935. 195 pp. Based on Vil'chur's previous book, RUSSKIE V AMERIKE (1918), this is an excellent account of Russian immigration in the United States.

PERIODICALS

AATSEEL NEWSLETTER. Mimeographed, six times in an academic year. Prints shorter articles, notes, statistics, etc., on the teaching of Russian.

THE MODERN LANGUAGE JOURNAL. Eight times a year. Devoted to methods, pedagogical research, and other topics of interest to all language teachers. Important for reviews of textbooks.

NEWS BULLETIN. Issued several times in the school year by The Russian Studies Center for Secondary Schools, The Choate School, Wallingford, Conn. Includes useful information, bibliographies, etc.

PMLA: PUBLICATIONS OF THE MODERN LANGUAGE ASSOCIATION OF AMERICA. Five times a year. Articles in the field of modern languages and literatures, bibliographies, statistics, and many other topics of interest.

RUSSIAN REVIEW. Four times a year. Prints articles on language, literature, and history; occasionally also articles of pedagogical nature.

THE SLAVIC AND EAST EUROPEAN JOURNAL. Quarterly of the American Association of Teachers of Slavic and East European Languages. It succeeded in 1957 the AATSEEL JOURNAL. Devoted to research in language and literature. Prints in each issue a number of textbook reviews.

SLAVIC REVIEW. A quarterly of the American Association for the Advancement of Slavic Studies. Prints articles dealing with the literature, history, geography, and political developments in the U.S.S.R. and other Slavic countries. Probably the most important periodical in the field.

Modern English Teaching with Oral Language Techniques

ELLEN NEWMAN
Washington, D.C.

Is THERE a relationship between foreign language teaching and the teaching of English to speakers of a non-standard English dialect?

Perhaps you are wondering why a chapter on the teaching of English to English speakers is included in a symposium on foreign language trends. In order to answer this question, one must look at the recent literature which describes the problems of teaching English effectively to people who speak a dialect other than the standard dialect.[1] Though there are many and varied theories explaining why the speaker uses a non-standard dialect, and almost as many theories describing the handicaps of the nonstandard speaker, all the available research seems to agree that the oral language or foreign language approach provides at least a partial solution to the problem.

Foreign language teachers realize that the student must learn to speak the new language before he can read and write it effectively. This, linguists tell us, is the natural way to learn a language. Foreign language teachers at all levels of instruction use the foreign language laboratory,[2] with its emphasis on oral language. Dialogues, substitution and transformation drills, and listening exercises are only a few of the techniques employed by foreign language teachers to help the student speak the new language first.

The possibility of using this approach and these devices in the English classrooms has only recently begun to be explored. As educators recognized that the traditional approaches to teaching English were unsuccessful in dealing effectively with the problems of nonstandard speakers, they began to explore the possibilities of using an oral language approach in the English classroom.

184

In the remainder of this paper I will attempt to explain why a modified oral language approach is valuable in the English classroom and what types of students can best profit from this program. I will also explore some of the current theories concerning nonstandard dialects and I will briefly summarize some of the many recent oral language experiments in the public schools. At this time it is too soon to draw any definite conclusions on the success of these techniques in the English classroom, but it is possible to take notice of the more successful trends.

Who Can Profit From an Oral Language Approach to the Teaching of English?

The culturally or socially disadvantaged learner is the most usual speaker of a nonstandard dialect.[3] To understand the current application of foreign language techniques in American English teaching, it is necessary to know something about the culturally disadvantaged student.

Whether we believe that his language is a cause or an effect of his isolation, it is true that the disadvantaged child and his family suffer social and economic discrimination in our society. The disadvantaged child comes from a family which is at the bottom of the American society in terms of income. The values and the patterns of his home life are usually different from those encountered by the middle class schools and are often in direct conflict with the values of the school. By necessity the disadvantaged child is more oriented to the here and now, and less interested in the future. He and his family appreciate knowledge for practical vocational ends and rarely value it for itself.

The disadvantaged child has experienced failure in the classroom. He does not like school and he feels insecure in a place where he is constantly being corrected. The disadvantaged child learns best through a physical concrete approach, not the conceptual approach of the traditionally quiet classroom. He is often a slow reader and is sometimes as much as four grade levels behind in his reading and communication skills.

The disadvantaged child lives in a separate social world. Separated from the larger society, he seldom hears the more standard English patterns. His teachers may speak standard

English, but his contact with the school is not as powerful nor is it as meaningful as his contacts at home. He hears a non-standard speech and therefore speaks a nonstandard speech.[4]

Differing Points of View
Concerning Non-Standard Speech[5]

Students from lower socio-economic groups do not use language with as full a range of potential as do those from higher socio-economic groups. The disadvantaged groups can use the full potential of language and its grammatical structures, but often do not.[6] People who live in lower socio-economic groups use language primarily for immediate nonabstract situations and are therefore able to use many partial sentences. The disadvantaged do not often use language to examine the future. These people are not in the habit of expressing subjective emotions and feelings, a very important function of language. It is not a part of their culture to look at feelings and examine them verbally. Vocabulary and usage of the nonstandard dialect is different, although the grammatical patterns are the same.

Another view of nonstandard speech suggests that the non-standard dialect is primarily a rural dialect which has been transported to the urban communities of the East and West coasts. In the rural environment these dialects were "in a structurally close and socially well defined relationship to the local varieties of standard English. . . . However, migration to the North and the West coast has taken the dialects out of that setting and brought them into direct contact with varieties of English—both standard and nonstandard—which are structurally very different, and into a new sociological environment where the intruding dialects are regarded with much less indulgence than they were at home."[7]

The nonstandard language is structurally different from the standard language. Certain phonemes[8] are lacking in the non-standard language and there is a different verb usage. The speaker of a nonstandard dialect uses such expressions as 'he be absent' instead of 'he is absent'; 'he go' instead of 'he goes'; or 'he goin'' instead of 'he is going'.

These differences reflect learning problems which are similar to the problems of learning a foreign language. Thus by using

186

foreign language techniques the standard usage could be taught effectively in the English classroom.

What Happens to the Speakers of a Nonstandard Dialect in the Traditional English Classroom?

Whether the child speaks a language which is grammatically different from the more standard dialect or whether he speaks a restricted standard dialect, his experiences in the classroom are unpleasant. Soon after the child enters school a knowledgeable but insensitive English teacher tells him his English is "bad." Instead of recognizing that all the languages and dialects are equal in merit, the English teacher unknowingly reacts as if any dialect which is different from the one he uses is inferior. The young student recognizes this attitude and is soon afraid to respond in class. Rather than expanding his knowledge of English, he remains limited in his ability to use standard English. He does not "know" what to write about when a theme is assigned, not because he has nothing to write but because he does not know an acceptable classroom dialect.

In addition to the psychological frustration suffered by the disadvantaged child, he also suffers from a curriculum with is not designed for him. Traditionally, English courses in the United States have been concerned with enrichment, additional vocabulary, more complex patterns of written expression, and, of course, reading. Much time is spent diagraming and dissecting sentences, learning the parts of speech, and learning the different sentence types. This type of English course is acceptable for students who are natural speakers of standard English. The course aims at polishing basic skills and is successful in its goals. However, this type of program does not adequately meet the needs of the student who speaks a nonstandard dialect. While it is true that this student is not learning a foreign language in the full sense and therefore would not profit from a course which employed only foreign language techniques, it is true that the changes in dialect between nonstandard and standard speech present enough differences to warrant a teaching approach which takes into account that "conflicts between different linguistic structures underlie many of the learner's difficulties."[9]

The disadvantaged child sees no point in diagraming sentences, underlining subjects and verbs, and various other tech-

187

niques which are designed to enrich his knowledge of English. For this student the study of English must employ practical, realistic techniques. The study of English must teach the disadvantaged child the more standard English patterns so that he may use them in appropriate situations. It must teach him the standard English patterns so that he may achieve his full potential socially and economically.[10] And it must do all this *without* destroying the child's own language. This is where the traditional English methods have failed, and it is for these reasons that English teachers must borrow from the foreign language teacher.

Changes are desperately needed in the English curriculum in the public schools if we are to educate each child to his fullest potential. These changes must stress oral language before written language. How can a child write a language he cannot speak? These changes must recognize that a quiet classroom does not always mean learning is taking place. These changes must recognize and respect the child's language. Rather than seeking to destroy that language, these changes must lead toward the mastery of a second language to be used with the first.

Practical Classroom Techniques and Experiments

In large urban centers throughout the country experiments in foreign or oral language techniques for teaching English to speakers of a nonstandard dialect are in process. The objectives behind these programs are clearly reflected in the extent and scope of their design. Some of these programs are much more sweeping in their aims, while others deal with the more minor problems and do not seek to eradicate all regional differences. As it would be impossible to describe all of the experiments and programs, the following represent only a brief sampling.[11]

One type of program currently being tested is a program which uses oral language techniques at the junior and senior high school levels. This program is incorporated into the regular English program. Every day a short portion of the regular classroom time is devoted to oral language. During this time the students participate in listening drills, question-and-answer drills, transformation drills, and exercises which work on the difficult or different phonemes.

The students might listen to a reading selection which concentrates on one area of difficulty, followed by drill work in that area. For example, to work on the sound and usage of the past tense a transformation drill might be used.

Teacher: I start school at eight.
Student's response: I started school at eight.

A transformation drill might be used to teach affirmative and negative responses also.

Teacher: I liked school.
Student's response: I didn't like school.
Teacher: I started school.
Student's response: I didn't start school.

Question and answer drills might also be used.

Teacher: Did you start school?
Student's response: Yes, I started school.
                No, I didn't start school.

Students may respond to these exercises either individually or as a group. If tape recorders and head sets are available, they may be used, otherwise the teacher can read the drills to the class. At times the students have copies of the reading materials or they may be required to respond orally without any written guide.

It is hoped that through constant drill, in addition to the regular classroom procedures, the students will incorporate the standard usage into their language patterns.[12]

Other junior and senior high school programs combine the above methods with additional oral language practices. In some schools an oral language program is used in place of the traditional English program. Other schools have tried teaching oral English as a separate class in addition to the regular English program.

In these more comprehensive programs the techniques described above are supplemented with exercises and discussions designed to improve the students' expression of ideas, of points of view, and of opinions. Students are also involved in role playing and socio-drama. They are placed in a problem situation and must work out the solution. Students act out real life situations. They must talk and act as if they were the "angry mother or

189

anxious salesman." Not only do these techniques help teach awareness of language but they also help the students understand how others respond to certain situations.

The students might be asked to read a short paragraph and express the thought in their own words. Tongue twisters are used to practice difficult sounds. Substitution drills are used to teach verb tense and increase vocabulary. Sentences such as: "Yesterday I washed my shirt" are placed on the board and the students must replace *washed* with another verb. Then the word *yesterday* is replaced by the word *tomorrow* and students must again make changes so that the sentence "makes sense". A similar technique is used to teach the word order of a sentence.

Special word lists are employed to help students with the pronunciation of difficult sounds.[13] Much can be accomplished by allowing students to work with each other. From time to time students evaluate their own progress. In the early stages of the programs most of the work is oral. As the students progress written work is introduced.[14]

When these programs are designed for junior or senior high school students, the importance of language can be stressed. Teachers can explain that this "new" or "second" language is to be learned in addition to the language the student normally speaks. This new language should be used in certain situations. The more mature student can understand this approach, and if he does not feel threatened, he can make great strides toward mastery of standard usage.

It is not necessary, however, to wait until high school to begin an oral language approach, nor is it desirable to do so. Programs have been designed and taught on the elementary level. The following is an outline of a comprehensive program which begins on the elementary school level and continues through high school.

At an early age students are encouraged to talk a great deal, regardless of dialectical differences. It is more important at this time to encourage oral responses than to emphasize the standard dialect. Too much emphasis at an early age may only confuse and inhibit the students. Throughout the primary grades students are given the opportunity for oral expression through sociodramas, oral reading, and play acting. Later on the students are exposed to various dialects so they realize that there are many sounds they can imitate. At this time standard language is introduced and the students are encouraged to imitate it. Records and tape recordings have been used with great success for these purposes. When the student is older, he is made aware of the importance of standard language. He should be told that standard language is necessary for social and economic success, not because this language is better than his, but because this language is the language spoken by the majority of society.

Throughout secondary school the student must expand his command of the standard language. Drills, tapes, and other language laboratory techniques must alternate with discussions and writing to achieve this end.[15]

All of the programs described so far deal with the problems of nonstandard speakers in the public schools. There is very little information available of work on the college level. A student who is in college has, for the most part, mastered a standard English dialect. This does not mean that the college student has forgotten his nonstandard speech, but rather that he is able to shift dialects in the appropriate situations.

There are programs on the college level which are designed to enrich and supplement the education of the disadvantaged youth. At Mount Diablo College in California high school students can participate in a three-month program in the language arts. This program is offered to students who expect to attend college in the near future. Writing skills and reading skills are especially emphasized. Yale University offers a program in cultural enrichment to students from slum schools who did not quite meet admission requirements. By participating in this program successfully, students are eligible for admission the following year.

While these programs and others like them are designed to help the culturally disadvantaged child achieve his full potential, they also assume that the child is fluent in the standard dialect. It remains therefore the responsibility of the public schools and especially the English teacher to develop in every student the ability to speak standard English.

Conclusion

At this time it is too early to say that oral language provides all the answers for a new English curriculum. The programs de-

191

scribed are still in the experimental stage. However, educators working in this field have noted improvement on most levels. Educators may differ in their views concerning the desirable dialectical changes, but they do agree that the speaker of a nonstandard dialect must learn a standard dialect.

When we compare the traditional English class and the oral language English class, it is clear that the oral language methods are better suited to the needs of certain types of students. The oral language class does not represent a threat to the disadvantaged student. He is not told that his English is poor or sloppy, but he is taught that there are many ways to speak, and each language should be used when appropriate. Through oral language techniques the disadvantaged learner can make language work for him.

ELLEN NEWMAN received a B.A. from the University of California at Los Angeles in 1963. She received her California General Secondary Teaching Credential from the University of California at Berkeley and has done additional graduate work at the University of Minnesota and San Francisco State College. She has taught English at James Madison Junior High School in Oakland, California. There she worked under a Ford Foundation grant to develop a pilot program in oral language. In 1965 Mrs. Newman was chairman of the Junior High School Committee on Language Development for the Disadvantaged at the Asilomar Conference of Central California Council of Teachers of English. In 1967 Mrs. Newman taught English at Dunbar High School in Washington, D.C., where she participated in an Urban Language Study at the Center for Applied Linguistics.

FOOTNOTES

1. Standard English is normal, correct grammatical usage for a given region. Nonstandard English is English which varies from the standard.
2. Where the term language laboratory is used in reference to English courses, it means a type of teaching approach regardless of the physical structure of the room. At this time it would be unrealistic to assume that the public schools had an elaborate language laboratory structure for their English classes.
3. This paper deals only with the culturally deprived or disadvantaged child. There is another group of students, the culturally different, who can also profit from the type of language approaches suggested. For a description of the culturally different, see Charlotte Brooks,

"Teaching English as a Second Language," DIALOG, Fall 1965, 1-7.

4. For More detailed information on the culturally disadvantaged see: Martin P. Deutsch, "The Disadvantaged Child and the Learning Process," A. Harry Passow, Ed., EDUCATION IN DEPRESSED AREAS. New York: Bureau of Publications, Columbia University, 1963, 163-179; Robert J. Havighurst, "Who are the Socially Disadvantaged?" in Joe L. Frost and Glenn R. Hawkes, eds., THE DISADVANTAGED CHILD. Boston: Houghton Mifflin Co., 1966, 15-23; Frank Reisman, THE CULTURALLY DEPRIVED CHILD. New York: Harper & Row, New York, 1962, Staten Webster, ed., THE DISADVANTAGED LEARNER: KNOWING, UNDERSTANDING, EDUCATING. San Francisco: Chandler Publishing Co., 1966.

5. There are many different points of view as to what constitutes a nonstandard dialect. This first description of nonstandard speech includes the speech of the American Indian, the Negro, and the Cajun in Louisiana, to mention just a few. The second description of nonstandard speech is based primarily on the speech of the Negro in large urban centers.

6. Walter Loban, "A Sustained Program of Language Learning." LANGUAGE PROGRAMS FOR THE DISADVANTAGED, National Council of Teachers of English, Illinois: 1965, 223; see also 221-224 for a more detailed description of nonstandard speech.

7. William A. Stewart, "Foreign Language Teaching Methods in Quasi Foreign Language Situations", William Stewart, ed., NON-STANDARD SPEECH AND THE TEACHING OF ENGLISH. Washington, D.C.: Center for Applied Linguistics of the Modern Language Association of America, 1964, 7.

8. Lee A. Pederson, "Non-Standard Negro Speech in Chicago," William Stewart, ed., NON-STANDARD SPEECH AND THE TEACHING OF ENGLISH. Washington, D.C.: Center for Applied Linguistics of the Modern Language Association of America, 1964, 18-19.

9. William A. Stewart, *Loc. Cit.*

10. Ruth I. Golden, "Ways to Improve Oral Communication of Culturally Different Youth." IMPROVING ENGLISH SKILLS OF CULTURALLY DIFFERENT YOUTH IN LARGE CITIES, United States Department of Health, Education, and Welfare, Washington, D.C.: United States Government Printing Office, 1964, 104.

11. See LANGUAGE PROGRAMS FOR THE DISADVANTAGED for a listing of current programs, 303-323.

12. A program of this type is now in progress in the Washington, D.C., schools. The Center for Applied Linguistics has prepared sample lessons which are being used on a trial basis in several junior and senior high schools.

13. Ruth I. Golden, IMPROVING PATTERNS OF LANGUAGE USAGE. Detroit: Wayne State University Press, 1960, 153-157.

14. For a more complete description of these programs see: *Ibid.,* 69-157; Ellen Newman, "An Experiment in Oral Language," ed., Staten Webster, ed., *Op. Cit.,* 510-514.

15. Walter Loban, *Op. Cit.,* 223-231, contains a detailed description of this type of program.

193

Selected Bibliography

BOOKS

Barrows, Marjorie Wescott, GOOD ENGLISH THROUGH PRAC-
TICE. New York: Henry Holt, 1956. English textbook with
materials designed to attack the problem areas of nonstandard
speakers. The drills are in the form of games which can be
adapted to all grade levels.

Conant, James B., THE EDUCATION OF AMERICAN TEACHERS.
New York: McGraw-Hill Book Co., 1963. A survey of teacher
education; stresses the areas of education, restrictions on the
hiring practices of local school boards, and recommendations
for change in these areas.

——, SLUMS AND SUBURBS. New York: McGraw-Hill Book Co.,
1961. A discussion of the problems of education found in the
slum school and the suburban school. Includes suggestions for
improving education in both areas.

Finocchiaro, Mary, TEACHING ENGLISH AS A SECOND LAN-
GUAGE. New York: Harper and Row, 1958. A description of
methods for teaching English as a second language to non-
English speakers.

Fries, Charles C., TEACHING AND LEARNING ENGLISH AS A
FOREIGN LANGUAGE. Ann Arbor: University of Michigan
Press, 1964. Presentation of foreign language teaching techniques, many of which are applicable for teaching standard
speech to nonstandard speakers.

Frost, Joe L., and Hawkes, Glenn R., eds., THE DISADVANTAGED
CHILD. Boston: Houghton Mifflin Co., 1966. A collection of
articles describing the disadvantaged child, his culture, and his
education.

Golden, Ruth, IMPROVING PATTERNS OF LANGUAGE USAGE.
Detroit: Wayne State University Press, 1960. A study of nonstandard language and its effects on the socio-economic level of
the speaker; includes methods for dealing with the problems
of the nonstandard speaker at the high school level.

Gunderson, Doris V., Mersand, Joseph, and Jewett, Arno, eds., IM-
PROVING ENGLISH SKILLS OF CULTURALLY DIFFER-
ENT YOUTH IN LARGE CITIES. United States Department of
Health, Education and Welfare, Office of Education, Washington,
D.C.; United States Government Printing Office, 1964. A series
of papers from a conference on improving English skills of
culturally different youth; includes descriptions of projects and
recommendations for future action.

Morse, Arthur D., SCHOOLS OF TOMORROW — TODAY. Garden
City, N.Y.: Doubleday, 1960. A collection of experiments in all
fields of education including the use of teacher aides, television,
and ungraded schools.

National Council of Teachers of English, Illinois, LANGUAGE PRO-

GRAMS FOR THE DISADVANTAGED. 1965. The Report of the NCTE Task Force on Teaching English to the Disadvantaged. A report of language programs for the disadvantaged from all sections of the United States; includes a description of the problems of the disadvantaged and recommendations for more effective education.

Passow, A. Harry, ed., EDUCATION IN DEPRESSED AREAS. New York: Bureau of Publications, Teachers College, Columbia University, 1963. A collection of articles covering teachers, schools, programs, and the psychological and sociological aspects of education in slum areas.

Reissman, Frank, THE CULTURALLY DEPRIVED CHILD. New York: Harper & Row, 1962. A discussion of the culture of the disadvantaged child; includes new approaches to the education of the deprived child.

Stewart, William A., ed., NON-STANDARD SPEECH AND THE TEACHING OF ENGLISH. Washington, D.C.: Center for Applied Linguistics of the Modern Language Association of America, 1964. Three articles dealing with differences and similarities between teaching English as a second dialect and teaching English as a second language, a study of dialect differences, and approaches to teaching English as a second language.

Strom, Robert D., TEACHING IN THE SLUM SCHOOL. Columbus; Charles E. Merrill Books, Inc., 1965. An overview of the issues which can influence progress or failure in the classroom and a discussion of the external forces influencing education.

Webster, Staten, ed., THE DISADVANTAGED LEARNER: KNOWING, UNDERSTANDING, EDUCATING. San Francisco; Chandler Publication Co., 1966. A description of the disadvantaged learner and his culture, and the effects of these characteristics in the classroom; stresses the importance of understanding the disadvantaged learner for successful teaching and includes learning programs designed for the disadvantaged.

ARTICLES

Bernstein, Basil, "Language and Social Class." BRITISH JOURNAL OF SOCIOLOGY, XI, 1960, 271-276. Compares the modes of expression of the working classes with those of the middle classes.

Brooks, Charlotte, "Some Approaches to Teaching Standard English as a Second Language." DIALOG, Fall 1966, 1-7. Points out the differences between the culturally different and the culturally disadvantaged child; urges an oral approach to the teaching of English to nonstandard speakers.

Cohen, Werner, "On the Language of Lower Class Children." SCHOOL REVIEW 67, Winter 1959, 433-440. Describes differences between the nonstandard and the standard dialects and urges steps toward greater teacher understanding in dealing with the nonstandard speaker.

Davis, Allison, "Socio-Economic Influence Upon Children's Learning." SCHOOL LIFE, XXXIII, 1951, 87, 93-94. Describes the effects of social class values upon motivation and learning.

Deutsch, Martin P., "The Disadvantaged Child and the Learning Process," A. Harry Passow, ed., EDUCATION IN DEPRESSED AREAS, New York: Bureau of Publications, Columbia University, 1963, 163-179. Discusses the impact of social factors on school learning; describes the values and attitudes of the disadvantaged child. Includes suggestions for making education more effective for the disadvantaged.

Golden, Ruth I., "Ways to Improve the Oral Communication of Culturally Different Youth." IMPROVING ENGLISH SKILLS OF CULTURALLY DIFFERENT YOUTH IN LARGE CITIES. United States Department of Health, Education, and Welfare, Office of Education, Washington, D.C.: United States Government Printing Office, 1964, 100-109. Stresses the importance of standard speech for socio-economic success and describes some practical classroom techniques for dealing with the problems of the nonstandard speaker.

Green, William D., "Language and the Culturally Different." ENGLISH JOURNAL, LIV, Number 8, November 1965, 724-733, 740. Summarizes six approaches to the problem of teaching English to nonstandard speakers.

Havighurst, Robert J., "Who are the Socially Disadvantaged?" in Joe L. Frost and Glenn R. Hawkes, eds., THE DISADVANTAGED CHILD, Boston: Houghton Mifflin and Co., 1966, 15-23. Describes the characteristics of the disadvantaged child with an emphasis on his family and social characteristics and compares his background with that of the middle-class child.

Loban, Walter, "A Sustained Program of Language Learning." LANGUAGE FOR THE DISADVANTAGED, National Council of Teachers of English, Illinois, 1965, 221-231. Describes a program of oral language for speakers of nonstandard dialects.

McDavid, Raven I., Jr., "American English Dialects," in W. Nelson Francis, ed., THE STRUCTURE OF AMERICAN ENGLISH. New York: Ronald Press Co., 1958. Describes the dialect differences in American English and the social, economic, and other forces behind these differences.

Newman, Ellen, "An Experiment in Oral Language," in Staten Webster, ed., THE DISADVANTAGED LEARNER: KNOWING, UNDERSTANDING, EDUCATING. San Francisco: Chandler Publishing Co., 1966, 510-514. Describes a program of oral language for the nonstandard speaker; discusses teacher attitudes which can help the child achieve success in the classroom.

Pederson, Lee A., "Non-Standard Negro Speech in Chicago," in William A. Stewart, ed., NON-STANDARD SPEECH AND

THE TEACHING OF ENGLISH. Washington, D.C.: Center for Applied Linguistics of the Modern Language Association of America, 1964, 16-23. Presents a study of dialectial differences in Chicago.

Scott, Charles T., "Teaching English as a Foreign Language." ENGLISH JOURNAL, LIV, Number 5, May 1965, 414-418. Describes differences in teaching English as a foreign language and English teaching to native speakers; describes the process of native language learning.

The Neglected Languages

JAMES E. IANNUCCI
St. Joseph's College, Philadelphia

IN THE last two decades interest and concern have been growing apace with regard to languages which have not been widely taught in the United States. These languages are referred to as "critical languages," "neglected languages," "non-Western languages," or simply "uncommonly taught languages" depending on the point of view or kind of concern. The concern has arisen in the main from two important facts of modern history: (a) the world-wide revolution which has seen dozens of new nations come into existence from former colonial status; and (b) the increasing involvement and leadership of the United States in world affairs. The United States has become increasingly conscious of the growing importance of these new nations in Africa and Asia, and increasingly aware of the American stake in knowing and understanding their cultures.

Response to Concern

The response to this concern has come from various sources. The National Defense Education Act has made possible the establishment of many Language and Area Programs in Arabic, Chinese, Hindi-Urdu, Japanese, Portuguese, and Russian, the six languages defined as having top priority. Enrollments have increased sharply in eighteen other languages designated second priority and in sixty languages designated third priority. The Foreign Language Program of the Modern Language Association of America has rendered a great service in conducting statistical studies and in disseminating information on manpower in the neglected languages.[1] The Center for Applied Linguistics performs an invaluable service as a clearing house of information on teaching materials and linguistic studies in the neglected languages.[2] The American Council of Learned Societies has for many years sponsored the development of teaching materials and reference works.[3] Foundations have become increasingly interested and have given increasing support to programs in the neglected languages.[4]

Indicative of the mounting interest in very recent years is the large number of top-level conferences on the subject of neglected languages since 1961. The first of these, the Conference on Neglected Languages, was held in Washington, D. C. in 1961.[5] It was sponsored jointly by the Modern Language Association of America and the United States Office of Education. This conference decided to establish a list of the major languages of the world and a classification of these languages based partly on generic and partly on areal criteria. It also made basic recommendations and established priorities in such areas as teaching materials, bilingual dictionaries, linguistic research, training of teachers, the establishment of chairs, and the establishment of language and area centers abroad. Subsequent conferences have in general confirmed these recommendations or expanded them with a view to more specific goals.

The focus of more recent concern has been the introduction of the study of critical or neglected languages in undergraduate curricula in colleges and universities. Typical of the thinking in this area are the formal recommendations of the Conference on Critical Languages in Liberal Arts Colleges, sponsored by the United States Office of Education and held at the University of Washington in 1965. The recommendations were:

1. Even with present limitations of staff and materials, as well as constraints of curriculum, it is feasible to introduce the study of critical languages into American liberal arts colleges so that it will be a valid component of liberal education.

2. Instruction in a critical language should be introduced in a liberal arts college only if the equivalent of at least two full years of work in a specialized university program can be offered.

3. Emphasis in the early stages of instruction should be on oral control, but in every case, work in reading should be introduced in the first year.

4. When languages present special learning problems because

of complicated writing systems or a classical-colloquial split, restricted objectives should be decided on to avoid dispersion of effort and discouraging results.

5. Of alternative patterns of instruction, the most desirable is a professional teacher of the language, regular class sessions at least four or five hours a week, and supplementary work in a language laboratory or with the instructor. It is also feasible to have a linguist or language specialist on the faculty supervise instruction by an informant, that is, a foreign student or a speaker of the language present on the campus. In this case some special training for the informant must be provided.

6. Where it is not feasible to set up a full program of instruction in a critical language, and where for some special purpose a more unusual language must be offered, a supervised program of individual study with special materials and tapes, like the Kalamazoo program, can be effective. It should be noted that while this is a promising means of meeting the special needs of a small fraction of the student body, it does not solve the problem of including one of the critical languages as a standard component in a liberal arts curriculum.

7. Valuable adjuncts to undergraduate instruction in critical languages now exist in the form of intensive summer courses at universities, the undergraduate year at Princeton and other institutions and provisions for study abroad for the undergraduate who has completed elementary preparation. Any liberal arts college which introduces study of the critical languages should take full advantage of these adjuncts.

8. It is desirable that standardized tests of proficiency in the critical languages be developed so that small colleges may have an effective means of measuring their work against that of other institutions.[6]

Special Problems

The neglected languages can of course share with the commonly taught languages the results of research in such general areas as the psychology of second language learning, the application of linguistics to language learning, language laboratory techniques, and the problem of ethnocentrism and culture conflicts. However, some problems are peculiar to individual languages, and the neglected languages frequently present special

200

problems not encountered in the commonly taught languages.

Chinese, for example, presents special problems in the teaching and learning of reading and writing since Chinese writing consists of characters that are morphemes. Furthermore, there are several script forms of these characters: the standard printed form, a modified form of the printed form used in handwritten representation, a cursive handwritten form for ordinary communication, in addition to various artistic and archaic forms. In the last ten years still another form has developed on the Chinese mainland, a simplified form of the traditional printed form, which is now almost universally used in all printed matter. Publications in Taiwan and in overseas Chinese areas, however, continue to be written in the traditional printed forms. Programs in Chinese differ widely in the time at which the writing system is introduced and also in the relative time devoted to audiolingual work and reading. Most programs do not give formal instruction in the various script forms.[7]

Arabic, in addition to having an alphabet different from that of English, presents the problem of a sharp cleavage between written and spoken forms. The student of Arabic must learn Classical Arabic for reading and writing, and Spoken Arabic (not generally written) for conversation. Furthermore, since the spoken forms vary considerably, the student may have to learn more than one spoken dialect in addition to the classical language. Because of these problems and because of the lack of teaching materials for the spoken forms, most courses in Arabic in the United States have concentrated primarily or exclusively on Classical Arabic. As teaching materials have become available, more institutions are teaching some form of Spoken Arabic before introducing Classical Arabic.[8]

Hindi and Urdu, or Hindi-Urdu as they are sometimes referred to, present still another type of problem. On the colloquial oral level these are not really two different languages but one language with considerable regional dialectal variations. Thus in any one particular region, one finds very slight differences between the speech of those who consider their language Hindi and those who consider it Urdu. On the formal, literary, and written levels there are important differences. The learned, literary, and technical vocabularies of the two languages differ considerably. Hindi draws its learned and literary vocabulary from Sanskrit while Urdu draws its learned and literary vocabulary from Persian. The writing systems are also entirely different. Hindi uses the Devanagari script derived from Sanskrit, while Urdu uses the Perso-Arabic script. Most courses do not differentiate between Hindi and Urdu on the elementary level since they are audio-lingually oriented and use a phonemic transcription. There is considerable variation of practice in the introduction of the writing systems and the formal or literary style. Ordinarily, the Devanagari script is introduced sometime during the first year, and Perso-Arabic later in advanced literary courses.[9]

Many universities, especially the larger ones, now offer a great variety of neglected languages. More than a hundred languages are now available somewhere in the United States.[10] Small colleges, however, find it difficult to introduce neglected or critical languages in their curricula for economic reasons, because of the difficulty of acquiring qualified teachers for such languages, and because of the uncertainty of undergraduate interest in any one neglected language in a given year on a given campus. Various approaches have been sought to the solution of this problem.

The Princeton Program

One solution is the establishment of cooperative programs between a major university center and a group of undergraduate institutions. Such a program has been instituted by Princeton University with about eighty Eastern and Midwestern colleges. The Princeton Program permits students from the participating colleges who wish to study a critical language to spend the summer between their sophomore and junior years at a summer intensive language program taking an elementary course in the language. During their junior year they continue their language instruction at Princeton, taking related area courses at the same time. After the junior year at Princeton they are encouraged to take a third-year course in an intensive summer program. They then return to their own college to complete their senior year. Students who have studied a critical language before may participate in the Princeton Program, following the same schedule but taking language instruction at a higher level. Some students spend two years at Princeton or one year at Princeton and one at an overseas study center. These students spend a fifth year at their home institution, after which they receive their undergraduate degree jointly from Princeton and their own college. During its first year, 1963-1964, the Princeton Program accommodated fourteen students from the participating colleges. In its second year there were twenty-five students enrolled in the program. A foundation grant provides scholarships for summer study and funds for administration. Princeton University assumes the responsibility for instructional costs and scholarship support for the academic year. Two main problems had to be dealt with in the Princeton Program, and they are problems likely to arise in any program of this type. Some colleges object to too much specialization on the undergraduate level at the expense of broad liberal arts training. This problem was met by demonstrating that the program, as it is constituted, actually strengthens the student's basic liberal education. Some colleges are reluctant to participate for fear of losing good students. This hesitancy was largely overcome by encouraging students to return to their home institutions for their senior year and by discouraging transfers.[11]

Another approach is the provision of overseas study of a neglected or critical language for undergraduates. This generally requires a fifth year of study for the undergraduate degree. Overseas programs are in operation in Lebanon, Taiwan, India, and Japan for the study of Arabic, Chinese, Hindi, and Japanese. Such programs are intended primarily for very well-qualified students with a sound preliminary foundation in the language they plan to study. Because there is still very little undergraduate instruction in neglected languages, very few students now qualify for these programs.

The Kalamazoo Program

A very different approach to providing undergraduates in small colleges with instruction in neglected languages is the Neglected Language Program of Kalamazoo College. This program has been in operation since 1963 under contract with the U. S. Office of Education. The program is largely self-instructional. Its objective is to lay a foundation of oral competence in a neglected language, roughly equivalent to the first three semesters of instruction as it is given in formal courses at other

203

institutions. Instruction is offered in any neglected language for which suitable audio-lingually oriented teaching materials with accompanying tapes are commercially available from such sources as the Foreign Service Institute and the Yale Institute of Far Eastern Languages. Teaching materials which are adequately designed for self-instruction are now available for Chinese, Japanese, Hindi-Urdu, Swahili, Persian, Portuguese, Yoruba, Hausa, and South Vietnamese. Similar course materials for other languages are being developed with NDEA support. The essential ingredients of the Kalamazoo Program are described as follows: (1) one or more highly motivated students of proven linguistic ability; (2) commercially available audio-lingual course materials with complete sets of accompanying tapes; (3) a portable tape recorder for loan to each participating student; (4) a native-speaking exchange student to serve as a pronunciation drill master; (5) regular academic credit; (6) a specialist from a leading university invited quarterly to evaluate progress and to furnish the grade for the quarter's work; (7) a faculty member, familiar with audio-lingual techniques, to serve as part-time coordinator for the entire program.

During the first two years of the Kalamazoo Program twenty-three liberal arts freshmen and sophomores had each taken, for regular academic credit, from two to four quarters of one of the six neglected languages offered: Mandarin Chinese, Japanese, Hindi-Urdu, Persian, Swahili, and Brazilian Portuguese. Each student worked at his own speed for eight to ten hours a week with the course materials and for another three to four hours a week with a foreign student drill master. Visiting specialists from the Department of Far Eastern Languages of the University of Michigan, from the African Studies Center at Michigan State University, and from the Peace Corps Training Center for Brazilian Portuguese at the University of Wisconsin in Milwaukee were invited to examine the students quarterly and to rate them on the same basis as their own regular students. In all but one language the course materials used by the Kalamazoo students were the same as the materials used by the specialists in their own courses. Thus there was a good basis for comparison. The students in the Kalamazoo Program consistently received excellent ratings from the visiting specialists. Since the program is largely self-instructional with expert guidance and evaluation, the cost is modest enough for small colleges. Its flexibility makes possible instruction in a large number of neglected languages even for the immediate benefit of only one interested student.[12]

Another possible solution (as yet unexplored to my knowledge) to the problem of making instruction available in neglected languages in small colleges is the organization of consortia. This would be possible in areas where a fairly large number of small colleges is clustered within an area small enough for easy commuting between the member colleges. Such a consortium might function as follows: Each member college would agree to develop regular courses up to at least the second-year level in one neglected language. These courses would then be made available to the students of the other participating colleges with credits mutually granted and accepted for these courses by the participating colleges. In this way a small college could make available to its students several (depending on the number of member colleges) neglected languages while having to provide the cost for only one.

Appraisal of Progress

The plans outlined above represent various means of providing under-graduate instruction in neglected languages to a very small number of highly selected and self-motivated students. These plans, however, do not provide a full answer to the consensus of the Conference on Critical Languages in Liberal Arts Colleges, namely, that "the study of such major world languages as Arabic, Chinese, Hindi-Urdu, Japanese, Portuguese and Russian should be included in American higher education not merely as a special purpose course for foreign area careers but in its own right as a valuable element in liberal education."[13]

While much progress has been made in the furthering of the study of neglected languages and cultures, there is general agreement that much more needs to be done. Perhaps one of the greatest obstacles is psychological, the difficulty of orienting to a vastly changed world situation. It is interesting that even geographical terminology established in the old order of things can produce problems and embarrassment in the new order. Apparently such problems can arise from the most well-intentioned sources. The Peace Corps recently changed the name of its Far East Division to East Asia and Pacific Region. The change was prompted by the objection of a Philippine senator, who asked, "Why Far East? Far from what?" The senator argued that the term "Far East" represents "archaic, paternalistic Euro-centrism." Peace Corps officials are now concerned about the title "North Africa and Near East Division." "Near what?" they ask. One also thinks of such negative terms as "non-Western" and "non-Indo-European" used so much by the very people who are most vitally concerned with promoting interest in these areas.

JAMES E. IANNUCCI has taught at Saint Joseph's College in Philadelphia since 1936, and since 1944 has been chairman of its Department of Modern Languages. He taught French Applied Linguistics at the NDEA Summer Language Institutes, University of Maine, 1960 and New York University, 1961. He is also chairman of the Test Construction Committee, MLA Foreign Language Proficiency Tests for Teachers and Advanced Students, French Speaking Tests. His works include a book, titled *Lexical Number in Spanish Nouns with Reference to their English Equivalents,* and articles in *Romance Philology, Modern Language Journal, Babel, Hispania.* In 1964-1965, Dr. Iannucci served as Consultant and Professor of Linguistics at Airlangga University, Malang, East Java, Indonesia.

FOOTNOTES

1. John Harmon, James Simms, and Hannelore Tierney, MANPOWER IN THE NEGLECTED LANGUAGES, Fall, 1962. New York: Modern Language Association of America, 1964. Hannelore Tierney; Gladys A. Lund, and Marjorie N. Ball, MANPOWER IN THE NEGLECTED LANGUAGE, Fall, 1963. New York: Modern Language Association of America, 1965.
2. Since 1959 the Center for Applied Linguistics has published six times a year its newsletter, THE LINGUISTIC REPORTER, which keeps the profession abreast of current developments in program, teaching materials, bibliography, current meetings, and conferences. The Center also publishes useful bibliographies and statistical studies.
3. Since 1953 the ACLS has sponsored an extensive Program in Oriental Languages for the production of basic descriptions, elementary textbooks, grammars, introductions to writing, graded readers, and dictionaries. This program has also made an important contribution to the development of American specialists in Asian languages.
4. George M. Beckman, "The Role of the Foundations in Non-Western Studies." THE ANNALS OF THE AMERICAN ACADEMY OF POLITICAL AND SOCIAL SCIENCE, Vol. 356, November 1964.
5. Austin E. Fife and Marion L. Nielsen, CONFERENCE ON NEGLECTED LANGUAGES. A REPORT. New York: Modern Language Association of America, 1961.

6. CONFERENCE ON CRITICAL LANGUAGES IN LIBERAL ARTS COLLEGES, Washington, D.C.: Association of American Colleges, 1965, 6-7.
7. *Ibid.*, 18-24.
8. *Ibid.*, 12-13.
9. *Ibid.*, 30-31.
10. UNIVERSITY RESOURCES IN THE UNITED STATES FOR LINGUISTICS AND TEACHER TRAINING IN ENGLISH AS A FOREIGN LANGUAGE, 5th rev. ed. Washington, D.C.: Center for Applied Linguistics, 1966.
11. UNDERGRADUATE INSTRUCTION IN CRITICAL LANGUAGES AND AREA STUDIES. Princeton, N.J.: Princeton University, 1964, 24-27.
12. CONFERENCE ON CRITICAL LANGUAGES IN LIBERAL ARTS COLLEGES. Washington, D.C.: Association of American Colleges, 1965, 7-11.
13. *Ibid.*, 5-6.

Selected Bibliography

Beckman, George M., "The Role of the Foundations in Non-Western Studies." THE ANNALS OF THE AMERICAN ACADEMY OF POLITICAL AND SOCIAL SCIENCE, Vol. 356, November 1964.

CONFERENCE ON CRITICAL LANGUAGES IN LIBERAL ARTS COLLEGES. Washington, D.C.: Association of American Colleges, 1965. A report of a conference held at the University of Washington, April 6-7, 1965. This includes annotated lists of available teaching materials for Arabic, Chinese, Hindi-Urdu, Japanese, Portuguese, and Russian.

Fife, Austin E. and Nielsen, Marion L., CONFERENCE ON NEGLECTED LANGUAGES. A REPORT. New York: Modern Language Association of America. 1961. Report of a conference held in Washington, D.C. Its purpose was to bring into a unified whole the deliberations and conclusions of a number of previous conferences dealing with specific problems of language development. It was sponsored jointly by the MLA and the U.S. Office of Education.

Harmon, John, Simms, James, and Tierney, Hannelore, MANPOWER IN THE NEGLECTED LANGUAGES, Fall, 1962. New York: Modern Language Association of America, 1964.

Miller, Andrew Roy, A SURVEY OF INTENSIVE PROGRAMS IN THE UNCOMMON LANGUAGES, Summer, 1964. New Haven, 1964.

NON-WESTERN STUDIES IN THE LIBERAL ARTS COLLEGE. Washington, D.C., 1964. A report of the Commission on International Understanding of the Association of American Colleges.

Parker, William R., THE NATIONAL INTEREST AND FOREIGN LANGUAGES, 3rd ed. Washington, D.C., 1961.

RETROSPECT AND PROSPECT ON THE NEGLECTED LAN-
GUAGES. Mimeographed. A report of a conference held at
Northwestern University, January 16-17, 1965. Its purpose was
to make an assessment of progress made to date and the establishment of needs, priorities and guidelines for research and development of instructional materials in the uncommonly taught
languages.

Rice, Frank A., STUDY AIDS FOR CRITICAL LANGUAGES.
Washington, D.C.: Center for Applied Linguistics. 1966. A briefly annotated bibliography of 275 items (tapes and records as
well as books) representing eighty languages arranged alphabetically by language from Afrikaans to Vietnamese.

Tierney, Hannelore, Lund, Gladys A., and Ball, Marjorie N., MAN-
POWER IN THE NEGLECTED LANGUAGES, Fall, 1963.
New York: Modern Language Association of America, 1965. A
photo-offset report in five parts on the teaching and study of all
languages except French, German, Italian, Russian, and Spanish
in U.S. colleges and universities.

UNDERGRADUATE INSTRUCTION IN CRITICAL LANGUAGES
AND AREA STUDIES. Mimeographed. A report of a conference held at Princeton University, October 12-13, 1964, with
support from the U.S. Office of Education. The conference
brought together sixty-eight scholars representing a variety of
skills bearing on undergraduate instruction in critical languages
and area studies.

THE UNIVERSITY LOOKS AHEAD: APPROACHES TO WORLD
AFFAIRS AT SIX AMERICAN UNIVERSITIES. New York:
Walker & Co., 1965. A report of Education and World Affairs, a
private nonprofit educational organization established in 1962
with basic support from the Ford Foundation and the Carnegie
Corporation of New York. Its chief concern is with the activities
of American colleges and universities in the international field.
The universities included in the report are Stanford, Michigan
State, Tulane, Wisconsin, Cornell, and Indiana.

UNIVERSITY RESOURCES IN THE UNITED STATES FOR
LINGUISTICS AND TEACHER TRAINING IN ENGLISH AS
A FOREIGN LANGUAGE, 5th rev. ed. Washington, D.C.:
Center for Applied Linguistics, 1966. Although not revealed in
the title, this is a useful guide for university resources, both
linguistic and pedagogic, in the neglected languages. An index
of over a hundred languages indicates in which universities each
is taught.

RELATED PROBLEMS

Intensive Language Training

ORRIN FRINK
Ohio University

THE CONCEPT OF intensive language training arose and flourished in two traditions, both traditions born of military expediency. One tradition grew under the Army Specialized Training Program (ASTP) and the Army's Civilian Affairs Training School (CATS) founded in 1943, descendants of which lingered on in one form or another at a number of civilian universities during the first post-Second World War decade. It is this tradition that produced so much controversy in our professional journals over the last twenty years. Attempts to apply the principles developed under the ASTP and CATS programs to semi-intensive civilian language courses meeting 8-12 hours per week gave rise to many misunderstandings concerning the nature of intensive language training.

In the other tradition, intensive language courses meeting 30-40 hours per week have been offered by the Army Language School and the Navy Language School for more than three decades. Although these programs received little attention in the professional journals, a great deal of our modern foreign language training methodology had its origin in these schools and their civilian adjuncts, where the earlier traditions of intensive language training are still carried on.

The historical background is nowhere clearly spelled out for intensive language training, and although none of them distinguished sufficiently clearly between the two traditions, the following five sources present a fairly good impression of the general trends in intensive language training.

William G. Moulton's splendid article "Linguistics and Language Teaching in the United States 1940-1960," which appeared in the inaugural issue of the *International Review of Applied Linguistics in Language Teaching* presents a general outline of the development of the intensive idea.[1] Moulton interprets and presents the development and growth of the new language methodology from the point of view of a linguist who was intimately involved with the application of the most modern theories of linguistics to the problem of fast, effective mass training in foreign languages for the military during the Second World War and in the postwar years. His chronicle draws on well over a hundred sources, following the new methodology from its inception under the guidance of the American Council of Learned Societies in 1941 through its extension under the ASTP and CATS programs in 1943, the expansion of the Army and Navy Language Schools, and other postwar civilian university language programs.

A second account appears in the form of an article, "The Application of Linguistics to Language Teaching," by Mary R. Haas in the anthology *Anthropology Today,* edited by A. L. Kroeber.[2] The author writes from the viewpoint of a linguist and traces the appearance and adoption of modern linguistic techniques by the ASTP and subsequent postwar semi-intensive programs initiated at a number of universities.

A third account tracing the development of the intensive idea is found in Jacob Ornstein's article "Structurally Oriented Texts and Teaching Methods Since World War II: A Survey and Appraisal."[3] Here we find structural linguistics again flourishing under the ASTP and subsequent civilian programs, and practically no mention of the Army and Navy Language Schools.

The two most detailed texts on the wartime language teaching methodology are *Armed Forces Foreign Language Teaching,* 1947 by Angiolillo, and *Area Studies in the Armed Services,* 1947 by Matthew.[4, 5] Both accounts stress the ASTP and CATS aspect of the programs, while the latter contains an excellent annotated bibliography with over two hundred source articles, books and documents prior to 1948 which are pertinent to intensive language training.

ASTP, CATS and Semi-Intensive

As stated in the Army directives issued June 23, 1943, the specific objectives were quite general. We find that any methodology which would achieve the objectives outlined was acceptable to the military, and that according to the directive, provision for seventeen contract hours of language study was to be made in the curriculum for the ASTP.[6] Professional criticism of the ASTP was quickly felt and quickly answered by Cowan and Graves. Their answer appeared in the February 1944 issue of *Hispania* and suggested that the "dribble method" of learning languages (three hours a week for years) was insufficient, that better results are obtained by more concentrated use of the students' time (a minimum of ten hours per week), that major emphasis at first should be placed upon the acquisition of spoken language, and that language instruction should be controlled by a trained technical linguist.[7]

Perhaps the clearest explanation of method was the one adopted by the Commission on Trends in Education of the Modern Language Association of America on May 27, 1944:

Many persons have been led to believe that these striking results were attained through the discovery of a magical new method. This is by no means true. On the contrary, they were the fruits of the application of well-tried practices. Nor were the results achieved under the direction of linguistic magicians. The entire language program was designed by teachers of foreign languages in consultation with the War Department, and in the fifty-five colleges and universities to which the trainees were assigned the program was entrusted to the foreign language departments, which organized the work, gave instruction to the student-soldiers, and engaged and supervised special assistants required for any emergency . . .[8]

Springer notes that in accordance with the wartime directives, intensive language study under the ASTP was to have the following specific features: a large number of instructional hours (contact hours) in a relatively short period of time, small numbers of students per class, a combination of presentation of

211

language structure and conversational practice, emphasis on drill and the formation of linguistic habits, phonemic analysis and transcription, employment of native informants, and a specific objective of command of the colloquial spoken form of the language.[9] It is not surprising then to find Haas noting in 1953 that some language teachers were delighted with the results achieved by the new methods, while others (particularly those who had little firsthand contact with them) hated the very thought of the innovations.[10] This feeling of hatred and suspicion persists twenty years later, and the reason is not difficult to understand. Few of the shorter, hence more popular, articles published during the twenty-year postwar period agree on the essential nature of intensive language training, and most of these attribute the innovations exclusively to the model of the ASTP.

The so-called "intensive language" courses developed by a score of American universities in the late 1940's and 1950's were patterned on the experiences of the ASTP program and finally resulted in standard "Intensive" courses such as the Intensive Russian 101-102 now offered by the Slavic Department of Indiana University. Such a course meets eight hours a week meeting one hour a day, five days a week with a native Russian drill instructor, with an additional three one-hour sessions under the guidance of a trained linguist or Russian specialist. Although eight hours per week is more than half of a student's normal fifteen-hour class load, this accounts for only a very small portion of the 168 hours per week that are available, and could be called "intensive" only after the model of the ASTP and CATS programs of the Second World War.

DLI and Intensive

By an act of Congress in February 1962, the Army Language School in California, and the Navy Language School in Washington, D.C. were combined under the jurisdiction of the newly created Defense Language Institute (DLI), the two language schools becoming respectively DLI-West Coast and DLI-East Coast. At this merger, DLI also assumed the responsibility of negotiating contracts with civilian universities to provide intensive language training for the Air Force. For the last several years, truly intensive language training based on maximum utilization of the available time has been carried on chiefly by DLI-West Coast, DLI-East Coast, by Yale, Syracuse and Indiana University for the Air Force, and by the Foreign Service Institute of the Department of State, Georgetown University, and the National Security Agency. The July 16, 1965 issue of *TIME* magazine devoted two columns to the Army Language School DLI-West Coast in an article which briefly describes the installation's business of training 2,500 military personnel a year in 27 languages and 33 dialects, in courses that range from a 12-week "quickie" in Vietnamese to a full 47 weeks in Chinese, Russian, Arabic and some 13 other languages.[11] It is in these institutions that intensive language training is carried on in its purest form, where it again serves the requirements of military expediency. No civilian university has elected to carry on the traditions characteristic of the intensive language training methodology which is displayed by the Defense Language Institute and its civilian adjuncts, Yale, Syracuse, and Indiana University.

While we have witnessed some striking changes in the structure and methodology of language teaching in our colleges and universities since the Second World War, these changes are but a small portion of the changes we can expect in the near future, and a smaller part of the changes we might expect when such progressive fields as education, psychology, and communication theory are brought to bear on the problems of effective foreign language teaching.

Intensive language training is currently based on three fundamental principles: the principle of a complete concentration on one purpose, the principle of a high degree of curriculum organization and planning, and the principle of the separation of the functions of teaching and drilling.

The first principle is that of one hundred per cent concentration on the task at hand, attaining mastery or fluency in a foreign language. In our decade a forty-hour work week is the current standard; one hundred per cent concentration means forty hours a week. Therefore, government and military personnel, for whom such a course of language training is often required, normally spend six hours a day, five days a week in a formal classroom environment, and then put in an additional two or three hours of homework each night. There is no natural reason why such a program could not be extended beyond this arbitrary forty hour per week limit. However, there is no basis to believe that forty hours a week actively studying a foreign language is not too much time over the long run. Nevertheless, the first salient characteristic of intensive language training is the principle that if you really want to master something, you can hardly do better than by spending most of your consciously directed time and effort trying to master that one thing. The principle of one hundred per cent concentration on the task at hand could probably be applied to gaining mastery of any particular phase of a foreign language. It is just as easy to imagine a group of students devoting all their time to learning to produce good abstracts of technical articles as it is to imagine them devoting all their time to learning to converse in a foreign language. It just happens that the emphasis required for most positions in the government or the military service has traditionally been an audio-lingual fluency.

The second principle is that an intensive language program is by nature highly organized. This is both a result of the large enrollments normal to intensive language programs, as well as a result of the great speed with which an intensive language program covers the material. If teachers and students in an intensive language program do not know what is required of them specifically and in great detail every moment, there is chaos and a great deal of lost time. If in a traditional three or four hours per week language course the student did not prepare for the lesson, he can often improvise his way through the class hour, and have a day or so to prepare the next hour more thoroughly. Intensive language training moves much too rapidly to accommodate any such improvisation unless it is specifically planned. The planning that goes into a traditional college fifteen-week course meeting four hours per week would be expended before the end of the second week in an intensive language course. Thus, a high degree of organization and planning is one of the natural prerequisites of an intensive language training course.

The third principle is that of the separation of the functions of teaching and drilling. Whereas we would never expect the professor of physics or chemistry to be both a lecturer and a laboratory, there has been a latent expectancy that the language teacher will be an excellent lecturer as well as an excellent drill instructor. This concept seems to be a notion well ingrained in our traditional thinking. By separating the responsibilities of academic lecturer and drill instructor, perhaps we can arrive at a situation analogous to that of the physics professor and the physics laboratory, and in so doing, insure optimum fulfillment of both functions.

In all other respects, the principles characteristic of the intensive language programs of the ASTP model are valid for the Defense Language Institute model.

The Changing Aspects of Language Training

In spite of our relatively recent experience with intensive language training, evoked in times of national crisis when it became a military necessity to bring foreign language training to its utmost efficiency, our modern foreign language teaching methodology at the college level has changed very little over the last several decades. That our colleges and universities are willing to perpetuate their traditional methods without further innovation and experimentation and without drawing more heavily on the new techniques developed with intensive language training, is a matter of concern for the teaching profession. Such ideas and principles as increased class contact hours, smaller class size, the audio-lingual approach with emphasis first placed on acquisition of the spoken language, the use of native informants, and linguistically guided patterned structural drills appear as firm recommendations of the Modern Language Association in the conference report prepared and edited by Mac-Allister on the preparation of college teachers of modern foreign languages finally only after twenty years since they were first used by Cowan, Graves and Springer to characterize intensive language training in 1944.[12]

It would be a credit to our institutions of higher learning to see a renewed effort and experimentation with intensive language training along the lines of the ASTP and DLI models. It would be equally pleasing to see some of the principles and characteristics of intensive language training of twenty years ago further implemented as fundamental bases of our current college-level language programs, as the MacAllister report urges.

ORRIN FRINK, born in 1932, earned a Bachelor of Arts degree in Russian at Haverford College, a Master of Arts degree in Russian at the Middlebury College Russian Summer School, a Doctor of Philosophy degree in Slavic Languages and Literature at Harvard University, and served a year as a Fulbright Scholar at the State University of Leiden, Netherlands. He was Assistant Professor of Russian and Director of the Russian Division of the University of Massachusetts for two years, and Assistant Professor of Linguistics and Director of the Intensive Language Training Center at Indiana University for three years, and has been Associate Professor of Modern Languages at Ohio University since 1964.

FOOTNOTES

1. William G. Moulton, "Linguistics and Language Teaching in the United States 1940-1960." INTERNATIONAL REVIEW OF APPLIED LINGUISTICS IN LANGUAGE TEACHING, I, No. 1, 1963, 21-41.
2. Mary R. Haas, "The Application of Linguistics to Language Teaching," in ANTHROPOLOGY TODAY, edited by A. L. Kroeber, The University of Chicago Press, Chicago, 1953, 807-818.
3. Jacob Ornstein, "Structurally Oriented Texts and Teaching Methods Since World War II: A Survey and Appraisal." THE MODERN LANGUAGE JOURNAL, XL, No. 5, May 1956, 213-222.
4. Paul F. Angiolillo, ARMED FORCES FOREIGN LANGUAGE TEACHING. New York: S. F. Vanni, 1947, vi + 440.
5. Robert John Matthew, LANGUAGE AND AREA STUDIES IN THE ARMED SERVICES; THEIR FUTURE SIGNIFICANCE. Washington, D.C.; 1947, ix + 211.
6. Otto Springer, "Intensive Language Study as a Part of the College Curriculum." THE GERMAN QUARTERLY, XVII, No. 4, November 1944, Part I, 225-227.
7. J. Milton Cowan and Mortimer Graves, "A Statement on Intensive Language Instruction." HISPANIA, XXVII, No. 1, February 1944, 65-66.
8. "Foreign Languages and the Army Program, A statement adopted by the Commission on Trends in Education of the Modern Language Association of America, Atlantic City, New Jersey, May 27, 1944." PUBLICATIONS OF THE MODERN LANGUAGE ASSOCIATION, LIX, No. 4, December 1944, 1317.
9. Otto Springer, Op. Cit.
10. Mary R. Haas, Op. Cit., 815.
11. "Education," TIME, LXXXVIII, No. 3, July 16, 1965, 54, 56.
12. Archibald T. MacAllister, "The Preparation of College Teachers of Modern Foreign Languages: A Conference Report." PUBLICATIONS OF THE MODERN LANGUAGE ASSOCIATION, LXXIX, No. 2, May 1964, 29-43, see especially 32b, 41b and 42a.

Selected Bibliography

BOOKS

Angiolillo, Paul F., ARMED FORCES FOREIGN LANGUAGE TEACHING. New York: S. F. Vanni, 1947. Presents the best detailed description of the planning involved in the ASTP and CATS programs.

Matthew, Robert John, LANGUAGE AND AREA STUDIES IN THE ARMED SERVICES: THEIR FUTURE SIGNIFICANCE. Washington, D.C.: American Council on Education, 1947. While chiefly concerned with a description of the ASTP and CATS programs, this book presents an excellent characterization of the Army and Navy Language Schools, and lists well over two hundred source articles, books and documents prior to 1948.

ARTICLES

Cowan, J. Milton and Graves, Mortimer, "A Statement on Intensive Language Instruction." HISPANIA, XXVII, No. 1, February 1944, 65-66. One of the best replies to exaggerated claims for the "new methodology."

"Education." TIME, LXXXVIII, No. 3, July 16, 1965. Contains an excellent capsule description of the current intensive language training activities of the Defense Language Institute.

"Foreign Languages and the Army Program, A statement adopted by the Commission on Trends in Education of the Modern Language Association of America, Atlantic City, New Jersey, May 27, 1944." PUBLICATIONS OF THE MODERN LANGUAGE ASSOCIATION, LIX, No. 4, December 1944, 1317. A brief but powerful assessment of the characteristics of intensive language training.

Haas, Mary R., "The Application of Linguistics to Language Teaching," in ANTHROPOLOGY TODAY, edited by A. L. Kroeber. Chicago: The University of Chicago Press, 1953, 807-818. Presents a good description of a linguist's impressions of his part in developing the new methodology.

MacAllister, Archibald T., "The Preparation of College Teachers of Modern Foreign Languages: A Conference Report." PUBLICATIONS OF THE MODERN LANGUAGE ASSOCIATION, LXXIX, No. 2, May 1964, 29-43. The strongest recent recommendation of a partial return to the principles characteristic of intensive language training.

Moulton, William G., "Linguistics and Language Teaching in the United States 1940-1960." INTERNATIONAL REVIEW OF APPLIED LINGUISTICS IN LANGUAGE TEACHING, I, No. 1, 1963, 21-41. The recent description of the postwar trends in

217

language teaching over the whole spectrum, with excellent documentation.

Ornstein, Jacob, "Structurally Oriented Texts and Teaching Methods Since World War II: A Survey and Appraisal." THE MODERN LANGUAGE JOURNAL, XL, No. 5, May 1956, 213-222. The best commentary on the application of modern linguistic methods in the classroom and the structural format of materials developed under the ASTP and during the subsequent decade.

Springer, Otto, "Intensive Language Study as a Part of the College Curriculum." THE GERMAN QUARTERLY, XVII, No. 4, November 1944, Part I, 225-227. A commentary on the feasibility of applying some of the new principles to the civilian university programs.

The Language Laboratory

CALVIN ANDRE CLAUDEL
West Virginia Wesleyan College

DURING THE PAST decade in the teaching of foreign languages in the United States, the meteoric rise of the language laboratory to its present prominence is worthy of critical study, since the glowing claims of its proponents have not been fulfilled, not because of any failure of this mechanical medium but because of its misapplication in our regimented methods. There is a crying need for more meaningful use of the laboratory with better teaching methods.

Ten or so years ago, the language laboratory was almost unknown, certainly to the traditional language teacher, who might have dismissed the idea of such an innovation as a fad or as a superficial approach, unworthy of scholarly attention. Yet because of the sudden demand for foreign languages and because of the invention of electronic devices coupled with their release and subsidization by the government, language laboratories mushroomed in most of our large metropolitan school systems.

Conservative teachers grudgingly cooperated with the growingly compulsive programs. "Even though you don't agree and don't like it, you'd better make use of this equipment, because it represents a tremendous investment of the taxpayer's money!" was a phrase sometimes heard. Some isolated school districts, without any plans for using such devices, might ask for them since they ostensibly cost nothing, except at first in casual commitments which were ultimately to bring on our present widespread lockstep method of teaching foreign languages in the officially accepted "New Key" or audio-lingual method. Thus an official government pamphlet recently proclaimed after some four reprintings: "The language laboratory makes its greatest contribution as an integral part of a program

219

in which audio-lingual instruction forms the basis for the progressive and continuous development of all the language skills."[1]

The language laboratory was to be the focal point and means of teaching by a kind of crash method whose presumed effectiveness was trumpeted far and wide. Among the many weaknesses now attributed to the audio-lingual approach, the main one is "too much reliance on mechanical devices for learning."[2]

A Scientific Allure

A sort of *mystique* developed around the language laboratory, investing it with almost magical possibilities. One writer aptly said: "The language laboratory can only create a superficial stimulus for those fascinated by its technical or 'scientific' allure."[3] However, this fascination is wearing off, and there is a need for a sober reassessment, if we are to make progress in the teaching of languages, as pointed out by Dr. Meras in his article cited above and by many other critics.

There is growing disenchantment with and criticism of the use of the language laboratory: "It is incumbent upon laboratory researchers, therefore, to interpret their findings conservatively and cautiously and to report all but incontrovertible findings at best."[4]

Machines are valuable aids in the teaching of languages, but only aids, and they will never replace the keen-minded and well-trained teacher.

Revolution in Language Teaching

Let us consider some of the factors in the rise and spread of the language laboratory. For years the student eager to learn the living spoken language, not only as found in literature but in all aspects of life, had begun to question the language pedagogue's insistence on only grammar memorization and translation of literary works. Conditions were sometimes worse on the higher university level where professors, complacent and indifferent, lectured in English and expatiated in course after course on the most abstruse philological points and esoteric questions while avoiding any practical aspect of the language. Certainly the ever-widening gulf between the student's dimmed hopes to master a language and the teacher's failure to meet his needs were to help spark a revolution in language teaching.

Perhaps to liven his boring chores, the inventive student in the past might have used language records. Indeed the phonograph recording of dialogues was the kernel idea of the language laboratory, and the wire and tape recorder gave further impetus to it.

Next, the multiplying media of communication, bringing every corner of the earth closer together, not only pointed up the importance of languages but also the possibility of better methods of teaching them. The many inventions, from the overhead projector to the broadcasting satellite, presented undreamed-of possibilities.

Is Language a Science?

The term "language laboratory" arose by analogy with the science laboratory, although languages and literature had not been conceived of as sciences such as biology and chemistry in the past: "An unstable E dropped at the wrong place will not turn up red, nor can we analyze rising and falling intonations as alkaline and acid."[5]

The scientific method did help to discover and explain the often regularly recurring sounds and structures of language. The ancients were aware of these facts. The influence of the scientific method on the study and teaching of languages became more pronounced in the nineteenth century in the field of philology and later spread to the field of literature, by way of literary classification and analysis, especially in our increasingly sterile literary research.[6]

The relating of liberal arts to sciences is no accident, for this has been a growing tendency, particularly in Germanic and American scholarship. This is especially true in totalitarian countries like Russia, where science with an emphasis on technology permeates every aspect of life. Our competitive concern with the latter nation is somewhat causing us to overemphasize technology.

In this century we see the even greater influence of science on linguistics and phonetics which gave rise to the phonetics laboratory, the predecessor of the language laboratory. Middlebury College was a pioneer.[7]

In the recent past there developed an *avant-garde* movement in linguistics, known as the school of "phonemic analysis," "structural linguistics," or lately "the new linguistics," etc., which sees language as a purely contemporary popular expression: "For both practical purposes and scientific analysis, a language is the way people talk, not the way someone thinks they ought to talk."[8]

The phonemicists or structural linguists are often referred to as the descriptivists. The traditionalists are called prescriptivists. The position of the structural or descriptive linguist is an inconsistent one, indeed, for while he regards language as a science, in practice he accepts no traditional norm but only a somewhat amorphous folk speech.[9] The well-trained scholar views language as slowly changing and developing through both popular and cultural influences. The extreme prescriptivist is in an equally untenable position when he refuses to recognize any change.

The new linguists claim a close relationship not only to natural sciences but also to the so-called "behavioral sciences." They have broken completely with the classical and humanistic traditions and explain language as a purely physical skill or habit to be taught and learned by mechanistic methods. They assume a biological and non-intellectual basis for language, which is "far more visceral than cerebral."[10]

The scientist is interested in the physical universe while the scholar of literature is interested in aesthetic and spiritual values. The good scientist and the good literary scholar are not mutually exclusive. The literary scholar should not be a vassal to the sciences nor be enslaved by technology. "But though we be the children of technology we must be its masters and not its slaves."[11]

Doctrinaire groups furnished much of the leadership for the officially accepted new language movement. Its adherents claim that language and its study is a "science." In the expressions "New Math," "New Language," "New Key," we see links with the teaching of mathematics and a mutual jargon in such words as "set," "frame," "pattern," etc. This would-be scientific approach is seen in even more extremist schools such as "psycholinguistics," "biolinguistics," and "mathematical linguistics." There is an ever-increasing amount of so-called "scientific" language in teaching and learning material emanating from "behavioral research laboratories."

Traditional scholars have been justly critical. Professor

Watkins plainly states in a previously cited article, "Language is by tradition, and rightly so, considered as one of the humanities rather than one of the sciences."[12] Indeed, language is not only the door to the humanities but also to the sciences, for civilization is inconceivable without language.

Laboratory Literature

There have been in the past few years numerous volumes and hundreds of articles written on the language laboratory, and some are continuing to appear. A bibliography of these would make a sizable tome. Some of them deal with the purely mechanical aspects and maintenance. Others deal with the laboratory and its use in the audio-lingual method, with emphasis on drill and repetition. While a number of these works voice approval of this mechanical medium associated with the mechanistic audio-lingual method, there is an ever-growing number of highly critical ones, questioning the validity of this method[13] and even the use of the laboratory itself as it is currently applied.[14] Finally, quite a few suggest its use with more meaningful and better methods, especially the direct audio-visual.[15]

Methods and Laboratory

When we discuss the language laboratory, we must necessarily think of it in terms of language teaching methods. In several current methods: 1) the traditional, 2) the audio-lingual, and 3) the direct audio-visual method. The first is the traditional method which uses texts that emphasize the study of grammar in English and the translating of numerous sentences from English into the foreign language. For the second year, this system is usually followed by a similar review grammar with even more English exercises to be translated. The third year may include a sort of review of review grammars, from which the student must translate whole themes. While this method is not completely bad, it is certainly inadequate to teach a foreign language effectively. However, this method is better than the dialogue-parroting one, the second method prevalent today, which is often represented as the audio-lingual, aural-oral, or "New Key" method, bolstered by laboratory hardware. The originators of this method seem to have chanced upon the words "New Key" from Susanne K. Langer's *Philosophy in a New Key*.

223

Expensive makeshift volumes, always accompanied by costly tapes for laboratory use, are creating a "textbook jungle."[16] Concerning these texts and tapes which are all "almost hypnotically boring and repetitious," one critic says: "Since 'poor' and 'mediocre' best describe the vast majority of each year's new and revised texts, the value of most tapes is obviously minimal."[17]

In spite of this patent situation, the writer has been shocked to note that the United States Office of Education has just recently made a grant of $159,525 to ascertain whether the audio-lingual method is more effective than the traditional method.[18]

As one language scholar writes, "The much-needed reassessment of our profession . . . set the stage for a general overhauling of foreign language teaching and led to a period of unprecedented activity — though not necessarily of unprecedented success."[19]

In initiating this stultifying method, based upon Pavlovian psychology, audio-lingualists required of students endless repetition and "relentless drill."[20]

The audio-lingual method not only does not require any intellectual effort on the part of the student, but its purpose "is to bring him 'not to think' in any language."[21] Thought is discouraged, although "it is the intelligence of the student which, it seems to me, we should cultivate more in the language classroom, and which has been overlooked by high-powered methodology."[22] In her severe criticism of the lack of using the intellect in the audio-lingual method, a writer says that "it now appears that the mind can take lessons from the tongue."[23] She also has another incisive comment: "Too often we're getting completely thoughtless responses — canned answers, probably, to canned questions."[24]

Language Institutes

The Language Institute Program was established through government subsidy. Growing numbers of these hastily-contrived institutes were launched, in which teachers have been trained to use the laboratory in the audio-lingual method. "A major application of the university language laboratory is for training teachers not only in the language they will teach but also in the use of the language laboratory."[25]

Concerning these programs, one teacher likens the lectures

to "wartime indoctrination sessions."[26] Myron gives a pessimistic description of the whole program tied in with the institutes: "At institutes, seasoned and less-experienced colleagues alike are now assembled and instructed in the jargon of the new language game."[27]

Discussing the future of the institutes, one writer seems to assume there is no other method but the audio-lingual.[28] Hocking says that "even some of the NDEA Institutes seem not to have heard of visuals."[29]

Groundswell of Criticism

There is a groundswell of criticism against our lockstep laboratory methods: "I do not believe that the cause of either language or of education is served when we use our expensive laboratory equipment to drill into the unwilling heads of our students endless sets of disconnected inanities."[30]

A teacher from France states, "We are training civilized and cultivated young people, not parrots that can only repeat phrases learned by rote or banalities fabricated in assemblyline fashion."[31] Another states that language "cannot be acquired by the mere parroting of dialogues and patterns without some sort of intellective process."[32]

It is difficult to explain our Juggernaut course in our somewhat "strange revolution," so aptly described by Myron: "If unchecked the overaccent and imbalance will lead, through its already anti-intellectual and illiberal trends, to the eventual mechanization of subject matter and regimentation of the human beings with whom we deal."[33]

One writer criticizes the one-school domination for the use of words out of their accepted meaning: "A further evidence of a drift toward the same kind of one-school domination which, until recently, shackled the public schools, is the trend for pre-empting common terms to compose a special jargon. Terms like 'conversational,' 'aural,' 'oral,' 'pattern,' 'linguistic' can no longer be used with impunity in their full legitimate meaning."[34] An amusing article has been written by John C. Merrill on the "New Language" jargon, which he dubs "Novalinguistication."[35]

Another critic commiserates with the students coerced into laboratory attendance: "There is nevertheless a considerable majority which, when herded in 'masses and lumps' into the beehive cells of the lab, slump and relax, then twist and squirm. No more aggressive protest in the guise of passive revolt could be witnessed within the educational precincts today."[36]

Another teacher has this to say: "Although foreign language teaching has become more of a science, it must not overlook the sensitivity of the learner." She asks: "Is the audiolingual approach to foreign languages increasing the sale of tranquilizers to college students?"[37]

While some of the articles voice an indirect disapproval of the laboratory, most of the criticisms, if we note well, are leveled at the audio-lingual method. Meras enumerates six glaring faults of this method including over-reliance on the laboratory, pattern drills, and repetition. The student is unable "to meet emergency needs in conversation," and his vocabulary is too limited in scope to read even modern literature. He finally points out that there is "less work accomplished than by previous methods although more time is spent in teaching and more time consumed in learning."[38]

Keating emphasizes that he is criticizing the current use of the laboratory, making it clear that the laboratory doubtless has untapped possibilities: "No attempt was made . . . to indicate what results would be obtained under some ideal . . . program . . . into which the laboratory has been integrated according to organizational principles not yet widely accepted . . . this study has attempted to assay the results that were obtained with the laboratory as it was actually being used."[39]

Researchers have emphasized the need for investigations to bring out undiscovered potential application: "Certain uses of the laboratory remain to be explored. . . . Use of the laboratory should not be limited to one type of exercise, nor one type of course, nor one grade level. Its application will differ in different learning situations."[40]

To solve our impasse Meras suggests a return to the direct method, with audio-visual aids and cited John Carroll, a psychologist, who found that "materials presented visually are more easily learned and more accurately than materials presented orally."[41] Although Meras finds many faults in the audio-lingual method, he remains an apologist for it and feels that it can be salvaged by being combined with the direct audio-visual. He seems to equate the audio-visual method with the so-called "Saint Cloud Method," which certainly leaves much to be desired.[42]

The Better Audio-visual Method

The third or best method, according to some language experts, is an entirely direct audio-visual method, used in the more up-to-date educational institutions in the teaching of French. This system emphasizes at the very outset the exclusive use of the foreign language by the visual method associated simultaneously with the spoken word and the concomitant study of living grammar and all the other aspects of culture.

This method still remains relatively unknown. Elton Hocking says: "Many teachers are unprepared to use such revolutionary materials; most schools still lack a language laboratory, and most of the labs do not provide for visuals."[43] He cites a number of experts who show that effective language teaching and effective use of the laboratory lie in audio-visual aids.[44]

The audio-visual method is really the way a mother teaches language to her child. She does it in a relevant and meaningful way, not by endless mechanical repetition. The well-trained teacher does not at all reject the laboratory but simply its misuse. Indeed, he welcomes it, giving it a much broader concept and function in both the visual and auditory sense. The visual elements are not only presented by way of pictures but also in the form of living examples, specimens, drawings, charts, music, sounds, movements, etc.

The resourceful teacher invents his own laboratory in his daily class, if need be. The electronic devices of the so-called language laboratory are not really basically necessary, although these are helpful in supplying numerous native voices.

This writer had the opportunity of witnessing the effective use of the audio-visual method in teaching French at the Alliance Française in Paris and at its branch in Mexico City. This program is built around the three-volume series of Gaston Mauger, entitled *Cours de langue et de civilisation françaises*. The native teacher uses filmstrips to show on a screen basic objects from the immediate environment which are identified by the spoken word and logically related to everyday activities. The pictures and written words of the beginning text relate directly to the images of the filmstrips. The first volume contains sixty-five lessons, and the filmstrips are used along with the first twenty-five lessons in an intensive audio-visual presentation.

Commercial tapes with native voices accompany filmstrips for the first twenty-five lessons. More tapes are being made. This writer is at present using these tapes, filmstrips, and also slides in his French classes.

When to Use the Laboratory

There is no settled opinion on how much or how often the laboratory should be used, whether it should be integrated with classwork or whether it should be used separately.[45] Research seems to show that about an hour a week is devoted to this purpose.[46] Some institutions, however, seem to require an excessive use of the laboratory.[47]

William S. Vincent believes the laboratory should be used for the first year only: "If a school wishes to employ the language laboratory, its best move in the light of these results is to schedule first year language students into the lab for frequent and intensive exercises in speech production. Once a student 'has the tongue in his head,' the value of the laboratory appears to have passed its peak."[48] In many institutions laboratory attendance is becoming optional or students put in a token appearance once or twice during the course.

The idea that a language student reaches a saturation point or peak in the use of such materials in language learning may be a reaction to the aimless laboratory work of the audio-lingual method, for certainly audio-visual materials, meaningfully planned and related to classroom work, are useful to all levels of language learning, as pointed out by Sarah W. Lorge.[49]

Thus far our large and expensive laboratories have been mostly listening centers, arranged in cubicles with earphones. Our problem lies in the limited exploitation of the laboratory. Although the laboratory of the future will include such acoustical facilities, other needs, such as the visual, will have to be taken into account.

We have considered the effective use of the language laboratory with the audio-visual method for the beginning level of learning a foreign language. However, a more sophisticated use of the language laboratory is not only conceivable but has been realized beyond this elementary level. In Mexico City at the

Institut Français audiovisuel et linguistique (IFAL) this writer attended classes with programmed audio-visual French materials presented effectively for all levels. Although writers loosely mention "visuals" or "visual aids" in language teaching, for the best and most effective foreign language teaching, we should think in terms of a sustained audio-visual method integrated with class work.

While the Mauger method is a truly audio-visual method when properly applied, there are other texts for secondary and elementary levels: Robin and Bergeaud's *Le Français par la méthode directe* and Mauger and Gougenheim's *Le Français élémentaire*. There are several commercial texts for teaching foreign languages through pictures, such as I. A. Richards' *French Through Pictures, Spanish Through Pictures,* etc., which offer possibilities for the imaginative teacher to use in a beginning course.

Programming

Some writers give rather glowing accounts of the possibilities of programmed teaching and learning through the language laboratory without sufficiently considering the question of methods.[50]

Our elementary language program needs reappraisal.[51] Programmed and televised classes are excellent when integrated with serious class work. One of our greatest lacks is a well-defined program that progresses logically and gradually in a well-articulated and coordinated curriculum. This lack of coordination stems from the lack of planning and from a general unawareness of where we are going in foreign languages.

After the initiation of Foreign Language in Elementary Schools (FLES) some fifteen years ago, language enrollment in elementary schools shot from several thousand to today's several millions. Obviously our staff and language program were not adequate to meet these mass demands. Therefore a makeshift program was used to pay lip-service to public demands. In many cases so-called "programmed" classes were set up with "piped-in" television programs once or twice a week. In these infrequent classes that lasted perhaps only fifteen or thirty minutes, the poorly trained teacher sometimes acted only as a sort of monitor, going through the motions and posturings of teaching a foreign language. Television programming and teaching machines may well become a curse instead of a blessing.[52]

The Audio-visual Laboratory

Yet the laboratory and its various teaching machines, if properly used, should be regarded by the language teacher as a blessing and not as a bane. However, it is better to begin with a modest outlay of inexpensive equipment. No device should be acquired unless there is real need for it. The first acquisition should be a tape recorder and a projector for both filmstrips and slides, which can be economically combined. Also pictures from various sources, relevantly portraying textual materials, are very useful. In fact, the enlisting of artistic talent in the class or in the school to make needed drawings is usually inexpensive and yet supplies excellent aids by adding further visual material to a lesson which may not be fully and adequately pictured in the text. Such pictures can be made into slides very reasonably and will serve for permanent use. A fault of the advanced Mauger texts is the lack of more pictures directly associated with reading passages. The student can solve this problem somewhat by acquiring a picture or visual dictionary. Finally we must not fail to mention the overhead projector as an important instrument for supplying visual aids.[53] The teacher should also make full use of the chalkboard as a visual teaching device. A moving picture projector with adequate space for showing various films will also serve to enrich a foreign language program.

The well-stocked laboratory should include maps, dolls in native costumes, puppets, picture postcards, pictures of castles and cathedrals, paintings by famous painters, photographs and paintings of great writers and personages, portrayals of games, sports, customs and traditions. All these and others, both mechanical and otherwise, might well contribute to a good laboratory in the broadest sense of the meaning. However, we must remember that better teaching has more often been done with fewer gadgets and less laboratory hardware, while much worse teaching has been done with a surfeit of these, as has, alas, been the case in our average American school. Our poverty is not of things, but of the spirit.

We should by all means make way for, and allow, the well-trained teacher to use his talents to the fullest in the most progressive methods along with a meaningful use of the laboratory facilities. Such a teacher, freed from the bondage of the routine audio-lingual method, could serve as an example in pilot projects here and there, which could eventually arouse and awaken others in less-developed states.

Stressing the need for teachers well-trained in audio-visual techniques, Dr. Scuorzo points out that the flaw in audio-visual teaching often lies not in laboratory "hardware" but in the "software" of the teaching material and its presentation. He warns that the audio-visual program can be given the kiss of death when the material presented is aimless and extraneous to the work at hand and not closely integrated with well-planned lessons.[54]

The anti-intellectual tendency of the audio-lingual method with its mechanistic habit-learning theory has been stressed and deplored. The purpose of all education should be the use of the intellect, including all the faculties of the mind. While memorization should be done, it must be done meaningfully and intelligently. The learning of a foreign language, when done properly, is an exciting and rewarding adventure into a new realm. We must not kill the enthusiasm and anticipation that young people have as they embark upon this new and important educational experience.

There has been much healthful and vigorous criticism, and there are visible signs of taking stock and of progressive growth. The language laboratory is a splendid aid, and it would be foolish to try to do away with it. This would be like trying to do away with automobiles and telephones. We must recognize and accept the fact that the language laboratory has its proper place, and it is most effective when used audio-visually and directly in the foreign language.

For biographical notes on CALVIN ANDRE CLAUDEL, see p. 141.

FOOTNOTES

1. Joseph C. Hutchinson, MODERN FOREIGN LANGUAGES IN HIGH SCHOOL: THE LANGUAGE LABORATORY. Washington, D.C.:

U.S. Department of Health, Education, and Welfare, Office of Education, 1965, 9.
2. Edmond Meras, "An Evaluation of Audio-Lingual Methods." BULLETIN OF THE KANSAS MODERN LANGUAGE ASSOCIATION, XL, No. 5, May 1966, 4.
3. Richard A. Mazzara, "Now That We Have a Language Laboratory, What Do We Do With It?" THE FRENCH REVIEW, XXXII, No. 6, May 1959, 565.
4. Jerald R. Green, "Language Laboratory Research: A Critique." THE MODERN LANGUAGE JOURNAL, XLIX, No. 6, October 1965, 369.
5. James H. Watkins, "The Library System and the Language Laboratory." THE FRENCH REVIEW, XXXIV, No. 1, October 1960, 61.
6. William Arrowsmith, "The Shame of the Graduate Schools." HARPER'S, Vol. 232, No. 1390, March 1966, 51-59.
7. George B. Watts, "The Teaching of French in the United States: A History." THE FRENCH REVIEW, XXXVII, No. 1, October 1953, 124.
8. Bernard Bloch and George L. Trager, OUTLINE OF LINGUISTIC ANALYSIS. Special Publications of the Linguistic Society of America, Linguistic Society of America, Baltimore: Waverly Press, Inc., 1942, 79.
9. James C. Bostain, "The Dream World of English Grammar." NEA Journal, Vol. 55, No. 6, September 1966, 20-22.
10. Chilton-Didier, "Foreign Language Newsletter, A Periodical Report of Interested Educators." Vol. 2, No. 3, Fall 1964, Philadelphia.
11. William N. Locke, "The Future of Language Laboratories." THE MODERN LANGUAGE JOURNAL, XLIX, No. 5, May 1965, 294.
12. James H. Watkins, Op. Cit., 61.
13. T. Earle Hamilton, "The Audio-Lingual Method in the University: Fad or Panacea?" HISPANIA, XLIX, No. 3, September 1966, 434-439.
14. Raymond F. Keating, A STUDY OF THE EFFECTIVENESS OF LANGUAGE LABORATORIES. Institute of Administrative Research, Teachers College, Columbia University, New York, 1963.
15. Calvin Andre Claudel, "Parroting and Progressive French Teaching." THE FRENCH REVIEW, XXXIX, No. 1, October 1965, 120-123.
16. Gifford P. Orwen, "Reflections on the Textbook Jungle." THE FRENCH REVIEW, XXXVII, No. 5, April 1964, 557-567.
17. John Green, "On Improvement in Teaching Oral Skills." THE FRENCH REVIEW, XXXIX, No. 5, April 1966, 753.
18. George J. Edberg, "Language Lab Study." HISPANIA, XLIX, No. 1, March 1966, 132-133.
19. Georges J. Joyaux, "Foreign Languages and the Humanities." THE MODERN LANGUAGE JOURNAL, XLIX, No. 2, February 1965, 102.
20. Albert Valdman, "From Structural Analysis to Pattern Drill." THE FRENCH REVIEW, XXXIV, No. 2, December 1960, 180.
21. Ibid., 180.
22. Clodius H. Willis, Jr., "After You Speak, Think." THE FRENCH REVIEW, XXXVIII, No. 5, January 1965, 398.
23. Lillian S. Adams, "Audio-Lingual? Yes, But Let's Think." THE FRENCH REVIEW, XXXVIII, No. 2, December 1964, 233.
24. Ibid., 235.
25. William N. Locke, Op. Cit., 298.
26. Clodius H. Willis, Jr., Op. Cit., 387.
27. Herbert B. Myron, Jr., "Languages, Cultures, and Belles-Lettres." THE

FRENCH REVIEW, XXXVII, No. 2, December 1963, 178-179.
28. Mildred F. Boyer, "Language Institutes and Their Future." PUBLICA-TIONS OF THE MODERN LANGUAGE ASSOCIATION OF AMER-ICA, LXXIX, No. 4, Part 2, September 1964, 11-17.
29. Elton Hocking, LANGUAGE LABORATORY AND LANGUAGE LEARNING. Monograph 2, Department of Audiovisual Instruction, National Education Association of the United States, Washingon, D.C., 1964, 59.
30. Germaine Bree, "The Double Responsibility of the Foreign Language Teacher: Proficiency in the Language and Mastery of the Literature and Culture." PUBLICATIONS OF THE MODERN LANGUAGE ASSOCIATION OF AMERICA, LXXVIII, No. 2, May 1963, 8.
31. Roger Asselineau, cited by Calvin Andre Claudel in "Parroting and Progressive French Teaching." THE FRENCH REVIEW, XXXIX, No. 1, October 1965, 122.
32. Paul A. Gaeng, rev. of Robert L. Politzer, "Foreign Language Learn-ing." THE MODERN LANGUAGE JOURNAL, L, No. 4, April 1966, 236.
33. Herbert B. Myron, Jr., *Op. Cit.*, 179.
34. Edward T. Heise, "Let's Talk Sense About Language Teaching." THE FRENCH REVIEW, XXXV, No. 2, December 1961, 179.
35. John C. Merrill, "The 'New Language' of Schools: Some Verbalization on." LOUISIANA SCHOOLS, XXXVIII, December 1960, 3, 31.
36. Herbert B. Myron Jr., *Op. Cit.*, 179.
37. Gertrude Moskowitz, "The Fearsome Foreign Language Hour." THE FRENCH REVIEW, XXXVIII, No. 6, May 1965, 781-786.
38. Edmond Meras, *Op. Cit.*, 4.
39. Raymond Keating, *Op. Cit.*, 37.
40. Sarah W. Lorge, "Language Laboratory Research Studies in the New York City High Schools: A Discussion of the Program and the Find-ings." THE MODERN LANGUAGE JOURNAL, XLVIII, No. 7, November 1964, 419.
41. John B. Carroll, "The Contributions of Psychological Theory and Edu-cational Research to the Teaching of Foreign Languages." THE MODERN LANGUAGE JOURNAL, XLIX, No. 5, May 1965, 280.
42. Edmond Meras, *Op. Cit.*, 4.
43. Elton Hocking, *Op. Cit.*, 48.
44. *Ibid.*, 88-89.
45. John A. Green, *Op. Cit.*, 749.
46. Raymond F. Keating, *Op. Cit.*, 13.
47. Edith Hiten et Renée Mikus-Perréal "La Bande Sonore." THE FRENCH REVIEW, XXXVII, No. 6, May 1964, 681.
48. William S. Vincent, Foreword to Raymond F. Keating, *Op. Cit.*, vi.
49. Sarah W. Lorge, *Op. Cit.*, 419.
50. F. Rand Morton, "The Teaching Machine and the Teaching of Lan-guages: A Report on Tomorrow." PUBLICATIONS OF THE MOD-ERN LANGUAGE ASSOCIATION OF AMERICA, LXXV, No. 4, part 2, September 1960, 1-6.
51. Jacob Ornstein, "A Frank Appraisal of the Foreign Language Program in Our Grade Schools." WOMAN'S DAY, Vol. 29, No. 4, January 1966, 46-47 and 86-88.
52. John C. Merrill, "TV in the Classroom: A Few Words of Caution." LOUISIANA SCHOOLS, XXXVII, No. 2, October 1959, 3, 38-39.

53. Karl S. Pond, "A Language Teaching Tool: The Overhead Projector."
THE MODERN LANGUAGE JOURNAL, XLVII, No. 1, January
1963, 30-33.
54. Herbert E. Scuorzo, "You Are Cordially Invited to Kill A-V." GRADE
TEACHER, Vol. 84, No. 3, November 1966, 85, 170-172.

Selected Bibliography

BOOKS

De Cecco, John P., EDUCATIONAL TECHNOLOGY: READINGS
IN PROGRAMMED INSTRUCTION. New York: Holt, Rinehart
and Winston, Inc., 1964. A wide collection on the many aspects
of programmed instruction.

Footlick, Jerrold K., EDUCATION—A NEW ERA. Silver Spring,
Md.: The National Observer, 1966. Part I of this volume tells
about the revolution in learning including the New English,
the New Math, etc.

Fourré, Pierre, PREMIER DICTIONNAIRE EN IMAGES. Paris:
Didier, 1957. A concise visual dictionary depicting the meaning
of 1,300 basic French words.

Hayes, Alfred S., LANGUAGE LABORATORY FACILITIES. Writ-
ten for the Electronic Industries Association. Washington, D.C.:
U.S. Department of Health, Education, and Welfare, Office of
Education, 1964.

Hocking, Elton, LANGUAGE LABORATORY AND LANGUAGE
LEARNING. Monograph 2, Department of Audiovisual Instruction. Washington, D.C.: National Education Association of the
United States. 1964. A description of the language laboratory
today and its use in American schools. One of the best volumes
available on the language laboratories.

Hutchinson, Joseph C., THE LANGUAGE LABORATORY . . . HOW
EFFECTIVE IS IT? Washington, D.C.: U.S. Department of
Health, Education, and Welfare, Office of Education, 1965.

Keating, Raymond F., A STUDY OF THE EFFECTIVENESS OF
LANGUAGE LABORATORIES. Institute of Administrative Research, Teachers College, Columbia University, New York, 1963.
This brochure questions the validity of the language laboratory
as generally used today and suggests a search for a better method.

Mauger, Gaston, COURS DE LANGUE ET DE CIVILISATION
FRANCAISE. Volume I. Paris: Librairie Hachette, Revised Edition, 1963. This is an excellent direct visual elementary French
text, to be used audio-visually in teaching adults.

Mauger, Gaston et Gougenheim, G., LE FRANCAIS ELEMEN-
TAIRE, PREMIER LIVRET. Paris: Librairie. 1955. An excel-
lent direct visual elementary French text designed to teach
French audio-visually to young people.

Mauger, Gaston et Gougenheim, G., LE FRANCAIS ELEMEN-
TAIRE. Paris: Deuxième Livre, Librairie Hachette, 1956. This
is volume two of the above text.

Richards, I. A., SPANISH THROUGH PICTURES, Book I. New York: Washington Square Press, Inc., 1962. This is the first volume of an elementary Spanish text designed to teach Spanish audio-visually by means of stick pictures.

Robin, C. et Bergeaud, C., LE FRANCAIS PAR LA METHODE DIRECTE, Premier Livre. Paris: Librairie Hachette, 1941. This and the following volume are excellent elementary French visual texts designed to teach French audio-visually to young people.

Robin, C. et Bergeaud, C., LE FRANCAIS PAR LA METHODE DIRECTE, Deuxième Livre. Paris: Librairie Hachette, 1941.

Stack, Edward, THE LANGUAGE LABORATORY AND MODERN LANGUAGE TEACHING. New York: Oxford University Press, 1966. This is a revised edition of the original edition of 1960.

Wittich, Walter A. and Schuller, Charles F., AUDIO-VISUAL MATERIALS: THEIR NATURE AND USE. New York: Harper and Row, 1962. A comprehensive study of the field of audio-visual materials, including television, language laboratories, and programmed learning.

ARTICLES

Adams, Lillian S., "Audio-Lingual? Yes, But Let's Think." THE FRENCH REVIEW, XXXVIII, No. 2, December 1964, 233-236. Deplores the lack of use of the thought processes in the audio-lingual method and urges that they be used somehow.

Claudel, Calvin Andre, "Parroting and Progressive French Teaching." THE FRENCH REVIEW, XXIX, No. 1, October 1965, 120-123. A presentation of the traditional, audio-lingual, and audio-visual methods of teaching French, emphasizing the superiority of the latter.

Green, Jerald R., "Language Laboratory Research: A Critique." THE MODERN LANGUAGE JOURNAL, XLIX, No. 6, October 1965, 367-369. A criticism of language laboratory research coupled with an appeal for factual data.

Hamilton, T. Earle, "The Audio-Lingual Method in the University; Fad or Panacea?" HISPANIA, XLIX, No. 3, September 1966, 434-439. A strong criticism of the audio-lingual method that is equivocal at the end and offers no valid alternative to this bad method.

Heise, Edward T., "Let's Talk Sense About Language Teaching." THE FRENCH REVIEW, XXXV, No. 2, December 1961, 176-184. A traditionalist's view of our growing lockstep methods.

Lorge, Sarah W., "Language Laboratory Research Studies in New York City High Schools: A discussion of the Program and the Findings." THE MODERN LANGUAGE JOURNAL, XLVIII, No. 7, November 1964, 409-419. A discussion of the use of the language laboratory with the suggestion that it should be used audio-visually.

Meras, Edmond, "An Evaluation of Audio-Lingual Methods." BULLETIN OF THE KANSAS MODERN LANGUAGE ASSOCIATION, XL, No. 5, May 1966, 2-5. The writer cites the many faults of the audio-lingual method and concludes it should be combined with the direct audio-visual method.

Merrill, John C., "TV in the Classroom: A Few Words of Caution." LOUISIANA SCHOOLS, XXXVII, No. 2, October 1959, 3, 38-39. This writer foresaw the danger of the aimless adoption of mechanical methods.

Moore, J. Michael, "Is It Time to Take Stock?" THE MODERN LANGUAGE JOURNAL, L. No. 5, May 1966, 269-272. This article says that it is time for foreign language teachers to take stock and be more concerned about text material and methods.

Moskowitz, Gertrude, "The Fearsome Foreign Language Hour." THE FRENCH REVIEW, XXXVIII, No. 6, May 1965, 781-786. An appeal for making foreign language teaching more human.

Myron, Herbert B., Jr., "Languages, Cultures, and Belles-Lettres." THE FRENCH REVIEW, XXXVII, No. 2, December 1963, 176-181. This is a traditionalist's view of the regimented procedures in foreign language teaching.

Page, Mary, "We Dropped FLES." THE MODERN LANGUAGE JOURNAL, L, No. 3, March 1966, 139-141. This is a pessimistic appraisal of foreign languages in elementary schools.

Palfrey, Thomas R., "How Far Off Key Is The New Key?" TEACHING OF MODERN FOREIGN LANGUAGES IN SECONDARY SCHOOLS, Bureau of Educational Research and Services, Arizona State University, August, 1965, 29-35. This article is another of many articles that are being written against the "New Key."

Scuorzo, Herbert E., "You Are Cordially Invited to Kill A-V." GRADE TEACHER, Vol. 84, No. 3, November 1966, 85, 170-172. This critic stresses the importance of using relevant material in an audio-visual program.

Smith, George E., "An Experiment in Statewide Development: The Indiana Language Program." THE FLORIDA FL REPORTER, Spring 1966. This article tells about the splendid program for the development of foreign language teaching in the Indiana schools.

Waltz, Ralph H., "Language Laboratory Administration." THE MODERN LANGUAGE JOURNAL, XVI, No. 3, December 1931, 217-227. One of the very first articles on the language laboratory.

Willis, Clodius H., Jr., "After You Speak, Think." THE FRENCH REVIEW, XXXVIII, No. 5, January 1965, 396-398. An amusing article on the audio-lingual method in which one speaks before thinking!

Intrinsic Programming of Foreign Languages

RICHARD BARRUTIA
University of California, Irvine

A Brief History of Our Present Concepts of
Programmed Instruction in America

THE PRESENT CONCEPTS of programmed instruction first appeared
as a budding art on the American scene in 1926 with the publication of S. L. Pressey's "A Simple Apparatus Which Gives Tests
and Scores — and Teaches."[1] About the same time, Edward
Sapir and Leonard Bloomfield were taking the incipient steps
which gave rise to what is now sometimes referred to as the
"American School of Linguistics." The latter pair of scholars
were instrumental in establishing still another minor revolution
in language instruction which has come to be called the "New
Key," or "Audio-lingual" method.[2]

Since the inception of these two relatively new but important American trends, each of them has developed separately
—the programmers mainly via the disciplines of psychology and
education, and the linguists mainly via the disciplines of modern
languages and anthropology. By 1958 the psychologist B. F.
Skinner had developed a theory and method of *linear* programming, while Norman L. Crowder had developed a slightly
divergent type called *branch* programming. American teachers
in 1958 were unprepared for the advent of programmed self-
teaching, but they rapidly became familiar with the rudiments
of programmed instruction chiefly through the mass media and
meetings of professional groups. Teachers on the whole are still
not equipped professionally for this revolutionary development
and, therefore, will require special training in the application and
evaluation of programmed materials. Not until experience grows
and until selected teachers begin to specialize in the technique

237

will formal courses in programmed instruction be initiated in large numbers of universities and teacher training institutions. In this context, it is also reasonable to predict that "teaching machines" will not be seriously considered for general use until low-cost, highly durable, and simple devices can be produced, distributed, and serviced with great ease.

Enthusiastic partisans of any promising new method in education all too frequently view it as a panacea for all educational problems. While programming is regarded here as a highly promising new development, it is only considered as one among many. There is still a more important place for textbooks, reference books, and libraries. What appears to be needed, therefore, is a continuing search for the particular combination of synthesis of materials and methods which will be most effective for the individual learner.

A surprising and disturbing development is not the proportionately small number of language programs but the lack of a modern linguistic orientation of virtually all of those existing to date.[3] It is even more surprising when one considers the close similarities of major principles in the two fields. Modern linguistic science advocates an oral-aural, habit-forming approach to language learning, and it analyzes languages by describing the distribution of minimal contrasts. Programmed instruction also advocates a behavioristic approach to learning, and its principle of reinforced minimal steps of learning makes it perhaps a logical vehicle for language instruction emphasizing a linguistically programmed audio course.

A notable lack of interest among language programmers in branch as opposed to linear programming exists partially because very few linguists have contributed programs to the auto-instructional field. Stanley M. Sapon, John B. Carroll, F. Rand Morton, and Sullivan Associates are among the few linguists who have ventured into the publishing of programmed materials. Of the available programmed language courses mentioned above, none are branch programs and only a few reluctantly admit to the use of some branching. Only several of the programs use some taped material, but all present the written form of the target language right from the beginning of the course. The marked prejudice in favor of Skinnerian linear programming has left a serious lacuna in the variety of materials still needed for the research necessary to prove the efficacy of programmed instruction. Another unsalutary development of the prejudice is that until very recently, it caused only the traditionally inclined language teachers to be drawn into the field of programmed text writing.

Programming as Related to Linear "Intrinsic," Branch "Extrinsic," and other Disciplines

Any teaching machine that employs a flexible program must have some means of controlling the selection of the material depending on the behavior of the student. Gustave J. Rath, Nancy S. Andersen, and R. C. Brainerd have described an experiment in which the student's response was automatically fed into an IBM 650 computer and this information, along with stored information in the computer, determined the next material to which the student was exposed.[4] In this case, the programming device is an external computer and the method, in our terms, would be one of *extrinsic* rather than *intrinsic* programming. *Intrinsic programming* simply refers to the fact that the necessary program of alternatives is built into the material itself in such a way that no external programming device is needed. *Extrinsic* is generally associated with linear programming and *intrinsic* with branch programming.

The *intrinsic* branch program as discussed in this study would require linguistically-sound alternative material to be recorded on the same tape for any given error that might be made. A diagram of such a program might look like Figure 1.

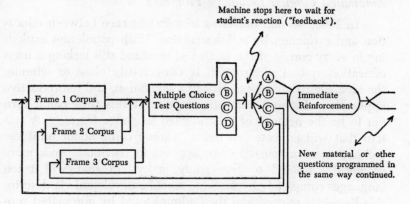

Figure 1. Branch Programming.

An important consideration of an intrinsic program is that all students must go through all portions of the right answer track and must successfully answer all the questions to all the tests in order to keep moving forward. The machine should only give more information on the same material or simply not move at all until the student responds correctly. This type of program would even differ from Dr. Norman Crowder's well-known branching programs (Tutor Texts). The Crowderian program might allow student A to bypass certain items and arrive at the same final point as student B via a different route. In the program discussed here, a student might by-pass only secondary alternative material designed for error correction.

The need for automated programmed instruction in many disciplines is clear. The need in language learning is as urgent as in many other subjects, which have received more attention from programmers. Ideally, education should be ahead of industry in all of its advancements. The sad fact is that in automation, industry has far outstripped education. It would undoubtedly be a boon to teachers and students alike if education could at least keep up with industry in the intelligent and imaginative use of nonhuman logic systems. An expanding industry, a growing populace, an increasingly complex world, and a greater need for understanding than ever before in man's history leave us no choice but to find ways to educate the masses as quickly and as economically as possible.

A Rationale of the Need for
Automated Foreign Language Programs

In 1968, we find ourselves in a serious race between education and extinction by self-destruction. With population exploding in every corner of the earth and mankind still lacking a mass education system, destruction is dangerously close to winning the race. Shortsightedness, lack of imagination, and unproductive application of sound linguistic theories at this time could turn out to be the nemesis of programmed language learning. A system that will educate "en masse" cannot come about until the techniques of automation are applied to teaching. And, more specifically related to this study, a system that will teach languages completely by machine must be developed via descriptive linguistic science and then administered by automated programs. By presentation of automated audio programming through properly constructed teaching machines, the skills of mimicry and memorization can be more widely developed. What is more, in most disciplines, by the use of proper questioning and "feedback" from student to machine and vice versa, we can even bring about *Gestalt* learning just as Socrates did with the slave boy Meno two thousand years ago.

Because of the ever-growing number of language classrooms, many teachers do not have the energy or the time to do the things that *only teachers* can do because they themselves are doing all the work of the machines. Instead, we should give the machine the task of teaching habitual behavior and the teacher that of teaching creative behavior. The machine can even be brought into play in teaching creativity. With the awe-inspiring numbers that will flood our language classrooms in the next decade, we should welcome any helpful device, even if it slightly encroaches upon our domain. Some teachers live in dread of automated teaching, but as with many apparent evils the danger is attributed to the wrong elements.

> Si no pasamos de ser máquinas instructoras no somos nada; y habremos merecido el destino que nos amenaza, de ser reemplazados por otras máquinas que se diferencian de nosotros principalmente en no ser de carne y hueso.[5]

The danger of the machine does not lie in the mechanization of the teaching process or the materials. The problem today is how to avoid the mechanization of the teacher himself. The present danger is the dehumanization of education, mainly because the teacher has insufficient time to perform his most important functions adequately.

In addition to reaching greater numbers, the machine has the purpose of relieving the teacher from some of the drudgery of teaching and of freeing him for those things for which only humans may serve as models. It can free the teacher to help correct the student's pronunciation by making an individual analysis of his problem. It can enable the teacher to help those who need help without disturbing the pace of the rest of the class. It can relieve the student of inhibitions and cloak him in

241

the anonymity of the device. It has infinite patience and absolute consistency in its delivery.

How We Can Meet the Unattained Goal

Paradoxically, the language laboratory is not yet a labor-saving device, nor is it a teaching machine. In 1960, F. Rand Morton aptly described the language laboratory as a teaching machine.[6] He discusses the teaching machine implications of the language laboratory and exposes the state of the art with reference to an original experiment of his own devising. Mr. Morton also makes some courageous speculations on the future teaching of languages and culture by machine. In 1962, Fernand Marty published a book on the prospects for self-instruction by programming a basic foreign language course. Here, also, Marty ends with the conclusion that a true teaching machine laboratory and program are still things of the future.[7]

Our present laboratories may not yet meet the requirements of an automated teaching machine system, but many of them do enable a good program to be used anywhere on any number of students. The coming years will be years of double effort for teachers with language laboratories. Not until a sufficient number of good automated programs are developed will the laboratories begin to be real teaching machines and the panacea everyone is dreaming about. In the development of these programs, it will be necessary to maintain a farsighted view in order to avoid their obsolescence because of the rapidly developing technological aspects of teaching machines.

As stated above, present-day language laboratories are far from being teaching machines. The main reason for this is that they simply go on and on whether or not the student is interacting. The only bit of feedback comes when a good student is reinforced by a recorded correct answer or when an occasional student has enough talent to glean something significant from a comparison of his recorded responses with the model. Even such cases cannot properly be called feedback, because the machine is not adjusting itself but merely moving on in the same way that it would with any student. Our labs are not acting as servo-mechanisms.

Present laboratory positions could be vastly improved by the minimal requirements of machine programming as men-

242

tioned above, e.g., a device that does not permit the student to move forward until he has mastered the previous step. A rough diagram of such a present program is as in Figure 2.

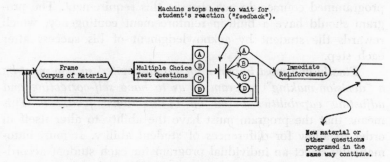

Figure 2. Minimal Linear Programming.

Even the minimal step suggested above would be a marked improvement on language laboratories in our country today. It could easily be built into all labs that have recording devices at individual booths by preparing programs that would tell the device merely when to start and stop. *Where an essential component of the behavior being taught is the making of accurate sound comparisons, it is necessary to have machines that do not advance until correct choices are made.*

Requirements for a Fully-Automated Intrinsic Program

It is necessary at this point to set up the minimal requirements of a genuine automated program.

Such a program must first be completely self-operational. That is, it must not require stopping, starting, or any other type of maneuver by student or teacher from one part of the program to the next. In order to accomplish this on tape, nothing short of a very careful "to the second radio-type" programming of the whole course will suffice. The drills, dialogues, instructions, pauses must all be pretimed and spliced together in their proper sequences. If, for instance, the course moves from a pronunciation exercise to a dialogue presentation, the teacher should not have to be concerned with making the change. All portions must be edited in such a way as to assure complete teacher freedom.

Secondly, the automated program must meet the rather strict requirements of teaching machine principles. That is, it must proceed by small steps called "frames" and test the student on

243

the learning of these frames. Ideally, it should have the capacity of not allowing the student to proceed to the next frame until the previous one has been mastered. At present, most available programmed courses do not observe this requirement. The program should have a built-in reinforcement contingency, which rewards the student by acknowledgment of his success after each step.

Finally and most importantly, an automated system must be a "decision-making" program so as to have self-correcting and adjusting capabilities based on bi-directional feedback. This means that the program must have the ability to alter itself in order to allow for differences of student ability. It must automatically select an individual program for each student according to a given student's errors. By so doing, the program and device are combining to function as a true servo-mechanism.

The manufacturers of language laboratory equipment do a great deal of propagandizing about accounting for individual differences and about letting a student learn at his own speed. But such claims are exaggerated when the problem is seen in the light of the above requirement.

Terminal Behavior, Method, and Branching Philosophy

For the past several years, there has been a dichotomy between the linear or Skinnerian approach and the branching or Crowderian approach to programmed instruction, which depends on cognitive processes as expounded by Noam Chomsky.[8] Recently, however, there has also been some thought given to the notion that the differing subject matter to be taught requires different techniques of programming. That is, the material to be learned and the specific objective should dictate the type of program to be used. The latter is the position held here.

The Skinnerian linear program holds to the premise of trial but no error, which is to say that steps should be so minimal and so simple that the student cannot make an error. In fact, many linear program exponents have rewritten their programs many times, eliminating each time those items that might cause any student trouble. They do not take advantage of utilizing the student error in the program, because they do not want or expect errors to occur.

244

It must be made clear at the outset, however, that the *main first* objective of a linguistically oriented program should be *only* the first two steps of the four ordered steps recommended for New Key, audio-lingual language teaching:

1. *Listening and Understanding*
2. *Speaking*
3. *Reading*
4. *Writing*

To predictably measure the attainment of listening and understanding, ways should be found for determining when and what portion of the result is achieved and for taking appropriate action on the basis of that determination.

Learning a foreign language involves not only a behavioral problem of habit forming, but also the acquisition of a new set of language habits against a background of different native language habits. As a child learns his native language, he learns not only to perceive the contrasts that function as signals in his language but also to ignore all those redundant features that do not make a difference. After the patterns of hearing and speaking have been firmly fixed in his nervous system, the native speaker will also have acquired certain blind spots that will prevent him, at first, from responding to the features that do not constitute the contrastive signals of his native language. We often hear people, even some linguists, talk glibly about learning a language just the way a child does. This is of course nonsense. The fact is that learning a second language is a significantly different task from learning one's first language. The basic problems do not arise so much out of mastering the features of the new language as out of the special "mental circuitry" or system created by the first language habits.

That the language student indeed *does* make mistakes, then, is more than an assumption. It is an observation of fact which supports and is supported by recent linguistic theory of language learning.

With this consideration in mind, an automated language program should not only anticipate errors based on pressures from the learner's native speech, but it also should further utilize those errors so as to signal the machine where to move next. By comparison, a linear program is passive and cannot alter itself or function with a student in this way. On the other hand, an intrinsic program will receive signals from one student or another for as many calculated errors as are written into it.

A clarification of the last statement is essential before going on. The so-called "errors" built into an intrinsic program are not errors at all in the normal sense of the word. *All* the multiple-choice alternatives should *always* be *correct* in syntax, intonation, and pronunciation. That is, the student should *never* hear a wrong form in itself. These correctly phrased and pronounced utterances, however, can be put by the student into the wrong environment. The errors occur because some rejoinders are more fitting than others. They more or less aptly satisfy the needs of the environment framed by the initial question. Only one rejoinder, of course, is completely correct in this way. In the present state of the art, the student must first imitate the rejoinder he has selected, then mechanically signal the machine which selection he has made.

A Skinnerian Versus Crowderian Approach to Foreign Languages

Intrinsic programming is clearly favored for teaching language by sound; but in order to expose the student to the fullest measure necessary, the program should also subject all students to its linear right answer track.

Holding to the notion, then, that the subject matter should dictate the best type of programming, it is conceded that certain subjects can be learned without committing errors at any point. Such programs must, of necessity, be presented in very minute steps. For these reasons, books like Buchanan's *A Programmed Instruction for Linguistics*[9] and Holland and Skinner's *The Analysis of Behavior*[10] will probably prove to be successful although quite boring for the student. These linear programs are often boring and even insulting to the intelligence of a bright student, mainly because the steps are made extremely minuscule in order to avoid error. Nevertheless, such programs can and do build up behavorial patterns as per their objectives.

Language learning, like the learning of some other subjects such as music, first requires discrimination of contrasts. It is this discrimination of contrasts, then, that must subsequently be habitualized until it is subconscious and automatic. Even if presented within the most minute steps, the target language will be misheard and mispronounced many times before it is fixed automatically. Errors and inaccuracies will occur until there has been sufficient listening and speaking practice to overcome the fixed patterns of one language system while adding to it all the new distributions of the phonemes, morphemes, and syntactic complexities of another.

On the Predictability of Error

In more specific terms, we can state that certain phonemes in Spanish are similar to their counterparts in English and have a similar distribution. In such cases, less difficulty arises and, consequently, less or perhaps only a minimum of practice, which will probably occur with fewer errors, is needed. Here learning occurs by simple transfer of one item in one system into the other. It is well to note that this is not a transfer of a like system into another like situation. The problem is that some phonemes are often identical, and even in closely related languages the distribution is often similar but seldom identical in all its positions. Similarity can sometimes be of great help by using it as a key to systematizing the target language. For instance, a literate Portuguese speaker studying Spanish needs to know among other things that the Spanish intervocalic /s/ is always [s] like his own double s or ç or c+i or c+e. Similarities between the target and native languages also present moderately difficult problems of distributional adjustment as witnessed by a different aspect of the above situation. A Spanish speaker does not have an intervocalic [z] as the Portuguese speaker does and will need considerable exposure and practice to learn to separate the Portuguese /s/, /z/ distribution.

Unfortunately, in most unrelated languages, there are a good many phonemes that are not only differently distributed but that also have differing points and manners of articulation. Persistent difficulty of many types will plague the student in these cases until the new phonology has become a part of his nervous system.

Conclusions

The short argument of this chapter suffices to show that either remote or related languages show a considerable number of differences simply by being distinct languages and mutually unintelligible. Although recognizing and distinguishing these contrasts are the first necessary steps in learning a second language, more and different steps are needed to make the new system one's own. Linear programs cannot provide all of the needed steps, because the program cannot adjust to the proper step to take. A branch program can be more complete in fulfilling the linguistically oriented requirements of second language learning.

Figure 3 shows a comparison of the features of the two most useful types of programming. It also gives a composite descrip-

COMPARATIVE MAJOR ELEMENTS OF

SKINNERIAN PROGRAMING		CROWDERIAN PROGRAMING
LINEAR		BRANCHING
ERROR AVOIDING		ERROR UTILIZING
UNIDIRECTIONAL		MULTIDIRECTIONAL
INFLEXIBLE PROGRAM		SELF-ADJUSTING
MINUTE STEPS	INTRINSIC PROGRAM	SMALL FRAMES
CONSTRUCTED RESPONSE		MULTIPLE CHOICE
MINIMAL FEEDBACK		MAXIMUM FEEDBACK
PASSIVE PROGRAM		PROGRAM INTERACTION
EXTRINSIC		INTRINSIC
REINFORCEMENT		REINFORCEMENT
COMPARE FEATURE		COMPARE FEATURE

Used in this program by the exceptional students

Used by most students

Used by all students

This outline illustrates the major elements of the two leading types of programming. In the intrinsic program suggested here, the specific needs of the subject matter based on linguistic criteria account for the omission of some of the weaker elements of the Skinnerian approach.

Figure 3. Two Types of Programming.

tion of those features which best fulfill the needs of a linguistically oriented language course. Such a language course presupposes that the student will be learning to *understand* and speak the language first. This means that the intrinsic nature of the program must be recorded on alternate tracks of a single tape. The tape recorder must hence be equipped to stop, start, and rewind automatically in response to a set of multiple-choice buttons. The program will give the learner many decisions to make, which test his comprehension of the recorded frames. The learner has the double task of repeating all items and responding orally to all the challenges offered by the program. When the test portion begins, the tape will stop after the questions and multiple-choice answers are put to the student. It will start again only after the student audibly answers and then presses the A, B, C, or D button, which matches his verbal response. At this time, the machine makes a decision and either reverses to another track of specific remedial drills or moves forward on the right answer track. The simple electronic equipment to drive such programs is fully described in "A Suggested Automated Branch Program for Foreign Languages."[11]

RICHARD BARRUTIA received his B.A. and M.A. degrees in Spanish from Arizona State University and his Ph.D. degree in Linguistics from the University of Texas. He is now Associate Professor of Foreign Languages and Linguistics and Director of the Language Laboratory at the University of California, Irvine. He is an associate editor of HISPANIA and in charge of the Shop Talk section. He is co-author of the Modern Language Association-sponsored text, *Modern Portuguese*. Professor Barrutia is also the author of numerous articles and reviews on language and language teaching. He previously taught at the American Institute for Foreign Trade, and was a Peace Corps Project Director and Language Coordinator at Arizona State University. He has served as the linguist or methodologist at National Defense Education Act Summer Language Institutes in the United States and abroad since the inception of the NDEA program.

FOOTNOTES

1. S. L. Pressey, "A Simple Apparatus Which Gives Tests and Scores—and Teaches." SCHOOL AND SOCIETY, XXIII, March 20, 1926, 373-76.
2. Edward Sapir, LANGUAGE: AN INTRODUCTION TO THE STUDY OF SPEECH. New York: Harcourt, Brace and World, Inc., 1921, 1-258; and Leonard Bloomfield, LANGUAGE. New York: Holt, Rinehart and Winston, 1933, 1-564.
3. PROGRAMS, '63—A GUIDE TO PROGRAMMED INSTRUCTION MATERIALS AVAILABLE TO EDUCATORS BY SEPTEMBER 1963, Lincoln F. Hanson, ed. The Center for Programmed Instruction, Inc., in cooperation with the U. S. Department of Health, Education, and Welfare, Washington, D.C.: U. S. Government Printing Office, 1963, 1-814.
4. Gustave J. Rath, Nancy S. Andersen, and R. C. Brainerd, "The IBM Research Center Teaching Machine Project." AUTOMATED TEACHING: THE STATE OF THE ART, Eugene H. Galanter, ed. New York: John Wiley and Sons, 1959, 117-30.
5. Dwight L. Bolinger, "Algo más que entrenamiento." HISPANIA, XLIV, March 1961, 17. [If we are no more than teaching machines, we are nothing; and we will have deserved the fate that threatens us, of

being replaced by other machines that differ from us principally by not being made of flesh and blood.]

6. F. Rand Morton, THE LANGUAGE LABORATORY AS A TEACHING MACHINE. Ann Arbor: The University of Michigan, 1961, 1-62.
7. Fernand Marty, PROGRAMMING A BASIC FOREIGN LANGUAGE COURSE. Hollins College, Va.: Hollins College, 1962, 69.
8. Noam Chomsky, CARTESIAN LINGUISTICS: A CHAPTER IN THE HISTORY OF RATIONALIST THOUGHT. New York: Harper and Row, 1966.
9. Cynthia D. Buchanan, A PROGRAMMED INTRODUCTION TO LINGUISTICS: PHONETICS AND PHONEMICS. Boston: D. C. Heath & Co., 1963.
10. James G. Holland and B. F. Skinner, THE ANALYSIS OF BEHAVIOR (programmed text), New York: McGraw-Hill Book Company, Inc., 1961.
11. Richard Barrutia, "A Suggested Automated Branch Program for Foreign Languages." HISPANIA, XLVII, May 1964, 342-50.

Selected Bibliography

Barrutia, Richard, "A Suggested Automated Branch Program for Foreign Languages." HISPANIA, XLVII, May, 1964, 342-50. To date, this article represents the only attempt at intrinsic branch programming strictly by sound for language laboratories. It employs simple devices and branching procedures, which are fully explained and diagrammed. There are also examples of selected frames of the actual program in Spanish.

Bloomfield, Leonard, LANGUAGE. New York: Holt, Rinehart and Winston, Inc., 1933. A classic text on language by one of the founders of modern linguistic science in the United States. Although recent developments go beyond it, most American works since its time have been based on it.

Bolinger, Dwight L., "Algo más que entrenamiento," HISPANIA, XLIV March 1961, 16-20. This was the presidential address delivered at the 42nd Annual Meeting of the American Association of Teachers of Spanish and Portuguese, San Diego, December 30, 1960. He defended the need for advancement in the use of good programs, teaching practices, and time-saving tools, lest we ourselves become machine-like.

Buchanan, Cynthia D., A PROGRAMMED INTRODUCTION TO LINGUISTICS: PHONETICS AND PHONEMICS. Boston: D. C. Heath and Co., 1963. A fine example of linear programming using written material only. Some recorded tapes and certain intrinsic branching steps would, no doubt, improve its effectiveness.

Chomsky, Noam, CARTESIAN LINGUISTICS: A CHAPTER IN THE HISTORY OF RATIONALIST THOUGHT. New York: Harper and Row, 1966. An essay which surveys the philosophical concerns with language in the period of the rationalist thinkers from Descartes to Humboldt. The central doctrine of Cartesian linguistics is that the general features of grammatical structure are common to all languages and reflect certain fundamental properties of the mind.

Holland, James G. and Skinner, B. F., THE ANALYSIS OF BEHAVIOR (programmed text). New York: McGraw Hill Book Company, Inc., 1961. This is still another example of rather unimaginative linear programming of a first-year college psychology text.

Marty, Fernand, PROGRAMMING A BASIC FOREIGN LANGUAGE COURSE. Hollins College, Virginia: Hollins College, 1962. Represents another early contribution to programming of French for our language laboratories. It also describes, with charts and pictures, the special applications and devices used in an experiment at Hollins College.

Morton, F. Rand, THE LANGUAGE LABORATORY AS A TEACHING MACHINE. Ann Arbor: The University of Michigan, 1961. This early work was one of the forerunners which aptly describes, among other innovations, a highly sophisticated and completely automated language laboratory of the future.

Pressey, S. L., "A Simple Apparatus Which Gives Tests and Scores—and Teaches." SCHOOL AND SOCIETY, XXIII, March 20, 1926, 373-76. Describes the original multiple-choice testing machine, which is the precursor to present more sophisticated devices.

PROGRAMS, '63: A GUIDE TO PROGRAMMED INSTRUCTIONAL MATERIALS AVAILABLE TO EDUCATORS BY SEPTEMBER 1963. Edited by Lincoln F. Hanson, The Center for Programmed Instruction, Inc., in cooperation with the U.S. Department of Health, Education, and Welfare. Washington, D.C.: U.S. Government Printing Office, 1963. A complete compilation of all existing published programs up to the date of printing (1963). It describes each program, pointing out its major features, and gives several examples of the actual frames used in each.

Rath, Gustave J., Andersen, Nancy S., and Brainerd, R. C., "The IBM Research Center Teaching Machine Project." AUTOMATED TEACHING: THE STATE OF THE ART. Edited by E. H. Galanter. New York: John Wiley and Sons, Inc., 1959, 117-30. This article describes, in a general way, the application of computers to programmed teaching and, in a specific way, the project alluded to in this paper.

Sapir, Edward, LANGUAGE: AN INTRODUCTION TO THE STUDY OF SPEECH. New York: Harcourt, Brace and World, Inc., 1921. Another classic in the study of language phenomena. It is outdated in part, but still full of important insights into the nature of language.

Tests and Measurement

ROBERT J. LUDWIG

Mont Pleasant High School, Schenectady, N.Y.

THE CONCEPT of language as a total communication experience and as a cultural synthesis revolving about the four skills of speech, aural comprehension, reading, and writing, is the order of the current decade. Hence tests and measurements, whether they have been designed within or without the classroom, whether to determine aptitude for language learning or achievement therein, whether to diagnose difficulties so that they may be remedied, whether to test the proficiency of the potential or practicing teacher, or whether to place students in a language sequence, must reflect not only what is, has been, or is to be taught, but also how that body of knowledge is, has been, or is to be taught.

As Nelson Brooks points out,

> Until the mid-1930's the traditional grammar-translation-composition exercise was the rule with the student writing out his answer in full. Then came the gradual introduction of fixed-response tests which were widely adopted in the early 1940's because of their apparent superiority with regard to brevity, economy and efficiency. . . . As for the role of the different skills, the earlier tests had involved reading alone. It was not until the mid-1950's that widely used tests began to be concerned with anything more than paper-and-pencil activity.[1]

Aptitude Tests

The question of which students have the greatest potential for foreign language learning, which should be grouped in fast and slower sections of language classes, the speed with which the student will learn the language, and for which students instruction should be postponed, as well as areas of difficulties that individual students may be expected to encounter, may be revealed from results of language aptitude tests.

The misuse of such tests occurs when students who may indeed benefit from foreign language study are eliminated from the study. Robert Lado states, "Aptitude tests are useful for the selection of students for foreign language training when final mastery rather than educational growth of the students is the primary aim."[2]

The factor of motivation in foreign language learning is a crucial one. The grouping of students permits differentiated curricula which enable students to produce at a pace commensurate with ability and to encompass those learnings in an articulated program. The phenomena of the underachiever and the "late-bloomer" are other special factors to be evaluated.

There can be no doubt that aptitude tests in foreign languages should include elements which take into account both aural-oral and visual-graphic factors in language learning. Two examples of such aptitude tests are the Modern Language Aptitude Test[3] and the Pimsleur Language Aptitude Battery.[4]

The Modern Language Aptitude Test, which evolved from the Harvard Language Aptitude Project, is a test which consists of practice exercises in learning an artificial language and exercises in other aspects of language learning. The five parts of the test measure the student's ability to learn words for numbers in an artificial language and to write these from dictation, to identify sounds and learn phonetic symbols for them, to decipher phonetically spelled English words, to recognize the structural parts of sentences, and to learn and recall words in an artificial language.

The Pimsleur Language Aptitude Battery is structured on six factors: grade point average in academic areas other than foreign languages; interest in learning a foreign language; vocabulary as an indicator of verbal intelligence; language analysis; sound discrimination; and sound/symbol association.

Classroom Testing

Testing is an essential ingredient in any teaching situation.

Wrong testing will encourage wrong learning. Nelson Brooks states,

> Tests are designed to aid learning. There are tests that enhance the learner's progress; there are also tests that deflect his progress from desired objectives to the point of negating the learning that is desired. Accurate measurement is just as possible with tests that aid learning as with those that negate it.[5]

The test is an index of student progress and proficiency as well as lack of progress and deficiency. It is a motivational device. It is a diagnostic tool which points up the student's strengths and weaknesses, and gives the teacher insights into areas which require re-entry and further elaboration. Edward M. Stack puts it, "Tests are a kind of academic radar, sending useful indications back to the teaching center, allowing the teacher to reorient his work to overcome weaknesses and difficulties."[6]

Before writing a test the teacher should have catalogued the purpose the test is to serve, the content areas it is to measure, and the relative weight of these items. The classroom quiz, unit test, mid-year and final examinations require a thorough knowledge of the aims and goals of instruction so that appropriate weight may be given to the various skills on the four levels.

Validity is a prime criterion in the classroom test. Remunda Cadoux states, "In constructing a classroom test we should have three considerations in mind: what it tests, how it tests, and how it can teach and test."[7]

Measuring the understanding of spoken utterances given at normal native speed is the focus of the aural comprehension test.

Aural comprehension is measured in the initial stages of language learning through the use of the action-response or body movement test in which commands given by the teacher are carried out by the student. A multiple-choice test in which both the question and the foils are given orally with the student circling A, B, C, or D is frequently employed. A true-false test is still another example of a test form in which the teacher gives an oral statement and the student may utilize a symbol to indicate his response. Another form requiring a nonverbal student response presents a group of pictures to the student who chooses the one which is linked to the teacher's statement.

As the student progresses he may be presented with an oral statement for which written foils are given and from which he makes a selection. This may be expanded to a short paragraph which he hears and upon which one or more multiple-choice questions are presented with written foils. The foils may answer a question, complete a statement, or be a rejoinder. Aural comprehension passages should not be too long so that what is involved is not a test of memory retention, but is in fact, a question of comprehension.

Aural comprehension may also be measured through sound discrimination. The student hears a statement and then is required to select the written representation of that statement. The incorrect foils represent very slight phonemic differences.

It is particularly important on early levels that the content of the questions reflect the unit of work being studied in combination with previously learned elements of vocabulary and structure so that the test may be used as a teaching instrument for these levels.

The testing of the speaking skill presents the most difficulty for the teacher. The problems include eliciting the desired response through the stimulus, objective scoring, and group administration. The classroom teacher, in calling on a student daily, will need to focus on various aspects of speech evaluation: pronunciation; intonation; speed of response; and fluency which includes vocabulary, syntax, and knowledge of forms; in short the ability to express one's thoughts intelligently to a native speaker.

Initially, we test lead-up phases to speech itself. Since speaking is expressing one's thoughts orally either in response to a stimulus or to initiate a conversation, we need first to test those spoken elements which when mastered will produce fluency. The ultimate goal is to produce an educated speaker of the language who can make himself understood by a native and carry on a conversation meaningfully. Before that point is reached, the linguistic elements have to be incorporated.

In the beginning, we utilize the obvious device of the mimic or echo test as a lead-up activity. The teacher rates specific phonemes which are being measured at that point in time and/or stress, intonation, and junctures. Obviously in daily practice, no more than three or four items can be attempted as we test one-third to one-half of the class, depending on its size, lesson plans, and circumstances. Asking questions of students will give us an index of the students' fluency and speed of response as well as aural comprehension-speech reflex. Structural drills do not measure speaking as such, but rather the scales which through mastery will lead to accurate production in spontaneous situations. The directed dialogue in which students are instructed to ask questions, give answers, or issue commands, tests the ability to express oneself in a variety of conversational situations under controlled conditions.

As the student progresses, spontaneity of speech is measured through such varied devices as: (1) response to picture stimuli based on learnings in the page, chapter or unit; (2) setting the content of a dialogue and then having the teacher play role A and the student role B; (3) silent reading of a newspaper article and then giving an oral précis of its contents; and (4) oral composition in which the student speaks extemporaneously on a topic under current study.

The administration and scoring of the speech test poses difficult problems. In the classroom situation in which speech is but one of the four skills developed during a given period, other than during the first level audio-lingual limited phase in which reading and writing are not included, it is evident that daily testing of speech will be integrated with other aspects of language learning. Hence, a portion of the class will be evaluated each day as part of the classroom activities. A scale is usually developed varying from 0-2 to 0-5 for each item to be tested. One such effort is the New York City Foreign Language Oral Ability Rating Scale which utilizes a scale of 0-2. The items measured are echo ability, recitation, drills, drill responses, and directed responses.[8] Patricia O'Connor outlines a similar procedure for measuring achievement during the strictly aural-oral phase of Level I.[9]

When recording machines are available, unit speech tests can be administered as a group test. When they are not, a shorter form must be utilized. While the class is involved in an aural comprehension-directed exercise in the laboratory, individual students can be tested. Several periods may be necessary depending upon the length of the test and the number of students to be tested. Alternate forms should be used when more than one period is used to test the same material.

Crucial to testing reading is the selection of vocabulary and structures. The linguistic content of reading involves vocabulary items which are re-entered, new items studied in the context of current materials, and items whose meanings can be inferred through intelligent guessing. The use of synonyms and antonyms, true cognates, and words in the same family is a steppingstone to lexical mastery.

One method of testing reading is to ask students questions in the target language requiring a complete answer in that language. The material may be presented simultaneously or may be based on a passage already completed and not in view. The Spanish Syllabus of the State of New York cautions:

> In testing pupils on reading done in class when they do not have the passage before them, the teacher might remember that the questions asked should (1) represent items of story content which might reasonably be re-called, (2) require that students supply vocabulary and idioms which have been emphasized in class, and (3) result in a work sample of pupil's comprehension of the story. If pupils are supplied with the reading passage, they are to answer in complete Spanish sentences questions put to them in Spanish, the passage should (a) contain some vocabulary and idioms which have already been studied and some which can be inferred from the context and (b) be a rearrangement of this language content into a new context. Caution should be exercised so that the questions asked require genuine understanding and not a mere copying of parts of the reading passage to form the answer.[10]

Mary Finnochiaro suggests that among various ways to test reading comprehension, the teacher may ask the children to select unrelated words from a group, place related words under categories, complete sentences where a choice of three or four words is given, tell whether a caption under a picture is true or false, or read several sentences about a "situation" and then choose the logical response from a list of possible responses.[11]

In his structural approach to French, Robert L. Politzer proceeds with the premise that since reading is a process of recognition rather than production, the completion of sentences is the essential element of the structure to be practiced that will signify a meaningful completion and indicate understanding of that construction.[12] This premise may be incorporated therefore in the testing phase by construction of such items based on a given passage.

In testing the writing skill, the progression is from that which is guided and imitative to that which is free and creative. It is important that writing be controlled on early levels. As the student achieves structural mastery, he becomes increasingly able to move forward in the progression. Spelling, punctuation, and vocabulary are elements which must be developed.

On the first level, writing should be based on what has been already experienced audio-lingually and through reading. Appropriate areas for testing include the ability to copy with precision, completion of structural drills in which transformations and substitutions are required, dictation, and replies to both oral and written questions.

Robert Lado suggests that "in testing spelling a better technique than dictation is one in which a sentence identifies an incomplete word which the student is asked to complete from memory or from several given choices. The letters omitted are those that constitute the spelling problem, thus giving more density of test elements."[13]

As the student progresses to level two, the structures become more complex. The principle of testing based on what has already been experienced audio-lingually and read continues in choosing items for the writing sample. The skill is integrated with reading and aural comprehension testing through such media as replying to questions based on a reading selection, answers to spoken questions, and completion of sentences requiring structural knowledge. A picture may be presented as a stimulus based on the learnings of a page, chapter or unit, in which key words are omitted from a descriptive paragraph or sentence, or dialogue segment. Sentences may be altered by requiring changes based, for example, on number or tense.

Guided writing should continue to be the principle of level-three writing tests. Premature expectations in the area of free composition should be avoided. A dialogue may be changed to a narrative or vice versa. Letters may be written in which the content is guided through topic items. A composition may be required in which the writing is controlled through direct stimuli such as questions to be answered in each sentence, or information to be very specifically included. More complex structural forms may be elicited.

It is on the fourth level that we move from the controlled to the creative. To be sure structures are reviewed through written exercises such as completions, substitutions, and alterations. As structural mastery is demonstrated, the student is ready for such test activities as book reports, note-taking on lectures, dictation from tape, a descriptive paragraph based on a picture stimulus, summarizing, and creative writing on specified topics.

It is important that teachers be aware of the weight of aural comprehension, speaking, reading and writing in arriving at a global grade for the student. Each level will have a variation in the weight of these items, and the synthesis of performance in the four areas, so weighted, will produce the grade.

What are the criteria language teachers use to determine whether the test meets their testing, teaching, and learning objectives? The performance of the student in the foreign language exclusively is a special guideline. On early levels English should be used in directions so that the student is not placed in double jeopardy. The use of translation as a test of comprehension should be avoided. In aural comprehension testing, passages should be read at normal native speed. The four skills should be tested separately in drawing up an accurate language profile.

Working Committee III of the 1961 Northeast Conference on the Teaching of Foreign Languages lists fifteen specific criteria for effective test construction. The report also suggests that the test writer raise the following questions:[14]

1. Have I made up the test in terms of what the students know, not what I know?
2. Are the questions appropriate to the limits and purposes of the test and the capacities of the group being tested?
3. Have I tested everything I announced I was going to test?

4. Have I acquainted the students with the techniques I have used?
5. Have I had the test read over and if possible, tried by someone else?
6. Have I made the assignment for study and review as specific as possible?

Achievement Tests

The achievement test measures learnings that have been acquired.

The College Board offers tests in both modern and classical languages. This achievement test focuses on reading comprehension, vocabulary, and usage. A supplementary listening comprehension test measures the skill of understanding a foreign language as spoken by native speakers. It is administered on tape. It utilizes conversation questions, logical-illogical questions, situation questions, single questions based on illustrations, and sets of questions based on longer spoken passages. A single test involving the skills of the present achievement and supplementary aural comprehension test is now projected. With the exception of the Greek tests, all scores are reported on a standard 200 to 800 scale. The Greek test is graded by examiners because of the smaller sample.

Since the College Board Test is administered to students with varying years of language study, percentile ranks for foreign language scores are published separately for candidates having two, three, or four years of study.[15]

The Regents Examination of the State of New York in Modern Foreign Languages is a third-level comprehensive examination. It measures aural comprehension, reading comprehension, and writing skills. The examination in Latin is given as a second-level examination.

Proficiency Tests

The proficiency tests measure the four skills, structure, vocabulary, and culture. Such tests are based on the use to which language is put without reference to specific curriculum items to which the student may have been exposed.

An example of a Level I proficiency test is the Common Concepts Foreign Language Test published by the California

Test Bureau. The student hears stimulus sentences in the foreign language and indicates his understanding of what he has heard by selecting from a set of four small pictures the one which is correctly described. Two forms are available and items are based on common concepts which are taught in Spanish, German, and French.[16]

The Modern Language Association Cooperative Foreign Language Tests provide examinations in French, Spanish, German, Russian, and Italian in four skills: listening, speaking, reading, and writing. There are two levels and two forms of each level. Forms LA and LB are for students with one to two full years of study in secondary school or with one to two semesters of study in college, while the MA and MB forms are for students with three to four full years of study in secondary school or with three to four semesters of study in college.

The Modern Language Association Proficiency Test for Teachers and Advanced Students[17] consists of a battery of seven tests. The Listening Comprehension test examines phonemic discrimination, idiomatic expressions, vocabulary and conversational structure. The Speaking test rates vocabulary, pronunciation, structure, and fluency. In the Reading test the candidate selects appropriate lexical, idiomatic or structural completions for incomplete sentences. The Writing test is based on a completion exercise and the correction of errors in poorly written texts. The Applied Linguistics test deals with questions on pronunciation, phonetics, orthography, morphology, general linguistics, and historical and comparative philology. The Civilization and Culture tests measure the knowledge of civilization and culture in such areas as geography, history, the arts, literature, and social institutions. The Professional Preparation test examines teaching methods and developments in the field of language teaching, including objectives, techniques, professional development, and evaluation.[18]

Miriam M. Bryan points out that results on the tests indicate more emphasis needs to be given to developing greater speaking competence on the part of the prospective teacher, that there is a higher correlation between listening and reading than between listening and speaking, and that college curricula in the different foreign languages do not make adequate allowance for work with the development of skill in writing.[19]

Prior to placing their students in student teaching situations, teacher training institutions might well consider an eligibility requirement which includes scores meeting the minimum qualifications of the Modern Language Association in the seven test categories described above. The use of such test, in the absence of such procedure by the teacher training institutions, by state bureaus of certification in determining eligibility for the certificate should also be given consideration.

Conclusion

The change in emphasis in the past decade from the reading-translation focus to that of total communication in language learning has resulted in the development of tests in the four basic skills. The greatest progress has been made in the evaluation of aural comprehension. The mass testing of speech continues to be the chief testing problem.

ROBERT J. LUDWIG, chairman of the Language Department of Mont Pleasant High School in Schenectady, New York, is serving his third term as President of the New York State Federation of Foreign Language Teachers. He was Visiting Assistant Professor of Education at the State University of New York at Albany. He has served as a consultant to the Bureau of Foreign Languages of the New York State Education Department, and conducts workshops for teachers throughout the State of New York under the auspices of the New York State Federation of Foreign Language Teachers and the New York State Education Department. Mr. Ludwig received the Librairie Larousse prize in 1965 as teacher of a national winner in the annual contest of the American Association of Teachers of French. He holds the M.A. degree from Columbia University and has continued graduate studies at the University of Paris, the University of Aix-Marseille and the Institut des Hautes Etudes of the Universities of Toulouse and Bordeaux at Pau. He was named chevalier dans l'ordre des Palmes Academiques by the French Government in 1967. He is also a member of the Academy of Certified Social Workers.

FOOTNOTES

1. Nelson Brooks, LANGUAGE AND LANGUAGE LEARNING, 2nd edition. New York: Harcourt, Brace and World, 1964, 200.
2. Robert Lado, LANGUAGE TESTING. London: Longmans, Green and Co., 1961, 370.
3. John B. Carroll, and Stanley M. Sapon, THE MODERN LANGUAGE APTITUDE TEST. New York: The Psychological Corporation, 1959.

4. Paul Pimsleur, PIMSLEUR LANGUAGE APTITUDE BATTERY. New York: Harcourt, Brace and World, 1966.
5. Nelson Brooks, LEARNING A MODERN FOREIGN LANGUAGE FOR COMMUNICATION. Modern Language Teaching in School and College, Northeast Conference on the Teaching of Foreign Languages, Foreword to the Reports of Working Committees. New York: New York University, 1961, 19-20.
6. Edward M. Stack, THE LANGUAGE LABORATORY AND MODERN LANGUAGE TEACHING. New York: Oxford University Press, 1960, 118.
7. Remunda Cadoux, THE CLASSROOM TEST. Unpublished address delivered at the New York State Federation of Foreign Language Teachers Annual Meeting, Syracuse, New York, October 1964.
8. Emilio L. Guerra, David Abrahamson and Maxim Newmark, "The New York City Foreign Language Oral Ability Rating Scale." THE MODERN LANGUAGE JOURNAL, XLIII, 8, December 1944, 486-489.
9. Patricia O'Connor, MODERN FOREIGN LANGUAGES IN HIGH SCHOOL: PRE-READING INSTRUCTION. Bulletin OE-27000, No. 9. Washington, D. C.: U. S. Department of Health, Education and Welfare, 1960, 42.
10. SPANISH FOR SECONDARY SCHOOLS. Bureau of Secondary Curriculum Development. New York: New York State Education Department, Albany, 1961, 227-228.
11. Mary Finnochiaro, TEACHING CHILDREN FOREIGN LANGUAGES. New York: McGraw-Hill Book Company, 1964, 138.
12. Robert L. Politzer, READING FRENCH FLUENTLY. Englewood Cliffs, N.J.: Prentice-Hall, Inc., 1965, Introduction, iii.
13. Robert Lado, LANGUAGE TEACHING. New York: McGraw-Hill Book Company, 1964, 168.
14. Working Committee III, THE TRANSITION TO THE CLASSROOM. Northeast Conference on the Teaching of Foreign Languages. New York: New York University, 1961, 50.
15. College Entrance Examination Board, ACHIEVEMENT TESTS. New York, 1966-1967, 41-69.
16. Bela Banathy, et al., COMMON CONCEPTS FOREIGN LANGUAGE TEST. Monterey, Calif.: California Test Bureau, 1962.
17. Modern Language Association Foreign Language Tests, DIRECTIONS FOR ADMINISTERING AND SCORING. Princeton, N.J.: Educational Testing Service Cooperative Test Division. 1964, 4.
18. "Description of MLA Proficiency Test." MODERN LANGUAGE JOURNAL, Vol. L, No. 6, October 1966, 395-397. (Reprinted from Bulletin of Information, 1966-67. Princeton, N. J.: Educational Testing Service, 1966.)
19. Miriam L. Byran, "Implications for Higher Education: Results of the New FL Tests." DFL BULLETIN, Vol. V, No. 3, May 1966, 1-3.

Selected Bibliography

BOOKS

Brooks, Nelson, LANGUAGE AND LANGUAGE LEARNING, 2nd edition. New York: Harcourt, Brace and World, Inc., 1964, 199-

226. Prognostic, progress, achievement, and proficiency tests are described. The author discusses the objective test, standardized tests, the writing of test items, pretesting and its analysis and test norming. Suggestions for the preparation of classroom tests are given and item types are analyzed and illustrated.

Carroll, John B. and Sapon, Stanley M., THE MODERN LANGUAGE APTITUDE TEST. New York: The Psychological Corporation, 1959. The test and its administration are described. Designed to predict how rapidly students will learn a foreign language, to identify students with special language talent, to place students in fast and slow language sections, and to aid in diagnosing student difficulties in language learning, the test consists of five parts and its range is grade nine and above. Norms are presented and analyzed.

College Entrance Examination Board ACHIEVEMENT TESTS. New York, 1966-1967, 41-69. Achievement tests in Latin, French, German, Hebrew, Russian, and Spanish are described and type questions are illustrated. Answer keys are included.

Educational Testing Service, MAKING THE CLASSROOM TEST: A GUIDE FOR TEACHERS. Evaluation and Advisory Service, Series No. 4, Second Edition, Princeton, N.J.: Educational Testing Service, 1961. Basic general principles for constructing tests to meet specific classroom needs are presented. Special problems in writing and scoring tests are described. Illustrations are given to aid the practitioner.

Finnochiaro, Mary, TEACHING CHILDREN FOREIGN LANGUAGES. New York: McGraw-Hill Book Company, 1964, 135-140. The author lists techniques for oral and written testing and annotates principles of classroom test construction as well as the reporting of the achievement of children. The focus is on the elementary school language learner.

FRENCH FOR SECONDARY SCHOOLS. Bureau of Secondary Curriculum Development. Albany, N.Y.: New York State Education Department, 1960, 186-200. Principles of test construction and varied examples of test questions for each of the four skills are illustrated. The testing of culture is also included.

Holton, J. S., et. al., SOUND LANGUAGE TEACHING: THE STATE OF THE ART TODAY, New York: University Publishers Inc., 1961, 57-65, 167-174, 221-227. The focus is on the testing of speech and aural comprehension with particular reference to the use of the language laboratory and on achieving objectivity in oral testing.

Huebener, Theodore, HOW TO TEACH FOREIGN LANGUAGES EFFECTIVELY. New York: New York University Press, 1959, 175-189. The author illustrates objective testing principles and briefly discusses validity, reliability, and the various types of tests.

264

Lado, Robert, LANGUAGE TEACHING. A SCIENTIFIC AP-
PROACH. New York: McGraw-Hill Book Company, 1964, 158-
170. Current views and practices are contrasted with the new
view in language testing which is rooted in the structural understanding of language. Reliability, validity, and norming are
explained and the author illustrates ways of testing the four
skills.

———, LANGUAGE TESTING: THE CONSTRUCTION AND
USE OF FOREIGN LANGUAGE TESTS, A TEACHER'S
BOOK. London: Longmans, Green and Co., 1961. All aspects
of testing language skills are elaborated upon in this work. Theoretical as well as practical considerations are detailed and a
thorough analysis is made of testing the integrated skills of
auditory and reading comprehension, speaking, writing, and
translation.

Mialaret, G. and Malandain, C., TEST C. G. M. 62, Pour Apprecier
le Niveau des connaissances linguistiques: Francais: Realisation
du Centre de Recherches et d'Etudes pour la Diffusion du
Francais. Paris: Didier, 1962. The procedures for administering
and the test itself are discussed in this battery which is utilized
for the placement of students of French. Six tests are described
which measure oral comprehension, oral expression, aural comprehension, written comprehension and written expression.
Scores are analyzed and interpreted.

New York City Foreign Language Program for Secondary Schools,
SPANISH LEVELS 1-5. Board of Education, City of New York:
Curriculum Bulletin 1965-66, Series No. 2b, Part III, 224-235.
Purposes of testing, characteristics of a good test, and the testing
of the four skills are described. An elaboration is presented of the
New York State Regents Examinations, the Modern Language
Association Cooperative Foreign Language Tests, and the Col-
lege Board examinations.

O'Connor, Patricia, MODERN FOREIGN LANGUAGES IN HIGH
SCHOOL: PRE-READING INSTRUCTION. Bulletin OE-
27000, No. 9. Washington, D.C.: U.S. Department of Health,
Education and Welfare, 1960, 42-43. Problems and suggestions
for measuring achievement during the aural-oral phase of language learning are described.

Pimsleur, Paul, PIMSLEUR LANGUAGE APTITUDE BATTERY.
New York: Harcourt, Brace and World, 1966. Designed for use
at the end of grade six and in grades seven through twelve, the
battery is intended for both predicting success in foreign language learning and for diagnosing language learning difficulties.
The administration and use of the battery and its rationale are
presented.

Stack, Edward M., THE LANGUAGE LABORATORY AND MOD-
ERN LANGUAGE TEACHING. New York: Oxford University
Press, 1960, 118-134. The author details examples of aural com-

prehension testing and analyzes oral examinations and their grading in terms of factors of immediacy of response, excellence of pronunciation and appropriateness of response. The dictation and written examination are described as well as reading comprehension and controlled composition.

ARTICLES

Bryan, Miriam L., "Implications for Higher Education: Results of the New FL Tests." DFL BULLETIN, V, No. 3, May 1966, 1-3. The author indicates that an analysis of results in the Modern Language Association Cooperative Foreign Language Tests have important implications for higher education, including: (1) the need for more effective articulation between college and high school curriculum offerings and student placement, (2) the necessity for greater speaking competence on the part of the prospective language teacher and appropriate consideration thereof in his training, and (3) the need for the college curriculum to make more adequate allowance for work with the development of skill in writing.

Guerra, Emilio L., Abramson, David, and Newmark, Maxim, "The New York City Foreign Language Oral Ability Rating Scale." THE MODERN LANGUAGE JOURNAL, XLVIII, No. 8, December 1964, 486-489. An oral ability rating scale which includes quality factors of echo ability recitation and drills and aptness factors of drill responses and directed responses utilizes a 0-2 scale. It was prepared as a Level II evaluatory instrument in the New York City schools.

Pimsleur, Paul, "A French Speaking Proficiency Test." THE FRENCH REVIEW, XXXIV, No. 5, April 1961, 470-479. The test is intended, according to the author, to represent the most significant aspects of the student's ability to speak French within the limitations of the content of his school course. It is divided into five parts: (1) concrete nouns, (2) abstract words, (3) pronunciation, (4) syntax, and (5) fluency. The reliability and validity of the test are discussed as well as practical considerations.

Politzer, Robert, "Toward a Practice-Centered Program for the Training and Evaluation of Foreign Language Teachers." THE MODERN LANGUAGE JOURNAL, L, No. 5, May 1966, 251-255. The author discusses the implications of the Modern Language Association Proficiency Tests for Teachers and Advanced Students for the training and evaluation of foreign language teachers and the need to supplement them by tests which measure the teacher's performance in the classroom.

Schatz, Roy, "A Great Step Forward: A Further Report on Oral Testing in Grade 13 French." THE CANADIAN MODERN LAN-

GUAGE REVIEW, XXIII, No. 1, Fall 1966, 7-9. An oral test (given at the end of grade thirteen for students of French) which has been developed by the Modern Language Inspectors of the Ontario Department of Education, utilizes anecdotes and pictures to determine oral competence. It is administered by the teacher.

Starr, Wilmarth H., "Proficiency Tests in Modern Foreign Languages." PMLA, LXXVI, No. 2, May 1961, 7-11. An explanation and description of the Modern Language Association Foreign Language Proficiency Tests in French, German, Italian, Russian and Spanish for Teachers and Advanced Students is elaborated.

The Articulation of Language Teaching

CONTINUITY FOR THE LEARNER FROM ELEMENTARY
SCHOOL THROUGH COLLEGE

THEODORE H. RUPP
Millersville State College

THE PROBLEM of the continuity of foreign language instruction from school to college and the articulation of this instruction at the juncture of the two levels was considered to be so pressing as to form one of the discussion topics of the 1965 Northeast Conference on the Teaching of Foreign Languages. Though the report[1] should be read in its entirety, it is summed up as follows in number 18 (August 1965) of *MLabstracts,* abstract 918:

> In spite of renewed interest in learning foreign languages, in spite of intensified efforts toward improving the quality of teaching at every level, secondary schools and colleges are still exchanging grievances and accusations. To remedy this situation the following propositions should be considered: (1) To encourage better communication and greater coordination between teachers of foreign languages, key universities and colleges in the Northeast Conference could sponsor meetings between their foreign language faculties and teachers of secondary schools in their areas. (2) Colleges should abandon any formula that sets a fixed ratio of secondary school years of study to college semesters. (3) Colleges should place students in language classes in accordance with their abilities as demonstrated in tests. (4) Colleges should grant full credit to any student who successfully completes any course in which he is

placed, whether he is "repeating" work done in second-ary school or not. (5) Test development has not kept pace with new methods of teaching foreign languages; there are very few standard tests which accurately test all four skills. Most tests still stress only reading ability. (6) The Northeast Conference should contribute to the improvement of communication and coordination by seeking ways of making available specific information about what is being taught in secondary schools and in colleges, and how it is being taught.

Note that the report does not deal with continuity from the elementary school through college. Margaret Eaton in the 1958 Northeast Conference describes an ideal continuous program running from grade 3 through grade 12.[2]

I am not aware of any studies dealing specifically with continuity from undergraduate through graduate school.

When I accepted the assignment for this chapter, I set about obtaining information on the present state of affairs by devising three questionnaires: the first divided into three sections for the elementary, junior high school and senior high school levels; the second for college level; and the third for graduate school level. Though certain questions appear which bear only slightly, if at all, upon the central problem and though there are the inevitable vaguely or ambiguously phrased questions, I think the reader will be able to trace the thread of relevance throughout. The essential question is whether or not there is any clearly definable philosophy of foreign language study remaining consistent from elementary through graduate school.

QUESTIONNAIRE FOR THE SCHOOL DISTRICT ON
ARTICULATION IN THE FOREIGN LANGUAGE
PROGRAM FROM ELEMENTARY SCHOOL TO COLLEGE

Part I — Elementary School

1. At what grade from 1 to 6 is instruction in FL (foreign language) first given in your district?
2. How many periods per week and of what length each?
3. Is the teaching done by the regular grade teachers or by specialists?
4. Is there a person designated as coordinator?

5. Do the teachers have a syllabus for each grade?
6. Who is responsible for the existence of syllabi?
7. Are they prepared locally or purchased elsewhere?
8. Is there a single course of study providing for progression from the first to the last year of FL instruction?
9. Whose responsibility is the course of study?
10. Was it written locally or purchased elsewhere?
11. Do all children in a given grade receive FL instruction?
12. If not, what is the basis for selection?
13. What coordination, if any, is there of the FL with other subjects?
14. If the teaching is done by specialists, what part, if any, does the regular teacher have in FL instruction?
15. In the elementary school program in general what percentage of emphasis is given to teaching the following: reading ————%, writing ————%, understanding ————%, speaking ————%, mechanics of the language ————%, (other) ————%?
16. What attempt, if any, is made to prepare the children for their junior high school FL course?

Part II — Junior High School

1. In what grade from 7-9 is FL instruction first given?
2. How many periods per week and how many minutes each?
3. Is there any articulation between the elementary FL program and the Junior High School program?
4. Who is responsible for providing this articulation?
5. How is it made possible (for example, sequential course of study, teacher conferences, etc.)?
6. Do all children who have had an FL in elementary school have one in Junior High School?
7. If not, what is the basis for selection?
8. Do some children begin an FL who have never had it before?
9. Are they placed in *separate* beginner's classes or with children who had the FL in elementary school?
10. If in separate classes, are the two groups kept in separate tracks through Junior High School?
11. If the answer to No. 10 is "no," in what grade do they merge?

12. If the two groups are not separated from the beginning, how does the instruction provide for the difference?
13. Who is responsible for the existence of a syllabus for each course?
14. Is there a course of study for the whole Junior High School sequence?
15. If so, who is responsible for its preparation or procurement?
16. What percentage of emphasis is given to the following areas: reading ——%, writing ——%, speaking ——%, mechanics of the language ——% understanding ——%, (other) —— ——%?
17. What attempt, if any, is made to prepare the pupils for their high school FL course?

Part III — High School

1. In what grade (9 or 10 to 12) is an FL first given?
2. How many years of one FL are offered?
3. How many years does the majority of students studying an FL take?
4. How many years does the majority of those going to college take?
5. Do most students taking an FL have it their senior year?
6. Their junior year?
7. Is there a person responsible for coordinating instruction in one or more FL's?
8. How much teaching does this person do?
9. Do you have a course of study to cover the whole high school sequence in each FL?
10. Whose responsibility are the syllabi and course of study?
11. Is there continuity in the FL between the Junior High School and High School?
12. Who is responsible for establishing and maintaining the continuity?
13. How is it accomplished (for example, through the course of study, teacher meetings, use of textbooks series, etc.)?
14. Where pupils have not had an FL in Junior High School are there beginning classes in High School?
15. Where they have had an FL in grade 7, 8, and 9, to what course are they assigned in High School (for example, beginning Spanish, second-year Spanish, etc.)?

16. In grades 8 and 9?
17. Do all pupils who have passed an FL in Junior High School take the FL in High School?
18. If not, what is the basis for selection?
19. In general in the High School sequence taken by *college-bound* pupils what percentage of your total time is spent teaching the following: speaking ——%, understanding ——%, mechanics of the language ——%, reading ——%, writing ——%, civilization ——%, literature ——%, (other) ——— ——%?
20. Do you have an advanced Placement Program in FL's?
21. By what means is it determined where to place the instructional emphasis for college-bound pupils (for example, CEEB tests, conducting surveys of colleges, former students)?
22. Who is responsible for keeping abreast of changing emphases in college FL study?
23. What do you think the colleges expect you to emphasize most in preparing your students for college FL courses?
24. How many years of one FL do you recommend as adequate preparation for college FL courses?
25. Does the school district possess a single course of study in each FL taught providing for year-to-year continuity in the program from the beginning in the elementary or junior high school to the end in High School?
26. Are copies available, and what is the cost?

QUESTIONNAIRE FOR COLLEGES AND GRADUATE SCHOOLS: ARTICULATION IN THE FOREIGN LANGUAGE PROGRAM FROM HIGH SCHOOL TO GRADUATE SCHOOL

Part I – College

1. Do you have an FL (foreign language) requirement for admission, and if so how many years of one FL?
2. Do you have an FL requirement for graduation, and if so, how many semester-hours?
3. May this figure (in No. 2) include a year of the beginners' FL course?
4. Do you use a test for placement purposes?

5. If you use the CEEB Reading Test, what score is required for placement in the intermediate course?
6. What use do you make of the CEEB Listening Test?
7. How many years of high school FL do you consider necessary for the student to do satisfactory work in the college intermediate course?
8. If a college student is a beginner in an FL, how many semester-hours does he need to enter the intermediate course?
9. What percentage of their total time do you think the high schools should spend teaching the following: reading: ——%, writing ——%, speaking ——%, understanding ——%, mechanics of the language ——%, civilization ——%, literature ——%, (other) —— ——%?
10. Of the phases you consider most important in high school teaching which one is most neglected or poorly taught in high school?
11. Do you think the high schools do a satisfactory job of teaching their students to speak with an acceptable accent?
12. To speak with grammatical correctness?
13. To understand the spoken language?
14. For your college intermediate course is there a common course of study for all sections?
15. Is there a person charged with the specific responsibility of coordinating the intermediate course?
16. Is your intermediate course articulated with the FL curricula of the high schools of your students?
17. How do the products of your college elementary course perform in the intermediate classes as compared with the products of the high school FL courses?
18. If the high school products were as well prepared as you would like, would you spend *less* time teaching your college courses?
19. *More* time?
20. What course normally follows your intermediate course?
21. Do you feel that the majority of the students taking the course are adequately prepared for it?
22. If not, why not?
23. Is English or the FL the language of the classroom in the following courses: elementary ——, intermediate ——,

course following intermediate ———, advanced courses ———?

24. In the instruction of your undergraduate *majors* on what one phase does your department place the greatest emphasis (for example, language skills, linguistics, civilization, literary texts, literary history and criticism, etc.)?

25. How important do you think it is for your majors upon graduation to be able to speak and understand the FL? Check one: very important ———, of medium importance ———, not important ———.

26. What will the majority of your majors do upon graduation?

27. Do you have a teacher-training program aimed specifically at future *college* FL teachers?

28. Do you see any need for such a program?

29. In what one phase of your college program do you think the graduate schools expect your graduates to have their greatest strength?

Part II – Graduate School

1. To what one phase of *undergraduate* FL instruction do you think the college should devote the greatest attention (see No. 24 of Part I)?

2. In what phase of FL knowledge are your graduate students most deficient upon entrance?

3. How important do you consider it to be for your students *upon entrance* to be able to speak and understand the FL? Check one: Very important ———, of medium importance ———, not important ———.

4. Upon obtaining the master's degree?

5. The doctor's degree?

6. What type of position do most of your students obtain upon termination of their graduate study (for example, college teaching and research, secondary school teaching, diplomacy, etc.)?

7. Of those who go into college teaching what percentage have had at least one semester of classroom teaching experience under supervision?

8. Do you consider such experience necessary for prospective college teachers?

274

9. For prospective college teachers is there any prerequisite of pedagogical training experience for *admission* to graduate school?

10. Are you in favor of such a prerequisite?

11. Do you have, and do you favor such a prerequisite for the granting of an advanced degree? (Two answers desired.)

12. In awarding your teaching fellowships do you give any special consideration to persons who have had teacher-training and experience?

13. Do your teaching fellows participate in a training program involving supervision and classroom visitation?

14. If not, do you favor such a program?

15. In the language examinations required for the Ph.D. in all fields are you in favor of requiring the candidate to demonstrate any other language skill besides reading, and if so what?

The first of these was sent to the 18 public school districts in Lancaster County, Pennsylvania, in which my institution, Millersville State College, is located, to 24 large population centers (including Philadelphia and Pittsburgh) throughout Pennsylvania, and to 12 suburban school districts around Philadelphia, a total of 54 school districts.

The second and, in some instances the third, were sent to the other 13 state colleges, to 28 other colleges and universities in Pennsylvania in all categories (public, private, church-related, liberal arts, all-male, all-female, coeducational, large, small, with and without graduate school) and to 14 universities scattered around the country from New England to California where I was acquainted with someone who had demonstrated an interest in the teaching of foreign languages in this country. For the institutions in Pennsylvania, the chairman of foreign languages was addressed if there was one and, if not, either the chairman of Romance languages or of German in about equal proportions, with no polling of other languages (such as Russian) because of the small numbers involved. In three instances within Pennsylvania more than one chairman was queried. The institutions having a graduate school were asked to fill out both the second and the third questionnaire.

Returns

Of the questionnaire mailed to the 54 public school districts in Pennsylvania, 40 were returned, or about 75 per cent. Of the 58 chairmen asked to fill out the *college* questionnaire, 41 complied, about 72 per cent. On the graduate level 15 out of 26 came back, about 55 per cent. Not everyone answered every question, and in a goodly number of cases the answers were so broad or so qualified that they could not be used in a statistical count. Thus the replies to each question will usually not add up to the number of questionnaires returned.

Results: *Elementary School*

Of the 40 public school districts returning the questionnaire 16 (or 40 per cent) sponsor some type of FLES program. Among the 16 are such large population centers as Pittsburgh, Philadelphia (though the program is not city-wide), Reading, and Allentown. Eight districts begin the language in fourth grade, 3 in third, 2 in fifth, 1 in second (after "brief exposure" in kindergarten and first), and 1 in sixth and 1 is ungraded and for gifted children only.

Concerning the number of periods per week and the length of each, the situation is terribly confused. One reports one 30-minute period a week, another two 1-hour periods per week, another reports two 40-minute periods. The number of periods per week may vary within the same district for different grades, as is perhaps reasonable, but it may even vary for the same grades. Four reported two 30-minute periods, 3 reported four 25-minute periods and 3 reported five 20-minute periods. It is this writer's belief that the most desirable situation is five periods per week progressing from 15 to 30 minutes from grade three upward. If this admittedly limited survey is at all representative of the country as a whole, it is understandable why there seems to be such disagreement as to the effectiveness of FLES. It is obvious that many districts are still experimenting. If FLES is to be judged fairly, it should occupy the same place in the curriculum as any other course and given the same weight.

For the most part (12) the teaching is done by a specialist, but two districts use a television course. In two cases the regular teacher does it, and two have a combination of television teacher and regular teacher. Most (11) have a coordinator, 11 of 16 have syllabi, most of which are locally prepared, and 11 have a course of study from the first to the last year of instruction. Opinion varies as to who is responsible for syllabi and courses of study with 5 thinking the syllabus is the teacher's responsibility and 5 thinking the course of study should be furnished by the foreign language supervisor, director, or coordinator. The difference of opinion may explain why some have neither syllabi nor courses of study.

In general, where FLES exists all children receive it, but in 4 cases a selection is made based on such factors as I.Q., parents' wishes, pupils' wishes and pupils' success.

There is little attempt to coordinate the language with other subjects, nor does the regular teacher (where there is a specialist) in most instances play any part in the FL instruction, only 4 assigning her an important role.

The question on emphasis in the instruction indicates that understanding and speaking in that order occupy the greatest percentage by far of the total teaching time, with reading, writing, and mechanics in that order following far behind. Only 5 devote as much as 5 per cent of their time to reading (4 give 10 per cent) and 7 give up to 5 per cent for writing (5 give 10 per cent).

The answers to the final question, asking what attempt is made to prepare for the junior high course, reveal some uncertainty but also in general an awareness of the desirability of continuity. Only one said there is no attempt at preparation, while another one said that the whole purpose of the FLES program was to prepare for junior high.

Results: Junior High School

On the 40 districts responding, 38 have foreign language instruction beginning in either seventh, eighth or ninth grade, with 24 beginning in seventh grade at least for one or two languages and for certain categories of pupils, such as the gifted or those who have had a FLES sequence. The situation in regard to the number of periods and minutes per week is completely chaotic, particularly in grades seven and eight, with variations within the same district. One district reports one 45-minute per week period for seventh and eighth grade, another reports one 50-

minute period for these grades, still another one 52-minute period for the same grades. Eight report two periods per week ranging from 45 to 90 minutes in length. Five have three periods per week of 24 to 50 minutes length, 4 have four per week from 25 to 50 minutes in length, and 10 have five per week, ranging from 25 to 50 minutes in length. Each of the rest reports some variation of the preceding for seventh and eighth grades. For ninth the pattern is generally five periods of 45 minutes each.

Where a FLES program exists, there is an almost 100 per cent affirmative answer concerning articulation between elementary school and junior high. Most state that this results from teacher conferences, the existence of a single course of study, or an integrated series of textbooks. Opinion varied somewhat as to whose responsibility it is, but most said the department head, coordinator, supervisor, or director of foreign languages.

Most districts having a FLES program answer negatively the question asking whether all children who have a foreign language in elementary school have one in junior high. Though the questionnaire failed to ask for the percentage, three districts indicated a 10 per cent drop. The principal basis for screening is ability, other bases being aptitude tests, pupil election, parent election, teacher recommendation, and English reading ability.

Most of the districts having FLES state that a pupil who has not had a language previously may start one in junior high school, but the picture is somewhat confused. The language of the FLES program is taught in grades seven, eight and nine, but in general the other languages do not begin until ninth or tenth grade. Thus it appears that the non-FLES pupils cannot in a majority of these districts start a foreign language before ninth grade, though an apt pupil wanting to take the language of the FLES program may be permitted to go into the seventh grade class along with the FLES products. It is true that a minority of these districts have beginning courses at the seventh and/or eighth grade levels where a non-FLES pupil may receive his introduction to a foreign language other than the FLES language. In scattered instances the non-FLES pupils are given a year of introduction to the language and merge with the FLES products the following year.

Thirty-three districts said they had a course of study for the junior high sequence, and most agreed this was the responsibility of the department head. As for the syllabi, opinion was divided about evenly between the department head and the teachers.

Concerning instructional emphasis, the great majority spend about 40 per cent of their total time teaching their pupils to speak and about 30 per cent on understanding, with reading receiving about 15 per cent of the emphasis, writing 10 per cent, and mechanics 5 per cent of the emphasis. All claim to prepare the pupil for the high school courses, chiefly as a result of following a prepared sequence.

Results: Senior High School

Of the 39 senior high schools participating 29 offer 4 years of at least one modern foreign language, 4 offer 3 years, 2 offer 6 years, 2 offer 5 years and 2 offer 2 years. In a number of cases, the information was volunteered that the same or shorter sequence applied to a second or third language. Nineteen report that a majority of those taking a language take two years, but 21 report, as follows: 9—3 years, 6—4 years, 4—2 to 3 years and 2—3 to 4 years. About their college-bound students, 27 report that the majority take at least 3 years (17—3 years, 8—4 years, 2—5 years), 10 say 2 years, and one says 2 to 3 years. Nineteen districts say most students taking a language do not have one in their senior year, 17 say they do, and 2 say maybe.

Most of the districts (33) have a person who is responsible for conducting foreign languages. In 8 districts he does no teaching; in 4 he teaches full-time. In one district he is released from teaching one day per week; in 7 he teaches 4 classes per day, in 2, 5 classes, in 1, 3 classes, and in another, 2 classes. Some districts give percentages of teaching time. However, if we reduce all the figures to percentages, the average amount of time the language coordinator spends teaching is about 53 per cent. Most of the districts (30) state they have a course of study to cover the high school sequence in each language and assign to the coordinator or department head responsibility for its existence.

Thirty-six districts say there is continuity in the FL between the junior high and senior high, but are divided in their belief as to who should establish and maintain it. Twelve say the department head; 9 say the curriculum coordinator; 6, administration and department head; 6, the teachers; 4, department head and teachers; and 2, the superintendent. They are also somewhat divided on how this is accomplished, but in general are in agreement on the necessity of a course of study and of meetings of the teachers; and apparently see value in the use of integrated series of textbooks.

Thirty-six districts offer beginning FL courses in high school for students who have not had a language in junior high. However, where the pupils have had the language in grades seven, eight, and nine, there is no clear pattern as to where they will be placed in high school. Thirteen districts say the second year, 9 say proper level based on the students' past performance, 4 say the third year, 1 says second or third year, and 3 put them in the beginning course. Other replies are too vague or too complicated to evaluate. The same applies to the question about where a pupil is placed who had a language in grades eight and nine. Some (9) put him in a beginning course, 7 in the "proper course" according to his previous work, 5 in the second-level course, 3 in the first- or second-level course, and 1 in the third-level course. Clear-cut answers are difficult to give to these questions because of the many variables resulting from the present status of foreign languages in the junior high school, particularly in the seventh and eighth grades, where they may meet only once or twice a week because they are considered "exploratory."

The responses to the question concerning the percentage of total teaching time devoted to the various aspects of the language average approximately as follows: speaking 25 per cent, understanding 25 per cent, reading 15 per cent, writing 10 per cent, literature 10 per cent, civilization 10 per cent and mechanics 5 per cent.

Seven out of 39 have an Advanced Placement program. In determining where to place the emphasis in the preparation of college-bound students, most of those who answered the question (about 10 did not) said they were guided by the College Board tests, by conversations with former students, by surveys, and by meetings with college professors and officials. They place the responsibility for staying abreast of changing emphases in college upon the teachers and department head or language coordinator. The answers to the question, What do you think the colleges expect you to emphasize most in preparing your students for college FL courses?, reflect a degree of uncertainty, with some hedging and reluctance to answer (a dozen did not). However, 9 said speaking; 6, oral and written comprehension; 5, aural comprehension; 4, all four major areas of language; 1, speaking and aural comprehension; and 5, said it depends on the college.

One of the most significant responses in the whole questionnaire is the one given to the question, How many years of one FL do you recommend as adequate preparation for college FL courses? Nineteen districts said 4 years, 17 said 3 years, 1 said 6 to 8 years, 1 said 6 years, 1 said 5 to 6 years, and only 1 said 2 to 3 years. *Thus, almost 100 percent recommend at least 3 years.*

Twenty-three (or about 55 per cent) districts say they possess a single course of study in each FL taught providing for year-to-year continuity in the program from beginning to end. Fourteen said they did not.

Results: College

Of the 41 colleges responding 18 have a foreign-language entrance requirement for everyone; 4 have one for certain curricula only—for example, arts and sciences, liberal arts, secondary education, and library science. The majority (13) specify at least 2 years, 4 ask for 3 years, and 3 for 4 years. Two do not have a requirement, but ask candidates to take the College Entrance Examination Board achievement test in a foreign language, and several volunteered percentages showing that from 90 to 99 per cent of their incoming students have had a foreign language in high school anyway. It would appear that even where there is no requirement the competition for admission is such that students having had a language are favored over the others.

One hundred per cent of the respondents have a foreign language requirement for graduation in at least the liberal arts curriculum and in some cases in other curricula too, such as teacher-preparation. The number of semester hours required for graduation varies from college to college and, in numerous instances within the colleges, by curriculum and even by language. The question is also complicated by use of the term

281

"semester hours." Some colleges reported by "semesters," some by "courses," some by "levels." Some state the requirement in terms of a level of proficiency demonstrated by passing courses at a certain level and/or passing a test. Since another complicating factor could be whether the semesters or semester hours which some of the students spend taking beginning language courses are counted toward the graduation requirement, this question was specifically asked.

In spite of the maze of varying requirements, of methods of reporting these requirements, and of difficulties posed by those whose requirements depend on the students' curriculum, it is possible to see a broad pattern. Practically all (40) require in one or more curricula that the student pass the second-year college course or demonstrate by examination the proficiency which should be attained by the end of the second-year college course. In general, this means a requirement of at least 2 semesters or 6 semester-hours, not counting the first-year course. Most give credit for the first-year course but add the credits, course units or semester-hours to the graduation requirement. A very few (4) give credit toward the requirement for the beginning course, and of these, 3 give credit only if the student has already passed a sequence in another foreign language in high school, but these three still require a *second* year of college language.

Ten colleges (about 25 per cent) require in one or more curricula the passing of a third-year college course, generally described as a survey of literature or in some instances a composition or conversation course. Thus, their requirement is tantamount to 12 semester-hours or 4 semesters above the elementary level.

In all cases where distinctions were made by curriculum, the liberal arts students have the heavier requirement. Some colleges have various options involving taking courses or proficiency tests, great depth in one language or lesser depth in two, continuing with the language of high school or starting a second one, and the like.

Thirty-three of the colleges use a test of some sort in some way as a means of placement. Five do not use a test, 2 use one for majors only, and 1 did not answer. About half (17) use the CEEB achievement test in reading, and about half of these use

282

the CEEB listening test to supplement the reading test. Two volunteered that they use certain parts of the MLA Cooperative test, both using the listening part.

As can be imagined, the question asking for the CEEB cut-off score for placement in the intermediate course evoked a multiplicity of answers, complicated even further by ranges within the cut-off scores and by qualifications based on the semester of the intermediate course, on the number of years of high school language, on high school achievement, and frequently on the language being studied. The lowest score is 350 (one college). The next lowest is 400 (3 colleges). Two reports 425, another 425-450, another 440, a fifth reports 450-500, and a sixth 480. Three report cut-off scores of 500, and one a score of 545. Two gave 575 and 650 respectively as scores *below* which their students are put into the intermediate course. Two specified scores of 540 and 575 respectively as qualifying students to enter the second half of the intermediate course. One, where the CEEB listening test is used as well as the reading test, gives a *combined* score of 850.

The answer to the question about how many years of high school FL are considered necessary for satisfactory work in the college intermediate course may provide a surprise in view of oft-heard complaints from the colleges about the preparation of their students. Twenty, or about 50 per cent, seem to feel that two years are sufficient. Another 6 say 2 to 3, and 1 says 2 to 4. Eight say 3 years. One says 3 to 4, and one says 4 years. (Three feel the number of years means little and that it is the quality of the student and the high school that count.) Even if we lump together all in favor of more than two years we have only a minority 18 in face of the *almost* 100 *per cent response from the high schools that they considered* 3 *years to be necessary, with* 55 *per cent recommending at least* 4.

Analysis of the replies submitted to the question concerning the percentage of time which the colleges think the high schools should devote to the various aspects of the language reveals that if the respondents' answers are pooled and averages are taken, the results are approximately as follows: speaking 25 per cent, understanding 20 per cent, reading 15 per cent, writing 10 per cent, mechanics 10 per cent, civilization 10 per cent, and literature 10 per cent.

Opinion varies as to which phases are most neglected or poorly taught, but a majority (23) indicate the speaking phase, and 11 are critical of the teaching of understanding. No more than 4 colleges are in agreement in their criticism of the various other aspects of high school language teaching. Opinion is, however, fairly well defined as to whether the high schools do a satisfactory job of teaching their students to speak with (a) an acceptable accent and (b) with grammatical correctness. To the first question, 20 say no, 12 say yes, and 9 will not generalize. To the second, 23 say no, 12 say yes, and 6 will not generalize. As to whether the high schools teach their students to understand the spoken language, opinion is about evenly divided, 17 saying no, 16 yes, and 8 refusing to generalize. Again, in view of the considerable dissatisfaction manifested with what they consider to be the chief jobs of the high school, it is difficult to understand why so many think that two years of high school foreign language are adequate preparation for satisfactory work in the college intermediate course.

One possible explanation is that, as the questionnaire reveals, where students begin a foreign language in college, they can go into the intermediate class the following year with, in most instances, no more than 6 semester-hours. There are, nevertheless, exceptions to this pattern, in which the elementary course may be a highly intensive one requiring 8 to 10 semester-hours. Certain other colleges have another "intermediate" or second-year course sandwiched between the elementary year and the conventional intermediate course to serve the needs of incoming freshmen whose college board FL scores are not good enough for the conventional course but too good for the elementary course.

Questions No. 14 to No. 23 deal primarily with continuity and articulation *within* the college FL program itself. Most (30) say they have a common course of study for all the intermediate courses, and most have either a person or a committee to do the coordinating. Only 11 claim any articulation between the intermediate course and the FL curricula of the high schools from which they receive their students. A number even intimate that the question is a bit on the foolish side, as well it may be, given the complex makeup of our educational system. It is, perhaps, surprising that 11 should give an affirmative answer. Yet, difficult as it may be, a way must be found to provide this much needed articulation, for as long as the college teachers and the high school teachers are not aware of what the other is doing and as long as they do not do more to solve their common problems than to indulge in mutual recriminations, the student will continue to be the one who pays the penalty.

Question No. 17 asks how the products of the college elementary course perform in the intermediate classes as compared with the products of the high school FL courses. Eighteen think the products of the college elementary course perform better, 10 say "about the same", 5 vote for the high school product, and 8 say the evidence is inconclusive. What would the college spend more time teaching if the high school products were better prepared? Pretty generally it would be literature, with civilization, composition, and advanced conversation following. What would they spend less time on? Generally, grammar and the other mechanical aspects of the language.

The course most frequently (23) named as following the intermediate course is introduction to literature; in 8 cases it is advanced composition; in 4, composition and conversation; in 3, advanced conversation; and in 3, advanced readings. Twenty-nine think their students are adequately prepared for this course; 12 do not, chiefly on the grounds that the intermediate course is not enough to overcome the inadequate preparation with which the student arrived at college.

The great majority (28) answer that the FL is the language of the elementary course; 9 state half and half; and 4 say mostly English. For the intermediate and advanced courses the FL is almost 100 per cent used, with some slight deviation reported for advanced literature courses.

On what one phase does the department place its greatest emphasis in the instruction of its majors? The replies were as follows: language skills, 19; literary texts, 11; literary history and criticism, 9; linguistics, 1; and even balance, 1.

There was 100 per cent agreement that it is *very important* for the major to be able to speak and understand the FL upon graduation. Of these graduates about half will teach and about half will go to graduate school. None of the colleges without a graduate school affiliation has a teacher-training program aimed specifically at future college teachers. Most see a need for such a program, but because the question is not precise, it is possible that many respondents who said yes would advocate such a program on the graduate level only and some of the few saying no meant not on the undergraduate level. In fact, some of those replying yes added "on the graduate level." The question was meant to find out whether some type of training of future college teachers might be considered feasible on the undergraduate level, perhaps in the form of supervised apprentice teaching of elementary and intermediate classes as preparation for teaching fellowships in graduate school.

Answers to the last question, In what one phase of your college program do you think the graduate schools expect your graduates to have their greatest strength?, are rather widely distributed. There is general agreement among 15, however, who beg the question a bit and opt for strong linguistic competence (particularly oral) and general knowledge of the literature. Six choose depth in literature; 5 choose thorough command of the language; 4 select a well-developed critical faculty; 4 hedged by stating that the graduate schools want the student to be strong in all areas; 3 think the students must be strong in literary criticism and history; 1 said it depends on the graduate school; 2 did not answer the question.

Returns: Graduate School

The sampling on this level is so small as to render the returns of little value in showing general tendencies or practices. However, since the graduate schools all have undergraduate schools affiliated with them and in most cases share a common faculty, continuity and articulation are not real problems except insofar as many of their students come from other colleges. Thus, this section of the questionnaire is not intended to do any more than to suggest one or two problems which some graduate schools may be facing now or soon in the future.

For the first question there are almost as many different answers as there are schools replying. The question is: To what one phase of undergraduate FL instruction do you think the college should devote the greatest attention? Three answered with language skills; 2, with language skills and literary texts; 2, with literature; and 2, with speaking proficiency. The following each received one vote: language skills and grounding in literature and civilization, literature and linguistics, methodology and teacher training, speaking and understanding and ability to interpret literary texts, grasp of nature and structure of FL, knowledge of literary texts and criticism.

In what one phase of FL knowledge are the graduate students most deficient upon entrance? Four answer speaking; 2, ability to analyze works of literature; and 2, writing. The following were individual choices: knowledge of literary texts and criticism, language skills and literary appreciation, linguistics, and audio-comprehension. Three did not acknowledge deficiencies in their students. All but one consider it very important for the student to be able to speak and understand the FL. The one considers them of medium importance. All are unanimous about these abilities on obtaining the master's and doctor's degrees. Practically all their graduates go into teaching, the Ph.D.'s into college, the M.A.'s into high school. Ten report that a majority up to all of their graduate students will have had at least one semester of teaching experience under supervision. Each of the rest reports 50 per cent, 33-1/3 per cent, 25 per cent, 20 per cent, and unknown. Eleven consider such experience necessary; 3, not necessary but desirable. Only 1 reports a prerequisite of pedagogical training and experience for *admission* to graduate school. Nine are opposed to such a prerequisite, and 5 in favor. Ten do not have such a prerequisite for the granting of advanced degrees; 5 do. Nine are in favor of one; 6 are not. Eleven indicate that in awarding their teaching fellowships some consideration is given to those who have had teaching experience, but several qualify their statement by saying, "all things being equal," or something similar. Three give no special consideration. One has no teaching fellows. Twelve state that their teaching fellows participate in a program involving teaching under supervision. Two expect to have teaching fellows and favor the idea. One has no teaching fellows.

Seven are not in favor of requiring the Ph.D. candidate in nonlanguage fields to demonstrate any other skill but reading ability. Four favor requiring demonstration of all four skills, but 2 would then reduce the number of languages tested to one. Two favor requiring a speaking knowledge, and 2 understanding of the spoken word.

Summary

My purpose in this chapter has been to acquaint the reader with the problems existing in the field of foreign languages from grade school through the university in the matters of articulation from one level to the next and in the continuity of experience. In order to obtain information on the subject I prepared and distributed questionnaires designed for each of the various levels to public school districts and to all types of colleges and universities in the state of Pennsylvania. In addition, I sent questionnaires to a very small sampling of universities scattered from New England to California.

My survey shows that though FLES classes are generally taught by specialists possessing syllabi and courses of study in programs having an established sequence, there are still districts where FLES is still "experimental" and not treated like the other parts of the curriculum. The survey shows that though the school districts are generally aware of the necessity for articulation between the elementary school and the junior high and between the junior high and the senior high, actual practice leaves much to be desired. In fact, it is in the junior high school where the foreign language picture is the most confused. Part of the problem lies in the fact that a number of the senior high schools appear to have done little to adjust their language programs to take advantage of the junior high school experiences of their students. Furthermore, though in a minority of instances it is possible, the dreamed-of sequence of six solid years of one language, meeting five days per week, from seventh to twelfth grade is only rarely a reality.

College-bound students are in general taking three years of a language and are being recommended by their high schools to take more, but fewer than half have a language their senior year and thus suffer from this hiatus when they undertake their college courses. This is only one of the problems of articulation, however. The rest are created primarily by the immense diversity among the high schools and among the colleges to which the high school products go, diversities resulting from our decentralized system of education.

In general, the colleges and the high schools agree on what the high schools should be doing in languages, but the colleges are not satisfied with the students which the high schools are sending them. Under the circumstances, it is difficult to understand why the majority of the colleges reporting think that two years of high school language are sufficient preparation for their intermediate college course. Since the high schools are recommending more and the students are taking more, perhaps the colleges would be wise to insist on more.

The colleges in general emphasize acquisition of speaking proficiency, and though in advanced courses the objective is essentially inculcation of literary knowledge and appreciation and critical sense, the colleges tend to agree, with numerous exceptions, that the language skills are the number one objective of the college. The fact that there are divergencies of opinion here is principally responsible for the problems in articulation which exist between the college and the graduate school.

The survey shows that there is general agreement on the need for some kind of training for prospective college teachers, but most colleges think this is the business of the graduate school. The sampling of graduate schools is too small to be valid, but those reporting indicate that they do in fact provide such training, which appears to be teaching under supervision. How effective this system is or whether something more is necessary the survey did not attempt to ascertain.

As a final word it seems safe to say that the survey shows no strong thread of continuity from grade school through graduate school. Given the state of flux in which foreign languages find themselves at this time and the diversity which pervades the American system of education, homogeneity is hardly to be expected.

THEODORE H. RUPP, born in Windham, New York, in 1915, was educated in the public schools of Connecticut and Pennsylvania, and was graduated from Franklin and Marshall Academy in 1931. He holds an A.B. from Franklin and Marshall College, from which he was graduated in 1935 with Phi Beta Kappa honors. He attended the Middlebury French Summer School and received his M.A. from the Institute of French Education of Pennsylvania State University in 1942. He studied at the Sorbonne and at the University of Montpellier as a Fulbright Scholar and was awarded the Ph.D. by the Department of Romance Languages of the University of Pennsylvania in 1954. He taught on the secondary level in Pennsylvania in Lancaster, New Hope, and Pittsburgh, served in the U.S. Navy as an officer in World War II, and has been on the faculty at Millersville (Pennsylvania) State College since 1946, serving as chairman of the Department of Foreign Languages since 1954. In 1964-1965, on leave of absence from Millersville, he served as resident director of a study-abroad program at the University of Besançon, where he also studied and did research. He has published a number of articles on foreign study and other subjects. He is immediate past president of the Pennsylvania State Modern Language Association, a member of the AATF, the MLA, and the International Arthurian Association.

FOOTNOTES

1. Micheline Dufau, "From School to College: The Problem of Continuity." REPORTS OF THE WORKING COMMITTEES, NORTH-EAST CONFERENCE ON THE TEACHING OF FOREIGN LANGUAGES, 1965, 103-128.
2. Margaret E. Eaton, "The FL Programs, Grades 3-12." REPORTS OF THE WORKING COMMITTEES, NORTHEAST CONFERENCE ON THE TEACHING OF FOREIGN LANGUAGES, 1958, 21-35.

Selected Bibliography

BOOKS

Brooks, Nelson, LANGUAGE AND LANGUAGE LEARNING: THE-ORY AND PRACTICE. New York: Harcourt, Brace, and World, 1960. Excellent guide to how to teach FL's. See particularly chapter 9, "Continuity for the Learner," which proposes a continuity from grade school through high school.

Cornfield, Ruth R., FOREIGN LANGUAGE INSTRUCTION. DIMENSIONS AND HORIZON. New York: Appleton-Century-Crofts, 1966. Another excellent guide. Chapter 10 gives a brief treatment of the "Foreign Language Continuum" and the problems of articulation.

Ericksson, Marguerite, et al., FOREIGN LANGUAGES IN THE ELEMENTARY SCHOOL. Englewood Cliffs, N.J.: Prentice-Hall, 1964. Contains a great deal of valuable information on FLES, particularly Chapter 9, "Administration: Planning, Organization and Articulation."

Finocchiaro, Mary, TEACHING CHILDREN FOREIGN LANGUAGES. New York: McGraw-Hill, 1964. Valuable for instruction on organizing a FLES program. Chapter 5 goes into the problem of articulation with the secondary school.

Mac Allister, Archibald T., ed., THE PREPARATION OF COLLEGE TEACHERS OF FOREIGN LANGUAGES. New York: Modern Language Association of America, 1963. Fundamental to any study on the preparation of college teachers. Points up a serious lacuna in our educational system.

ARTICLES

Beam, C. Richard, ed., "Continuity in German from School to College
—A Blueprint for Action." NEWSLETTER OF THE AMERI-
CAN ASSOCIATION OF TEACHERS OF GERMAN, CEN-
TRAL PENNSYLVANIA CHAPTER, November 1965. A sym-
posium of German teachers produced an intelligent approach to
the articulation problem.

Dannerbeck, Francis J., "Towards a Methods Course Requirement at
the Graduate Level." MODERN LANGUAGE JOURNAL, L,
May 1966, 273-274. Persuasive argument for improving the
pedagogical preparation of the future college instructor.

Dufau, Micheline, "From School to College: The Problem of Continuity." REPORTS OF THE WORKING COMMITTEES,
NORTHEAST CONFERENCE ON THE TEACHING OF FOR-
EIGN LANGUAGES, 1965, 103-128. Basic to any research on
the problems of continuity.

Eaton, Margaret E., "The FL Program, Grades 3-12." REPORTS OF
THE WORKING COMMITTEES, NORTHEAST CONFER-
ENCE ON THE TEACHING OF FOREIGN LANGUAGES,
1958, 21-35. Describes an ideal sequence of foreign language
study, which if adopted throughout the country, would produce
revolutionary improvement.

Guerra, Emilio L., "The Problem of Articulation between the Junior
and Senior High Schools." HISPANIA, XLVIII, September 1965,
506-510. Particularly knowledgeable exposition of the subject by
an expert working in the school system of New York City.

Hadlich, Roger L., "Foreign Languages in Colleges and Universities."
REPORTS OF THE WORKING COMMITTEES, NORTH-
EAST CONFERENCE ON THE TEACHING OF FOREIGN
LANGUAGES, 1964, 39-57. Excellent portrayal of, and suggested remedies for, the tensions in language teaching resulting
from demands of graduate schools on the colleges and those
of the colleges on the high schools.

Schmitt, Conrad J., "Foreign Languages in the Elementary School."
REPORTS OF THE WORKING COMMITTEES, NORTH-
EAST CONFERENCE ON THE TEACHING OF FOREIGN
LANGUAGES, 1964, 3-18. Exceptionally good presentation of
an ideal program, which anticipates problems and offers solu-
tions. A "must" for administrators.

Silber, Gordon R., "A Six-Year Sequence from Grade Nine through
the Second Year of College." REPORTS OF THE WORKING
COMMITTEES, NORTHEAST CONFERENCE ON THE
TEACHING OF FOREIGN LANGUAGES, 1959, 9-32. Interesting attempt to resolve problems resulting from present lack of
articulation between high school and college.

Stein, Jack M., "The Preparation of College and University Teachers."
REPORTS OF THE WORKING COMMITTEES, NORTHEAST

CONFERENCE ON THE TEACHING OF FOREIGN LAN-
GUAGES, 1961, 33-41. Presents a workable plan which merits
more consideration than it seems to be receiving.

"The Preparation of College FL Teachers." PSMLA, LXX, September, 1955, 57-68. An unsigned report issued by a group of interested people recognizing at an early date the weaknesses inherent in the way we prepare, or do not prepare, college teachers.

Walsh, Donald D., "Articulation in the Teaching of Foreign Languages." CURRICULUM CHANGES IN THE FOREIGN LAN-
GUAGES. Princeton, N.J.: College Entrance Examination Board,
1963, 62-67. Essential for complete understanding of the necessity for articulation.

The Teaching of Other Cultures

SAMUEL GOMEZ

Salem State College, Salem, Massachusetts

THERE HAS BEEN a recent general awakening in American schools and colleges to stimulate the study of other peoples, to learn more about them and their ways, and to bring about efforts to improve international knowledge, understanding, and communication. Increasingly, attention in education is focusing upon teaching in the field of international relations and comparative studies in education, philosophy, and the social sciences, as well as developments in the teaching of foreign languages and English as a second language. American education is being called upon to promote a wider and deeper understanding of world affairs among not only the American people, but schools and educational planning have emerged as vital and significant international lifelines as well. The urgency of the world situation is a real and penetrating influence in living, and all present and prospective teachers need a better understanding of the various life styles that divide and unite the peoples of the world. Special efforts need to be made to develop a greater sense of individual concern and responsibility for grappling with the critical issues of international affairs. And if school graduates are to be really effective, they must be able to look in two directions at once; they must always have the inside, local view of their own situation and circumstances while at the same time they must have that enlarging world perspective of those forces surging about them which alter the local context. By this combination of insights and endeavors they will come to know themselves, to improve their own conditions, and to cope effectively with new international responsibilities.

Since World War II and particularly since orbiting of the first spaceship, there has been a powerful development in the

United States devoted to the general objectives of promoting international understanding. Currently, there seems to be an ever-increasing concern with the study of international relations. The number of organizations engaged in this type of effort has multiplied rapidly, and the number of colleges and universities offering courses in international affairs has grown remarkably. With the introduction of foreign languages into the elementary school curriculum, a new era has been reached in the consideration of the international dimension in education, a new period with markedly differing conceptions regarding the approach to world problems. In a more important sense, education is being seen as that dynamic force which can shatter the barriers to real world awareness and truly bring men together through a profound understanding of the epic of man. The realities of contemporary life require nothing less than a new "humanitas" which can contemplate things in all directions.

This is no simple task, for being reared in any particular culture brings about a perceptual framework which is fragmented in that it is both inclusive and at the same time exclusive. A matrix of perceptions predisposes itself to include those objects and events that are qualitatively similar and parcel out for exclusion those experiences perceived as dissimilar. Certain tensions are set into motion, and cultural gaps occur. The dynamics of this phenomenon are essentially the same whether one analyzes the fragmentation pinpointed by the recent discussion of Sir Charles Snow's "two cultures," the dissociations inherent in the encounter between individuals representing different socio-economic backgrounds within the same culture, the lack of understanding that exists between adults and the teenage culture, or the lack of communication resulting from the encounters of people with diverse cultural backgrounds. Perceptions, the basis of which are assumptive, respond selectively and have a highly specialized capacity for appropriation.[1] When perceptual maps do not fit the territory, disjunctures result. We see what we want to see even if it means changing the territory to fit our maps whether or not the alterations of the territory result in warping it—and distortions that occur become reinforcing in a circular feedback pattern. Out of the myriads of transactions with experience, we build up our worlds, worlds in which we can act with equanimity. In the words of

John Dewey, "We bring to the simplest observation a complex apparatus of habits, of accepted meanings and techniques. Otherwise observation is the blankest of stares, and the natural object is a tale told by an idiot."[2]

That this seems to be the fact of the matter we do not deny. We would attempt to see in this reality a portent and convert it into an instrumentality to realize the consequences of cultural enhancement by transcending cultural constrictions whereby out of the drama of diverse cultural transactions, new possibilities and choices are created if the trappings of idiosyncratic isolation and the leveling down of cultures can be avoided or overcome. Hence, reducing the circumambience of man between man. The teaching of other cultures would have the realization of this consequence as its ultimate goal. At the outset we would propose a model to serve as a theoretical underpinning to this notion. This model would point to a multidimensional approach to the teaching of cultures that purports to breach the cultural cleavages which are now major features of the world background. Since the crisis of our time is profound and unique, presenting us with many complex challenges calling for speed in contriving solutions, we must make every effort to maintain confidence and nerve and to develop a solid framework as referent for any proposed solutions. The crux of the multidimensional model focuses upon the role of shared experience and stresses the construction of sets of assumptions that can be widely shared and well meaning in promoting the ends of enhancement of the human person and the human condition. It would ultimately strive to transcend the inclusiveness of specialized cultural differences and deliberately fashion out of the welter of varying life styles the agora for the proper study of mankind. *Hoc opus est.*

The Multidimensional Model

There are two dimensions to the teaching and learning of other cultures. At one level the explorations of other cultures can begin in the immediacies of childhood experience. Starting early in the elementary school, experiences will be provided to bring closer to children the notion of a rapidly expanding universe through early learning experiences with other cultures compounded throughout the school years. The advantages of a

295

recurring program of increasing complexity and meaning are becoming clear. As in any other learning situation, the provision of an optimal learning environment as early as possible for as long as possible seems to be the most appropriate and effective strategy. Using a core of common elements within the disciplines to serve as the thread for continuity, structure, and integration, concepts and values can be effectively taught regarding other cultures. While it seems to be that few schools are re-orienting their curriculum in this direction, we would propose that there exist now some scattered models to help serve this purpose. For example, some insights could be had by analysis of the strategies of teaching other social patterns to the disadvantaged child. The following reveal some insights: projects and research in intercultural education;[3] the training of Peace Corps workers; and the logistics of military training. It is the task of this discussion to offer a coordinating model to serve as the basis for a strategy for the teaching of other cultures. We would call this dimension of the early and recurring introduction of other cultures into the idea environment of children the "gradual immersion approach." While there does not exist common agreement on whether or not elementary school children can understand the different influences of cultural customs and the value and personality determinants of the variety of patterns of human life,[4] new work in psychology on the effects of early learning experiences leads one to conclude that early learning deprivation handicaps the formation of positive and adequate cognitive sets for enhanced coping with the environment.[5] Moreover, there is growing indication that elementary school children possess broad, extensive interests and some understanding of a variety of concepts in the social disciplines.[6] Justification for early and regularized involvement with other cultures can be found in the concepts of early learning experiences and developmental tasks. Although the problem why children can or cannot engage in conceptualizing in international understanding is complex, the point to be made is that the deprivation of early learning experiences is a variable to be considered. This phase of the model is predicated upon the idea of long-term continuity.

The second feature of the multidimensional model would focus upon a shorter range approach to the teaching of other cultures as defined by two purposes: (1) to provide an ongoing program with international dimensions at a higher level of learning, the secondary school or the college and university, with the expressed purpose of developing understandings and appreciations of the common humanity of all men everywhere; (2) to provide knowledge and understanding of other cultures in a short period of time as called for in such cases as the training of foreign language teachers, students in comparative education, Peace Corps workers, or military personnel. We would label this the "total immersion approach." In this second aspect of stage two of the multidimensional model, the approach is conditioned by limitation in time and by whatever specific purposes are operating, such as to know as much as possible about a culture in a relatively short time prior to taking up some role within that culture. But we would like to state plainly that within the framework of this paper these would be subsidiary objectives subsumed under the basic and ultimate end. The *terminous ad quem* of the impact of other cultures would be to achieve free and authentic personal commitment on the part of the individual to the idea of mankind as the self-orchestration of multiverse cultures and ways of being. From the idea of mankind one would enter into the building of a sense of community, an "I and Thou" relationship, where one could bet on human survival, individual accentuation, and enhanced possibilities for existence and becoming. The conditions here are those designed to carry one beyond the superficialities of toleration and acceptance to confrontations toward greater realities.

The Teaching of Other Cultures in The Elementary School

The planning of experiences furthering the communion of men requires vision, but then just plain good teaching calls for the same. Knowledge and understanding of other cultures is born of good teaching, as is any other knowledge and understanding. In this dimension of the model we should like to consider specific modalities for structuring the learning environment in relationship to other cultures at the elementary school level. While many curriculum areas lend themselves easily to the study of other peoples and societies, we shall attempt to describe how this problem can be approached through the social studies. Obviously, the investigations launched deliberately via the social studies can be powerfully reinforced by other disciplines. As a case in point, there has been for some time a whole development in children's literature emphasizing the concept of "one world." Although the theme here is a projection toward the image of mankind, a notion that perhaps goes beyond earlier ideas, fruitful utilization can be made of the availability of children's literature.[7] The newer developments in the field aim toward the understandings of the realities of other cultures and to enhance the notion that all men are brothers under the skin.[8] Increasingly, a rich variety of resource materials about other lands and peoples are becoming easily obtainable even for children at the primary school level. This trend is consistent with the idea that even kindergarten children are ready for stories about other peoples if the problems and themes are common and if appropriate methodologies are utilized.[9] It is generally accepted that literature provides a richness of offering to both enhance and reinforce other studies and, of course, to be used for its own sake.

Other opportunities present themselves for the teaching of other cultures. The inquiry can be approached through the development of appropriate unit activities in a variety of learning experiences, for example, folk dancing or the study of other folk customs.[10] While the matter of resources and materials is always more or less problematic, the emergence of a variety of tools indicates that this problem is not insoluble. The writer has had occasion recently to observe the basic idea, expressed in this paper, implemented by a student teacher with a fourth grade class centering on a unit of activities on the topic "Holiday Customs" with emphasis upon the unique and universal features of human experiences.[11] The student teacher focused primarily on Christmas holiday customs in France, correlating the activities with the elementary school French program which children study via television and with a visiting teacher of French. An in-depth study of this aspect of French folklore was carried out in a realistic style. Although it so happened that in this particular case the student teacher was proficient in the French language, similar experience units can be explored with other cultures and customs in order to extend meanings beyond the classroom borders towards perspectives of mankind.[12]

We would like to turn to an additional exemplar for the teaching of other cultures through the planning and development of conditions for learning focusing upon the ideal of the image of man.

General Structure of Learning Experiences in the Teaching of Other Cultures

One would find common agreement that all teachers are responsible in one way or another for the development of the idea of humanity. This ideal is not inconsistent with the underlying objective of education in a democratic society; for if in the enterprise of learning within the framework of democracy, teachers establish a climate where education as inquiry fulfills and enhances itself, eventually learners will be confronted not only with localized problems but with concerns of all mankind. The individual styles and modes of classroom teachers have a singularly significant influence on curriculum, and any teacher worth his salt must extend meanings to increasingly wider commitments.[13] Teachers are in a unique position; they are "gatekeepers"[14] in shaping perspectives toward humanity.

A significant body of research is available to show that children are aware of racial and ethnic differences but that children can learn to cope effectively with intergroup problems.[15] They can learn to move in larger circles. It is within the conceptual framework of concern and care for the idea of man that we offer the following exemplar of the study of another culture. It should be emphasized that there would be two other sets of objectives working which focus upon intellectual processes and the handling of ideas. One class of objectives would promise to enhance the several aspects of critical thinking: the analysis of statement meanings; clarification of issues and problems; clarification of purpose; collection and evaluation of information; probing assumptions; utilization of structures, models, and theories; organization and evaluation of conclusions in some systematic way; evaluation of effectiveness of facts and conclusions in light of purposes; presentation and sharing of facts, ideas, and experiences; an attitude of openness to ideas and experience; and identification of additional issues and problems.[16] Particularly pertinent to these skills and abilities are a second category of objectives directly related to the unit of experience set forth below. The integrating ideas are these: to build broader understandings of the world; to ascertain factors which determine the quest of different peoples for existence; different individuals perceive the world in their own way, and these differing perceptions result in uniqueness and present a potentially rich source for growth and enhancement in the dialectic of cultural encounters; interdependence is a fact in man's world; what do we have in common with other peoples; the role of culture and society in shaping styles of thinking, perceiving, feeling, and acting. We direct our attention now to the sketching of an experience unit for the study of an overseas country in depth.

We shall entitle this sample activity, "The Teaching of Portuguese Culture": *

I. Initiation of the study. Display and discussion of typical Portuguese costumes, artifacts, and art objects. Some of the following are part of the author's own collection of "Portugalia": ceramic symbolic rooster; various provincial costumes; paintings; photographs and slides; flag and shield emblems; recordings of typical folk music; texts in literature, such as Camoes' Lusiads; schoolbooks and maps.

II. The first basic problem for consideration would be "Portuguese Social Customs and Family Life." Groups would be organized to frame guiding questions and procedures. Departures could be made from the above and from such sources as films ("Portugal Today") available from Casa de Portugal, 547 Madison Avenue, New York City. Contact could be established with resource agencies such as Casa de Portugal and perhaps correspondence exchanged with an elementary school in Portugal. Folk music could be studied; food and eating habits discussed (perhaps even a Portuguese dessert could be arranged with the cafeteria). It might be profitable to engage in a comparison of schooling. Portuguese textbooks could be examined and a "pen" school could be established.

III. "Highlights of History" would be the next topic. This study would provide opportunities for "post-holing" and depth analysis. Certainly, the age of discovery should be covered.

IV. "The Role of Portugal in the World Today" could be

---

*Portugal is selected because of the author's own background and familiarity with the language, resources, and cultural patterns. Portugal is usually studied (briefly) as part of "The Age of Discovery" in the intermediate grades and an activity such as suggested here would provide opportunity for a study in depth.

pursued next. Here would be explored its present economic and geo-political structure and problems.

V. "The Contributions of the Portuguese." Some suggestions are navigation, sailing, language, race relations, music, and literature.

These features suggest a model for the study of Portuguese culture, a structure which could easily provide the morphology for the study of any other culture. The task of the next section is to describe the basic features of what we have called the "total immersion approach."

The Total Immersion Approach

This aspect of the model is designed to provide a structure for the experience of meeting another culture "head on," in direct contact. It is geared to inundate the student with a variety of stimulus patterns in a situation simulating the components of the culture to be taught and learned through a high-powered culture shock situation where responses are reinforced and shaped according to "S = R" learning principles.[17] The major principles involved are derived from reinforcement theory. Through the structuring of the total learning situation in simulation of the culture to be learned, a variety of apparatus for stimulus presentation is designed. Literally, the attempt is to see an actual culture in operation (through simulation techniques) and to "rub the students' noses in it." Simulation techniques would be contrived with specific reference to the eliciting of responses and the control of stimulus conditions governing responses.[18] Situations would be engineered so that the learner would meet in constant contact a culture in a multitude of real life situations requiring response to a variety and number of practical problems. The theoretical schema can be represented diagrammatically in the following manner:

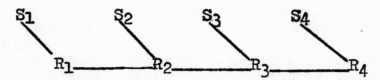

The explanation proceeds thus: the learner responds in controlled situations to the various units of cultural experiences

301

represented by the sequence of stimuli. The student learns to respond in the desired manner, building a hierarchy of responses along the way. Here we have the organization of behavior framed into a paradigm which renders itself effective in dealing with the problem at this stage of the multidimensional model, offering these advantages: (1) It is built upon an empirically oriented behavioral science reducing the behavior to manageable units, that is, stimulus and response variables and their interactions.[19] That this is no idle movement should be well understood by teachers by this time as earlier concepts and research have been bolstered in a powerful way by a host of significant developments, particularly training research in the military and industry and the development of an educational technology.[20] (2) The design proceeds from specific purposes and task analysis. (3) The structure gives full play to learning principles that are becoming well tested, namely, (a) responses are better acquired and retained if they are learned under conditions similar to those in which they will be used; and (b) the principle of reinforcement.

A strong attraction of the total immersion approach is that it permits a student through simulation techniques to travel through a society. The learner is confronted with a variety of stimuli and reinforcers within the cultural pattern. He walks through the market place; enters into intercourse with the inhabitants; walks the streets, enters the homes, restaurants, and shops; and reacts to the real facts of the culture's philosophical notions, politics, economics, social arrangements, and problems. After all, these are the significant life experiences of a culture. These are the things that one needs to have one's nose rubbed in. It is in direct contact with human problems that one comes to know the people and their culture and it is in the arena of life as one strives toward attaining solutions to these problems that one can say with meaning that one knows another culture.

The total immersion approach can be supported by one other consideration, namely, it could utilize fully new technological devices for stimulus presentation and response reinforcement. A chamber could easily be constructed for this purpose. We are not suggesting a complex and expensive teaching machine but rather a chamber built of plywood or some such material and arranged so as to provide various experimental contingencies. The contingencies would focus primarily upon a number of problem and conflict situations and would lend itself as well to the utilization of concepts and techniques from "games theory." The "theory of games" and the special mathematical techniques developed within that theory seem to offer possibilities for the analysis of conflict situations.[21, 22] The one significant advantage presented by this approach is that it possesses precision and proceeds from the general application of known learning principles while working in another direction, the experimental analysis of the total methodology itself. Experimental methods and learning principles have attained a stage of development where they can be utilized in the teaching of more complex learnings such as those involved here. One caution is uttered in concluding the description of this approach: Any experimental and pedagogical modality abstracts itself at a level removed from practical affairs and human transactions, so at regular intervals the student would have to return to immersion in the flesh and blood world of reality as close as we could simulate it.

In Retrospect

Having examined certain notions regarding the teaching of other cultures, we attempt to carry this discussion forward. The discussion centers around two ideas, namely, (a) the need and purposes of teaching other cultures, and (b) a model for the teaching of culture with some specific suggestions for an in-depth study of a particular culture. In this section we will attempt to attain a consummation so that the examination launched here will remain as an open-ended inquiry for those concerned with the study of education. We have indicated the purposes for the study of other cultures and a methodology for doing such. At this point we should like to go beyond that and deliberately commit ourselves to the conception expressed earlier and its implications; that is, that the 'sine qua non' for the teaching of other cultures is the enhancement of the human condition, the human image. It is our view that out of the myriads of cultural transactions, emerge the perceptions that liberate man from the circumambience of specialties toward the creation of the image of mankind as the living wholeness man is. Education as inquiry rightfully searches for the integral unity of all human knowledge, and this function is given impetus from the interplay of cultural diversity. The realities of these transactions are such that from "listening" to them, man composes the harmony that is the unity of the human image.

The current educational scene is fraught with many possibilities for this kind of thing to occur, albeit the larger background is an extremely viable one which in and of itself need not lead us into pessimistic portraits of crisis and of man, Hobbesian or otherwise. Man himself is viable; he copes heartily with viability. Some positive events are occurring. Witness these. In a recent stay in Portugal the writer's attitude was piqued in this direction in conversations with teachers of foreign languages in that country by the claim that a teacher of a foreign language is expected to sojourn and study in the country of the language of specialization for which financial assistance was easily available. In some unforgettable conversations with the philosopher Professor Delfim Santos, who held the chair in pedagogy at the University of Lisbon, the ideal of the human image was uppermost in his mind. Professor Santos' recent and untimely passing away has saddened my heart but the ideal lives on.

We cited above a teaching episode wherein a student teacher at Salem State College in Salem, Massachusetts, strived deliberately to establish contact points with another culture. In this instance the teacher was guided by the broader value ends of the teaching of other cultures as set forth here. Clear and definite unification areas for confrontations were located. And yet another: from Salem, Oregon, the State Department of Education curriculum plan for social studies in the secondary school reveals similar themes.[23] Emphasis is on the study of man's relationships to his fellow man through a sequence of courses on cultures of the world. In a recently published collection of poems by the Russian poet Yevtushenko the same ideal and dream comes alive in one of his verses.[24] Certain existential writers have grasped the essence of this notion when they describe the heroic struggles and joys of every man building for all.[25]

So from Moscow to Lisbon to Salem, Massachusetts, to Salem, Oregon, the theme resounds—across half a world. The possibilities are coming into existence; it requires man 'qua' intelligence to realize them. If unification points could be located, the reality of the encounter is such that the unity of man-

304

kind floats through it. The teaching of other cultures purports to locate such points. Inquiry by its very abstraction leads to a view of knowledge that is free from the perspective of any one person, society, or culture. In the study of what is uniquely human—the joys and sufferings, values, and aspirations, beauty, language, laws, and arts—what we can come to call the human condition, the totality of the unification of man is envisioned. The human experience is a reality *'sui generis.'* Call it what you will— the ideal of mankind, philosophical anthropology, religious anthropology—we have chosen to call it the human image. We are all in it together. No one is alienated; no one is the chosen. There is emerging from the human experience a new symbolism of the human image feeding back and enhancing the human condition. The idea of mankind is becoming clear. *'Per gradus, per ambages, per angusta, per fas et nefas vincet veritas hominus.'* The way is not easy. There will be much groping, with some leaps forward, some falling back, for it seems that we like to have our cultural cake and eat it too. But the ends are clear and we are beginning to know how to fashion the means. I would wager on it.

SAMUEL GOMEZ, Associate Professor of the Philosophy of Education at Salem State College, Salem, Massachusetts, received his bachelor's and master's degrees from Bridgewater State College, and is a candidate for the Ph.D. at the University of Connecticut. Professor Gomez has studied at the University of Florida and has traveled and studied in Portugal. His experiences in public school education include elementary school teaching and administration. He has taught at Glassboro State College and the University of Bridgeport.

FOOTNOTES

1. For depth analysis of the role of culture in personality, see: A. Irving Hallowell, CULTURE AND EXPERIENCE. Philadelphia: University of Pennsylvania Press, 1955; Abraham Kardiner, THE INDIVIDUAL AND HIS SOCIETY. New York: Columbia University Press, 1939; Dorothy Lee, FREEDOM AND CULTURE. Englewood Cliffs, N. J.: Spectrum Books, 1959; and selected writings of Linton, Kluckhohn, and George H. Mead.
2. Quoted in Ernest Becker, THE BIRTH AND DEATH OF MEANING. New York: The Free Press of Glencoe, 1962, 44. Becker, a psychiatrist, writing on the relationships between psychiatry and anthropology

adopts the Deweyan and Mead notion of "meaning" which is consistent with the transactional frame of reference used in this paper.

3. An extensive treatment of some of these basic problems is provided in the following: The Intergroup Education Series, Hilda Taba, ed., DIAGNOSING HUMAN RELATIONS NEEDS (1951), ELEMENTARY CURRICULUM IN INTERGROUP RELATIONS (1950), INTERGROUP EDUCATION IN PUBLIC SCHOOLS (1952). Washington, D. C.: American Council on Education; Frost and Hawkes, THE DISADVANTAGED CHILD. Boston: Houghton Mifflin Co., 1966; Long and King, IMPROVING THE TEACHING OF WORLD AFFAIRS: THE GLENS FALLS STORY. Washington, D. C.: National Council for the Social Studies, Bulletin No. 35, 1964; Franklin Patterson, ed., CITIZENSHIP AND A FREE SOCIETY: EDUCATION FOR THE FUTURE. Washington, D. C.: The National Council for the Social Studies, 30th Yearbook, 1960.

4. Ralph C. Preston, TEACHING SOCIAL STUDIES IN THE ELEMENTARY SCHOOL. New York: Holt, Rinehart and Winston, 1962, 211.

5. Jerome Bruner, "The Cognitive Consequences of Early Sensory Deprivation," in THE DISADVANTAGED CHILD (edited by Frost and Hawkes). Boston: Houghton Mifflin Co., 1966, 137-44.

6. Ronald O. Smith and Charles F. Cardinell, "Challenging the Expanding-Environment Theory." SOCIAL EDUCATION, XXVIII, March 1964, 141-143.

7. American Library Association, A BASIC BOOK COLLECTION FOR THE ELEMENTARY GRADES. Chicago: The Association, 1956.

8. May Hill Arbuthnot, TIME FOR TRUE TALES. Fair Lawn, N. J.: Scott, Foresman and Co., 1961.

9. May Hill Arbuthnot, CHILDREN AND BOOKS, Fair Lawn, N. J.: Scott, Foresman and Co., 1964, 499.

10. G. Andrews, "Cultural Understanding Through Folk Dance." JOURNAL OF HEALTH, PHYSICAL EDUCATION AND RECREATION, XXXVI, September 1965, 65-66.

11. Some helpful cues were offered by: "Folklore: France." THE INSTRUCTOR, December 1966, 52-3, and a series of similar articles in that same number.

12. The writer is indebted to Miss Susan Anderson of Salem State College, the student teacher who cooperated in carrying out this teaching episode.

13. For a discussion of the problems involved, see: R. S. Peters, AUTHORITY, RESPONSIBILITY AND EDUCATION. London: Allen and Unwin, 1959.

14. Kurt Lewin, et al., AUTHORITY AND FRUSTRATION. University of Iowa, Studies in Child Welfare, Vol. XX, 1944, 22.

15. Trager and Yarrow, THEY LEARN WHAT THEY LIVE. New York: Harper and Brothers, 1952.

16. For an attempt to provide a comprehensive discussion of inquiry from another perspective, see the author's: "The Teaching of History in the Elementary School," in THE TEACHING OF HISTORY, edited by Joseph S. Roucek. New York: The Philosophical Library, 1967.

17. Arthur W. Staats and Carolyn K. Staats, COMPLEX HUMAN BEHAVIOR. New York: Holt, Rinehart and Winston, 1963, Chapter 10.

18. Robert Glaser, "Implications of Training Research For Education," in

THEORIES OF LEARNING AND INSTRUCTION. The Sixty-third Yearbook of the National Society for the Study of Education, Part I, edited by Ernest R. Hilgard. Chicago: University of Chicago Press, 1964, Chapter VII.

19. B. F. Skinner, SCIENCE AND HUMAN BEHAVIOR. New York: Macmillan, 1953.
20. For a definite attempt to coordinate the work being done, see: Robert Glaser, ed., TRAINING RESEARCH AND EDUCATION. Pittsburgh: University of Pittsburgh Press, 1962; A. A. Lumsdaine and Robert Glaser, TEACHING MACHINES AND PROGRAMMED LEARNING (2 Vols.). Washington, D. C.: National Education Association, 1960 and 1964; and John P. DeCecco, ed., EDUCATIONAL TECHNOLOGY. New York: Holt, Rinehart and Winston, 1964.
21. E. S. Venttsel, AN INTRODUCTION TO THE THEORY OF GAMES, Boston: D. C. Heath and Co., 1963.
22. John G. Kemeny and J. Laurie Snell, MATHEMATICAL MODELS IN THE BEHAVIORAL SCIENCES. New York: Ginn and Co., 1962.
23. SOCIAL STUDIES IN OREGON SECONDARY SCHOOLS. Salem: Oregon State Department of Education, 1955.
24. Yevgeny Yevtushenko, YEVTUSHENKO POEMS (translated by Herbert Marshall). New York: Dutton Press, 1966.
25. Albert Camus, DISCOURS DE SUEDE, Paris: Gallimard, 1958.

Selected Bibliography

Arbuthnot, May Hill, CHILDREN AND BOOKS. Fair Lawn, N.J.: Scott, Foresman and Co., 1964. An extremely valuable and almost indispensable resource book in the field of children's literature, containing a wide array of summaries and suggestions for using books in terms of children's needs and the purposes of literature.

Becker, Ernest, THE BIRTH AND DEATH OF MEANING. New York: The Free Press of Glencoe, 1962. A fascinating study by a psychiatrist on the psychiatric perspectives of culture, society, anthropology, and perception drawing heavily from John Dewey and George Herbert Mead. Becker makes the statement that the "age of Dewey" has barely begun—we would concur wholeheartedly.

Bruner, Jerome, THE PROCESS OF EDUCATION. Cambridge, Mass.: Harvard University Press, 1963. Offers a comprehensive treatment of the "discovery" method and the role of early learning experiences and a critical analysis of learning and its relation to the structures of the disciplines.

Dewey, John, DEMOCRACY AND EDUCATION. New York: The Macmillan Co., 1916. Dewey's analysis of the relationship between means and ends in education and his discussion of the school and society is a classic and still timely as is the discussion of thinking in education.

Frost, Joe L. and Hawkes, Glen R. THE DISADVANTAGED CHILD. Boston: Houghton Mifflin Co., 1966. Perhaps the most complete and useful compilation of the literature relating to the education and characteristics of the disadvantaged.

Glaser, Robert, TRAINING RESEARCH AND EDUCATION. Pittsburgh: University of Pittsburgh Press, 1962. Detailed discussion of the issues, problems, achievements, and promises in this field.

Gomez, Samuel, "The Teaching of History in the Elementary School," in THE TEACHING OF HISTORY (edited by Joseph S. Roucek). New York: The Philosophical Library, 1967. An attempt to offer a definitive analysis of the role of inquiry in the social studies and the concept of early learning experiences. Includes some models.

Hallowell, A. Irving, CULTURE AND EXPERIENCE. Philadelphia: University of Pennsylvania Press, 1955. An excellent work in anthropology providing deep understandings on the role of culture in constituting meaning, behavior, and the self.

Kardiner, Abram, THE INDIVIDUAL AND HIS SOCIETY. New York: Columbia University Press, 1939. An early work on the relationship of ego to culture and society, and the establishment of a flexible notion of the ego; one of the pioneers in this development.

Kemeny, John G. and Snell, J. Laurie, MATHEMATICAL MODELS IN THE BEHAVIORAL SCIENCES. New York: Ginn and Co., 1962. Itself a model in the use of mathematical models and techniques in the solution of problems in the social sciences.

Kilpatrick, Franklin P., ed., EXPLORATIONS IN TRANSACTIONAL PSYCHOLOGY. New York: New York University Press, 1961. One of the few attempts to establish a transactional psychology which is the basic frame of reference of this paper —through transactional experiences man creates his world. The implications are peculiarly pertinent to the task of the paper, the transactions with other cultures.

Lee, Dorothy, FREEDOM AND CULTURE. Englewood Cliffs, N.J.: Spectrum Books, 1959. Standard work on the interactions of culture, personality, behaving, and perceiving.

Long, Harold M. and King, Robert N., IMPROVING THE TEACHING OF WORLD AFFAIRS: THE GLENS FALLS STORY. Washington, D.C.: The National Council for the Social Studies, Bulletin No. 35, 1964. A case study of how one community implemented action research to set up and improve teaching world affairs at all grade levels. This work could serve as a useful model for other such projects.

Patterson, Franklin, ed., CITIZENSHIP AND A FREE SOCIETY: EDUCATION FOR THE FUTURE. Washington, D.C.: The National Council for the Social Studies, 30th Yearbook, 1960. A discussion in depth of the issues, problems, and developments in the social studies with emphasis upon the future citizen with the need for ever wider and larger commitments and responsibilities.

Preston, Ralph C., TEACHING SOCIAL STUDIES IN THE ELEMENTARY SCHOOL. New York: Holt, Rinehart, and Winston, 1962. This is a standard in the field. Particularly useful is the discussion of the issues involved in the teaching of other cultures.

Pritzkau, Philo T., DYNAMICS OF CURRICULUM IMPROVEMENT. Englewood Cliffs, N.J.: Prentice Hall, Inc., 1959. A scholarly, highly intellectualized analysis of curriculum issues and problems particularly valuable for its total philosophical perspective toward inquiry and the existential concern for the individual. One of the most exciting and provocative of its kind, perhaps way ahead of its time.

Smith, Ronald O. and Cardinell, Charles F., "Challenging the Expanding-Environment Theory." SOCIAL EDUCATION, XXVIII, March 1964, 141-143. Indicates that children possess broad and extensive social learning concepts. Supports our position that younger children can experience the encounter with other cultures in positive ways.

Staats, Arthur W. and Staats, Carolyn K., COMPLEX HUMAN BEHAVIOR. New York: Holt, Rinehart, and Winston, 1963. An empirically oriented analysis of human behavior—social, verbal, perceptual, cognitive—based upon "S-R" principles and the theory of reinforcement; comprehensive, well organized.

Strauss, Anselm, THE SOCIAL PSYCHOLOGY OF GEORGE HERBERT MEAD. Chicago: University of Chicago Press, Phoenix Books, 1956. Mead (and Dewey) are originators of the extra-individual nature of the self and mind, the basis for the transactional notion of experience and perception described here. Particularly insightful is Mead's social-personal view of meaning.

Venttsel, E. S., AN INTRODUCTION TO THE THEORY OF GAMES, Boston: D. C. Heath and Co., 1963. A basic, concise introduction to the theory of games, an area as yet unexplored in pedagogical fields but a field offering some promise for technique and method particularly in conflict and puzzle situations.

Sociological Interpretation of International Education: Experiments in Studying Abroad

ERNEST M. KUHINKA

Hahnemann Medical College, Philadelphia

FROM A sociological point of view, the study of international education in the midst of a profound process of change in contemporary societies is a challenging task, especially since societies have some definite ideas about the kind of man their members should become. In such a projection all the peculiarities of an educational organization are reflected, especially the transfer of knowledge on a higher level.

Education in the above sense is a national undertaking, but as the results of scientific endeavor cannot be isolated, national education is a *contradictio in terminis.* Natio-centric education, which lacks the bounds of interdependence of human culture, limits its people's horizons by political geography and thereby develops a knowledge involving only a nation's own knowledge. Hence, there is no need for a scientific doctrine formulated in terms of some ideology which will enable persons unknown to each other to engage in an exchange of ideas through which they will achieve a consensus of knowledge. Contemporary societies, as one knows, are influenced by this international consensus due to the revolution in communication and mobility. Progressive governments, however, recognize that education as a process within a national society comes about in response to international forces. These forces—forming the consensus of knowledge—do exist, widening men's horizon and enriching them with realistic alternatives. This development includes not only the economic forces influencing men's expectations but far-reaching changes in men's views of the world and their place within it. Men begin seriously to contemplate not only new freedoms, new social and political organizations, new careers, but also new access to knowledge and new values, from which national governments evolve.[1]

Of course, nations have been exposed to change throughout the history and their cultures diffused: education is largely the result of what we call international consensus based upon modern science and technology; modern standards and communication and modern practices of organization.

Historically, especially in the field of higher learning, education is becoming more and more international in character liberating itself from national controls. While in the olive groves of Greece and in the *grammaticus* of Rome, individuals were educated to subordinate themselves to collectivity, need later arose during the Hellenistic Age in the field of education to assist individuals to become autonomous. In the Middle Ages, education again depended upon a single centralized system, international in methodology and language, a system of theological control from which the scholars of the Renaissance departed when they assumed a secular scientific character. This emancipation continues today and even natio-centric dictatorial systems cannot isolate the mind of educated man.

It is science that emerges freely, elaborating on the cardinal notions that govern men's thought and form the basis of education: notions of cause, of law, of space, of body, of number, of kind, of conscience, and of society. The comprehension of these ideas are perpetually evolving because they are the results of men's scientific effort. Today, we do not conceive ideas in orthodoxy, as during the Renaissance, Middle Ages, Hellenistic or Roman and Greek periods. This is because our knowledge, understanding, methods, and technologies are no longer the same, implying that science is truly international in character: presupposing a cooperation of all scientists and their own findings not only during their own time but all the successive epochs of history.

In the Middle Ages wandering scholars helped to create a community of learning fragmented by barriers of distance. In today's world distance is no longer a barrier and even national divisions and loyalties do not impede the growth of exchange scholar movements. This has resulted in a most enlightening growth of education and science and started a series of modern-

311

izations. For example, Emperor Meiji of Japan, who announced in 1868, that "knowledge shall be sought among the nations of the world" started to send students and civil servants to Europe and America. Europe, for centuries, was the Mecca for foreign students. In the 1880's, it was reported that there were 387 Russian students in German Universities, by 1911, there were 2,000. During the same period nearly half the students in Swiss Universities were foreigners and half of these were Russians. The industrial development of the Soviet Union owes much to the Soviet scientists and technicians who were trained abroad and to the foreign engineers and advisers brought into the country.

Today, the figures of foreign students in Europe are between 35,000-40,000, the same is true for the United States. It is an alarming number of persons seeking any knowledge anywhere. It is not a question anymore that one student visits the scholar of great fame as in the past. It is not a question anymore if "education is for the masses or for the selected few." Since decolonization started, especially after the Second World War, the number of foreign students has increased to the present high level. This requires a newly designed exchange program: a movement of "development exchange"—wherein the diversity and interdependence of culture and science becomes the operating principle of international education.

To understand these exchange programs and to see them as an experiment, one must eliminate the ideological or national aspects of international education especially, since some governments think that the exchange program should use education as a cold war weapon in the ideological struggle for the minds of men. The 'People's Friendship University,' now called the Lumumba University, in Moscow was established for political aims, expecting to operate with a 3,000 to 4,000 student body composed of tuition-free students from Africa, Asia, and Latin America. As a reaction to this Soviet move, some Americans have proposed a "Free University of the West," perhaps on Ellis Island in New York. Fortunately, this plan never left the drawing board.

The contest for the minds of the future leaders of the developing countries, however, is not limited only to the two great powers. Many other nations, such as France, Israel, Japan, People's Republic of China, the United Arab Republic, United

312

Kingdom, and West Germany, to mention the most significant ones, are competing and devoting manpower and financial resources in increasing amounts to the development of exchange—permeated with a sense of urgency. Further, these exchanges are often placed against a background of rapid social, economic, and political change, lacking the understanding that education abroad is a long-term investment which will pay its dividends in later years. Both the immediate shortages of trained manpower in most of the developing countries and the social and political needs ten and twenty years from now are seldom considered.[2]

The development toward a value-free foreign exchange program in a classical sense, therefore, is wishful thinking. The real world is still motivated by national conventions, prejudices, lairs and interests and will be for a long time. Even at international centers, such as the United Nations, UNESCO, World Bank, International Monetary Funds, nations are pressing and bargaining around the points of national policies and pressures. International education still lies in teaching students how to grasp their own national interests and policies and how, at best, to understand another people and to know why they are different. However, one may not underestimate the trend toward better international education. During the last few years one may clearly observe an intensified effort to take at least science out of a national context and establish a world dialogue. The formal international institutions, such as UNESCO, are not entirely fitted for the task, since they operate within the guidelines of governmental agreements. One thinks here of professional meetings where scientists convene not as representatives of any particular country but as a community of scientific interest and concern. PUGWASH meetings, for example, are based upon the assumption that a scientific community transcending national frontiers does exist.[3] This is the level of science where the search and winnowing for knowledge is accepted as an opportunity, the scientist responding to the challenges and only there where the scientist, in a willing community, wills himself. The influence of such an environment exerting on him, notably through education, does not have as its object and its effect to repress him, to diminish him or to denature him, as national education does, but on the contrary to make him grow and to make him truly a human being thoroughly permeated with the instincts, the hopes,

313

and the ideas of humanity, full of aspiration for the improvement of knowledge by all peoples for knowledge sake. Beyond this, no wise man will go, and short of it, hardly any unprejudiced man will stop.

American Experiments in International Education

The development and the success of the educational system of the United States, as one knows, is the result of the free exchange of ideas as well as educators. Not only did the first teachers and scholars actually come from the outside, but when they became "American" in the eighteenth and nineteenth centuries they continued to look back to Europe for educational ideas, innovations, and practices respecting the opinions of mankind.[4] Jefferson, a nationalist at heart, but concerned enough about education stated that "there should be brought home to the people the knowledge that trade, commerce, finance, debts, communications, have a bearing on peace. In all our countries, we have scholars who can demonstrate these facts; let them not be silent."[5] Following these suggestions we have benefited from the flow of people, scholarships, and ideas not only from Europe but from the rest of the world as well. We have received and now we are willing to give, give freely to anybody; hereby liberalizing existing and nonexisting educational systems throughout the world. The full-scale involvement and experimentation of today, however, did not come overnight. International education is becoming more regimented and complex, while many students still go on their own, an increasing number are taking part in different sorts of organized programs which started in the nineteenth century.

We have records as early as 1849 indicating when the Smithsonian Institute established an International Exchange Service. This service exchanged official documents with other countries depositing foreign documents in the Library of Congress. The National Bureau of Standards was authorized in 1892 to receive qualified foreign scientists and technicians as guest workers. While in 1900 Harvard University offered a special summer session for 1,400 Cuban teachers who were transported by the Army. Just eight years later the State Department created the Boxer Indemnity Fund in 1908, which utilized reparations paid to the U.S. government by the Chinese government to finance study of Chinese students in the United States. This impressive experiment of interchange of scholars and students lasted many years.

After World War I, the image that the first educational institutions in America lacked intellectual depth and that pragmatism does not deserve the name of a university became modified as a result of demonstrated economic strength and educational accomplishments. European countries began to establish cultural and educational exchanges formalizing by signing cultural agreements the present operational student exchange. By 1929, there were more than 700 official and unofficial organizations in Europe and some 115 in the United States that were directly or indirectly involved in cultural programs and academic exchange.

To expand the successful exchange programs in Latin America, the United States proposed the "Facilitation by Government Action of the Exchange of Students and Teachers," in Buenos Aires in 1936. Just prior to the establishment of the Cultural Relations Division, President Roosevelt created the Interdepartmental Committee for Scientific and Cultural Cooperation. The function of the Committee was to determine what knowledge and skills each executive department had that could be made available to Latin American governments. On July 28, 1938, the Division of Cultural Relations was established in the U.S. Department of State to facilitate exchanges with Latin America. In 1939, Public Law 355 of the 76th Congress incorporated the passage of the act "to render closer and more effective the relationships between the American Republics" and established an official exchange of persons and programs with Latin America; this represented the first permanent legislation of this kind.[6]

Since 1941, the State Department has assigned cultural officers to our diplomatic missions, first in Latin America and later in other areas of the world as well. Their duties were defined as informing the missions and the Department of State about the cultural developments in the countries of their assignments.

After the Second World War, the United States with the passage of legislation, sponsored by Senator J. William Fulbright (P.L. 584, 79th Congress) laid the groundwork for the using of foreign currencies owed to, or owned by, the United

States for a cooperative program of education exchanges. This large-scale effort was destined to become one of the world's largest and most respected cooperative educational programs for the interchange of graduate students, teachers, and scholars.

Further, a Board of Foreign Scholarships was created by the Congress to supervise the educational exchange programs of the Fulbright Act. The intent of Congress was to establish an impartial and nonofficial body, which would assure respect and cooperation of the academe, for the educational exchange program through the selection of grantees from educational institutions here and abroad and for their placement in American or foreign schools. The Board was responsible not only in setting policies and procedures for the administration of the program, but also has the final responsibility of approval of grantees and the supervision of the program which has been the key to successful operation. A new impetus was given to the Fulbright Act in 1948, when the United States Information and Educational Exchange Act (P.L. 402, 80th Congress) became operative. One of the provisions of this act authorized financing cultural activities from the sale of American publications in certain countries.

The problems of the postwar period however, were not only educational but also economic and social. Technical know-how was needed for reconstruction, especially in Europe. The technical assistance of the United States achieved worldwide prominence when Secretary of State, George C. Marshall, set forth a plan for the economic recovery of Europe. He proposed that United States capital and technical skills be put at the disposal of war-torn countries in an effort to "revive a working economy in the world so as to permit the emergence of political and social conditions in which free institutions can exist."[7] President Truman in Point IV of his 1949 inaugural address extended the technical assistance concept to other parts of the world, stressing the sharing of technical know-how rather than the export of American capital and credit.[8]

It is in the tradition of the United States to offer asylum for those who are oppressed because of religious or political beliefs. The first settlers were guided to the colonies under the same principle. During the last decades many German and Austrian exchange students became refugees during the Nazi period, as did Czechs, Hungarians, Poles, and other East Europeans during the early postwar period when Communist regimes rose to power. One of the highly publicized examples of refugee students were Chinese students in residence within the United States when the Chinese Communists took over the mainland of China. Of the 4,000 Chinese students enrolled in American institutions more than two-thirds remained in the United States.

The growth of legal acts as related to educational, technical, and cultural exchanges can be seen from the ever-increasing expenses. A budget of less than $6 million for exchange persons in 1948, increased to about $21 million in 1958. The number of foreign countries participating in the programs under the Fulbright Act has grown from 4 in 1948 to 33 in 1958. No funds at all were available for cultural presentations overseas in 1948, while in 1958 they amounted to more than $2 million. As compared to 98 libraries, cultural institutes, and information centers in 1948, there were 234 in 75 countries in 1958; in 1965, the program included over 5,200 new exchanges with 110 countries. To date over 70,000 Americans and foreign nationals have been among its participants. These exchanges, as significant as they are, are only a small percentage of the total flow of students and scholars. Private programs continue to account for the vast majority of educational exchanges.

The experiment of assisting students and scholars to study abroad or to assist them to study here is most significant. A formal institutionalized Junior Year Abroad program, which was started by the University of Delaware in 1923, is mushrooming. The idea was taken up not only by Ivy League schools but by other larger state and private institutions of higher learning as well. These colleges still offer credit programs of study in foreign countries, mostly in Europe, to their own undergraduates and often to those of other colleges. In 1960, we had more than 3,000 American students participating in these programs.

The University of Maryland went abroad under the name of University College in 1947, to educate our military personnel. The College now operates in 142 centers, most of them in Europe. The Atlantic Division has offered courses in eight centers since 1951, and the Far East Division, established in 1956, operates 50 centers in Asia. Course enrollments per term are within the range of from 16,000 to 20,000 at all centers. Students may earn the degree of Bachelor of Arts in General Studies. In addition to

317

its evening classes abroad—as well as for some 6,000 students in the Pentagon or in military or civilian locations in Maryland—the University College maintains in Munich a two-year daytime resident college program, with dormitory facilities available, for dependents of armed services personnel.

Training courses for foreign military personnel, selected here in the United States or at our military schools, are also successfully operated. These students are handpicked by their own countries to become instructors when they return home. These trainees follow through three stages of orientation: (1) orientation before departure, (2) orientation at special centers in the United States, and (3) orientation at the trainee's assigned base of training. Possibly the greatest return on our military-assistance investment comes from the training of these selected groups who in the long run will become the leaders in their nation. No one should underestimate the importance of firsthand knowledge of how Americans operate and think as experienced by these trainees.[9]

The development of international education and experimentation in this field came so rapidly, so recently and so urgently that the efforts have often been uncoordinated, some of the programs in favorable cases indifferent to each other or even hostile to one another. International education is too precious to allow these relationships to become patterned since we need them all: the task is of such proportion that everyone's individual or organizational effort is needed so that American education may be mobilized for the benefit of other nations as well as for our own. Already in 1950, a number of questions were raised about mutual understanding and the objectives of international education and the value of experimentation. For example, The Social Science Research Council pointed out the lack of knowledge about the effectiveness of exchange programs as a means of extending the field of knowledge since "we do not yet know whether it is effective as an instrument of foreign policy."[10] Since 1953 several private foundations have invested large sums in investigating just how much international education has contributed to world understanding. Social scientists came up with an array of findings especially in the field of foreign students' acculturation difficulties here and abroad. The insight must prevail that without commitment, the experiment in the field of international education (our relationship with the underdeveloped countries) shall either continue to find it impossible to apply hard and meaningful standards in granting our aid or we shall discover that our insistence upon standards will be seen as insulting and degrading.[11]

American policy in the field of international education may recognize that the direction of future development of uncommitted peoples may depend not only upon what America does in economic, technical, military, political, and diplomatic fields but also mainly in the field of education: education not as a weapon of national propaganda but as a means of national and international improvement. Therefore with several federal agencies engaged in international education and cultural activities, the necessity for central policy guidance, joint planning, and coordination of the total national effort is obvious. The effective conduct of these programs requires coordination to ensure the maximum use of available resources; to assist administrators maintain awareness of all the needs and effects, while at the same time keep their own programs in perspective; to continue uniformity in making and executing general policies, and to promote cooperation between public and private agencies.[12]

Participation by the United States in intergovernmental organizations engaged in educational and cultural activities, increased in both scope and importance during the fiscal year 1964. The Multilateral Policy Planning Staff, which has the primary function of defining objectives, planning and coordinating policy, and formulating positions on multilateral educational and cultural programs, has used traditional channels to advance the nation's aims.[13]

Under contract with the Department of State, for example, the Institute of International Education (IIE) arranges placement of almost all foreign students; it handles day-to-day supervision of foreign student grantees in the United States and assists in a preliminary review of American students competing for awards. Further, IIE representation keeps in touch with foreign students' advisors on U. S. campuses through reports and personal visits to colleges and universities during the academic year.[14]

Of course, while important steps have been taken in coordinating international exchange programs and clarifying objectives, it is not a closed system but an open one since clarification and coordination is a continuing process. However, certain principles in international education are crystallizing around three main propositions: (1) development exchange programs should be closely related to over-all U.S. government development operation, (2) development exchange programs should, to the maximum extent possible, be on a long-term basis and must be insulated from day-to-day political influences; and (3) development exchange programs, like other exchange programs, should use the administrative services and facilities of qualified private agencies, as provided by existing legislation.[15]

After twenty years of intensified international educational experimentation with a shift from individual voluntary exchanges of scholars to organized and institutionalized exchanges we must recognize that numbers alone, even if impressive, do not justify strict governmental control. As the Assistant Secretary of State for Education and Cultural Affairs observed during a Columbia University symposium on "Diversity and Interdependence Through International Education," September 9-10, 1966, it *would* be urgently needed if the U.S. Senate should follow the House in adopting the International Education Act of 1966. This bill, he continued, would get the government behind the effort in a new imaginative fashion but would also get it out of the way by turning large projects over to universities. A most appropriate evaluation of the last twenty years of the Fulbright Program was given by Fulbright himself, who searched for "new rules." "We need," he said, "a new game." It's a mystery to me why we feel we have the final truth about human relations. That's what his exchange program is all about. The problem of how to find ways to retain and conciliate diversity among people while they live and learn peaceably is as old as mankind. To this task the exchanges must be increasingly dedicated in the years to come. It must, for scholarly interest, bind the academic community together and encourage the continuing flow of scholars across national boundaries. The strong web of scholarship exists between countries. The world community of scholars, long-heralded and earnestly sought, is becoming a reality independent from political and national controls. In this sense American programs, strong in self-criticism, are still growing and evolving. They have shown a steady increase in size and scope, as we have seen in this discussion of the different experimental programs over the past twenty years, and will probably continue to grow for sometime to come as the universities increasingly assume a greater share of this experiment. In the final analysis, international education based upon consensus is individualistic. It is composed of two distinct groups: one who learns and one who teaches. Even so, their dialogue is removed from the olive groves to the sophisticated laboratories of modern universities. Individuals who participate in educational exchanges must serve as representatives of their respective intellectual and scholarly communities and not as spokesmen or advocates for official political ideologies. As Secretary Rusk has pointed out: "There is no field in which nationality plays a more restrained role, no field in which fraud is more easily detected and more simply punished because discipline is imposed by integrity and the criterion of truth."[16]

Some Theoretical Considerations on International Education

Without postulating the transcultural character of international education and the experiments within this field, one could not account for the possibility of understanding between two persons of different cultures—between any two persons. International education enables one to reason, to understand on the basis of free exchange of ideas. It is a forum into which conflicts may enter from one side, but is transmitted to the other only in an objective form. It permits the institution of higher learning to carry its basic educational function: the development of the intellectual and moral excellence of the individual on a worldwide scale. It creates educational opportunities for those who have the capacity and inclination to learn. Equally important, it strengthens the scholarly function of the university, the advancement of knowledge and learning throughout the world. It facilitates and maintains the two-way communication and research between scholars and students and thereby contributes to the intellectual growth of future scholars.

As we have seen, academic exchanges are sponsored by private and public organizations to assist the flow of students and scholars in both directions: exchange, mutual understanding, and cooperation on a basis of reciprocity. The very concept of exchange, which originally involved a student in one country exchanging places with a student in another, implies returning home. The round-trip aspect of foreign study is an integral part of the total experiment in international education. Returning home completes a normal cycle and brings the exchange to a logical conclusion. It is assumed that the student who returns from study and travel abroad is a vital link between nations in a fragmented world: rich with new and stimulating ideas useful both to himself and his society.

A one-way exchange experience can be considered only a partial success from the point of view of international education which has certain defined objectives: that is, that the student shall return home promptly upon completion of his studies. If he fails to return, the knowledge that he acquires may benefit himself and his host country, but will not usually reach his home country; the insight he has developed into the ways of another people may broaden his own perspective but not that of his academic and professional friends.[17] And both the loss of an opportunity to see beyond narrow national boundaries and the loss of a trained person may have serious consequences in some areas of the world.

However, international education is not only a question of a round-trip or one-way trip; the foreign exchange person himself expects, experiences, and hopes.[18] With these psychological complexities the foreign student who arrives at the institute of learning is still fresh with the initial unsorted impressions of custom officials, cabdrivers, traveler-companions, hotels, and the welcome at the institute, where he will operate. This set of circumstances places the foreign exchange person in the role of being a "stranger." The socio-cultural pattern of the host country presents itself through the foreign exchange person. The socio-cultural pattern is composed of all social institutions, systems of orientation where habits, customs, folkways, mores and laws are comprehended in a given place and time. Of course, the socio-cultural pattern of the host country has a different meaning for those who have lived in the country, having a "we-consciousness," and for those who just arrived, having a "they-consciousness."

The host, who has lived in the country a long time, arranges the socio-cultural pattern of his environment in terms of relevance to his pattern of living. This arrangement presents stratified layers of relevance: each of them requiring a different degree of knowledge. This implies that the system of knowledge in relation to the socio-cultural pattern is not uniform but offers a sufficient change to every member of the host country as an unquestionable pattern system, along with the identity of the ritual regimentation of life, which normally occurs within the community and is taken for granted.

At the time of arrival, the exchange person, who brings with him his own country's idiosyncratic qualities of socio-cultural patterns, does not view the host country's way of life as relevant. He is one who must question the unquestionable, the self-evident, due to a lack of a long period of socialization and of the comprehension of local norms. For him, the host country's socio-cultural pattern lacks authority since he has not been a part of the historical development of the host country. In addition to these difficulties, the foreign exchange person comes to learn or to teach. As a student, he is the scientist of the future, as a scientist, he fertilizes the minds of the scientist of the future in the host country.[19]

The full value of the exchanges was not evaluated in its complexity in terms of international context. The major objectives of exchange programs have been to broaden the vision of students and teachers, to give them the warm feeling of belonging to a fellowship of mankind which cuts across the national, racial and geographical frontiers, and to quicken their social sensitiveness of the human scene. The issues we face today are so intricate that they cannot be left to the political elite; they have to be brought home to everyone. The world citizens of tomorrow need to become aware that such problems as combating ill-health and poverty or achieving freedom and independence are part of human striving everywhere. The educated and those to be educated also need to see how developments, no matter how remote, affect them and how the things happening in their own immediate environment have repercussions elsewhere. This is important to bear in mind when confronted with the opportunities that international education offers through the building of a sense of world community of knowledge and an awareness of the tangible working of interdependence.

ERNEST M. G. KUHINKA is Associate Professor of Community Medicine, Hahnemann Medical College, Philadelphia, and director of The Behavioral Sciences Research Laboratory, Carlisle. He formerly served as Public Health Behavioral Scientist and Hospital and Health Facility Planner for the Commonwealth of Pennsylvania, and previously was visiting Professor of Sociology, University of Wisconsin, Madison. Dr. Kuhinka received his B.A. from the University of Debrecen (1945), his M.A. (1950) and his Ph.D. from the University of Utrecht. He also engaged in postdoctoral study in sociology at the Graduate Faculty of the New School for Social Research (1956). He is the author of three books and of articles and book reviews for leading national and foreign journals in the field of sociology. He conducted research for The Netherlands Committee for Research of the European Refuge Problem, The Hague; Provincial Country and Town Planning, Haarlem; Research Bureau of the National Council of Churches, New York City. Dr. Kuhinka is a member of various professional associations and is well-known through his research activities in the field of regional public health, mental health hospitals and social welfare planning and community development.

FOOTNOTES

1. Max F. Millikian, ed., THE EMERGING NATIONS: THEIR GROWTH AND UNITED STATES POLICY. Boston: Little, Brown and Co., 1961, 94-95.
2. Committee on Educational Interchange Policy, EDUCATIONAL EXCHANGE IN THE ECONOMIC DEVELOPMENT OF NATIONS. New York: Institute of International Education, 1961, 7.
3. Barbara W. Jackson, "A Stevenson Memorial," in SATURDAY REVIEW. July 9, 1966, 19.
4. R. F. Butts, EDUCATION IN INTERNATIONAL DEVELOPMENT. New York: Harper and Row, 1963, 1.
5. Francis J. Colligan, TWENTY YEARS AFTER: TWO DECADES OF GOVERNMENT-SPONSORED CULTURAL RELATIONS. Washington, D. C.: The Department of State Publications, 6689, 1958, 19-20.
6. a. Francis J. Colligan, TWENTY YEARS AFTER: TWO DECADES OF GOVERNMENT-SPONSORED CULTURAL RELATIONS. Washington, D. C.: The Department of State Publications, 6689, 1958, 4.
   b. Board of Foreign Scholarships, EXCHANGE SCHOLARS: A NEW DIMENSION IN INTERNATIONAL UNDERSTANDING. Washington, D. C.: U. S. Government Printing Office, 1965, 3.
7. Speech by George C. Marshall, Secretary of State, Harvard University, June 5, 1947; Implemented under the Economic Cooperation Act of 1948, P. L. 472, 80th Congress, April 13, 1948.
8. Inaugural Address by President Truman, January 20, 1949, Implemented Under Title IV, Foreign Economic Assistance Act of 1950, P. L. 535, 81st Congress, June 5, 1950.
9. Committee on Educational Interchange Policy, MILITARY ASSISTANCE TRAINING PROGRAMS OF THE U. S. GOVERNMENT. New York: Institute of International Education, 1964, 7.
10. Guy Metreaux, EXCHANGE OF PERSONS: THE EVOLUTION OF

CROSS-CULTURAL EDUCATION. New York: Social Science Research Council, June 1962, p. 24.

11. Lucian W. Pye, POLITICS, PERSONALITY, AND NATION BUILDING. New Haven: Yale University Press, 1962, 300.

12. The Department of State, EDUCATIONAL AND CULTURAL DIPLOMACY — 1964. Washington, D.C.: U. S. Government Printing Office, 1964, 87.

13. Committee on Educational Interchange Policy, EDUCATIONAL EXCHANGE IN THE ECONOMIC DEVELOPMENT OF NATIONS. New York: Institute of International Education, 1961, 16.

14. Board of Foreign Scholarship, EXCHANGE SCHOLARS: A NEW DIMENSION IN INTERNATIONAL UNDERSTANDING. Washington, D. C.: The U. S. Government Printing Office, 1965, 19.

15. Committee on Educational Exchange Policy, EDUCATIONAL EXCHANGE IN THE ECONOMIC DEVELOPMENT OF NATIONS. New York: Institute of International Exchange, 1961, p. 17.

16. Board of Foreign Scholarship, EXCHANGE SCHOLARS: A NEW DIMENSION IN INTERNATIONAL UNDERSTANDING. Washington, D. C.: U. S. Government Printing Office, 1965, p. 5.

17. Joseph S. Roucek, "The Sociological Implications of the International Exchange of Academic Personnel," in V.O.E. JOURNAL OF EDUCATION, II, August 1962, 8.

18. Ernest M. Kuhinka, "The Foreign Exchange Student Looks at the United States," Prepared for the Committee for the International Exchange of Persons and the Conference Board of Associated Research Councils, Washington, D. C. Report No. 12. Carlisle, Pa.: The Behavioral Sciences Research Laboratory, 1961.

19. Ernest M. Kuhinka, "Community and Public Health: An Essay in Social Phenomenology." Working Paper No. 15, Division of Behavioral Science, Harrisburg, Pa.: Pennsylvania Department of Health, 1964.

Selected Bibliography

Anderson, Arnold C., and Bowman, Mary J., EDUCATION AND ECONOMIC DEVELOPMENT. Chicago, Ill.: Aldine, 1966. This volume is the outgrowth of a 1963 conference sponsored by the Committee on Economic Growth of the Social Science Research Council and the Comparative Education Center of the University of Chicago. The authors are social scientists in the fields of history, economics, sociology, education, and geography. The book deals with criteria for the allocation of resources among alternative investments: analyzes the way human capital is formed and the way schooling and other innovations spread through a population, and present historical evidence between the development of international education and economic growth.

Ashby, Eric, AFRICAN UNIVERSITIES AND WESTERN TRADITION. Cambridge, Mass.: Harvard University Press, 1965. In this book, based on the Godkin Lectures, and delivered at Harvard University on April 7, 8, and 9, 1964, the author reflects on the interaction of higher education and African society as he experienced it in Ghana and Nigeria.

Coleman, James S., ed., EDUCATION AND POLITICAL DE-
VELOPMENT. Princeton, N.J.: Princeton University Press, 1966.
This volume, devoted to education, is one of a number of studies sponsored by the Committee of Comparative Politics of the
Social Science Research Council. There are four parts in this
book. The first deals with cases of educational underdevelop-
ment in Asia, Africa, and South America. This is followed by
examples of "polity-directed" educational developments in the
Soviet Union, Japan, and the Philippines. The third part discusses
the development of political leadership and the training of government officials in various fields. The last section makes a summary and offers suggestions with reference to educational planning, international exchange, for integrated social and political
progress.

Curti, Merle, AMERICAN PHILANTHROPY ABROAD. New Brunswick, N.J.: Rutgers University Press, 1963. The author describes
American philanthropy on the international plane, both private
and governmental, from colonial days to the present. Among the
philanthropies covered are American relief for the Greeks in
their struggle for independence when such aid was overshadowed
by Byron's romantic activities; for the Irish during the "hungry
forties"; for the Russians during one of their regular famines in
the 1819's; for Cuba after she loosened her tie with Spain; for
all Western Europe immediately after both World Wars in this
century; for all displaced persons after the Second World War: for
the victims of all natural disasters all over the world; and for
various categories of Jews in various places and at varying times.

Hilsman, Roger, and Good, R.C., eds., FOREIGN POLICY IN THE
SIXTIES: THE ISSUES AND THE INSTRUMENTS. Baltimore:
Johns Hopkins Press, 1966. A *Festschrift* in honor of Arnold
Wolters is organized into three parts: the contemporary arena,
the instrumentalities of foreign policy, and statecraft and moral
theory.

Hughes, John, ed., INTERNATIONAL CONFERENCE ON
WORLD EDUCATIONAL PROBLEMS, Poughkeepsie, N.Y.,
1961. New York: Harpers, 1962. This volume grew out of the
International Conference on World Educational Problems at
Vassar College. The book includes both a record of the conference and the fourteen papers and addresses that provided the
framework for the discussions. Following the opening address:
"How Can Our Varied Culture Contribute to Living in an Interdependent World?" panel discussions considered economic and
social development, political relationships in a revolutionary
world and their challenge to education.

Johnson, Walter, and Colligan, F. J., THE FULBRIGHT-PROGRAM:
A HISTORY. Chicago: University of Chicago Press, 1966. After
a general introduction explaining the purpose of the program,
giving necessary historical and legislative background, and re-

viewing the problems encountered in starting and maintaining the exchange projects, the authors evaluate the program in representative countries; discuss its impact on the American people both as grantees and as host; and comment on the significance of the program in years ahead.

King, Edward J., WORLD PERSPECTIVES IN EDUCATION. Indianapolis: Bobbs, 1963. Making use of a topical, rather than national approach, the author treats in comparative terms such questions as the selection of students, the interrelationship of technology change and education. He refers in his analysis to education in various European and Asian countries as well as to the United States. The bibliography is somewhat too brief but is adequate for the general readers.

Platt, John R., THE EXCITEMENT OF SCIENCE. Boston: Houghton, 1962. The book is a series of reflections on interaction between science and society. The purpose here has been to go beyond facts as such and to begin to examine some deeper and more permanent questions applicable to international education: the fundamental relations between science and technology and the intellect of man which creates them; and their relations to the purposes of society which they serve or ought to serve.

Ulich, Robert, ed., EDUCATION AND THE IDEA OF MANKIND. New York: Harcourt, 1965. The volume of eleven essays by educators considers the ends of education—the fundamental purpose for which schools exist. A nation transmits its ideology to new generations through its schools. In the opinion of the educators represented here, the interdependence of nations demands that this ideology be broad enough to include those universal values common to mankind.

Modern Trends In Teaching
Foreign Languages

PETER F. OLIVA
Indiana State University

IN THE LAST twenty years there has been a veritable revolution in the field of foreign languages. Language instruction in the high school has moved from an all time low in the 1940's to a place of national prominence in the 1960's. The inclusion of modern foreign languages in the National Defense Education Act of 1958 proved a milestone in the history of foreign languages in the schools. Through Title III funds of the NDEA monies were channeled to the states and ultimately to the public schools for equipment for the foreign language departments. Under Title VI of the NDEA thousands of teachers have attended language institutes where they have been able to perfect their language skills. The foreign languages have received continuing support from the federal government since 1958.

Federal aid has stimulated state and local school systems to employ supervisors of foreign languages, to expand offerings in foreign languages, and to incorporate latest methods of instruction. The last twenty years have brought to the foreign languages striking changes. There have been changes in (1) goals, (2) curriculum, and (3) methodology.

Changes in Goals

Prior to the Second World War reading was the principal objective of foreign language instruction. Little stress was given to the spoken tongue. The language teacher gave lip service to the goals of speaking, understanding, and writing but reading was the principal emphasis. The language student's goal was the development of sufficient language skill to enable him to read the pieces of literature taught in college classes.

American tourists had not begun to travel, study, and work abroad in such large numbers as they do today. World War II changed this picture entirely. Suddenly the world seemed smaller. America broke the bonds of isolation and began to be aware of the world around her. Her servicemen came into contact with peoples around the world. The ability to communicate on a person-to-person basis became essential. It is no longer unrealistic to believe that the average American will come into contact with foreign nationals in their own countries. Barring a great war or depression, Americans will continue to travel in unprecedented numbers. A reading knowledge of a language does not meet the needs of a world which grows increasingly smaller as modes of transportation and communication improve.

Today all professional associations in the modern languages have endorsed stress on the spoken tongue. A priority in goals has been agreed upon by the majority of language teachers. The language teacher gives top priority to the ability to understand the spoken language. This is followed in order by the ability to speak, the ability to read, and the ability to write the foreign language. Included in language instruction and permeating all materials of instruction is the development of an understanding and appreciation of people of other cultures.

The change in goals has not been without its stresses and strains. There are those who believe that students will not have firsthand contacts with persons who speak a particular language they are studying. They ask further what use a speaking knowledge of French will be to the person who travels in Italy.

The study of a foreign language—any language—sensitizes a person to linguistic problems. It gives him a depth of understanding about foreign peoples that he does not gain in other ways. It makes him realize that different peoples have different ways of expressing themselves. Added to this is the supreme pleasure and inner satisfaction that is experienced when a human being who speaks one language is able to make his thoughts known to a human being who speaks another language.

Students today are learning to speak a foreign language as never before and they are deriving personal satisfaction and a feeling of confidence from their ability to speak the language. The goals of modern language instruction today are clearly defined with speaking and understanding topping the list.

Changes in the Foreign Language Curriculum

The foreign languages have grown both vertically and horizontally. We have programs in a single foreign language from first grade through the last year of high school. It is possible for a student in some school systems to take twelve years of a foreign language and to continue with the study of the language in college.

Foreign languages are an accepted part of the elementary school curriculum in many parts of the country. At this level emphasis is on the enjoyment of a foreign language, simple oral skills and development of the desire on the part of the young student to continue the study of a foreign language. Some elementary schools require the study of foreign language of all their pupils. Others limit instruction to a selected few. Language teachers as a rule would prefer that foreign languages be required of all elementary schoolchildren rather than limited to the more gifted.

On the junior and senior high school level three, four and six year sequences are now common. Twenty years ago it was the prevailing custom for those high school students who took foreign language to take it for only two years. These two years provided the barest smattering of the language. Students were not able to gain a sufficient mastery of the language. Three years of high school instruction are now considered an absolute minimum for developing an adequate knowledge of a modern foreign language. Four years are strongly recommended.

Some schools are able to offer a six-year sequence starting in the seventh grade. The exploratory courses in general language, popular at the junior high level some thirty years ago, have all but disappeared. In those courses students were generally given a small taste of several different languages, usually Latin, French, Spanish, and German. The purpose of the exploratory course was to aid students in choosing the language they would like to study in high school. Unfortunately, it was difficult to find qualified teachers who could handle well all the languages involved. Further, the general language course delayed a student in his study of one particular language. A few schools still hold on to the general language requirement but its popularity has dropped to almost nil.

One of the problems in language teaching in the public

schools today is the lack of articulation between levels. There are great gaps between programs in the elementary schools and junior high; between the junior high and senior high, and between the senior high and the university. There needs to be much greater coordination between levels. Students frequently go through one type of language program, for example an audio-lingual program at one level, and are then confronted with an entirely different type of program, for example, a grammar-translation type, at another level. The better school systems have found ways to articulate their programs in such a way that the learner follows a coordinated sequence from the point where he enters to the point where he leaves. Language teachers in these better school systems work together in deciding the content, methods, and materials to be used in the coordinated sequence.

Horizontally, the foreign languages have expanded beyond the traditional offerings of Spanish, Latin, and French. Large schools are providing, among other languages, instruction in German, Russian, and Chinese. This is in addition to the teaching of Hebrew, Swedish, Italian, and Japanese which have been offered for many years in various parts of the country where large ethnic groups live.

There are schools which boast the offering of six or seven foreign languages. They take pride in the number of offerings rather than the depth of each offering. No school should add additional languages until it has a well-developed sequence in each language which it has already started. Some schools are beginning to consider offering selected subjects in the foreign language itself. For example, it is not unrealistic to expect to find some high schools offering a course in Latin American history or in French literature or even in science or mathematics in a foreign language. Needless to say such a course would be open to only those students who had a thorough knowledge of the language. The course would have to be taught by a person who has not only a command of the language but an expertise in the subject field as well.

Enrollments in the foreign languages continue to grow. Some of the increase in enrollment comes from the reinstitution of college requirements of a foreign language for admission. Some of the increase comes from the desire of young people to participate in international affairs and to serve in varying capacities abroad in later years. Some of the increase derives from the favorable climate for foreign language study. Federal support has lent status to language study. Some of the increase stems from the willingness of guidance counselors to advise students to take a foreign language. Some of the increase arises from the efforts of language teachers themselves. They have, for one thing, cast off a kind of aloofness by joining the ranks of the National Education Association. For years language teachers were one of the few groups of professional teachers not allied with the National Education Association. The formation of the Department of Foreign Languages within the NEA's organization in 1961 was a milestone for foreign language teachers. The goals and needs of language teachers can now be more readily understood by teachers in other fields. Further, language teachers can understand the aspirations and problems of teachers in other fields. They can feel a part of the mainstream of American education, which they have not always felt before.

The foreign language curriculum has expanded in two directions: vertically with a longer sequence and horizontally with additional languages.

Changes in Methodology

Most significant change in methodology is the use of the audio-lingual approach. Audio-lingual techniques are used to attain the new primary goals of language instruction. Today more foreign language is or should be heard in the classroom than English. In former years an observer in the language classroom might not have been sure whether he was visiting a class in foreign language or in English. The teacher spoke in English, asked questions in English, and permitted students to respond a great deal of the time in English.

Today there is no question of the class's being one in foreign language. Almost everything is in the foreign language except for a few inevitable explanations or assistance given in English. The students become accustomed to hearing and speaking the language from the very first day of instruction. The language is spoken to them at a normal rate of speed not at a deliberately slow artificial rate.

The teacher today introduces the spoken language immediately. He carries his students through a period of "pre-reading instruction," which may vary from teacher to teacher from a few days to a few weeks. No printed materials are used during the pre-reading instruction.

An effort is made to approximate the way in which students have learned their own native language. Students listen to the teacher. They repeat what they hear and they try to imitate the teacher. It is true that we cannot nor should we try to duplicate the way students have learned their own language. They have a certain maturity. They have developed certain language and study skills. Printed materials are introduced in due course along with other kinds of visual and electronic aids which students did not have in learning their own language.

A startling change—one disconcerting to some teachers—has come about in the teaching of grammar. Grammar is taught inductively, by analysis, in the language for the most part. Students encounter countless examples of a grammatical principle. They learn the rule through the practice they have undergone. Grammar is taught largely through the use of pattern practices. The teacher gives the students a model or pattern. Students apply the pattern in many different kinds of exercises. After they have had sufficient practice and seem to have grasped the principle, the student may be told the rule by the teacher. The teacher strives to keep grammatical explanations as brief as possible.

This process reverses the historic method of teaching a foreign language. In prewar days and in a decreasing number of classrooms today the teacher introduced a grammar rule first. He gave students an explanation of the rule, then some examples of the rule. Most often he gave too few examples to reinforce the principle. Students then were set to working exercises, usually translations from English to the foreign language, in which they had opportunities to employ the rule.

Translation, except in the classical languages, is now kept to a minimum. Students are instructed in such a way that they do not have to translate. They learn to understand, speak, read, and write without resorting to translation.

Teachers of foreign languages are making use of the new technology. The language laboratory is an accepted part of modern language instruction. Prior to 1958 few schools had a tape recorder for the exclusive use of the language teacher. In less than ten years hundreds of schools have invested in language laboratory equipment of one kind or another. It is safe to say that many schools have more equipment than they have learned to use effectively.

Teachers are using newer text materials built on audio-lingual principles.[1] These materials present the language in a carefully integrated sequence. They progress from elementary levels of speech to advanced levels of reading and writing. They contain ample pattern drills. They are supplemented with tapes or records and various visual aids. These newer materials are rapidly supplanting the older-type textbooks prepared by the grammarian.

Today's text materials and techniques of instruction are based on linguistic principles. Linguistic scientists have subjected the various spoken languages to intensive analysis. They have recorded the sounds and structures of a language. The language teacher applies linguistic principles in the classroom. At the outset the language teacher agrees with the linguist that the spoken language should be stressed.

The linguist aids the language teacher by finding out which sounds and structures are most frequently used by native speakers of the language. He identifies sounds and structures which are different from those in the students' mother tongue. These, then, become points which the language teacher must stress. Once sounds and structures are identified along with the intonation patterns and the ways in which native speakers put together their language, the teacher can create and employ drills designed to teach the various elements of the language.

Since the linguist is concerned with the spoken language, the teacher who applies linguistic principles places great stress on auditory aids. He makes tapes for use in classroom and laboratory. He has students listen to recordings and make tapes of their own voices.

The linguist is concerned with the question of how a native speaker expresses himself. He is not concerned with the question, why does a speaker express himself as he does? The question of why is left to the philologist, the psychologist, and the philosopher. For this reason language teachers are urged to minimize discussions of why people say things as they do.

The most significant change in modern language instruction

has been the substitution of the audio-lingual approach for older grammar-translation and reading-oriented methods.

Needed Research

In spite of the long way we have come in language instruction, we have yet a long way to go. There is a great need for some high quality research in the field of foreign languages. Many of the practices which we now follow are based on logic and considered judgment. Much of the research has been of the survey variety. Twenty-one studies were reported in a recent document issued by the Modern Language Association of America.[2] These are all surveys and reports of the status of foreign languages at various levels and in various types of schools. We find a multitude of articles in the professional journals in which a language teacher or professor relates some technique he uses or states his opinions on how languages should be taught. We are woefully short on research in depth. What is needed is some long-term experimental research which would confirm or refute some of the practices and programs we now follow.

To begin with we need some intensive research on how human beings learn a language. Further, we need more specific research on the way human beings learn a second language. The literature on the psychology of language learning is rather limited when compared to that of reporting studies of other kinds of human behavior.

We need to determine through experimentation the best place to begin instruction in a foreign language. We have varying opinions on the best place to begin instruction. Some tell us in high school; others, junior high; others, fourth grade; still others, kindergarten. Some language teachers adopt the single-minded attitude that the earlier foreign language instruction begins, the better. Logically, this may sound defensible. Experimentally, we may find this position to be erroneous. It may very well be that students will learn a language quicker and better when they begin at some particular point along the academic ladder than at an earlier point.

In a similar vein we need some long-term research on achievement of students after three years, four years, six years, nine years and twelve years of language instruction. We now assume that the more instruction students have had, the higher their language achievement will be. It would be disconcerting if we find that students who have had only three years of high school language instruction achieve better results than those who have had twelve years of instruction.

It is now the folklore that students who go through an audio-lingual program ultimately achieve as well in reading and writing as those who have gone through a more traditional program. We need more conclusive evidence of this, if only to allay the anxieties of many language instructors.

We need more evidence on the optimum time to allot to various kinds of language activities. How long can students profitably undergo specific kinds of pattern drills? At what point does fatigue become a serious handicap? How much time should be allotted to the language laboratory? For how long should we conduct prereading instruction at the beginning of language study? Will we, for example, achieve just as good results when we present written materials to students on the first day as on the eleventh day? Are three weeks of prereading instruction better than one week? We have opinions. We have little solid experimental evidence.

We need research studies on the most effective ways to utilize language laboratories. We need experimentation with different kinds of laboratory equipment. We need to know what are the best kinds of laboratories. We might decide upon a particular set of language competencies and seek to develop them by using different kinds of laboratory equipment. We could then determine what kinds of equipment were best to achieve the particular competencies we have in mind.

We should have more evidence in the use of visual aids in the classroom. What kinds of visual aids are effective? Is the combination of visual aids plus audio aids better than audio alone? Do color, size, and authenticity make a big difference? Are films better than slides, charts, filmstrips, and pictures?

Some schools should be trying out some of the newer programmed materials in foreign languages. We need to determine the place and use of programmed materials in language instruction. We need to learn whether we can develop programmed materials which will teach the audio-lingual aspects of language as well as reading and writing.

Some organization should take the responsibility to disseminate research findings. This may be the task of the Modern Language Association or the Department of Foreign Languages of the National Education Association or the U.S. Office of Education. Whatever agency undertakes the role, significant findings should be made known throughout the country. Experimental evidence will help us to improve our language programs.

Summary

The modern foreign languages have undergone considerable change in the past twenty years. The languages have changed in goals, curriculum, and methodology. Top priority in goals today is given understanding and speaking the language. The foreign language curriculum has expanded both vertically and horizontally. Schools have lengthened the sequence of language instruction. Many school systems begin language instruction in the elementary school.

Schools have added additional and, in some cases, unusual languages to their curriculum. The audio-lingual approach is the approach to methodology preferred by the majority of modern language teachers.

In spite of the gains in foreign language instruction much more needs to be done. There is a great need for research which will bear out or negate some of the current programs and practices of foreign language teaching.

PETER F. OLIVA is Professor of Education at the School of Education, Indiana State University. He received his A.B. from Cornell University, M.A. in Teaching from Harvard University, and Ed.D. from Teachers College, Columbia University. Dr. Oliva has taught French and Latin in Maryland and New York State. He has taught at the University of Florida, the University of Mississippi, Western Michigan University, Miami University (Ohio), Portland State College (Oregon), and the University of Hawaii. He served with the binational centers branch of the U.S. Information Agency in Teheran, Iran. He has traveled extensively in Europe and Latin America. He is author of *The Teaching of Foreign Languages* (Prentice-Hall), in press.

FOOTNOTES

1. Among others: The Harcourt, Brace and World series, A-LM, and the Holt, Rinehart, Winston AURAL-ORAL SERIES.

2. Modern Language Association of America, REPORTS OF SURVEYS AND STUDIES IN THE TEACHING OF MODERN FOREIGN LANGUAGES, 1959-1961. New York: Modern Language Association Foreign Language Research Center, 1961.

Selected Bibliography

Brooks, Nelson. LANGUAGE AND LANGUAGE LEARNING, THEORY AND PRACTICE, 2nd edition, New York: Harcourt, Brace and World, 1964. A comprehensive work covering various aspects of language learning and methodology of language teaching based on an audio-lingual approach.

Douglass, Harl, R., ed., THE HIGH SCHOOL CURRICULUM, 3rd edition. New York: Ronald Press, 1964. In Chapter 21 of this book Walter V. Kaulfers discusses enrollments, offerings, objectives, trends, and problems of the foreign languages.

Fraser, Dorothy M., CURRENT CURRICULUM STUDIES IN ACADEMIC SUBJECTS. Washington, D.C.: National Education Association, 1962. Chapter V of this booklet provides information about recent developments, changes, and programs in modern foreign languages.

Lado, Robert, LANGUAGE TEACHING, A SCIENTIFIC APPROACH, New York: McGraw-Hill, 1964. An introduction to various aspects of language learning and teaching, including theory of language and language learning, principles of language teaching based on an audio-lingual approach, and the use of technological aids.

Parker, William Riley, THE NATIONAL INTEREST AND FOREIGN LANGUAGES, 3rd edition. Department of State Publication 7324, International Organization and Conference Series 26, 1962, Washington, D.C.: U.S. Government Printing Office. A discussion guide to stimulate thinking about foreign languages and the need for study of foreign languages.

Remer, Ilo, A HANDBOOK FOR GUIDING STUDENTS IN MODERN FOREIGN LANGUAGES. Bulletin 1963, No. 26, Washington, D.C.: U.S. Office of Education, 1963. Written to help guidance workers, teachers, principals, and parents who are advising students about foreign language programs.

Stack, Edward M., THE LANGUAGE LABORATORY AND MODERN LANGUAGE TEACHING, Rev. ed. New York: Oxford University Press, 1966. A detailed treatment of specific techniques of foreign language instruction with emphasis on the audio-lingual approach and use of the language laboratory.

Valdman, Albert, ed., TRENDS IN LANGUAGE TEACHING. New York: McGraw-Hill, 1966. A collection of fourteen papers written by authorities on various aspects of modern language teaching and learning.